SECOND EDITION

Research Methods
A Modular Approach

Sherri L. Jackson
Jacksonville University

WADSWORTH
CENGAGE Learning

Australia • Brazil • Japan • Korea • Mexico • Singapore • Spain • United Kingdom • United States

Research Methods: A Modular Approach, Second Edition
Sherri L. Jackson

Publisher: Linda Schreiber-Ganster

Acquisitions Editor: Tim Matray

Editorial Assistant: Alicia McLaughlin

Production Technology Analyst: Lori Johnson

Senior Marketing Manager: Jessica Egbert

Manufacturing Director: Marcia Locke

Media Editor: Mary Noel

Senior Marketing Communications Manager: Talia Wise

Content Project Manager: Pre-PressPMG

Senior Art Director: Vernon Boes

Print Buyer: Linda Hsu

Rights Specialist/Text: Roberta Broyer

Rights Specialist/Image: Dean Dauphinais

Production Service: Pre-PressPMG

Cover Designer: Denise Davidson

Cover Photo: DK & Dennie Cody/Masterfile

Compositor: Pre-PressPMG

Printer: RR Donnelley

Library of Congress Control Number: 2010925784

ISBN-13: 978-0-495-81119-0

ISBN-10: 0-495-81119-X

Wadsworth
20 Davis Drive
Belmont, CA 94002-3098
USA

Cengage Learning is a leading provider of customized learning solutions with office locations around the globe, including Singapore, the United Kingdom, Australia, Mexico, Brazil, and Japan. Locate your local office at **www.cengage.com/global**.

Cengage Learning products are represented in Canada by Nelson Education, Ltd.

To learn more about Wadsworth, visit **www.cengage.com/Wadsworth.**

Purchase any of our products at your local college store or at our preferred online store **www.CengageBrain.com.**

Printed in the United States of America
1 2 3 4 5 6 7 14 13 12 11 10

To my parents, Kenneth and Eleanor,
for all they have done

ABOUT THE AUTHOR

SHERRI L. JACKSON is Professor of Psychology at Jacksonville University, where she has taught since 1988. At JU she has won the Excellence in Scholarship (2003), University Service (2004), and Teaching Awards (2009), the university-wide Professor of the Year Award (2004), the Woman of the Year Award (2005), and the Institutional Excellence Award (2007). She received her M.S. and Ph.D. in cognitive/experimental psychology from the University of Florida. Her research interests include human reasoning and the teaching of psychology. She has published numerous articles in both areas. In 1997 she received a research grant from the Office of Teaching Resources in Psychology (APA Division 2) to develop *A Compendium of Introductory Psychology Textbooks 1997–2000*. She is also the author of *Research Methods and Statistics: A Critical Thinking Approach*, 3rd edition (Belmont, CA: Wadsworth/Cengage, 2009) and *Statistics Plain and Simple*, 2nd edition (Belmont, CA: Wadsworth/Cengage, 2010).

BRIEF CONTENTS

CONTENTS

CHAPTER NINE SUMMARY AND REVIEW: INFERENTIAL STATISTICS II

CHAPTER 10 APA Communication Guidelines

Module 21 Communicating Research Findings

Module 22 APA Sample Manuscript 337
CHAPTER TEN SUMMARY AND REVIEW: APA COMMUNICATION GUIDELINES 354

PREFACE

This text was written to provide students and instructors with a simple approach to learning and teaching research methods. One of my writing goals was to be **concise yet comprehensive.** The text is organized into ten chapters, each divided into modules. The modular format allows students to digest smaller chunks and allows teachers to enjoy greater flexibility in reading assignments and class coverage. Most modules are brief: 7 to 15 pages in length. However, even using a modular presentation, most of the text is comprehensive in its coverage of research methods and some statistics. Each module is divided into subsections, which further serve to break the material down into even smaller digestible chunks for ease of understanding and assimilation.

In addition, I have made every attempt to use a straightforward, easy-to-understand **writing style,** presenting information in a simple and direct fashion. Because the research methods course is often one of the more difficult ones for many students, I also try to write in an engaging, conversational style, much as if the reader were a student seated in front of me in my classroom. Through this writing style, I hope to help students better understand some of the more troublesome concepts without losing their interest and attention.

PEDAGOGICAL AIDS

The text utilizes several pedagogical aids at the chapter and modular levels. Each chapter begins with a **chapter outline.** Within the modules are:

- A **running glossary in the book margin**
- **Learning objectives** at the beginning of each module

- **In Review summary matrices,** which are at the end of major subsections and which provide a review of the subsection's main concepts in a tabular format
- **Critical Thinking Checks,** which vary in length and format, with most involving a series of application questions concerning the module subsection information, that are designed to foster analytical/critical thinking skills in students in addition to reviewing the module subsection information (students can thus use the In Review summary after reading a module subsection and then engage in the Critical Thinking Check on that information)
- **Module Exercises,** which are at the end of each module and which enable students to further review and apply the knowledge in the module.

At the end of each chapter, there is a **chapter summary and review—** essentially a built-in study guide consisting of a chapter review, Fill-In Self-Test, Multiple-Choice Self-Test, and Key Terms review. Answers to the Critical Thinking Checks are provided at the end of each module. Answers to the odd-numbered Module Exercises and all Chapter Review Exercises are included in Appendix A.

Additional study resources, including practice quizzes, chapter-by-chapter flashcards, research methods workshops, and more, can be found on the companion website at **www.cengage.com/psychology/jackson**.

NEW TO THIS EDITION

In this second edition, the APA manuscript style guidelines have been updated to bring them in line with the newest edition of the APA style guide (2009). In addition, learning objectives have been added to each module, the coverage of the qualitative methods and the survey methods has been expanded and updated, and the text has been reorganized from seven sections to ten chapters. Further, there is an additional appendix which shows students how to use Excel, SPSS, or the TI84 calculator to compute the statistics that are covered in the text.

ACKNOWLEDGMENTS

I must acknowledge several people for their help with this project. I thank my husband for his careful proofreading and insightful comments as well as Henry for the encouragement of his ever-present wagging tail. Additionally, I would like to thank those who reviewed the text in its various stages. The reviewers include Dr. Ibtihaj Arafat, City College of the City University of New York; Dr. Eric Bressler, Westfield State College; Dr. Bruce J. Diamond, William Paterson University and UMDNJ-NJ Medical School; Dr. Hyun-Jeong Kim, Rhodes College; Dr. Gary McCullough, the University of Texas of the Permian Basin; Dr. Anne Moyer, Stony Brook University; Dr. Todd Nelson, California State University, Stanislaus; and Dr. Frances M. Sessa, Penn State Abington.

Special thanks to the team at Wadsworth: Tim Matray, Acquisitions Editor; Alicia McLaughlin, Editorial Assistant; Sini Sivaraman, Content Project Manager; Jessica Egbert, Senior Marketing Manager; Talia Wise, Senior Marketing Communications Manager; Vernon Boes, Senior Art Director; and Roberta Broyer, Permissions Editor. Finally, thanks to James A. Corrick for his excellent copyediting skills.

Sherri L. Jackson

CHAPTER 1

Thinking Like a Scientist

Welcome to what is most likely your first research methods class. If you are like most psychology students, you are probably wondering what in the world this class is about—and, more importantly, why you have to take it. Most psychologists and the American Psychological Association (APA) consider the research methods class especially important in the undergraduate curriculum. In fact, along with the introductory psychology class, the research methods class is required by most psychology departments (Messer, Griggs, & Jackson, 1999). Why is this class considered so important, and what exactly is it all about? These are the questions we address in this chapter.

Science and Psychology

LEARNING OBJECTIVES

- Identify and describe the areas of psychological research.
- Identify and differentiate between the various sources of knowledge.
- Describe the three criteria of the scientific (critical thinking) approach.
- Explain the difference between basic and applied research.
- Explain the goals of science.

Before answering the two questions above, I will ask you to complete a couple of exercises related to your knowledge of psychology. I usually begin my research methods class by asking the students to do them. I assume that you have had at least one other psychology class. Thus these exercises should not be difficult.

Exercise 1: Name five psychologists. Make sure your list does not include "pop" psychologists such as Dr. Ruth or Dr. Laura. These latter individuals are considered by most psychologists to be pop psychologists because although they are certified to do some sort of counseling, neither completed a degree in psychology. Dr. Ruth has an Ed.D. in the interdisciplinary study of the family, whereas Dr. Laura has a Ph.D. in physiology and a postdoctoral certification in marriage, family, and child counseling.

Stop reading at this point, make your list, and then read on.

Okay, who is first on your list? If you are like most people, you named Sigmund Freud. In fact, if we were to stop 100 people on the street and ask them the same question, we would probably find that, other than pop psychologists, Freud is the most commonly named psychologist (Stanovich, 2007). What do you know about Freud? Do you believe that he represents all that psychology encompasses? Most people on the street think so, and in fact, they equate what psychologists "do" with what they see pop psychologists do and what they believe Freud did. That is, they believe that most psychologists listen to people and help them solve their problems. If this belief represents your schema for psychology, this class should help you see the discipline in a very different light.

Exercise 2 (from Bolt, 1998): Make two columns on a piece of paper: label one "Scientist" and one "Psychologist." Now write five descriptive terms for each. You may include terms or phrases that you believe describe the "typical" scientist's or psychologist's appearance, dress, behavior, or personal characteristics.

Stop reading at this point, make your list, and then read on.

Once you finish this task, evaluate your descriptions. Do the lists differ? Again, if you are like most students—even psychology majors—you have probably written very different terms to describe a scientist and a psychologist.

First, consider your description of a scientist. Most students see the scientist as a middle-aged man, usually wearing a white lab coat with a pocket protector. The terms for the scientist's personality typically include "analytical," "committed," and "introverted." He is regarded as having poor people or social skills. How do all these characteristics compare with your description?

Now let's turn to your description of a typical psychologist. Once again, a majority of students tend to picture a man, although some picture a woman. They definitely see the psychologist in professional attire, not in a white lab coat. The terms for personality characteristics tend to be "warm," "caring," "empathic," and "concerned about others." Is this description similar to what you have written?

What is the point of these exercises? First, they illustrate that most people have misconceptions about psychologists and psychology. In other words, most people believe that the majority of psychologists do what Freud did—try to help others with their problems. They also tend to see psychology as a discipline devoted to the mental health profession. As you will soon see, psychology includes many other areas of specialization, some of which may actually involve wearing a white lab coat and working with technical equipment.

Why do I ask you to describe a scientist and a psychologist? The reason is that I hope you will realize that a psychologist *is* a scientist. "Wait a minute," you may be saying, "I decided to major in psychology because I don't like science." What you are failing to recognize is that what makes something a science is not *what* is studied but *how* it is studied. Psychology as a science is precisely what we will be learning about in this course as we study how to use the scientific method to conduct research in psychology. Because the scientific method relies on the use of statistics, you may have had to take statistics as a pre- or corequisite to this class. In addition, statistics are also covered in this text because doing research requires an understanding of how to use statistics. In this text you will learn mainly about research methods; however, some of the statistics most useful for these methods are also covered.

––––––––––––

AREAS OF PSYCHOLOGICAL RESEARCH

As noted, psychology is not just about mental health. Psychology is a very diverse discipline that encompasses many areas of study. To illustrate this point, examine Table 1.1, which lists the divisions of the American Psychological Association (APA). Notice that the areas of study in psychology range from those that are close to the so-called hard sciences (chemistry, physics, and biology) to those close to the so-called soft social sciences (sociology, anthropology, and political science). The APA has 54 divisions, each representing an area of research or practice. To understand psychology, you have to appreciate its diversity. In the following sections, we briefly discuss some of the more popular research areas within the discipline of psychology.

Psychobiology

One of the most popular research areas in psychology today is psychobiology. As the name implies, this research area combines biology and psychology. Researchers in this area typically study brain organization or the chemicals in the brain (neurotransmitters). Using the appropriate research methods, psychobiologists have discovered, for example, links between illnesses such as schizophrenia and Parkinson's disease and various neurotransmitters in the brain. These findings have led in turn to research on possible drug therapies for these illnesses.

Cognition

Researchers who study cognition are interested in how humans process, store, and retrieve information; solve problems; use reasoning and logic; make decisions; and use language. Understanding and employing the appropriate research methods have enabled scientists in these areas to develop models of how memory works, ways to improve memory, methods to improve problem solving and intelligence, and theories of language acquisition. Whereas psychobiology researchers study the brain, cognitive scientists study the mind.

Human Development

Psychologists specializing in human development conduct research on human physical, social, and cognitive development. This work might involve research from the prenatal development period throughout the life span to research on the elderly (gerontology). Research on human development has led, for instance, to a better understanding of prenatal development and hence better prenatal care, greater knowledge of cognitive development and limitations in children, and a greater awareness of the effects of peer pressure on adolescents.

Social Psychology

Social psychologists are interested in how we view and affect one another. Research in this area combines the disciplines of psychology and sociology, in that social psychologists are typically interested in how being part of a group affects the individual. Some of the best-known studies in psychology represent work by social psychologists. As an example, Milgram's (1963, 1974) classic experiments on obedience to authority and Zimbardo's (1972) classic prison simulation are social psychology studies.

TABLE **1.1**

Divisions of the American Psychological Association

1. Society for General Psychology
2. Society for the Teaching of Psychology
3. Experimental Psychology
5. Evaluation, Measurement, and Statistics
6. Behavioral Neuroscience and Comparative Psychology
7. Developmental Psychology
8. Society for Personality and Social Psychology
9. Society for Psychological Study of Social Issues
10. Society for the Psychology of Aesthetics, Creativity, and the Arts
12. Society for Clinical Psychology
13. Society for Consulting Psychology
14. Society for Industrial and Organizational Psychology
15. Educational Psychology
16. School Psychology
17. Society for Counseling Psychology
18. Psychologists in Public Service
19. Society for Military Psychology
20. Adult Development and Aging
21. Applied Experimental and Engineering Psychology
22. Rehabilitation Psychology
23. Society for Consumer Psychology
24. Society for Theoretical and Philosophical Psychology
25. Behavior Analysis
26. Society for the History of Psychology
27. Society for Community Research and Action: Division of Community Psychology
28. Psychopharmacology and Substance Abuse
29. Psychotherapy
30. Society for Psychological Hypnosis
31. State, Provincial, and Territorial Psychological Association Affairs
32. Humanistic Psychology
33. Mental Retardation and Developmental Disabilities
34. Population and Environmental Psychology
35. Society for the Psychology of Women
36. Psychology of Religion
37. Society for Child and Family Policy and Practice
38. Health Psychology
39. Psychoanalysis
40. Clinical Neuropsychology
41. American Psychology–Law Society
42. Psychologists in Independent Practice
43. Family Psychology
44. Society for the Psychological Study of Lesbian, Gay, and Bisexual Issues
45. Society for the Psychological Study of Ethnic and Minority Issues
46. Media Psychology
47. Exercise and Sport Psychology

(*continued*)

TABLE **1.1**
Divisions of the American Psychological Association (*continued*)

48. Society for the Study of Peace, Conflict, and Violence: Peace Psychology Division
49. Group Psychology and Group Psychotherapy
50. Addictions
51. Society for the Psychological Study of Men and Masculinity
52. International Psychology
53. Society of Clinical Child and Adolescent Psychology
54. Society of Pediatric Psychology
55. American Society for the Advancement of Pharmacotherapy
56. Trauma Psychology

Note: There are no divisions 4 and 11.

Psychotherapy

Psychologists also conduct research to evaluate psychotherapies. Such research is designed to assess whether a therapy is really effective in helping individuals. Accordingly, researchers ask whether patients would have improved without the therapy, or did they perhaps improve simply because they thought the therapy was supposed to help? Given the widespread use of various therapies, it is important to have an estimate of their effectiveness.

SOURCES OF KNOWLEDGE

There are many ways to gain knowledge, and some are better than others. As scientists, psychologists must be aware of these methods. Let's look at several ways of acquiring knowledge, beginning with sources that may not be as reliable or accurate as scientists might desire. We then consider sources that offer greater reliability and ultimately discuss using science as a means of gaining knowledge.

Superstition and Intuition

knowledge via superstition: Knowledge based on subjective feelings, belief in chance, or belief in magical events.

Gaining **knowledge via superstition** means acquiring knowledge based on subjective feelings, belief in chance, or belief in magical events. Thus you may have heard someone say, "Bad things happen in threes." Where does this idea come from? As far as I know, no study has ever supported the hypothesis that bad events occur in threes; yet you frequently hear people say this and act as if they believe it. Some people believe that breaking a mirror brings 7 years of bad luck or that the number 13 is unlucky. These are all examples of superstitious beliefs that are not based on observation or hypothesis testing. As such, they represent a means of gaining knowledge that is neither reliable nor valid.

knowledge via intuition: Knowledge gained without being consciously aware of its source.

When we gain **knowledge via intuition**, we have knowledge of something without being consciously aware of where it came from. You have probably heard people say things like "I don't know, it's just a gut feeling" or "I don't know, it just came to me, and I know it's true." These statements are examples of intuition.

Sometimes we intuit knowledge based not on a "gut feeling" but on events we have observed. The problem is that the events may be misinterpreted and not representative of all events in that category. For example, many people believe that more babies are born during a full moon than at other times of the month or that couples who have adopted a baby are more likely to conceive after the adoption. These are examples of *illusory correlation*—the perception of a relationship that does not exist. More babies are not born when the moon is full, nor are couples more likely to conceive after adopting (Gilovich, 1991). Instead, we are more likely to notice babies born after a full moon or couples who conceive after adopting and to ignore the counter examples.

Authority

knowledge via authority: Knowledge gained from those viewed as authority figures.

When we accept what a respected or famous person tells us, we are gaining **knowledge via authority**. You may have gained much of your own knowledge through authority figures. As you were growing up, your parents provided you with information that for the most part you did not question, especially when you were very young. You believed that they knew what they were talking about, and so you accepted their answers. You probably also gained knowledge from teachers whom you viewed as authority figures, at times blindly accepting what they said as truth. Most people tend to accept information imparted by those they view as authority figures. Historically authority figures have been primary sources of information. For instance, in some time periods and cultures, organized religion and its leaders were responsible for providing much of the knowledge that individuals gained throughout the course of their lives.

Even today, many individuals gain much of their knowledge from perceived authority figures; such knowledge may not be a problem if the figure truly is an authority. However, problems may arise when the perceived authority figure really is not knowledgeable in the subject area. A good example is the infomercial in which celebrities are often used to deliver the message or a testimonial about a product. Cindy Crawford may tell us about a makeup product, or Jessica Simpson may provide a testimonial regarding an acne product. Do either of them have a degree in dermatology? What do they actually know about dermatology? These individuals may be experts on modeling, acting, or singing, but they are not authorities on the products they are helping to advertise. Yet many individuals readily accept what they say.

Accepting the word of an authority figure may be a reliable and valid means of gaining knowledge but only if the individual is truly an authority on the subject. Thus we need to question "authoritative" sources of knowledge and develop an attitude of skepticism so that we do not blindly accept whatever we hear.

Tenacity

knowledge via tenacity: Knowledge gained from repeated ideas and stubbornly clung to despite evidence to the contrary.

Gaining **knowledge via tenacity** involves hearing a piece of information so often that you begin to believe it is true and then, despite evidence to the contrary, clinging stubbornly to that belief. This method is often used in political campaigns in which a slogan is repeated so often that we begin to believe it. Advertisers also use the method of tenacity by repeating a slogan for a product over and over until people associate it with the product and believe the product meets the claims. As an example, the makers of Visine advertised for over 40 years that "it gets the red out," and although Visine recently changed its slogan, most of us have heard the original so many times that we probably now believe it. The problem with gaining knowledge through tenacity is that we do not know whether the claims are true. As far as we know, the accuracy of such knowledge may not have been evaluated in any valid way.

Rationalism

knowledge via rationalism: Knowledge gained through logical reasoning.

Gaining **knowledge via rationalism** involves logical reasoning. With this approach ideas are precisely stated and logical rules are applied to arrive at a reasoned and sound conclusion. Rational ideas are often presented in the form of a syllogism. Take the example

All humans are mortal;

I am a human;

Therefore I am mortal.

The conclusion is logically derived from the major and minor premises in the syllogism.

Consider, however, the following syllogism:

Attractive people are good;

Nellie is attractive;

Therefore Nellie is good.

This syllogism reflects the problem with gaining knowledge by logic. Although the syllogism is logically sound, the content of both premises is not necessarily true. If the content were true, the conclusion would be true in addition to being logically sound. However, if the content of either premise is false (as is the premise "Attractive people are good"), then the conclusion is logically valid but empirically false, and it is therefore of no use to a scientist. Logic deals only with the form of the syllogism and not its content. Obviously, researchers are interested in both form and content.

Empiricism

knowledge via empiricism: Knowledge gained through objective observations of organisms and events in the real world.

Knowledge via empiricism involves gaining knowledge through objective observation and the experiences of the senses. An individual who says that "I believe nothing until I see it with my own eyes" is an empiricist. The empiricist gains knowledge by seeing, hearing, tasting, smelling, and touching. This method dates back to the age of Aristotle, an empiricist who made observations about the world in order to know it better. Plato, in contrast, preferred to theorize about the true nature of the world without gathering data.

Empiricism alone, however, is not enough. It leads to a collection of facts. Thus, as scientists, if we rely solely on empiricism, we have nothing more than a long list of observations or facts. For these facts to be useful, we need to organize them, think about them, draw meaning from them, and use them to make predictions. That is, we need to use rationalism together with empiricism to make sure that our observations are logical. As we will see, this melding is what science does.

Science

knowledge via science: Knowledge gained through a combination of empirical methods and logical reasoning.

Gaining **knowledge via science** then involves a merger of rationalism and empiricism. Scientists collect data (make empirical observations) and test hypotheses with these data (assess them using rationalism). A **hypothesis** is a prediction regarding the outcome of a study. Often the prediction concerns the relationship between two variables (a **variable** is an event or behavior that has at least two values). By merging rationalism and empiricism, we have the advantage of using a logical argument based on observation. We may find that our hypothesis is not supported, and thus we have to reevaluate our position. On the other hand, our observations may support the hypothesis being tested.

hypothesis: A prediction regarding the outcome of a study that often involves the relationship between two variables.

variable: An event or behavior that has at least two values.

In science the goal of testing hypotheses is to arrive at or to test a **theory**, which is an organized system of assumptions and principles that attempts to explain phenomena and how they are related. Theories help us organize and explain the data gathered in research studies. In other words, theories allow us to develop a framework regarding facts. For example, Darwin's theory organizes and explains facts related to evolution. To develop his theory, Darwin tested many hypotheses. In addition to helping us organize and explain facts, theories help in producing new knowledge by steering researchers toward specific observations of the world.

theory: An organized system of assumptions and principles that attempts to explain certain phenomena and how they are related.

Students are sometimes confused about the difference between a hypothesis and a theory. A hypothesis is a prediction regarding the outcome of a single study. On a given topic many hypotheses may be tested, and several research studies conducted before a comprehensive theory is put forth. Once a theory is developed, it may aid in generating future hypotheses. That is, researchers may pose additional questions regarding the theory that help them to generate new hypotheses. If the results from additional studies support the theory, we are likely to have greater confidence in it. However, further research can also expose weaknesses in a theory that may lead to future revisions.

IN REVIEW Sources of Knowledge		
Source	**Description**	**Advantages/Disadvantages**
Superstition	Gaining knowledge through subjective feelings, belief in chance, or belief in magical events	Not empirical or logical
Intuition	Gaining knowledge without being consciously aware of where the knowledge came from	Not empirical or logical
Authority	Gaining knowledge from those viewed as authority figures	Not empirical or logical; authority figure may not be an expert in the area
Tenacity	Gaining knowledge by clinging stubbornly to repeated ideas, despite evidence to the contrary	Not empirical or logical
Rationalism	Gaining knowledge through logical reasoning	Logical but not empirical
Empiricism	Gaining knowledge through observation of organisms and events in the real world	Empirical but not necessarily logical or systematic
Science	Gaining knowledge through empirical methods and logical reasoning	The only acceptable way for researchers and scientists to gain knowledge

<table>
<tr>
<td>

CRITICAL
THINKING
CHECK 1.1
</td>
<td>

Identify the source of knowledge in each of the following examples:
1. A celebrity is endorsing a new diet program, noting that she lost weight on the program and so will you.
2. Based on several observations that Pam has made, she feels sure that cell phone use does not adversely affect driving ability.
3. A friend tells you that she is not sure why, but because she has a feeling of dread, she thinks that you should not take the plane trip you were planning for next week.
</td>
</tr>
</table>

THE SCIENTIFIC (CRITICAL THINKING) APPROACH AND PSYCHOLOGY

How do we apply what we know about science to the discipline of psychology? As already mentioned, many students are attracted to psychology because they think it is *not* a science. The error in their thinking is that they believe subject matter alone defines what is and what is not science. Instead, what defines science is how something is studied. Science is a way of thinking about and observing events in order to achieve a deeper understanding of them. Psychologists apply the scientific method to their study of human beings and other animals.

The scientific method requires developing an attitude of skepticism. A **skeptic** is a person who questions the validity, authenticity, or truth of something purportedly factual. In our society being described as a skeptic is not typically thought of as a compliment, but for a scientist it is. Being a skeptic means that you do not blindly accept any new idea being promoted at the time. Instead, the skeptic needs data to support an idea and insists on proper testing procedures when the data are collected. Being a skeptic and using the scientific method involve applying three important criteria that help define science: systematic empiricism, public verification, and empirically solvable problems (Stanovich, 2007).

skeptic: A person who questions the validity, authenticity, or truth of something purporting to be factual.

Systematic Empiricism

As we have seen, empiricism is the practice of relying on observation to draw conclusions. Before the 17th century most people relied more on intuition, religious doctrine provided by authorities, and reason than they did on empiricism. Most people today would probably agree that the best way to learn about something is to observe it. However, empiricism alone is not enough; it must be **systematic empiricism**. Therefore simply observing a series of events does not lead to scientific knowledge. The observations must be made systematically to test a hypothesis and to refute or develop a theory. As an example, if a researcher is interested in the relationship between vitamin C

systematic empiricism: Making observations in a systematic manner in order to test hypotheses and refute or develop a theory.

and the incidence of colds, she does not simply ask people haphazardly whether they take vitamin C and how many colds they have had. This approach is empirical but not systematic. Instead, the researcher might design a study to assess the effects of vitamin C on colds. Her study would probably involve using a representative group of individuals, who are then randomly assigned to either take or not take vitamin C supplements. She would then observe whether the groups differ in the number of colds they report. This approach would be empirical *and* systematic. (We go into more detail on designing such a study in the next module.) By using systematic empiricism, researchers can draw more reliable and valid conclusions than they can from observation alone.

Public Verification

public verification:
Presenting research to the public so that it can be observed, replicated, criticized, and tested.

Scientific research is research that is open to **public verification**. The research is presented to the public in such a way that it can be observed, replicated, criticized, and tested for veracity by others. Commonly the research is submitted to a scientific journal for possible publication. Most journals are peer reviewed, that is, other scientists critique the research in order to decide whether it meets the standards for publication. If a study is published, other researchers can read about the findings, attempt to replicate them, and through this process demonstrate that the results are reliable. We should be suspicious of any claims made without the support of public verification. For instance, many people have claimed that they were abducted by aliens. These claims do not fit the bill of public verification; they are simply the claims of individuals with no evidence to support them. Other people claim that they have lived past lives. Once again, there is no evidence to support such claims. These types of claims are unverifiable; there is no way that they are open to public verification.

Empirically Solvable Problems

empirically solvable problems: Questions that are potentially answerable by means of currently available research techniques.

Science always investigates **empirically solvable problems**—questions that are potentially answerable by means of currently available research techniques. If a theory cannot be tested using empirical techniques, then scientists are not interested in it. For example, the question "Is there life after death?" is not an empirical question and thus cannot be tested scientifically. However, the question "Does an intervention program minimize rearrests of juvenile delinquents?" can be empirically studied, and thus it is within the realm of science.

principle of falsifiability:
Stating a scientific theory in such a way that it is possible to refute or disconfirm it.

When solvable problems are studied, they are always open to the **principle of falsifiability**, meaning that a scientific theory must be stated in such a way that it is possible to refute or disconfirm it. That is, the theory must predict not only what will happen but also what will not happen. A theory is not scientific if it is irrefutable. You may be thinking that if a theory is irrefutable, it must be really good. However, in science, an irrefutable theory is not good. Read on to see why.

pseudoscience: A claim that appears to be scientific but that actually violates the criteria of science.

Pseudoscience, a claim that appears to be scientific but that actually violates the criteria of science, is usually irrefutable and is also often confused with science. As an example, those who believe in extrasensory perception (ESP, a pseudoscience) often make an argument of the fact that no publicly verifiable example of ESP has ever been documented through systematic empiricism. The reason they offer is that the conditions necessary for ESP to occur are violated by controlled laboratory conditions. This argument means that they have an answer for every situation. If ESP were ever demonstrated under empirical conditions, they might say their belief is supported. However, when ESP repeatedly fails to be demonstrated in controlled laboratory conditions, they say their belief is not falsified because the conditions were not "right" for ESP to be demonstrated. Thus, because ESP believers have set up a situation in which they claim falsifying data are not valid, the theory of ESP violates the principle of falsifiability.

You may be thinking that the explanation provided by the proponents of ESP makes some sense. Let me give you an analogous example from Stanovich (2007). Stanovich jokingly claims he has found the underlying brain mechanism that controls behavior and that you will soon be able to read about it in the *National Enquirer*. According to him, two tiny green men reside in the left hemispheres of our brains. These little green men have the power to control the processes taking place in many areas of the brain. Why have we not heard about these little green men before? Well, that's easy to explain. According to Stanovich, the little green men have the ability to detect any intrusion into the brain, and when they do, they become invisible. You may feel that your intelligence has been insulted with this foolish explanation of brain functioning. However, you should see the similarity of this explanation to the one offered by proponents of ESP, despite any evidence to support it and much evidence to refute it.

IN REVIEW The Scientific Method		
Criteria	**Description**	**Purpose**
Systematic empiricism	Making observations in a systematic manner	To refute or develop a theory or to test hypotheses
Public verification	Presenting research to the public so that it can be observed, replicated, criticized, and tested	To determine the veracity of a theory
Empirically solvable problems	Stating questions in such a way that they are answerable by means of currently available research techniques	To determine whether a theory can potentially be tested using empirical techniques and whether it is falsifiable

CRITICAL THINKING CHECK 1.2

1. Explain how a theory such as Freud's, which attributes much of personality and psychological disorders to unconscious drives, violates the principle of falsifiability.
2. Identify a currently popular pseudoscience and explain how it might violate each of the criteria identified above.

BASIC AND APPLIED RESEARCH

basic research: The study of psychological issues in order to seek knowledge for its own sake.

Some psychologists conduct research because they enjoy seeking knowledge and answering questions. This work is referred to as **basic research**—the study of psychological issues to seek knowledge for its own sake. Most basic research is conducted in university or laboratory settings. Its intent is not immediate application but the gaining of knowledge. However, many treatments and procedures that have been developed to help humans and other animals began with researchers asking basic research questions that later led to applications. Examples of basic research include identifying differences in capacity and duration in short-term memory and long-term memory, identifying whether cognitive maps can be mentally rotated, determining how various schedules of reinforcement affect learning, and determining how lesioning a certain area in the brains of rats affects their behavior.

applied research: The study of psychological issues that have practical significance and potential solutions.

A second type of research is applied. **Applied research** is the study of psychological issues that have practical significance and potential solutions. Scientists who conduct applied research are interested in finding an answer to a question because the answer can be immediately applied. Much applied research is conducted by private businesses and the government. Examples of applied research include understanding how stress affects the immune system, determining the accuracy of eyewitness testimony, developing and identifying the most effective therapies in treating depression, and identifying factors associated with weight gain.

Some people think that most research should be directly relevant to a social problem or issue. That is, they favor *only* applied research. However, much of what started out as basic research has eventually led to some sort of application. If researchers stopped asking questions simply because they wanted to know the answer (that is, stopped engaging in basic research), they would undoubtedly lose many great ideas and eventual applications.

GOALS OF SCIENCE

Scientific research has three basic goals: (1) to describe behavior, (2) to predict behavior, and (3) to explain behavior. All of these goals lead to a better understanding of behavior and mental processes.

Description

description: Carefully observing behavior in order to describe it.

Description begins with careful observation. Psychologists might describe patterns of behavior, thought, or emotions in humans. They might also describe the behavior(s) of other animals. Accordingly, researchers might observe and describe the type of play behavior exhibited by children or the mating behavior of chimpanzees. Description allows us to learn about behavior as well as when it occurs. Let's say, for example, that you are interested in the channel-surfing behavior of men and women. Careful observation and description would be needed to determine whether there were any gender differences in channel surfing. Description allows us to observe that two events are systematically related to one another. Without description as a first step, predictions cannot be made.

Prediction

prediction: Identifying the factors that indicate when an event or events will occur.

Prediction allows us to identify the factors that indicate when an event or events will occur. In other words, knowing the level of one variable allows us to predict the approximate level of the other variable. We know that if one variable is present at a certain level, then the other variable is likely to be present at a certain level. Therefore if we observed that men channel-surf with greater frequency than women, we could then make predictions about how often men and women might change channels when given the chance.

Explanation

explanation: Identifying the causes that determine when and why a behavior occurs.

Finally, **explanation** allows us to identify the causes that determine when and why a behavior occurs. To explain a behavior, we need to demonstrate that we can manipulate the factors needed to produce or eliminate it. For instance, if gender predicts channel surfing, why is that? The cause could be genetic or environmental. Maybe men have less tolerance for commercials and thus channel-surf at a greater rate. Maybe women are more interested in the content of commercials and are thus less likely to change channels. Maybe the attention span of women is longer. Maybe something associated with having a Y chromosome increases channel surfing, or something associated with having two X chromosomes leads to less channel surfing. Obviously there is a wide variety of possible explanations.

As scientists we test possibilities to identify the best explanation of why a behavior occurs. When we try to identify the best explanation, we must systematically eliminate any alternative explanations, and to do that, we must impose control over the research. We will discuss control and alternative explanations in the next module.

SUMMARY

We began the module by stressing the importance of research in psychology. We identified such research areas in the discipline of psychology as psychobiology, cognition, human development, social psychology, and psychotherapy. We discussed sources of knowledge, including intuition, superstition, authority, tenacity, rationalism, empiricism, and science. We stressed the importance of using the scientific method to gain knowledge in psychology. The scientific method is a combination of empiricism and rationalism; it must meet the criteria of systematic empiricism, public verification, and empirically solvable problems. Lastly, we outlined the three goals of science: description, prediction, and explanation. In the next module these goals will be related to the research methods used by psychologists.

REVIEW OF KEY TERMS

knowledge via superstition	knowledge via rationalism	theory	pseudoscience
knowledge via intuition	knowledge via empiricism	skeptic	basic research
knowledge via authority	knowledge via science	systematic empiricism	applied research
knowledge via tenacity	hypothesis	public verification	description
	variable	empirically solvable problems	prediction
		principle of falsifiability	explanation

MODULE EXERCISES

(Answers to odd-numbered exercises appear in Appendix A.)

1. Identify a piece of information that you have gained through each of the sources of knowledge discussed in the module (superstition or intuition, authority, tenacity, rationalism, empiricism, and science).
2. Provide an argument for the idea that basic research is as important as applied research.
3. Why is it a compliment for a scientist to be called a skeptic?
4. An infomercial asserts, "A study proves that Fat-B-Gone works, and it will work for you also." What is wrong with this statement?
5. What are the advantages of basic research and applied research?

CRITICAL THINKING CHECK ANSWERS

1.1

1. Knowledge via authority
2. Knowledge via empiricism
3. Knowledge via superstition or intuition

1.2

1. A theory such as Freud's violates the principle of falsifiability because it is not possible to falsify or test the theory. The theory is irrefutable. Freud attributes much of personality to unconscious drives, and there is no way to test whether this is so or for that matter whether there is such a thing as an unconscious drive.
2. Belief in paranormal events is currently a popular pseudoscience (spurred on by the popularity of such shows as *The X-Files* and *Ghosthunters*), but it violates all three criteria that define science. First, the ideas must be supported by systematic empiricism. Most "authorities" in this area do not test hypotheses but rather offer demonstrations of their abilities. Second, there has been little or no public verification of claims. There is little reliable and valid research on the topic, and what there is does not support the claims. Instead, most evidence tends to consist of testimonials. Third, many of the claims are stated in such a way that they are not solvable problems. That is, they do not open themselves to the principle of falsifiability ("My powers do not work in a controlled laboratory setting" or "My powers do not work when skeptics are present").

WEB RESOURCES

Check your knowledge of the content and key terms in this module with a practice quiz and interactive flashcards at **www.cengage.com/ psychology/jackson,** or for step-by-step practice and information, check out the Statistics and Research Methods Workshops at **www. cengage.com/psychology/workshops.**

An Introduction to Research Methods

LEARNING OBJECTIVES

- Identify and compare descriptive methods.
- Identify and compare predictive (relational) methods.
- Describe the explanatory method. Your description should include independent variable, dependent variable, control group, and experimental group.
- Explain how we "do" science and how proof and disproof relate to doing science.

The goals of science discussed in the previous module very closely track the research methods scientists use. In other words, there are methods that are descriptive in nature, predictive in nature, and explanatory in nature. We briefly introduce these methods in this module; the remainder of the text covers them in far greater detail. Descriptive methods are covered in Chapter Four, predictive methods in Chapter Five, and explanatory methods in Chapter Six.

DESCRIPTIVE METHODS

observational method: Making observations of human or other animal behavior.

naturalistic observation: Observing the behavior of humans or other animals in their natural habitats.

laboratory observation: Observing the behavior of humans or other animals in a contrived and controlled situation, usually the laboratory.

case study method: An in-depth study of one or more individuals.

survey method: Questioning individuals on a topic or topics and then describing their responses.

sample: The group of people who participate in a study.

population: All the people about whom a study is meant to generalize.

random sample: A sample achieved through random selection in which each member of the population is equally likely to be chosen.

Psychologists use three types of descriptive methods. First, in the **observational method** the researcher simply observes human or other animal behavior. Psychologists approach observation in two ways. **Naturalistic observation** involves observing how humans or other animals behave in their natural habitats. Observing the mating behavior of chimpanzees in their natural setting is an example. **Laboratory observation** entails observing behavior in a contrived and controlled situation, usually the laboratory. Bringing children to a laboratory playroom to observe play behavior is an example. Observation involves description at its most basic level. One advantage of the observational method, as well as of other descriptive methods, is the flexibility to change what we are studying. A disadvantage of descriptive methods is that we have little control. As we use more powerful methods, we gain control but lose flexibility.

A second descriptive method is the **case study method**. A case study is an in-depth study of one or more individuals. Freud used case studies to develop his theory of personality development. Similarly, Jean Piaget used case studies to develop his theory of cognitive development in children. This method is descriptive in nature because it involves simply describing the individual(s) being studied.

The third method that relies on description is the **survey method**, which involves questioning individuals on a topic or topics and then describing their responses. Surveys can be administered by mail, over the phone, on the Internet, or in a personal interview. One advantage of the survey method over the other descriptive methods is that it allows researchers to study larger groups of individuals more easily.

This method, however, has disadvantages. One concern is whether the group of people who participate in the study (the **sample**) is representative of all the people about whom the study is meant to generalize (the **population**). This concern can usually be overcome through random sampling. A **random sample** is achieved when through random selection each member of the population is equally likely to be chosen as part of the sample. Another concern has to do with the wording of questions. Are the questions easy to understand? Are they written in such a manner that they bias the respondents' answers? Such concerns affect the validity of the data collected.

PREDICTIVE (RELATIONAL) METHODS

correlational method: A method that assesses the degree of relationship between two variables.

Two methods allow researchers not only to describe behaviors but also to predict from one variable to another. The first, the **correlational method**, assesses the degree of relationship between two measured variables. If two variables are correlated with each other, then we can predict from one variable to the other with a certain degree of accuracy. For example, height and weight are correlated. The relationship is such that an increase in one variable (height) is generally accompanied by an increase in the other variable (weight). Knowing this relationship, we can predict an individual's approximate weight with a certain degree of accuracy based on our knowledge of the person's height.

One problem with correlational research is that it is often misinterpreted. Frequently people assume that because two variables are correlated, there must be some sort of causal relationship between them. This is not so. *Correlation does not imply causation.* A correlation simply means that the two variables are related in some way. For instance, being a certain height does not cause you to be a certain weight. It would be nice if it did because then we would not have to worry about being either under- or overweight. What if I told you that watching violent TV and displaying aggressive behavior were correlated? What could you conclude based on this correlation? Many people might conclude that watching violent TV causes one to act more aggressively. Based on the evidence given (a correlational study), however, we cannot draw this conclusion. All we can conclude is that those who watch violent television programs also tend to act more aggressively. It is possible that violent TV causes aggression, but we cannot draw this conclusion based only on correlational data. It is also possible that those who are aggressive by nature are attracted to violent television programs or that another (third) variable is causing both aggressive behavior and watching violent TV. The point is that observing a correlation between two variables means only that they are related.

positive relationship: A relationship between two variables in which an increase in one is accompanied by an increase in the other.

negative relationship: A relationship between two variables in which an increase in one is accompanied by a decrease in the other.

The correlation between height and weight or between violent TV and aggressive behavior is a **positive relationship**: as one variable (height) increases, we observe an increase in the second (weight). Some correlations indicate a **negative relationship**: as one variable increases, the other systematically decreases. Can you think of an example of a negative relationship between two variables? Consider this: as elevation increases, temperature decreases. Negative correlations also allow us to predict one variable based on another. Knowing the elevation of a mountain helps me predict the approximate temperature.

quasi-experimental method: Research that compares naturally occurring groups of individuals; the variable of interest cannot be manipulated.

A second method, the **quasi-experimental method**, also allows us to describe and predict by permitting us to compare naturally occurring groups of individuals. For example, we can examine whether alcohol consumption by students in a fraternity or sorority differs from that of students not in such organizations. You can see in a moment that this method differs from the experimental method, which is described in the next section, in that the groups studied occur naturally, that is, we do not control whether people join Greek organizations. Individuals choose to join or not, and we simply look for differences between the naturally occurring groups (in this case in the amount of alcohol typically consumed).

The type of variable used in quasi-experimental research and described above is often referred to as a **subject** or **participant variable,** a characteristic of the participants that cannot be changed. Because we are using groups that occur naturally, any differences we find may be due to the variable of being or not being a Greek member, or they may be due to other factors that we are unable to control in this study. Thus perhaps those who like to drink are also more likely to join a Greek organization. Once again, if we find a difference between the groups in the amount of alcohol consumed, we can use this finding to predict which type of student (Greek member or nonmember) is likely to drink more. However, we cannot conclude that belonging to a Greek organization *causes* one to drink more because the participants came to us after choosing to belong to these organizations. In the end what is missing when we use predictive methods such as the correlational and quasi-experimental methods is control.

When using predictive methods, we do not systematically manipulate the variables of interest; we only measure them. Although we may observe a relationship between variables (such as between drinking and Greek membership), we cannot conclude that it is a causal relationship. Why not? There could be *alternative explanations* for this relationship. An **alternative explanation** is the idea that it is possible some other uncontrolled, extraneous variable may be responsible for the observed relationship. Accordingly, maybe those who choose to join Greek organizations come from higher-income families and have more money to spend on such things as alcohol. Or maybe those who choose to join such organizations are more interested in socialization and drinking alcohol before they even join. Thus because these methods leave the possibility for alternative explanations, we cannot use them to establish cause-and-effect relationships.

participant (subject) variable: A characteristic of the participants that cannot be changed.

alternative explanation: The idea that another uncontrolled, extraneous variable may be responsible for an observed relationship.

EXPLANATORY METHOD

When using the experimental method, researchers pay a great deal of attention to eliminating the possibility of alternative explanations by using the proper controls. As a result, the **experimental method** allows researchers not only to describe and predict but also to determine whether there is a cause-and-effect relationship between the variables of interest. This method therefore enables researchers to know when and why a behavior occurs. Many preconditions must be met for a study to be experimental in nature, and we discuss many of these conditions in detail in later modules. Here, we simply consider the basics—the minimum requirements needed for an experiment.

experimental method: a research method that allows a researcher to establish a cause-and-effect relationship through manipulation of a variable and control of the situation.

The basic premise of experimentation is that the researcher controls as much as possible to determine whether there is a cause-and-effect relationship between the variables being studied. Let's say, for example, that a researcher is interested in whether taking vitamin C supplements leads to fewer colds. When using the experimental method, the researcher manipulates at least one

independent variable: The variable in a study that is manipulated by the researcher.

dependent variable: The variable in a study that is measured by the researcher.

control group: The group of participants who do not receive any level of the independent variable and serve as the baseline in a study.

experimental group: The group of participants who receive some level of the independent variable.

random assignment: Assigning participants to conditions in such a way that each has the same probability as all others of being placed in any condition.

variable (known as the **independent variable**) and measures at least one variable (known as the **dependent variable**). What should the researcher manipulate in our study? If you identified the amount of vitamin C, you are correct. If the amount of vitamin C is the independent variable, then the number of colds is the dependent variable.

For comparative purposes the independent variable has to have at least two groups, or conditions, typically referred to as the control group and the experimental group. The **control group** serves as the baseline or "standard" condition. In our vitamin C study the control group consists of those who do not take vitamin C supplements. The **experimental group** receives the treatment; in this case they take vitamin C supplements. Thus one thing that researchers control in an experiment is the level of the independent variable that participants receive.

What else should researchers control to help eliminate alternative explanations? They need to control the type of participants in each of the treatment conditions. They should begin by drawing a random sample of participants from the population. Once they have the sample, they have to decide who serves in the control group and who in the experimental group. To gain as much control as possible and to eliminate as many alternative explanations as possible, they should use **random assignment**, that is, assigning participants to conditions in such a way that each has the same probability as any other participant of being placed in any condition. How does random assignment help gain control and eliminate alternative explanations? Random assignment should minimize or eliminate differences between the groups. In other words, the two groups of participants should be as alike as possible. The only difference we want between the groups is that of the independent variable we are manipulating: the amount of vitamin C. Once participants are assigned to conditions, researchers keep track of the number of colds they have over a specified time period (the dependent variable).

Let's review some of the controls used in the present study. We have controlled who is in the study (we want a sample representative of the population about whom we are trying to generalize), who participates in each group (we should randomly assign participants to the two conditions), and the treatment each group receives as part of the study (some take vitamin C supplements and some do not). Randomly assigning participants also helps to control for participant differences between the groups. Can you identify other variables that we might need to consider for greater control in the present study? How about the amount of sleep participants receive each day, the type of diet, and the amount of exercise (all variables that might contribute to general health and well-being)? There are undoubtedly other variables we would need to control if we were actually to conduct this study. We discuss control in greater detail in later modules, but the basic idea is that when using the experimental method, we try to **control** as much as possible by manipulating the independent variable and limiting any other extraneous variables that could affect results.

control: manipulating the independent variable in an experiment or any other extraneous variables that could affect the results of a study.

What does all this control gain us? After completing this study with the proper controls, if we found that those in the experimental group (those who took vitamin C supplements) did in fact have fewer colds than those in the control group, we would have evidence supporting a cause-and-effect relationship between these variables. Thus we could conclude that taking vitamin C supplements reduces the frequency of colds.

IN REVIEW	An Introduction to Research Methods	
Goal Met	**Research Methods**	**Advantages/Disadvantages**
Description	Observational method	Descriptive methods allow description of behavior(s)
	Case study method	Descriptive methods do not support reliable predictions
	Survey Method	Descriptive methods do not support cause-and-effect explanations
Prediction	Correlational method	Predictive methods allow description of behavior(s)
	Quasi-experimental method	Predictive methods support reliable predictions of one variable based on another
		Predictive methods do not support cause-and-effect explanations
Explanation	Experimental method	Allows description of behavior(s)
		Supports reliable predictions of one variable based on another
		Supports cause-and-effect explanations

CRITICAL THINKING CHECK 2.1

1. In a recent study researchers found a negative correlation between income level and the incidence of psychological disorders. Jim thinks that this correlation means that being poor leads to psychological disorders. Is he correct in his conclusion? Why or why not?

2. In a study designed to assess the effects of exercise on life satisfaction, participants were assigned to groups based on whether or not they reported exercising. All participants then completed a life satisfaction inventory.
   a. What is the independent variable?
   b. What is the dependent variable?
   c. Is the independent variable a participant variable or a true manipulated variable?

3. Which type of method would you recommend using to answer the following questions?
   a. What percentage of cars run red lights?
   b. Do student athletes spend as much time studying as student nonathletes?
   c. Is there a relationship between the type of punishment used by parents and aggressiveness in children?
   d. Do athletes who use imaging techniques perform better than those who do not?

(continued)

4. Your mother claims that she has found a wonderful new treatment for her arthritis. She read "somewhere" that rubbing vinegar into the affected area for 10 minutes twice a day helps. She tried this remedy and is convinced that her arthritis pain has been lessened. She now thinks that the medical community should recommend this treatment. What alternative explanation(s) might you offer to your mother for why she feels better? How would you explain to her that her evidence is not sufficient for the medical or scientific community?

DOING SCIENCE

Although the experimental method can establish a cause-and-effect relationship, most researchers do not wholeheartedly accept a conclusion based on only one study. Why not? Any number of problems can occur in a study. For instance, there may be control problems. Researchers may believe that they have controlled everything but may have missed something, and the uncontrolled factor may affect the results. In other words, a researcher may believe that the manipulated independent variable caused the results when in reality something else did.

Another reason for caution in interpreting experimental results is that a study may be limited by the technical equipment available at the time. For example, in the early part of the 19th century many scientists believed that studying the bumps on a person's head allowed them to know something about the mind of the individual. This movement, known as phrenology, was popularized through the writings of physician Joseph Gall (1758–1828). Today we know that phrenology is a pseudoscience. However, at the time it was popular, phrenology appeared very "scientific" and "technical." Obviously with hindsight and with the technological advances we have today, phrenology seems somewhat laughable to us now.

Finally, we cannot completely rely on the findings of one study because a single study cannot tell us everything about a theory. Science is not static; the theories generated through science change. As an example, we often hear about new findings in the medical field such as "Eggs are so high in cholesterol that you should eat no more than two a week." Then, a couple of years later, we might read, "Eggs are not as bad for you as originally thought. New research shows that it is acceptable to eat them every day." People may complain when confronted with such contradictory findings: "Those doctors, they don't know what they're talking about. You can't believe any of them. First they say one thing, and then they say the complete opposite. It's best to just ignore all of them." The point is that when testing a theory scientifically, we may obtain contradictory results. The contradictions may lead to new and very valuable information that subsequently leads to a theoretical change. Based on the consensus of the research, theories evolve and change over time. Support of an idea or theory by data from one study does not mean that we just accept the theory as it currently stands and never do any more research on the topic.

PROOF AND DISPROOF

When scientists test theories, they do not try to prove them true. Theories can be supported by the data collected, but obtaining support does not mean a theory is true in all instances. Proof of a theory is logically impossible. Consider the following problem, adapted from Griggs and Cox (1982) and known as the Drinking Age Problem (the reason for the name will become apparent).

Imagine that you are a police officer responsible for making sure that the drinking age rule is being followed. The four cards below represent information about four people sitting at a table. One side of a card indicates what the person is drinking, and the other side of the card indicates the person's age. The rule is "If a person is drinking alcohol, then the person is 21 or over." In order to test whether the rule is true or false, which card or cards below would you turn over? Turn over only the card or cards that you need to check to be sure.

Drinking a beer	16 years old	Drinking a Coke	22 years old

Does turning over the beer card and finding that the person is 21 years of age or older prove that the rule is always true? No. The fact that one person is following the rule does not mean that it is always true. How then do we test a hypothesis? We test a hypothesis by attempting to falsify or disconfirm it. If it cannot be falsified, then we say we have support for it.

Which cards would you choose in an attempt to falsify the rule in the Drinking Age Problem? If you identified the beer card, you are correct. If you turn over the beer card and find that the individual is under 21 years of age, then the rule is false. Is there another card that could also falsify the rule? The 16 years of age card can. If you turn that card over and find that the individual is drinking alcohol, then the rule is false. These are the only two cards that can potentially falsify the rule. Thus they are the only two cards that need to be turned over.

Even though disproof or disconfirmation is logically sound in terms of testing hypotheses, falsifying a hypothesis does not always mean that the hypothesis is false. There may be design problems in the study, as already described. Thus even when a theory is falsified, we need to be cautious in our interpretation. We do not want to discount a theory completely based on a single study.

THE RESEARCH PROCESS

The actual process of conducting research involves several steps, the first of which is to identify a problem. Accomplishing this step is discussed more fully in Chapter Two. The other steps include reviewing the literature, generating hypotheses (Chapters Two and Three), designing and conducting the study (Chapters Four, Five, and Six), analyzing the data and interpreting the results (Chapters Seven, Eight, and Nine), and communicating the results (Chapter Ten).

SUMMARY

In this module we discussed the three categories of research methods used by psychologists: descriptive methods, predictive methods, and the explanatory method. Descriptive methods include observation, case study, and survey methods. Predictive methods include correlational and quasi-experimental methods. The experimental method allows for the explanation of cause-and-effect relationships. Finally, we introduced some practicalities of doing research, discussed proof and disproof in science, and noted that testing a hypothesis involves attempting to falsify it.

REVIEW OF KEY TERMS

observational method

naturalistic observation

laboratory observation

case study method

survey method

sample

population

random sample

correlational method

positive relationship

negative relationship

quasi-experimental method

participant (subject) variable

alternative explanation

experimental method

independent variable

dependent variable

control group

experimental group

random assignment

control

MODULE EXERCISES

(Answers to odd-numbered exercises appear in Appendix A.)

1. Many psychology students believe that they do not need to know about research methods because they plan to pursue careers in clinical/counseling psychology. What argument can you provide against this view?

2. In a research project intended to gather data on the effects of type of study method on examination performance, participants are randomly assigned to one of two conditions. In one condition they study alone, using notes they took during class lectures. In a second condition participants study in interactive groups with notes from class lectures. The amount of time spent studying is held constant. All students then take the same exam. In this study:
   a. What is the independent variable?
   b. What is the dependent variable?
   c. Identify the control and experimental groups.
   d. Is the independent variable manipulated, or is it a participant variable?

3. Researchers interested in the effects of caffeine on anxiety have randomly assigned participants to one of two conditions in a study: the no-caffeine condition or the caffeine condition. After drinking two cups of either regular or decaffeinated coffee, participants take an anxiety inventory. In this study:
   a. What is the independent variable?
   b. What is the dependent variable?
   c. Identify the control and experimental groups.
   d. Is the independent variable manipulated, or is it a participant variable?

4. Gerontologists interested in the effects of age on reaction time have two groups of participants take a test in which they must indicate as quickly as possible whether a probe word is a member of a previous set of words. One group of participants is between the ages of 25 and 45, whereas the other group is between the ages of 55 and 75. The time it takes to make the response is measured. In this study:
   a. What is the independent variable?
   b. What is the dependent variable?
   c. Identify the control and experimental groups.
   d. Is the independent variable manipulated, or is it a participant variable?

CRITICAL THINKING CHECK ANSWERS

2.1

1. Jim is incorrect because he is inferring causation based on correlational evidence. He is assuming that because the two variables are correlated, one must be causing changes in the other. In addition, he is assuming the direction of the inferred causal relationship: that a lower income level causes psychological disorders rather than that having a psychological disorder leads to a lower income level. The correlation simply indicates that these two variables are related inversely. That is, those with psychological disorders also tend to have lower income levels.

2. a. The independent variable is exercise.
   b. The dependent variable is life satisfaction.
   c. The independent variable is a participant variable.

3. a. Naturalistic observation
   b. Quasi-experimental method
   c. Correlational method
   d. Experimental method

4. An alternative explanation might be that simply rubbing the affected area makes it feel better, regardless of whether she is rubbing in vinegar. Her evidence is not sufficient for the medical or scientific community because it was not gathered using the scientific method. Instead, it is simply a testimonial from one person.

WEB RESOURCES

Check your knowledge of the content and key terms in this module with a practice quiz and interactive flashcards at **www.cengage.com/ psychology/jackson**, or for step-by-step practice and information, check out the Statistics and Research Methods Workshops at **www. cengage.com/psychology/workshops**.

CHAPTER ONE SUMMARY AND REVIEW: THINKING LIKE A SCIENTIST

We began the chapter by stressing the importance of research in psychology. We identified such areas in the discipline of psychology in which research is conducted as psychobiology, cognition, human development, social psychology, and psychotherapy. We discussed sources of knowledge: intuition, superstition, authority, tenacity, rationalism, empiricism, and science. We stressed the importance of using the scientific method to gain knowledge in psychology. The scientific method is a combination of empiricism and rationalism; it must meet the criteria of systematic empiricism, public verification, and empirically solvable problems.

We outlined the three goals of science—description, prediction, and explanation—and related them to the research methods used by psychologists. Descriptive methods include observation, case study, and survey methods. Predictive methods include correlational and quasi-experimental methods. The experimental method allows for the explanation of cause-and-effect relationships. Finally, we introduced some practicalities of doing research, discussed proof and disproof in science, and noted that testing a hypothesis involves attempting to falsify it.

CHAPTER ONE REVIEW EXERCISES

(Answers to exercises appear in Appendix A.)

Fill-in Self-Test

Answer the following questions. If you have trouble answering any of the questions, restudy the relevant material before going on to the multiple-choice self-test.

1. To gain knowledge without being consciously aware of where it comes from is gaining knowledge via _____.

2. To gain knowledge from repeated ideas and to cling stubbornly to them despite evidence to the contrary is to gain knowledge via _____.

3. A _____ is a prediction regarding the outcome of a study that often involves a prediction regarding the relationship between two variables in a study.

4. A person who questions the validity, authenticity, or truth of something purporting to be factual is a _____.

5. _____ are questions that are potentially answerable by means of currently available research techniques.

6. _____ involves making claims that appear to be scientific but that actually violate the criteria of science.

7. The three goals of science are _____, _____, and _____.

8. _____ research involves the study of psychological issues that have practical significance and potential solutions.

9. A _____ is an in-depth study of one or more individuals.

10. All of the people about whom a study is meant to generalize make up the _____.

11. In the _____ method the degree of relationship between at least two variables is assessed.

12. A characteristic inherent in the participants that cannot be changed is known as a _____ variable.

13. The variable in a study that is manipulated is the _____ variable.

14. The _____ group is the group of participants who serve as the baseline in a study. They do not receive any level of the independent variable.

Multiple-Choice Self-Test

Select the single best answer for each of the following questions. If you have trouble answering any of the questions, restudy the relevant material.

1. A belief that is based on subjective feelings is to knowing via _____ as stubbornly clinging to knowledge gained from repeated ideas is to knowledge via _____.
   a. authority; superstition
   b. superstition; intuition
   c. tenacity; intuition
   d. superstition; tenacity

2. Tom did really well on his psychology examination last week, and he believes it is because he used his lucky pen. He has now decided that he must use this pen for every written examination because he believes it will make him lucky. This belief is based on _____.
   a. superstition
   b. rationalism
   c. authority
   d. science

3. A prediction regarding the outcome of a study is to _____ as an organized system of assumptions and principles that attempts to explain certain phenomena and how they are related is to _____.
   a. theory; hypothesis
   b. hypothesis; theory
   c. independent variable; dependent variable
   d. dependent variable; independent variable

4. _____ involves making claims that appear to be scientific but that actually violate the criteria of science.
   a. The principle of falsifiability
   b. Systematic empiricism
   c. Being a skeptic
   d. Pseudoscience

5. The study of psychological issues to seek knowledge for its own sake is to _____ as the study of psychological issues that have practical significance and potential solutions is to _____.
   a. basic; applied
   b. applied; basic
   c. naturalistic; laboratory
   d. laboratory; naturalistic

6. Ray was interested in the mating behavior of squirrels; so he went into the field to observe them. Ray is using the _____ method of research.
   a. case study method
   b. laboratory observational
   c. naturalistic observational
   d. correlational

7. Negative correlation is to _____ as positive correlation is to _____.
   a. increasing or decreasing together; moving in opposite directions
   b. moving in opposite directions; increasing or decreasing together
   c. independent variable; dependent variable
   d. dependent variable; independent variable

8. Which of the following is a participant (subject) variable?
   a. the amount of time given to study a list of words
   b. fraternity membership
   c. the number of words in a memory test
   d. all of the above

9. If a researcher assigns participants to groups based, for example, on their earned GPA, the researcher is employing _____.
   a. a manipulated independent variable
   b. random assignment
   c. a participant variable
   d. a manipulated dependent variable

10. In an experimental study of how time spent studying affects grade, time spent studying is the _____.
   a. control group
   b. independent variable
   c. experimental group
   d. dependent variable

11. Baseline is to treatment as _____
    is to _____.
    a. independent variable; dependent
       variable
    b. dependent variable; independent variable
    c. experimental group; control group
    d. control group; experimental group

12. In a study of the effects of alcohol on
    driving performance, driving performance
    is the _____.
    a. control group
    b. independent variable
    c. experimental group
    d. dependent variable

KEY TERMS

Here are the terms from the glossary for Modules 1–2. Go through the list and see if you
can remember the definition of each.

Alternative
    explanation
Applied research
Basic research
Case study method
Control
Control group
Correlational method
Dependent variable
Description
Empirically solvable
    problems
Experimental group
Experimental method

Explanation
Hypothesis
Independent variable
Knowledge via
    authority
Knowledge via
    empiricism
Knowledge via
    intuition
Knowledge via
    rationalism
Knowledge via science
Knowledge via
    superstition

Knowledge via
    tenacity
Laboratory
    observation
Naturalistic
    observation
Negative relationship
Observational method
Participant (subject)
    variable
Population
Positive relationship
Prediction

Principle of
    falsifiability
Pseudoscience
Public verification
Quasi-experimental
    method
Random assignment
Random sample
Sample
Skeptic
Survey method
Systematic empiricism
Theory
Variable

CHAPTER **2**

Getting Started

4 | ETHICAL RESEARCH

Ethical Standards in Research with Human Participants
Institutional Review Boards
Informed Consent
Risk
Deception
Debriefing

Ethical Standards in Research with Children
Ethical Standards in Research with Animals

SUMMARY
REVIEW OF KEY TERMS
MODULE EXERCISES
CRITICAL THINKING CHECK ANSWERS
WEB RESOURCES

CHAPTER TWO SUMMARY AND REVIEW: GETTING STARTED

In the preceding chapter we described the nature of science and of thinking critically like a scientist. In addition, we offered a brief introduction to the research methods used by psychologists. In this chapter we discuss issues related to getting started on a research project, beginning with library research and moving on to conducting research ethically. We explain how to use some of the resources available through most libraries, and we cover the guidelines set forth by the APA (American Psychological Association) for the ethical treatment of both human and nonhuman participants used in research. The APA has very specific ethical guidelines for the treatment of humans used in research that are set forth in the APA's *Ethical Principles of Psychologists and Code of Conduct* (2002). In presenting these guidelines, we pay particular attention to several issues: obtaining approval for a research project, the meaning of informed consent, minimizing risk to participants, the acceptability of using deception in a research study, debriefing your participants, and detailing the special considerations when using children as participants. We also review the APA guidelines for using animals in research.

Research Ideas

LEARNING OBJECTIVES

- Use resources in the library to locate information.
- Understand the major sections of a journal article.

Getting started on a research project begins with selecting a problem. Some students find selecting a problem the most daunting task of the whole research process, whereas other students have so many ideas that they do not know where to begin. If you fall into the first category and are not sure what topic you want to research, you can get ideas from a few places. If you have trouble generating research ideas, you can start with what others have already done. Go over past research on a topic instead of just jumping in with a completely new idea of your own. For example, if you are interested in treatments for depression, you should begin by researching some of the treatments currently available. While reading about these treatments, you may find that one or more journal articles raise questions that have yet to be addressed. Thus looking at the research already completed in an area gives you a firm foundation from which to begin your own research, and it may lead to a hypothesis that your research project might address.

A second way to generate research ideas is to review past theories on a topic. A good place to find a cursory review of theories on a topic is in your psychology textbooks. For instance, when students tell me they are having trouble coming up with an idea for a research project, I have them identify which psychology class they found most interesting. I then have them look at the textbook from that class and pick the chapter they found the most interesting. After that, they focus on the topic in the chapter that was most interesting; the topical coverage in the chapter usually provides details on several theories.

A third source of ideas for a research project is observation. We are all capable of observing behavior, and our observations may give rise to questions. For example, you may have observed that some students cheat on examinations or papers, whereas most never consider doing such a thing. Or you may have observed that certain individuals overindulge in alcohol, whereas others know their limits. Or maybe you believe, based on observation, that a person's mood is affected by the type of music he or she listens to. Any of these observations may lead to a research project.

Finally, ideas for research projects are often generated from the practical problems encountered in daily life. This type of idea should sound familiar to you from Module 1 because research designed to find answers to practical problems is called applied research. Many students easily develop research ideas based on practical problems that they or someone they know have encountered. Here are two ideas generated by students based on practical problems they encountered: Do alcohol awareness programs lead to more responsible alcohol consumption by college students? Does art therapy improve the mood and general well-being of those recovering from surgery?

REVIEWING THE LITERATURE

Once you decide on a topic, the next step is to conduct a literature review. A literature review is a search for the published studies that are relevant to your topic in order to ensure that you have a grasp of what has been done in your area of intended study. This task may sound overwhelming, but several resources are available that help you simplify the process. Notice that I did not say the process is simple—only that these resources help you simplify it. A thorough literature review takes time, but the resources discussed in this section help you make the best use of that time.

LIBRARY RESEARCH

Usually the best place to begin your research is at the library. Several resources available through most libraries are invaluable when you are conducting a literature review. One important resource, often overlooked by students, is the library staff. Reference librarians have been trained to find information; this is their job. If you give them a sufficient description of what you are looking for, they should be able to provide you with numerous resources. Do not, however, expect them to provide this information on the spot. Plan ahead and give the librarian enough time to help you.

Journals

Most published research in psychology appears in the form of journal articles. See Table 3.1 for a list of the major journals in psychology. Notice that the titles listed in this table are journals, not magazines such as *Psychology Today*. The difference is that a paper published in these journals goes through a process called *peer review*. The paper is first submitted to the editor of the journal, who sends it out for review by other scientists who are specialists in the subject area of the paper. Based on the reviews, the editor then decides whether to accept the paper for publication. Because of the limited space available in a journal, most of the papers submitted are ultimately rejected. Thus the research published in journals represents a fraction of the research conducted in an area, and because of the review process, it should be the best research.

"THAT'S IT? THAT'S PEER REVIEW?"

As you can see in Table 3.1, a great many journals publish psychology papers. Obviously it is not possible to keep up with all the research published in these journals. In fact, it would even be very difficult to read all of the studies published in a limited subject area. As a researcher then how can you identify the papers most relevant to your topic? It would take forever to browse through the psychology journals in your library to find articles of interest to you. Luckily, such browsing is not necessary.

Psychological Abstracts

Besides the reference librarian, your other best friend in the library is *Psychological (Psych) Abstracts*. *Psych Abstracts* is a reference resource published by the American Psychological Association that contains abstracts, or brief summaries, of articles in psychology and related disciplines. Updated monthly, it can be found in the reference section of the library. To use *Psych Abstracts*, look in the index at the back of each monthly issue for the topic in which you are interested. Next to the topic you will find numbers referencing abstracts in that issue. You can then refer to each of these abstracts to find where the full article is published, who wrote it, when it was published, the pages on which it appears, and a brief summary of the article.

PsycINFO and PsycLIT

Most libraries now have *Psych Abstracts* in electronic form. If your library has such a resource, you will probably find it easier to use than the printed version. PsycINFO is an electronic database that provides abstracts and citations to the

TABLE **3.1**

Some Journals Whose Articles Are Summarized in *Psychological Abstracts*

Applied Psychology
Applied Cognitive Psychology
Consulting Psychology Journal: Practice and Research
Educational and Psychological Measurement
Educational Psychologist
Educational Psychology Review
Environment and Behavior
Health Psychology
Journal of Applied Behavior Analysis
Journal of Applied Developmental Psychology
Journal of Applied Psychology
Journal of Educational Psychology
Journal of Environmental Psychology
Journal of Experimental Psychology: Applied
Journal of Occupational Health Psychology
Journal of Sport Psychology
Law and Human Behavior
Psychological Assessment
Psychology, Public Policy, and Law
School Psychology Quarterly

Biological Psychology
Behavioral and Brain Sciences
Behavioral Neuroscience
Biological Psychology
Brain and Language
Experimental and Clinical Psychopharmacology
Journal of Comparative Psychology
Neuropsychology
Physiological Psychology

Clinical/Counseling Psychology
Clinician's Research Digest
Counseling Psychologist
Journal of Abnormal Child Psychology
Journal of Abnormal Psychology
Journal of Clinical Child Psychology
Journal of Clinical Psychology
Journal of Consulting and Clinical Psychology
Journal of Contemporary Psychotherapy
Journal of Counseling Psychology
Journal of Psychotherapy Integration
Professional Psychology: Research and Practice
Psychoanalytic Psychology
Psychological Assessment
Psychological Services
Psychotherapy: Theory, Research, Practice, Training
Training and Education in Professional Psychology

(continued)

TABLE **3.1**

Some Journals Whose Articles Are Summarized in *Psychological Abstracts* (*continued*)

Developmental Psychology
Child Development
Developmental Psychobiology
Developmental Psychology
Developmental Review
Infant Behavior and Development
Journal of Experimental Child Psychology
Psychology and Aging

Experimental Psychology
Cognition
Cognition and Emotion
Cognitive Psychology
Cognitive Science
Dreaming
Journal of Experimental Psychology: Animal Behavior Processes
Journal of Experimental Psychology: Applied
Journal of Experimental Psychology: General
Journal of Experimental Psychology: Human Perception and Performance
Journal of Experimental Psychology: Learning, Memory, and Cognition
Journal of Memory and Language
Journal of the Experimental Analysis of Behavior
Learning and Motivation
Memory and Cognition
Perception
Quarterly Journal of Experimental Psychology

Family Therapy
American Journal of Family Therapy
Families, Systems, & Health
Journal of Family Psychology

General Psychology
American Psychologist
Contemporary Psychology
History of Psychology
Psychological Bulletin
Psychological Methods
Psychological Review
Psychological Science
Review of General Psychology

Personality and Social Psychology
Basic and Applied Social Psychology
Journal of Applied Social Psychology
Journal of Experimental Social Psychology
Journal of Personality
Journal of Personality and Social Psychology

(*continued*)

TABLE **3.1**
Some Journals Whose Articles Are Summarized in *Psychological Abstracts* (*continued*)

Journal of Personality Assessment
Journal of Social and Personal Relationships
Journal of Social Issues
Personality and Social Psychology Bulletin
Personality and Social Psychology Review

Treatment
Addictive Behaviors
Behavior Modification
Behavior Therapy
International Journal of Stress Management
Journal of Anxiety Disorders
Journal of Behavioral Medicine
Psychology of Addictive Behaviors
Rehabilitation Psychology

scholarly literature in the behavioral sciences and mental health. The database, which is updated monthly, includes relevant material of use to psychologists and professionals in related fields such as psychiatry, business, education, social science, neuroscience, law, and medicine. With the popularity of the Internet, most libraries now have access to PsycINFO. PyscLIT is the CD-ROM version of *Psych Abstracts*. Although PsycLIT is no longer published, the library at your school may still have copies of it. It was updated quarterly during its publication period.

To use either of these resources, you simply enter your topic of interest into the Find box, and the database provides a listing of relevant abstracts. When you use these resources, do not make your topic either too broad or too narrow. In addition, try several phrases. When students type in their topic and cannot find anything on it, their keyword may not be the word used by researchers in the field. To help you choose appropriate keywords, you might use the APA's *Thesaurus of Psychological Index Terms* (2007). This resource, based on the vocabulary used in psychology, directs you to the terms necessary to locate articles on your topic. Ask your reference librarian for help in finding and using this resource.

You will probably find, when using PsycINFO, that you need to complete several searches on a topic using different words and phrases. For example, if you were to enter the word "depression" in the Find box, you would discover a very large number of articles because PsycINFO looks for the key word in the title of the article and in the abstract itself. Thus you need to limit your search by using Boolean operators, such as AND, OR, and NOT as well as the limiters available through PsycINFO.

As an example, a search using the key word "depression" in the Find box and limited to articles published in 2008, with the word depression somewhere in the title of the article, returned abstracts for 2,322 articles—obviously too many to review. Limiting the search further by using the Boolean operator AND ("depression AND college students") and once again restricting the search to articles published in 2008 yielded abstracts for 34 articles—a much more manageable number.

Further refinements are possible by using the Boolean operators NOT and OR. For example, some of the 34 journal articles returned in the second search were about scales used to measure depression. If this aspect of depression is not of interest, the search can be limited further by typing the following into the Find box: "depression AND college students NOT (measures OR scales)." When the search is conducted with this restriction, the number of relevant journal articles published in 2008 drops to 29. With a little practice you can make PsycINFO an invaluable resource in searching the literature.

Social Science Citation Index and *Science Citation Index*

Other valuable resources in a literature review are the *Social Science Citation Index* (SSCI) and the *Science Citation Index* (SCI). Whereas *Psych Abstracts* helps you work backward in time (find articles published on a certain topic within a given year), the SSCI helps you work from a given article (a *key article*) to see what has been published on the topic since the key article was published. The SSCI includes disciplines from the social and behavioral sciences, whereas the SCI includes disciplines such as biology, chemistry, and medicine.

Both resources are used in a similar way. Suppose you find a very interesting paper on the effects of music on mood that was published in 2000, and you need to know what has been published since then on the topic. The SSCI and the SCI enable you to search for subsequent articles that cite the key article as well as for articles published by its author(s). If a subsequent article cites your key article, the chances are good that it is on the same topic and is therefore of interest to you. Moreover, if the author(s) of the key article has since published additional papers, those would also likely be of interest to you. Thus the SSCI and the SCI allow you to fill in the gap between 2000 and the present. In this way you can compile an up-to-date reference list and become familiar with most of the material published on a topic. When using the SSCI or the SCI, you may also find that one of the "new" articles you discover is another key article on your topic, and you can then look for subsequent articles that cite it or were written by its author(s). The SSCI and the SCI are often available online through your library's home page.

Other Resources

Another resource often overlooked by students is the set of references provided at the end of a journal article. If you have found a key article of interest to you, begin with the papers cited in the key article. The reference list provides information on where the cited papers were published, enabling you to obtain any that appear to be of interest.

In addition to the resources already described, several other resources and databases may be helpful to you.

- *PsycArticles* is an online database that provides full-text articles from many psychology journals and is available through many academic libraries.
- *ProQuest* is an online database that searches both scholarly journals and popular media sources. Full-text articles are often available. ProQuest is available through most academic libraries.
- *Sociological Abstracts* are similar to *Psych Abstracts*, except they summarize journal articles on sociological topics.
- The Educational Resources Information Center (ERIC) is a clearinghouse for research on educational psychology, testing, counseling, child development, evaluation research, and related areas. It is available online through most academic libraries.
- *Dissertation Abstracts International*, published monthly, includes Abstracts of doctoral dissertations from hundreds of universities in the United States and Canada.

In addition to these resources, interlibrary loan (ILL) is a service that is provided by most libraries that allows you to borrow resources from other libraries if your library does not hold them. For instance, if you need a book that your library does not have or an article from a journal to which your library does not subscribe, you can use interlibrary loan to obtain it. Through this service, your library borrows the resources needed from the closest library that has them. See your reference librarian to use this service.

Finally, the World Wide Web may also be used as a resource. Many of the resources already described, such as PsycINFO, the SSCI, and ERIC, are available online through your library's home page. Be wary, however, of information you retrieve from the Web through a source other than a library. Bear in mind that anyone can post anything on the Web. Even information that looks scientific and appears to be written in the same form as a scientific journal article is not necessarily reliable. Use the resources available through your library's home page. Like the resources available on the library shelves, these resources have been chosen by the librarians, and they have most likely been reviewed by editors and other specialists before they were published. Information on the Web is frequently placed there by the author without any review by others.

IN REVIEW Library Research	
Tool	**What It Is**
Psych Abstracts	A reference resource published by the American Psychological Association that contains abstracts, or brief summaries, of articles in psychology and related disciplines
PsycINFO	The online version of *Psych Abstracts*, updated monthly
PsycLIT	The CD-ROM version of *Psych Abstracts*, updated quarterly
Social Science Citation Index (SSCI)	A resource that allows you to search for subsequent articles from the social and behavioral sciences that have cited a key article

(*continued*)

IN REVIEW	Library Research (*continued*)	
Tool	**What It Is**
Science Citation Index (SCI)	A resource that allows you to search for subsequent articles in disciplines such as biology, chemistry, or medicine that have cited a key article
Interlibrary loan (ILL)	A service provided by most libraries that allows you to borrow resources from other libraries if your library does not hold them
Sociological Abstracts	A reference that contains abstracts or brief summaries of articles in sociology and related disciplines
PsycArticles	An online database that contains full-text articles from many psychology journals
ProQuest	An online database that searches both scholarly journals and popular media sources; full-text articles are often available
ERIC	A clearinghouse for research on educational psychology, testing, counseling, child development, evaluation research, and related areas
Dissertation Abstracts	Abstracts of doctoral dissertations from hundreds of universities in the United States and Canada, published monthly

READING A JOURNAL ARTICLE: WHAT TO EXPECT

Your search for information in the library provides you with many journal articles. Research articles have a specific format that consists of five main sections: Abstract, Introduction, Method, Results, and Discussion. The following is a brief description of what to expect from each of these sections.

Abstract

The Abstract is a brief description of the entire paper and typically discusses the other sections (Introduction, Method, Results, and Discussion). It should be somewhere between 150 and 250 words depending on the restrictions of the journal in which it is published. The Abstract describes the problem under investigation and the purpose of the study, the participants and general methodology, the findings (including statistical significance levels), and the conclusions and implications or applications of the study. If your manuscript is published, the Abstract appears in the *Psychological Abstracts*.

Introduction

The Introduction has three components: (1) an introduction to the problem under study; (2) a review of relevant previous research, which cites works that are pertinent to the issue but not works of marginal or peripheral significance; and (3) the purpose and rationale for the study.

Method

The Method section describes exactly how the study was conducted and provides sufficient detail that a person who reads the Method section could replicate the study. The Method section is generally divided into subsections.

Although the subsections vary, the most common ones are Participants or Subjects, Materials or Apparatus, and Procedure. The Participants subsection includes a description of the participants and how they were obtained. A Materials subsection usually describes any testing materials used such as a particular test or inventory or a type of problem that participants were asked to solve. An Apparatus subsection describes any specific equipment used. The Procedure subsection summarizes each step in the execution of the research, including the groups used in the study, instructions given to the participants, the experimental manipulation, and specific control features in the design.

Results

The Results section summarizes the data collected and the type of statistic used to analyze the data. In addition, the results of the statistical tests used are reported with respect to the variables measured and/or manipulated. This section should include only a description of the results, not an explanation of them. In addition, the results are often depicted in tables or figures.

Discussion

In the Discussion section the results are evaluated and interpreted. Typically this section begins with a restatement of the predictions of the study and tells whether they were supported. It also usually includes a discussion of the relationship between the results and past research and theories. Finally, criticisms of the study and implications for future research are presented.

SUMMARY

In this module we discussed many elements relevant to getting started on a research project. We began with how to select a problem and how to conduct a literature search. This discussion included an examination of several library resources: *Psych Abstracts*, PsycINFO, the *Social Science Citation Index*, and the *Science Citation Index*, among others. Finally, we discussed the basic structure of a psychological journal article. The major sections in an article include the Abstract, Introduction, Method, Results, and Discussion.

MODULE EXERCISE

(Answers to odd-numbered exercises appear in Appendix A.)

1. Select a topic of interest to you in psychology and use *Psych Abstracts*, PsycLIT, or PsycINFO to search for articles on it. Try to find at least five journal articles relevant to your topic.

WEB RESOURCES

Check your knowledge of the content and key terms in this module with a practice quiz and interactive flashcards at **www.cengage.com/ psychology/jackson,** or for step-by-step practice and information, check out the Statistics and Research Methods Workshops at **www. cengage.com/psychology/workshops**.

MODULE 4

Ethical Research

LEARNING OBJECTIVES

- Briefly describe APA ethical standards in research with human participants.

- Explain what an IRB is.

- Explain when deception is acceptable in research.

- Identify what it means to be a participant at risk versus a participant at minimal risk.

- Explain why debriefing is important.

- Briefly describe the ethical standards in research with animals.

When conducting research with human (or nonhuman) participants, the researcher is ultimately responsible for their welfare.
Thus it is the researcher's responsibility to protect them from
harm. What harm you may be wondering could a participant suffer in a
simple research study? Let's consider some of the research studies that
helped to initiate the implementation of ethical guidelines for using human
participants in research.

ETHICAL STANDARDS IN RESEARCH WITH HUMAN PARTICIPANTS

The ethical guidelines we use today have their basis in the Nuremberg Code.
This code lists 10 principles, which were developed in 1948 for the Nazi war
crimes trials following World War II. The Nazis killed and abused millions
of Jews, many of whom died in the name of "research." For example, Nazi
doctors used many Jews for inhumane medical research projects that involved
determining the effects on humans of viruses, poisons, toxins, and drugs.

The Nazis were not the only researchers who conducted unethical research. Researchers who conducted the Tuskegee syphilis study, which began
in 1932 and continued until 1972, examined the course of the disease in untreated individuals. The participants were approximately 400 black men living in and around Tuskegee, Alabama. The individuals, most of whom were
poor and illiterate, were offered free meals, physical examinations, and
money for their eventual burial for participating in the study (Jones, 1981).
They were told that they were being treated for the disease by the U.S. Public
Health Service (USPHS). In reality they were never treated, nor were they ever
told the real purpose of the study—to observe the progression of syphilis in
an untreated population. Some of the participants realized that something
was amiss and consulted other doctors in the area. Those who did so were
eliminated from the study. In addition, the USPHS told doctors in the sur-
rounding area not to treat any of the participants should they request treatment, even though penicillin, an effective treatment for syphilis, was discovered
by the 1940s. The Tuskegee study continued until 1972, providing little new
knowledge about syphilis but costing about 400 lives.

Obviously the Nuremberg Code established in 1948 had little effect on the
researchers who conducted the Tuskegee study. In any case, the Nuremberg
Code applied only to medical research. In 1953, therefore, the members of the
APA decided to develop their own ethical guidelines for research with human
participants.

In 1963 Stanley Milgram's paper detailing some of his research on obedience to authority brought ethical considerations to the forefront once again. In
Milgram's study each participant was assigned the role of "teacher" and given
the responsibility for teaching a series of words to another individual, called the
"learner." What the teachers did not realize was that the learner was really

an accomplice of the experimenter. The teachers were told that the study was designed to investigate the effects of punishment on learning. Thus they were instructed to deliver an electric shock each time the learner made a mistake. They were also told that the shocks were not of a constant voltage level but rather increased in voltage for each mistake made. The learner (who was located in a separate room from the teacher and was working for the experimenter) purposely made mistakes. Milgram was interested in whether the teachers would continue to deliver stronger and stronger electric shocks given that (1) the learner appeared to be in moderate to extreme discomfort, depending on the level of shock administered, and (2) the experimenter repeatedly ordered the teachers to continue administering the electric shocks. In reality the learners were not receiving electric shocks; however, the teachers believed they were. Milgram found that nearly two-thirds of the teachers obeyed the experimenter and continued to deliver the supposed electric shocks up to the maximum level available.

Although the results of this experiment were valuable to society, the study was ethically questionable. Was it ethical to place human participants in a situation in which they were put under extreme psychological stress and may have learned things about themselves that they would have preferred not to know? This type of study is not allowed today because the APA has continually revised and strengthened its ethical guidelines since 1953, the latest revision occurring in 2002. You can find the most recent information at *http://www.apa.org/ethics*. Some of the principles outlined in 2002 are provided in Table 4.1. In addition to the APA guidelines, federal guidelines (Federal Protection Regulations), developed in 1982, are enforced by Institutional Review Boards at most institutions.

"IT'S FROM THE PROTOZOA RIGHTS COMMITTEE. THEY WANT TO KNOW WHAT YOU'RE USING THEIR CLIENTS FOR."

TABLE **4.1**

APA Principles Covering the Treatment of Human Participants

3.04. Avoiding Harm

Psychologists take reasonable steps to avoid harming their clients/patients, students, supervisees, research participants, organizational clients, and others with whom they work, and to minimize harm where it is foreseeable and unavoidable.

4. Privacy and Confidentiality
4.01. Maintaining Confidentiality

Psychologists have a primary obligation and take reasonable precautions to protect confidential information obtained through or stored in any medium, recognizing that the extent and limits of confidentiality may be regulated by law or established by institutional rules or professional or scientific relationship. (See also Standard 2.05, Delegation of Work to Others.)

4.02. Discussing the Limits of Confidentiality

(a) Psychologists discuss with persons (including, to the extent feasible, persons who are legally incapable of giving informed consent and their legal representatives) and organizations with whom they establish a scientific or professional relationship (1) the relevant limits of confidentiality and (2) the foreseeable uses of the information generated through their psychological activities. (See also Standard 3.10, Informed Consent.)

(b) Unless it is not feasible or is contraindicated, the discussion of confidentiality occurs at the outset of the relationship and thereafter as new circumstances may warrant.

(c) Psychologists who offer services, products, or information via electronic transmission inform clients/patients of the risks to privacy and limits of confidentiality.

4.03. Recording

Before recording the voices or images of individuals to whom they provide services, psychologists obtain permission from all such persons or their legal representatives. (See also Standards 8.03, Informed Consent for Recording Voices and Images in Research; 8.05, Dispensing with Informed Consent for Research; and 8.07, Deception in Research.)

4.04. Minimizing Intrusions on Privacy

(a) Psychologists include in written and oral reports and consultations, only information germane to the purpose for which the communication is made.

(b) Psychologists discuss confidential information obtained in their work only for appropriate scientific or professional purposes and only with persons clearly concerned with such matters.

4.05. Disclosures

(a) Psychologists may disclose confidential information with the appropriate consent of the organizational client, the individual client/patient, or another legally authorized person on behalf of the client/patient unless prohibited by law.

(continued)

TABLE **4.1**

APA Principles Covering the Treatment of Human Participants (*continued*)

(b) Psychologists disclose confidential information without the consent of the individual only as mandated by law, or where permitted by law for a valid purpose such as to (1) provide needed professional services; (2) obtain appropriate professional consultations; (3) protect the client/patient, psychologist, or others from harm; or (4) obtain payment for services from a client/patient, in which instance disclosure is limited to the minimum that is necessary to achieve the purpose. (See also Standard 6.04e, Fees and Financial Arrangements.)

4.06. Consultations

When consulting with colleagues, (1) psychologists do not disclose confidential information that reasonably could lead to the identification of a client/patient, research participant, or other person or organization with whom they have a confidential relationship unless they have obtained the prior consent of the person or organization or the disclosure cannot be avoided, and (2) they disclose information only to the extent necessary to achieve the purposes of the consultation. (See also Standard 4.01, Maintaining Confidentiality.)

4.07. Use of Confidential Information for Didactic or Other Purposes

Psychologists do not disclose in their writings, lectures, or other public media, confidential, personally identifiable information concerning their clients/patients, students, research participants, organizational clients, or other recipients of their services that they obtained during the course of their work, unless (1) they take reasonable steps to disguise the person or organization, (2) the person or organization has consented in writing, or (3) there is legal authorization for doing so.

8. Research and Publication
8.01. Institutional Approval

When institutional approval is required, psychologists provide accurate information about their research proposals and obtain approval prior to conducting the research. They conduct the research in accordance with the approved research protocol.

8.02. Informed Consent to Research

(a) When obtaining informed consent as required in Standard 3.10, Informed Consent, psychologists inform participants about (1) the purpose of the research, expected duration, and procedures; (2) their right to decline to participate and to withdraw from the research once participation has begun; (3) the foreseeable consequences of declining or withdrawing; (4) reasonably foreseeable factors that may be expected to influence their willingness to participate such as potential risks, discomfort, or adverse effects; (5) any prospective research benefits; (6) limits of confidentiality; (7) incentives for participation; and (8) whom to contact for questions about the research and research participants' rights. They provide opportunity for the prospective participants to ask questions and receive answers. (See also Standards 8.03, Informed Consent for Recording Voices and Images in Research; 8.05, Dispensing with Informed Consent for Research; and 8.07, Deception in Research.)

(*continued*)

TABLE **4.1**

APA Principles Covering the Treatment of Human Participants (*continued*)

(b) Psychologists conducting intervention research involving the use of experimental treatments clarify to participants at the outset of the research (1) the experimental nature of the treatment; (2) the services that will or will not be available to the control group(s) if appropriate; (3) the means by which assignment to treatment and control groups will be made; (4) available treatment alternatives if an individual does not wish to participate in the research or wishes to withdraw once a study has begun; and (5) compensation for or monetary costs of participating including, if appropriate, whether reimbursement from the participant or a third-party pay or will be sought. (See also Standard 8.02a, Informed Consent to Research.)

8.03. Informed Consent for Recording Voices and Images in Research

Psychologists obtain informed consent from research participants prior to recording their voices or images for data collection unless (1) the research consists solely of naturalistic observations in public places, and it is not anticipated that the recording will be used in a manner that could cause personal identification or harm, or (2) the research design includes deception, and consent for the use of the recording is obtained during debriefing. (See also Standard 8.07, Deception in Research.)

8.04. Client/Patient, Student, and Subordinate Research Participants

(a) When psychologists conduct research with clients/patients, students, or subordinates as participants, psychologists take steps to protect the prospective participants from adverse consequences of declining or withdrawing from participation.

(b) When research participation is a course requirement or an opportunity for extra credit, the prospective participant is given the choice of equitable alternative activities.

8.05. Dispensing with Informed Consent for Research

Psychologists may dispense with informed consent only (1) where research would not reasonably be assumed to create distress or harm and involves (a) the study of normal educational practices, curricula, or classroom management methods conducted in educational settings; (b) only anonymous questionnaires, naturalistic observations, or archival research for which disclosure of responses would not place participants at risk of criminal or civil liability or damage their financial standing, employability, or reputation, and confidentiality is protected; or (c) the study of factors related to job or organization effectiveness conducted in organizational settings for which there is no risk to participants' employability, and confidentiality is protected or (2) where otherwise permitted by law or federal or institutional regulations.

8.06. Offering Inducements for Research Participation

(a) Psychologists make reasonable efforts to avoid offering excessive or inappropriate financial or other inducements for research participation when such inducements are likely to coerce participation.

(*continued*)

TABLE **4.1**

APA Principles Covering the Treatment of Human Participants (*continued*)

(b) When offering professional services as an inducement for research participation, psychologists clarify the nature of the services, as well as the risks, obligations, and limitations. (See also Standard 6.05, Barter with Clients/Patients.)

8.07. Deception in Research

(a) Psychologists do not conduct a study involving deception unless they have determined that the use of deceptive techniques is justified by the study's significant prospective scientific, educational, or applied value and that effective nondeceptive alternative procedures are not feasible.

(b) Psychologists do not deceive prospective participants about research that is reasonably expected to cause physical pain or severe emotional distress.

(c) Psychologists explain any deception that is an integral feature of the design and conduct of an experiment to participants as early as is feasible, preferably at the conclusion of their participation, but no later than at the conclusion of the data collection, and permit participants to withdraw their data. (See also Standard 8.08, Debriefing.)

8.08. Debriefing

(a) Psychologists provide a prompt opportunity for participants to obtain appropriate information about the nature, results, and conclusions of the research, and they take reasonable steps to correct any misconceptions that participants may have of which the psychologists are aware.

(b) If scientific or humane values justify delaying or withholding this information, psychologists take reasonable measures to reduce the risk of harm.

(c) When psychologists become aware that research procedures have harmed a participant, they take reasonable steps to minimize the harm.

8.09. Humane Care and Use of Animals in Research

(a) Psychologists acquire, care for, use, and dispose of animals in compliance with current federal, state, and local laws and regulations, and with professional standards.

(b) Psychologists trained in research methods and experienced in the care of laboratory animals supervise all procedures involving animals and are responsible for ensuring appropriate consideration of their comfort, health, and humane treatment.

(c) Psychologists ensure that all individuals under their supervision who are using animals have received instruction in research methods and in the care, maintenance, and handling of the species being used, to the extent appropriate to their role. (See also Standard 2.05, Delegation of Work to Others.)

(d) Psychologists make reasonable efforts to minimize the discomfort, infection, illness, and pain of animal subjects.

(e) Psychologists use a procedure subjecting animals to pain, stress, or privation only when an alternative procedure is unavailable and the goal is justified by its prospective scientific, educational, or applied value.

(f) Psychologists perform surgical procedures under appropriate anesthesia and follow techniques to avoid infection and minimize pain during and after surgery.

(*continued*)

TABLE **4.1**

APA Principles Covering the Treatment of Human Participants (*continued*)

(g) When it is appropriate that an animal's life be terminated, psychologists proceed rapidly, with an effort to minimize pain and in accordance with accepted procedures.

8.10. Reporting Research Results

(a) Psychologists do not fabricate data. (See also Standard 5.01a, Avoidance of False or Deceptive Statements.)
(b) If psychologists discover significant errors in their published data, they take reasonable steps to correct such errors in a correction, retraction, erratum, or other appropriate publication means.

8.11. Plagiarism

Psychologists do not present portions of another's work or data as their own, even if the other work or data source is cited occasionally.

8.12. Publication Credit

(a) Psychologists take responsibility and credit, including authorship credit, only for work they have actually performed or to which they have substantially contributed. (See also Standard 8.12b, Publication Credit.)
(b) Principal authorship and other publication credits accurately reflect the relative scientific or professional contributions of the individuals involved, regardless of their relative status. Mere possession of an institutional position, such as department chair, does not justify authorship credit. Minor contributions to the research or to the writing for publications are acknowledged appropriately, such as in footnotes or in an introductory statement.
(c) Except under exceptional circumstances, a student is listed as principal author on any multiple-authored article that is substantially based on the student's doctoral dissertation. Faculty advisors discuss publication credit with students as early as feasible and throughout the research and publication process as appropriate. (See also Standard 8.12b, Publication Credit.)

8.13. Duplicate Publication of Data

Psychologists do not publish, as original data, data that have been previously published. This does not preclude republishing data when they are accompanied by proper acknowledgment.

8.14. Sharing Research Data for Verification

(a) After research results are published, psychologists do not withhold the data on which their conclusions are based from other competent professionals who seek to verify the substantive claims through reanalysis and who intend to use such data only for that purpose, provided that the confidentiality of the participants can be protected and unless legal rights concerning proprietary data preclude their release. This does not preclude psychologists from requiring that such individuals or groups be responsible for costs associated with the provision of such information.

(continued)

TABLE **4.1**
APA Principles Covering the Treatment of Human Participants (*continued*)

(b) Psychologists who request data from other psychologists to verify the substantive claims through reanalysis may use shared data only for the declared purpose. Requesting psychologists obtain prior written agreement for all other uses of the data.

8.15. Reviewers

Psychologists who review material submitted for presentation, publication, grant, or research proposal review respect the confidentiality of and the proprietary rights in such information of those who submitted it.

Source: American Psychological Association (2002). *Ethical principles of psychologists and code of conduct.* Copyright 2002 by the American Psychological Association. Reprinted with permission.

Institutional Review Boards

Institutional Review Board (IRB): A committee charged with evaluating research projects in which human participants are used.

An **institutional review board (IRB)** is typically made up of several faculty members, usually from diverse backgrounds, and members of the community who are charged with evaluating research projects in which human participants are used. IRBs oversee all federally funded research involving human participants. Most academic institutions have either an IRB (if they receive federal funding) or some other committee responsible for evaluating research projects that use human participants. In the evaluation process the researcher completes an application form detailing the method to be used in the study, the risks or benefits related to participating in the study, and the means of maintaining participants' confidentiality. In addition, the researcher provides an informed consent form (discussed in the next section). The purpose of the IRB is not necessarily to evaluate the scientific merit of the research study but rather the treatment of participants to ensure that the study meets established ethical guidelines.

Informed Consent

informed consent form: A form given to individuals before they participate in a study to inform them of the general nature of the study and to obtain their consent to participate.

When participants in a study are at risk, an informed consent form is needed. (We discuss exactly what "at risk" means later in the module.) The **informed consent form** is given to individuals before they participate in a research study in order to inform them of the general nature of the study and in order to obtain their consent to participate. The informed consent form typically describes the nature and purpose of the study. However, to avoid compromising the outcome of the study, the researcher obviously cannot inform participants about the expected results. Thus informed consent forms often make only broad, general statements about the nature and purpose of a study. When deception is used in the study of course, the informed consent form tells participants nothing about the true nature and purpose of the study. (We address the ethical ramifications of using deception later in the module.) The participants are also informed of what they will be asked to do as part of the study and are assured that the researchers will make every effort to maintain confidentiality with respect to their performance in the study. Participants are told that they have the right to refuse to participate in the study and to change their mind about participation at any point during it. Participants sign the form, indicating that they give their informed consent to participate. Typically the form is also signed by a witness. Researchers should normally keep informed consent forms on file for two to three years after completion of a study and should also give a copy of the form to each participant. If participants in a study are under 18 years of age, informed consent must be given by a parent or legal guardian. (Qualifications on using children in research are covered in more detail later in the module.) A sample informed consent form appears in Figure 4.1.

Risk

Typically participants in a study are classified as being either "at risk" or "at minimal risk." Those at minimal risk are placed under no more physical or emotional risk than would be encountered in daily life or in routine physical or psychological examinations or tests (U.S. Department of Health and Human Services, 1981). In what types of studies might a participant be classified as being at minimal risk? Studies in which participants are asked to fill out paper-and-pencil tests such as personality inventories or depression inventories are classified as minimal risk. Other examples of minimal risk studies are most research projects on memory processes, problem-solving abilities, and reasoning in which participants are asked simply to answer questions. In such studies, the participants are considered at minimal risk because the physical and emotional risk they encounter when participating in the study is similar to that encountered in daily life. If the participants in a study are classified as at minimal risk, an informed consent is not mandatory, but it is probably best to have the form signed anyway.

In contrast, the participants in the Tuskegee study and in Milgram's (1963) obedience study would definitely be classified as at risk. Studies in which the participants are at risk for physical or emotional harm fit the definition of putting participants at risk. When proposing such a study, the researcher and the members of the IRB must determine whether the benefits of the knowledge gained outweigh the risk to participants. Clearly Milgram believed that this was the case; members of IRBs today might not agree.

Participants are also often considered at risk if their privacy is compromised. Participants expect researchers to protect their privacy and keep their participation in and results from the study confidential. In most research studies there should be no need to tie data to individuals. Thus in such cases, privacy and confidentiality are not issues because the participants have anonymity. However, when it is necessary to tie data to an individual (for example, when data are collected from the same participants over many sessions), every precaution should be made to safeguard the data and keep them separate from the identities of the participants. In other words, a coding system should be used that allows the researcher—and no one else—to identify the individual. The information identifying participants should be kept separate from the data so that if seen by anyone, they could not be linked to particular individuals. In studies in which researchers need to be able to identify the participants, an informed consent form should be used because anonymity and confidentiality are at risk.

Informed Consent Form

You, _____, are being asked to participate in a research project titled _____. This project is being conducted under the supervision of _____ and was approved by _____ University/College's IRB (or Committee on the Use of Human Participants) on _____.

The investigators hope to learn _____ from this project.

While participating in this study, you will be asked to _____ for _____ period of time.

The nature of this study has been explained by _____. The anticipated benefits of your participation are _____. The known risks of your participation in this study are _____.

The researchers will make every effort to safeguard the confidentiality of the information that you provide. Any information obtained from this study that can be identified with you will remain confidential and will not be given to anyone without your permission.

If at any time you would like additional information about this project, you can contact _____ at _____.

You have the right to refuse to participate in this study. If you do agree to participate, you have the right to change your mind at any time and stop your participation. The grades and services you receive from _____ University/College will not be negatively affected by your refusal to participate or by your withdrawal from this project. Your signature below indicates that you have given your informed consent to participate in the above-described project. Your signature also indicates that:

⇨ You have been given the opportunity to ask any and all questions about the described project and your participation and all of your questions have been answered to your satisfaction.

⇨ You have been permitted to read this document and you have been given a signed copy of it.

⇨ You are at least 18 years old.

⇨ You are legally able to provide consent.

⇨ To the best of your knowledge and belief, you have no physical or mental illness or weakness that would be adversely affected by your participation in the described project.

_____   _____
Signature of Participant   Date

_____   _____
Signature of Witness   Date

FIGURE **4.1** Sample informed consent form

Deception

deception: Lying to the participants concerning the true nature of a study because knowing the true nature of the study might affect their performance.

Besides the risk of emotional harm, you may be wondering about another aspect of Milgram's (1963) study. Milgram deceived participants by telling them that the experiment was about the effects of punishment on learning, not about obedience to authority. **Deception** in research involves lying to participants about the true nature of a study because knowing its true nature might affect their performance. Thus in some research studies it is not possible to fully inform participants of the nature of the study because this knowledge might affect their responses. How then do researchers obtain informed consent when deception is necessary?

They give participants a general description of the study rather than a detailed description of the hypothesis being tested. Remember that participants are also informed that they do not have to participate, that a refusal to participate incurs no penalties, and that they can stop participating at any time. Given these precautions, deception can be used when necessary without violating ethical standards. After the study is completed, however, researchers should debrief the participants (see the next section), informing them of the deception and the true intent of the study.

Debriefing

debriefing: Providing information about the true purpose of a study as soon after the completion of data collection as possible.

A final ethical consideration concerns the debriefing of participants. **Debriefing** means providing information about the true purpose of the study as soon as possible after the completion of data collection. In the Milgram study, for example, debriefing entailed informing participants of the true nature of the study (obedience to authority) as soon as possible after completion of the study. Based on immediate debriefings and 1-year follow-up interviews, Milgram (1977) found that only about 1% of the participants wished they had not participated in the study and that most were very glad they had participated.

Debriefing is necessary in all research studies, not just those that involve deception. Through debriefing, participants learn more about the benefits of the research to them and to society in general, and the researcher has the opportunity to alleviate any discomfort the participants may be experiencing. During debriefing the researcher should try to bring participants back to the same state of mind they were in before they engaged in the study.

ETHICAL STANDARDS IN RESEARCH WITH CHILDREN

Special considerations arise in research studies that use children as participants. For instance, how does informed consent work with children, and how do researchers properly debrief a child? Informed consent must be obtained from the parents or legal guardians for all persons under the age of 18. Also, with children who are old enough to understand language, the researcher should try to inform them of the nature of the study, explain what they will be asked to do, and tell them that they do not have to participate and can stop participating at any time. The question remains, however, whether children really understand this information and whether they would feel comfortable exercising their rights. Thus the researcher must use especially good judgment when deciding whether to continue collecting data from children or whether to use a particular child in a research project.

Ethical Standards in Research with Animals

Using animals in research has become a controversial issue. Some people believe that no research should be conducted on animals, whereas others believe that research with animals is advantageous but that measures should be taken to ensure humane treatment. Taking the latter position, the APA has developed *Guidelines for Ethical Conduct in the Care and Use of Animals* (1996). These guidelines are presented in Table 4.2.

TABLE **4.2**

APA Guidelines for Ethical Conduct in the Care and Use of Animals: Developed by the American Psychological Association's Committee on Animal Research and Ethics (CARE)

I. Justification of the Research

A. Research should be undertaken with a clear scientific purpose. There should be a reasonable expectation that the research will (a) increase knowledge of the processes underlying the evolution, development, maintenance, alteration, control, or biological significance of behavior; (b) determine the replicability and generality of prior research; (c) increase understanding of the species under study; or (d) provide results that benefit the health or welfare of humans or other animals.

B. The scientific purpose of the research should be of sufficient potential significance to justify the use of animals. Psychologists should act on the assumption that procedures that would produce pain in humans will also do so in other animals.

C. The species chosen for study should be best suited to answer the question(s) posed. The psychologist should always consider the possibility of using other species, nonanimal alternatives, or procedures that minimize the number of animals in research, and should be familiar with the appropriate literature.

D. Research on animals may not be conducted until the protocol has been reviewed by an appropriate animal care committee—for example, an institutional animal care and use committee (IACUC)—to ensure that the procedures are appropriate and humane.

E. The psychologist should monitor the research and the animals' welfare throughout the course of an investigation to ensure continued justification for the research.

II. Personnel

A. Psychologists should ensure that personnel involved in their research with animals be familiar with these guidelines.

B. Animal use procedures must conform with federal regulations regarding personnel, supervision, record keeping, and veterinary care.[1]

C. Behavior is both the focus of study of many experiments as well as a primary source of information about an animal's health and well-being. It is therefore necessary that psychologists and their assistants be informed about the behavioral characteristics of their animal subjects, so as to be aware of normal,

(continued)

TABLE **4.2**

APA Guidelines for Ethical Conduct in the Care and Use of Animals: Developed by the American Psychological Association's Committee on Animal Research and Ethics (CARE) (*continued*)

species-specific behaviors and unusual behaviors that could forewarn of health problems.

D. Psychologists should ensure that all individuals who use animals under their supervision receive explicit instruction in experimental methods and in the care, maintenance, and handling of the species being studied. Responsibilities and activities of all individuals dealing with animals should be consistent with their respective competencies, training, and experience in either the laboratory or the field setting.

III. Care and Housing of Animals

The concept of psychological well-being of animals is of current concern and debate and is included in Federal Regulations (United States Department of Agriculture [USDA], 1991). As a scientific and professional organization, APA recognizes the complexities of defining psychological well-being. Procedures appropriate for a particular species may be inappropriate for others. Hence, APA does not presently stipulate specific guidelines regarding the maintenance of psychological well being of research animals. Psychologists familiar with the species should be best qualified professionally to judge measures such as enrichment to maintain or improve psychological well-being of those species.

A. The facilities housing animals should meet or exceed current regulations and guidelines (USDA, 1990, 1991) and are required to be inspected twice a year (USDA, 1989).

B. All procedures carried out on animals are to be reviewed by a local animal care committee to ensure that the procedures are appropriate and humane. The committee should have representation from within the institution and from the local community. In the event that it is not possible to constitute an appropriate local animal care committee, psychologists are encouraged to seek advice from a corresponding committee of a cooperative institution.

C. Responsibilities for the conditions under which animals are kept, both within and outside of the context of active experimentation or teaching, rests with the psychologist under the supervision of the animal care committee (where required by federal regulations) and with individuals appointed by the institution to oversee animal care. Animals are to be provided with humane care and healthful conditions during their stay in the facility. In addition to the federal requirements to provide for the psychological well-being of nonhuman primates used in research, psychologists are encouraged to consider enriching the environments of their laboratory animals and should keep abreast of literature on well-being and enrichment for the species with which they work.

IV. Acquisition of Animals

A. Animals not bred in the psychologist's facility are to be acquired lawfully. The USDA and local ordinances should be consulted for information regarding regulations and approved suppliers.

(*continued*)

TABLE **4.2**

APA Guidelines for Ethical Conduct in the Care and Use of Animals: Developed by the American Psychological Association's Committee on Animal Research and Ethics (CARE) (*continued*)

B. Psychologists should make every effort to ensure that those responsible for transporting the animals to the facility provide adequate food, water, ventilation, space, and impose no unnecessary stress on the animals.
C. Animals taken from the wild should be trapped in a humane manner and in accordance with applicable federal, state, and local regulations.
D. Endangered species or taxa should be used only with full attention to required permits and ethical concerns. Information and permit applications can be obtained from:
    Fish and Wildlife Service
    Office of Management Authority
    U.S. Dept. of the Interior
    4401 N. Fairfax Dr., Rm. 432
    Arlington, VA 22043
    703-358-2104

Similar caution should be used in work with threatened species or taxa.

V. Experimental Procedures

Humane consideration for the well-being of the animal should be incorporated into the design and conduct of all procedures involving animals, while keeping in mind the primary goal of experimental procedures—the acquisition of sound, replicable data. The conduct of all procedures is governed by Guideline I.

A. Behavioral studies that involve no aversive stimulation to, or overt sign of distress from, the animal are acceptable. These include observational and other noninvasive forms of data collection.
B. When alternative behavioral procedures are available, those that minimize discomfort to the animal should be used. When using aversive conditions, psychologists should adjust the parameters of stimulation to levels that appear minimal, though compatible with the aims of the research. Psychologists are encouraged to test painful stimuli on themselves, whenever reasonable. Whenever consistent with the goals of the research, consideration should be given to providing the animals with control of the potentially aversive stimulation.
C. Procedures in which the animal is anesthetized and insensitive to pain throughout the procedure and is euthanized before regaining consciousness are generally acceptable.
D. Procedures involving more than momentary or slight aversive stimulation, which is not relieved by medication or other acceptable methods, should be undertaken only when the objectives of the research cannot be achieved by other methods.
E. Experimental procedures that require prolonged aversive conditions or produce tissue damage or metabolic disturbances require greater justification and surveillance. These include prolonged exposure to extreme environmental conditions, experimentally induced prey killing, or infliction of physical trauma or

(continued)

TABLE **4.2**

APA Guidelines for Ethical Conduct in the Care and Use of Animals: Developed by the American Psychological Association's Committee on Animal Research and Ethics (CARE) (*continued*)

tissue damage. An animal observed to be in a state of severe distress or chronic pain that cannot be alleviated and is not essential to the purposes of the research should be euthanized immediately.

F. Procedures that use restraint must conform to federal regulations and guidelines.

G. Procedures involving the use of paralytic agents without reduction in pain sensation require particular prudence and humane concern. Use of muscle relaxants or paralytics alone during surgery, without general anesthesia, is unacceptable and should be avoided.

H. Surgical procedures, because of their invasive nature, require close supervision and attention to humane considerations by the psychologist. Aseptic (methods that minimize risks of infection) techniques must be used on laboratory animals whenever possible.

1. All surgical procedures and anesthetization should be conducted under the direct supervision of a person who is competent in the use of the procedures.

2. If the surgical procedure is likely to cause greater discomfort than that attending anesthetization, and unless there is specific justification for acting otherwise, animals should be maintained under anesthesia until the procedure is ended.

3. Sound postoperative monitoring and care, which may include the use of analgesics and antibiotics, should be provided to minimize discomfort and to prevent infection and other untoward consequences of the procedure.

4. Animals cannot be subjected to successive surgical procedures unless these are required by the nature of the research, the nature of the surgery, or for the well-being of the animal. Multiple surgeries on the same animal must receive special approval from the animal care committee.

I. When the use of an animal is no longer required by an experimental protocol or procedure, in order to minimize the number of animals used in research, alternative uses of the animals should be considered. Such uses should be compatible with the goals of research and the welfare of the animal. Care should be taken that such an action does not expose the animal to multiple surgeries.

J. The return of wild-caught animals to the field can carry substantial risks, both to the formerly captive animals and to the ecosystem. Animals reared in the laboratory should not be released because, in most cases, they cannot survive or they may survive by disrupting the natural ecology.

K. When euthanasia appears to be the appropriate alternative, either as a requirement of the research or because it constitutes the most humane form of disposition of an animal at the conclusion of the research:

1. Euthanasia shall be accomplished in a humane manner, appropriate for the species, and in such a way as to ensure immediate death, and in accordance with procedures outlined in the latest version of the American Veterinary Medical Association (AVMA) Panel on Euthanasia.[2]

2. Disposal of euthanized animals should be accomplished in a manner that is in accord with all relevant legislation, consistent with health, environmental, and aesthetic concerns, and approved by the animal care committee. No animal shall be discarded until its death is verified.

(*continued*)

TABLE **4.2**

APA Guidelines for Ethical Conduct in the Care and Use of Animals:
Developed by the American Psychological Association's Committee on
Animal Research and Ethics (CARE) (*continued*)

VI. Field Research

Field research, because of its potential to damage sensitive ecosystems and ethologies,
should be subject to animal care committee approval. Field research, if strictly observational, may not require animal care committee approval (USDA, 1989, pg. 36126).

A. Psychologists conducting field research should disturb their populations as little as possible—consistent with the goals of the research. Every effort should be
made to minimize potential harmful effects of the study on the population and
on other plant and animal species in the area.
B. Research conducted in populated areas should be done with respect for the
property and privacy of the inhabitants of the area.
C. Particular justification is required for the study of endangered species. Such research
on endangered species should not be conducted unless animal care committee
approval has been obtained and all requisite permits are obtained (see IV. D).

[1]U.S. Department of Agriculture (1989, August 21). Animal welfare: Final rules. Federal Register. U.S. Department of Agriculture. (1990, July 16). Animal welfare: Guinea pigs, hamsters, and rabbits. Federal Register.
U.S. Department of Agriculture. (1991, February 15). Animal welfare: Standards: Final rule. Federal Register.

[2]Write to AVMA, 1931 N. Meacham Road, Suite 100, Schaumburg, IL 60173, or call (708) 925-8070.

Source: American Psychological Association (1996). *Guidelines for ethical conduct in the care and use of
animals.* Copyright 1996 by the American Psychological Association. Reprinted with permission.

There is little argument that animal research has led to many advances for
both human and nonhuman animals, especially in medical research. Research
with animals has led to blood transfusions; advances in painkillers, antibiotics,
behavioral medications, and drug treatments as well as knowledge of the brain,
nervous system, and psychopathology. However, animal rights activists believe
that the cost of these advances is often too high.

The APA guidelines address several issues with respect to animal welfare.
Accordingly, the researcher must:

• Provide a justification for the study.
• Be sure that the personnel interacting with the animals are familiar with
the guidelines and well trained.
• Ensure that the care and housing of the animals meet federal regulations.
• Acquire the animals lawfully.

The researcher must also ensure that all experimental procedures are humane, that treatments involving pain are used only when necessary, that alternative procedures to minimize discomfort are used when available, that surgical
procedures use anesthesia and techniques to avoid pain and infection, and that
all animals are treated in accordance with local, state, and federal laws. As
an additional measure to make sure that animals are treated humanely, the
U.S. Department of Agriculture is responsible for regulating and inspecting animal facilities. Finally, the Animal Welfare Act of 1985 requires that institutions
establish animal care and use committees. These committees function in a manner

similar to IRBs, reviewing all research proposals that use nonhuman animals in order to determine whether the animals are being treated in an ethical manner.

CRITICAL THINKING CHECK 4.1	1. In what type of research might an investigator argue that deception is necessary? How can informed consent be provided in such a situation? 2. What is the purpose of an IRB? 3. When is obtaining informed consent necessary and not necessary?

SUMMARY

In this module we discussed the APA's ethical principles. In reviewing ethical guidelines for using humans for the proposed research, we discussed the importance of IRBs and obtaining informed consent, which is a necessity when participants are at risk. We also explained the use of deception in research along with the nature and intent of debriefing participants. Finally, we outlined the special considerations when using children as research participants and presented the APA guidelines on the use of animals in research.

REVIEW OF KEY TERMS

Institutional Review Board (IRB)	informed consent form	deception	debriefing

MODULE EXERCISES

(Answers to odd-numbered exercises appear in Appendix A.)

1. What should be accomplished by the debriefing of participants?
2. Describe what is meant by "at risk" and "at minimal risk."
3. In addition to treating animals in a humane manner during a study, what other guidelines does APA provide concerning using animals for research purposes?
4. What special ethical considerations must be taken into account when conducting research with children?

CRITICAL THINKING CHECK ANSWERS

4.1

1. The researcher could argue that deception is necessary if the participants' knowledge of the true nature or hypothesis of the study might alter their behavior or responses. Informed consent is provided by giving participants a general description of the study, by informing them that they do not have to participate, and by advising them that they can withdraw from the study at any time.

2. IRBs are charged with evaluating research projects in which humans participate to ensure their ethical treatment.

3. In any study in which a participant is classified as at risk, informed consent is necessary. Although it is not necessary when participants are classified as at minimal risk, it is usually wise to obtain informed consent anyway.

WEB RESOURCES

Check your knowledge of the content and key terms in this module with a practice quiz and interactive flashcards at **www.cengage.com/psychology/jackson,** or for step-by-step practice and information, check out the Statistics and Research Methods Workshops at **www. cengage. com/psychology/workshops.**

CHAPTER TWO SUMMARY AND REVIEW: GETTING STARTED

In the preceding chapter we discussed many elements relevant to getting started on a research project. We began with how to select a problem and conduct a literature search. This discussion included examination of several library resources: *Psych Abstracts*, PsycINFO, the *Social Science Citation Index,* and the *Science Citation Index*, among others. In Module 4 we discussed the APA's ethical principles. In reviewing ethical guidelines for using humans for research purposes, we discussed the importance of IRBs and obtaining informed consent, which is a necessity when participants are at risk. We also considered the use of deception in research along with the nature and intent of debriefing participants, outlined the special considerations when using children as research participants, and presented the APA guidelines on the use of animals in research.

CHAPTER TWO REVIEW EXERCISES

(Answers to exercises appear in Appendix A.)

Fill-in Self-Test

Answer the following questions. If you have trouble answering any of the questions, restudy the relevant material before going on to the multiple-choice self-test.

1. _____ and _____ are electronic versions of the Psychological Abstracts.
2. The _____ can help you to work from a given article to see what has been published on that topic since the article was published.
3. The form given to individuals before they participate in a study in order to inform them of the general nature of the study and to obtain their consent to participate is called a(n) _____.
4. Lying to the participants concerning the true nature of the study because knowing the true nature of the study would affect how they might perform in the study involves using _____.
5. A(n) _____ is the committee charged with evaluating research projects in which human participants are used.

Multiple-Choice Self-Test

Select the single best answer for each of the following questions. If you have trouble answering any of the questions, restudy the relevant material.

1. The Milgram obedience to authority study is to _____ as the Tuskegee syphilis study is to _____.
   a. the use of deception; participant selection problems
   b. failure to use debriefing; the use of deception
   c. the use of deception; failure to obtain informed consent
   d. failure to obtain informed consent; the use of deception
2. Debriefing involves:
   a. explaining the purpose of a study to subjects after completion of data collection.
   b. having the participants read and sign an informed consent before the study begins.
   c. lying to the participants about the true nature of the study.
   d. none of the above.

3. An institutional review board reviews research proposals to ensure:
   a. that ethical standards are met.
   b. that the proposal is methodologically sound.
   c. that enough participants are being used.
   d. that there will be no legal ramifications from the study.

4. _____ is to research involving no more risk than that encountered in daily life as _____ is to being placed under some emotional or physical risk.
   a. Moderate risk; minimal risk
   b. Risk; minimal risk
   c. Minimal risk; risk
   d. Minimal risk; moderate risk

KEY TERMS

Here are the terms from the glossary for Modules 3–4. Go through the list and see if you can remember the definition of each.

| Debriefing | Deception | Informed Consent | Institutional Review Board (IRB) |

CHAPTER **3**

Variables

6 | RELIABILITY AND VALIDITY

Reliability
Error in Measurement
How to Measure Reliability: Correlation Coefficients
Types of Reliability
Test/Retest Reliability
Alternate-Forms Reliability
Split-Half Reliability
Interrater Reliability

Validity
Content Validity
Criterion Validity
Construct Validity
The Relationship between Reliability and Validity

SUMMARY
REVIEW OF KEY TERMS
MODULE EXERCISES
CRITICAL THINKING CHECK ANSWERS
WEB RESOURCES

CHAPTER THREE SUMMARY AND REVIEW: VARIABLES

In the preceding chapter we discussed library research, how to read journal articles, and ethics. In this chapter we will discuss the definition, measurement, and manipulation of variables. As noted in Chapter One, we typically refer to measured variables as dependent variables and manipulated variables as independent variables. Hence some of the ideas addressed in this chapter are how we define independent and dependent variables and how we measure variables as well as the types of measures available to us and the reliability and validity of the measures.

Defining, Measuring, and Manipulating Variables

LEARNING OBJECTIVES

- Explain and give examples of an operational definition.
- Explain the four properties of measurement and how they are related to the four scales of measurement.
- Identify and describe the four types of measures.

DEFINING VARIABLES

An important step when beginning a research project is to define the variables in the study. Some variables are fairly easy to define, manipulate, and measure. For example, if a researcher is studying the effects of exercise on blood pressure, she can manipulate the amount of exercise either by varying the length of time that individuals exercise or by varying the intensity of the exercise (and monitoring target heart rates). She can also periodically measure blood pressure during the course of the study; a machine already exists that takes this measurement in a consistent and accurate manner. Does the fact that a machine exists to take this measurement mean that the measurement is always accurate? No. (We discuss this issue in Module 6 when we address measurement error.)

Now let's suppose that a researcher wants to study a variable that is not as concrete or as easily measured as blood pressure. For instance, many people study abstract concepts such as aggression, attraction, depression, hunger, or anxiety. How would a researcher either manipulate or measure any of these variables? One person's definition of what it means to be hungry may be vastly different from someone else's. If the researcher decides to measure hunger simply by asking participants in an experiment if they are hungry, the measurement is not accurate because each individual may define hunger in a different way.

operational definition:
A definition of a variable in terms of the operations (activities) a researcher uses to measure or manipulate it.

What such a study lacks is an **operational definition** of hunger, that is, a definition of the variable in terms of the operations the researcher uses to measure or manipulate it. Because this definition is somewhat circular, let's reword it in a way that may make more sense. An operational definition specifies the activities of the researcher in measuring and/or manipulating a variable (Kerlinger, 1986). In other words, the investigator might define hunger in terms of specific activities such as not having eaten for 12 hours. Thus one operational definition of hunger could be that simple: Hunger occurs when 12 hours have passed with no food intake. Notice how much more concrete this definition is than simply saying hunger is that "gnawing feeling" that you get in your stomach. Specifying hunger in terms of the number of hours without food is an operational definition; defining hunger as that "gnawing feeling" is not.

Researchers must operationally define all variables: those measured (dependent variables) and those manipulated (independent variables). One reason for so doing is to ensure that the variables are measured or manipulated consistently during the course of the study. Another reason is to help communicate ideas to others. As a consequence, if a researcher says he measured anxiety in his study, the question becomes how did he operationally define anxiety because it can be defined and therefore measured in many different ways? Anxiety can be defined as the number of nervous actions displayed in a 1-hour time period, as heart rate, or as a person's score on a GSR (galvanic skin response) machine or on the Taylor Manifest Anxiety Scale. Some measures are better than others, "better" meaning more reliable and valid (concepts we discuss in Module 6). Once other investigators understand how a researcher has operationally defined a variable, they can replicate the study if they so desire. They can better understand the study and whether it has problems. They can also better design their own studies based on how the variables were operationally defined.

PROPERTIES OF MEASUREMENT

identity: A property of measurement in which objects that are different receive different scores.

magnitude: A property of measurement in which the ordering of numbers reflects the ordering of the variable.

equal unit size: A property of measurement in which a difference of 1 is the same amount throughout the entire scale.

absolute zero: A property of measurement in which assigning a score of zero indicates an absence of the variable being measured.

In addition to operationally defining independent and dependent variables, we must consider the level of measurement of the dependent variable. There are four levels of measurement, each based on the characteristics, or properties, of the data: identity, magnitude, equal unit size, and absolute zero. When a measure has the property of **identity**, objects that are different receive different scores. Thus if participants in a study have different political affiliations, they receive different scores. Measurements have the property of **magnitude** (also called *ordinality*) when the ordering of the numbers reflects the ordering of the variable. That is, numbers are assigned in an order such that different numbers reflect more or less of the variable being measured.

Measurements have an **equal unit size** when a difference of 1 is the same amount throughout the entire scale. As an example, the height difference between people who are 64 inches tall and 65 inches tall is the same as the difference between those who are 72 inches tall and 73 inches tall. The difference in each situation (1 inch) is identical. Notice how this measurement differs from the property of magnitude. If we simply lined up and ranked a group of individuals based on their height, our scale would have the properties of identity and magnitude but not equal unit size. Why is this so? We would not actually measure people's height in inches but simply order them according to how tall they appear, from the shortest (the person receiving a score of 1) to the tallest (the person receiving the highest score). Therefore our scale would not meet the criterion of equal unit size because the difference in height between the two people receiving scores of 1 and 2 might not be the same as the difference in height between the two people receiving scores of 3 and 4.

Finally, measures have an **absolute zero** when assigning a score of zero indicates an absence of the variable being measured. For instance, time spent studying has the property of absolute zero because a score of zero means an individual spent no time studying. However, a score of zero is not always equal to the property of absolute zero. An example is the Fahrenheit temperature scale. Although that measurement scale has a score of zero (the thermometer can read 0 degrees), does the score indicate an absence of temperature? No, instead it indicates a very cold temperature. Hence it does not have the property of absolute zero.

SCALES OF MEASUREMENT

The level, or scale, of measurement depends on the properties of the data. There are four scales of measurement: nominal, ordinal, interval, and ratio. Each of these scales has one or more of the properties described in the previous section. We discuss the scales in order, from the one with the fewest properties to the one with the most, that is, from the least to the most sophisticated. As we see in later modules, it is important to establish the scale of data measurement in order to determine the appropriate statistical test to use when analyzing the data.

Nominal Scale

nominal scale: A scale in which objects or individuals are assigned to categories that have no numerical properties.

In a **nominal scale** objects or individuals are assigned to categories that have no numerical properties. Nominal scales have the characteristic of identity but lack the other properties. Variables measured on a nominal scale are often referred to as *categorical variables* because the data are divided into categories. However, the categories carry no numerical weight. Some examples of categorical variables, or data measured on a nominal scale, are ethnicity, gender, and political affiliation.

We can assign numerical values to the levels of a nominal variable. Take ethnicity for example: we could label Asian-Americans as 1, African-Americans as 2, Latin Americans as 3, and so on. Yet these scores do not carry numerical weight; they are simply labels for the categories. In other words, the scores are used for identity but not for magnitude, equal unit size, or absolute value. We cannot order the data and claim that 1s are more or less than 2s in any way. We cannot analyze these data mathematically. It would not be appropriate to report that the mean ethnicity was 2.56, and we cannot say that there is a true zero, that is, that someone has no ethnicity.

Ordinal Scale

ordinal scale: A scale in which objects or individuals are categorized and the categories form a rank order along a continuum.

In an **ordinal scale** objects or individuals are categorized, and the categories form a rank order along a continuum. Data measured on an ordinal scale have the properties of identity and magnitude but lack equal unit size and absolute zero. Ordinal data are often referred to as *ranked data* because they are ordered from highest to lowest or from biggest to smallest. For example, reporting how students did on an examination based simply on their rank (highest score, second highest, and so on) involves an ordinal scale. This variable carries identity and magnitude because each individual receives a rank (a number) that carries identity, and the rank also conveys information about order or magnitude (how many students performed better or worse in the class). However, the ranking score does not have equal unit size: The difference in performance on the examination between the students ranked 1 and 2 is not necessarily the same as the difference between those ranked 2 and 3. Nor does this scale have an absolute zero that indicates an absence of the variable being measured.

Interval Scale

interval scale: A scale in which the units of measurement (intervals) between the numbers on the scale are all equal in size.

In an **interval scale** the units of measurement (intervals) between the numbers on the scale are all equal in size. An interval scale meets the criteria for identity, magnitude, and equal unit size. For example, the Fahrenheit temperature scale is an interval scale of measurement. A given temperature carries:

- Identity—days with different temperatures receive different scores on the scale.
- Magnitude—cooler days receive lower scores, whereas hotter days receive higher scores.
- Equal unit size—the difference between 50 and 51 degrees is the same as that between 90 and 91 degrees.

The Fahrenheit scale, however, does not have an absolute zero. Because of this lack, we are not able to form ratios based on this scale (for example, a temperature of 100 degrees is not twice as hot as a temperature of 50 degrees). We can still perform mathematical computations on interval data, as we will see in later modules.

Ratio Scale

ratio scale: A scale in which in addition to order and equal units of measurement there is an absolute zero that indicates an absence of the variable being measured.

In a **ratio scale** in addition to order and equal units of measurement, there is an absolute zero that indicates an absence of the variable measured. Ratio data have all four properties of measurement (identity, magnitude, equal unit size, and absolute zero). Examples of ratio scales of measurement include weight, time, and height. Each of these scales has (1) identity (individuals with different weights receive different scores), (2) magnitude (those who weigh less receive lower scores than those who weigh more), and (3) equal unit size (1 pound is the same unit of weight anywhere along the scale). Ratio scales also have an absolute zero, meaning that a score of zero reflects an absence of the variable. For instance, all bathroom scales start at a weight of zero, and, although a person obviously cannot weigh zero, when the scale reads zero it reflects an absence of the variable.

Also, ratios can be formed. Thus a weight of 100 pounds is twice as much as a weight of 50 pounds. As with interval data mathematical computations can be performed on ratio data. Because interval and ratio data are very similar, many psychologists simply refer to the category as *interval-ratio data* and typically do not distinguish between the types. You should be familiar with the difference between interval and ratio data, but you should also be aware that because they are so similar, they are often referred to as one type of data.

IN REVIEW   Features of Scales of Measurement

	Scales of Measurement			
	Nominal	**Ordinal**	**Interval**	**Ratio**
Examples	Ethnicity	Class rank	Temperature	Weight
	Religion	Letter grade	(Fahrenheit and Celsius)	Height
	Sex		Many psychological tests	Time
Properties	Identity	Identity	Identity	Identity
		Magnitude	Magnitude	Magnitude
			Equal unit size	Equal unit size
				Absolute zero
Mathematical operations possible	None	Rank order	Add	Add
			Subtract	Subtract
			Multiply	Multiply
			Divide	Divide

1. Provide several operational definitions of anxiety. Include nonverbal measures and physiological measures. How would your operational definitions differ from a dictionary definition?
2. Identify the scale of measurement for each of the following variables:
   a. zip code
   b. grade of egg (large, medium, small)
   c. reaction time
   d. score on the SAT
   e. class rank
   f. number on a football jersey
   g. miles per gallon

DISCRETE AND CONTINUOUS VARIABLES

discrete variables: Variables that usually consist of whole number units or categories and are made up of chunks or units that are detached and distinct from one another.

Another means of classifying variables is in terms of whether they are discrete or continuous in nature. **Discrete variables** usually consist of whole number units or categories. They are made up of chunks or units that are detached and distinct from one another. A change in value occurs a whole unit at a time; decimals do not make sense in discrete scales. Most nominal and ordinal data are discrete. For example, gender, political party, and ethnicity are discrete scales. Some interval or ratio data can be discrete. For instance, the number of children someone has is reported as a whole number (discrete data), yet it is also ratio data (you can have a true zero and form ratios).

continuous variables: Variables that usually fall along a continuum and allow for fractional amounts.

Continuous variables usually fall along a continuum and allow for fractional amounts. The term *continuous* means that it "continues" between the whole number units. Examples of continuous variables are age (22.7 years), height (64.5 inches), and weight (113.25 pounds). Most interval and ratio data are continuous in nature. Discrete and continuous data will have increased importance in later modules when we discuss research design and data presentation.

TYPES OF MEASURES

When psychology researchers collect data, the types of measures used can be classified into four basic categories: self-report measures, tests, behavioral measures, and physical measures. We discuss each category, noting its advantages and possible disadvantages.

Self-Report Measures

self-report measures: Usually questionnaires or interviews that measure how people report that they act, think, or feel.

Self-report measures are typically administered as questionnaires or interviews to measure how people report that they act, think, or feel. Thus self-report measures aid in collecting data on behavioral, cognitive, and affective events (Leary, 2001).

Behavioral self-report measures typically ask people to report how often they do something such as how often they eat a certain food, eat out at a restaurant, go to the gym, or have sex. The problem with this and the other types of self-report measures is that we are relying on the individuals to report on their own behaviors. When collecting data in this manner, we must be concerned with the veracity of the reports and with the accuracy of the individual's memory. Researchers much prefer to collect data using a behavioral measure, but direct observation of some events is not always possible or ethical.

Cognitive self-report measures ask individuals to report what they think about something. You have probably participated in a cognitive self-report measure of some sort. You may have been stopped on campus and asked what you think about parking, food services, or residence halls. Once again, we are relying on the individual to make an accurate and truthful report.

Affective self-report measures ask individuals to report how they feel about something. You may have participated in an affective self-report measure if you ever answered questions concerning emotional reactions such as happiness, depression, anxiety, or stress. Many psychological tests are affective self-report measures. These tests also fit into the category of measurement tests described in the next section.

Tests

tests: Measurement instruments used to assess individual differences in various content areas.

Tests are measurement instruments used to assess individual differences in various content areas. Psychologists frequently use two types of tests: personality tests and ability tests. Many *personality tests* are also affective self-report measures; they are designed to measure aspects of an individual's personality and feelings about certain things. Examples of such tests include the MMPI II or the Beck Depression Inventory.

Ability tests, however, are not self-report measures and generally fall into two different categories: aptitude tests and achievement tests. *Aptitude tests* measure an individual's potential to do something, whereas *achievement tests* measure an individual's competence in an area. In general, intelligence tests are aptitude tests, and school exams are achievement tests.

Most tests used by psychologists have been subjected to extensive testing themselves and are therefore considered an objective, unbiased means of collecting data. Keep in mind, however, that any measuring instrument has the potential for problems, which may range from the state of the participant on a given day to scoring and interpretation.

Behavioral Measures

behavioral measures: Measures taken by carefully observing and recording behavior.

Psychologists take **behavioral measures** by carefully observing and recording behavior. Behavioral measures are often referred to as *observational measures* because they involve observing what a participant does. Briefly (because we discuss observational research studies in detail in the next chapter), behavioral measures can be applied to anything a person or an animal does—a pigeon pecking a disk, the way men and women carry their books, or how many cars actually stop at a stop sign. The observations can be direct (while the participant is engaging in the behavior) or indirect (via audio- or videotape).

When taking behavioral measures, a researcher usually employs some sort of coding system, which is a means of converting the observations to numerical data. A very basic coding system involves simply counting the number of times that participants do something. How many times does the pigeon peck the lighted disk, or how many cars stop at the stop sign? A more sophisticated coding system involves assigning behaviors to categories. For example, a researcher might watch children playing and classify their behavior into several categories of play such as solitary, parallel, and cooperative. In the example of cars stopping at a stop sign, simply counting the number of stops might not be adequate. What is a stop? The researcher might operationally define a full stop as the car not moving for at least 3 seconds. Other categories might include a complete stop of less than 3 seconds, a rolling stop, and no stop. The researcher then has a more complex coding system consisting of various categories.

Also think about the problems of collecting data at a stop sign. If someone is standing there with a clipboard making notes, how might the presence of the data collector affect the behavior of drivers approaching the stop sign? Are researchers going to get a realistic estimate of how many cars actually stop at the sign? Probably not. For this reason measures are sometimes taken in an unobtrusive manner. Observers may hide what they are doing, hide themselves, or use a more indirect means of collecting the data (such as videotape). Using an unobtrusive means of collecting data reduces **reactivity**, that is, participants reacting in an unnatural way to being observed. This issue is discussed more fully in the next chapter.

reactivity: A possible reaction by participants in which they act unnaturally because they know they are being observed.

Finally, let's note some of the possible problems with behavioral measures. First, they rely on humans observing events. How do we know that the observers perceived the events accurately? Second, the observers must then code the events into a numerical format. There is tremendous potential for error in this coding. Finally, if the observers are visible, there is the possibility that participants may not be acting naturally because the latter know they are being observed.

Physical Measures

physical measures: Measures of bodily activity such as pulse or blood pressure that may be taken with a piece of equipment.

Most **physical measures**, or measures of bodily activity, are not directly observable. Physical measures are usually taken by means of equipment. Weight is measured with a scale, blood pressure with a sphygmomanometer, and temperature with a thermometer. Sometimes the equipment is more sophisticated. Psychologists, for instance, frequently use the galvanic skin response (GSR) to measure emotional arousal, electromyography (EMG) recordings to measure muscle contractions, and electroencephalogram (EEG) recordings to measure electrical activity in the brain.

Physical measures are much more objective than behavioral measures. A physical measure is not simply an observation (which may be subjective) of how a person or animal is acting. Instead, it is a measure of a physical activity that takes place in the brain or body. This is not to say that physical measures are problem free. Keep in mind that humans are still responsible for running the equipment that takes the measures and ultimately for interpreting the data provided by the measuring instrument. Thus even when using physical measures, a researcher needs to be concerned with the accuracy of the data.

IN REVIEW   Features of Types of Measures

Types of Measures

	Self-Report	Tests	Behavioral	Physical
Description	Questionnaires or interviews that measure how people report that they act, think, or feel	A measurement instrument used to assess individual differences	Careful observations and recordings of behavior	Measures of bodily activity
Examples	Behavioral self-report Cognitive self-report Affective self-report	Ability tests Personality tests	Counting behaviors Classifying behaviors	Weight EEG recordings GSR recordings Blood pressure
Considerations	Are participants being truthful? How accurate are participants' memories?	Are participants being truthful? How reliable and valid are the tests?	Is there reactivity? How objective are observers?	Is the individual taking the measure skilled at using the equipment? How reliable and valid is the measuring instrument?

CRITICAL THINKING CHECK 5.2

1. Which types of measures are considered more subjective? Which are more objective?
2. Why might there be measurement error even when a researcher uses an objective measure such as a blood pressure cuff? What would you recommend to control or to minimize this type of measurement error?

SUMMARY

We discussed many elements important to measuring and manipulating variables. We learned the importance of operationally defining both the independent and the dependent variables in terms of the activities involved in measuring or manipulating each variable. It is also important to determine the scale, or level, of measurement of a variable based on its properties (identity, magnitude, equal unit size, and absolute zero). Once established, the level of measurement (nominal, ordinal, interval, or ratio) helps determine the appropriate type of statistics to be used. Data can also be classified as discrete (whole number units) or continuous (allowing for fractional amounts). We next described several types of measures, including self-report measures (reporting on how you act, think, or feel), tests (ability or personality), behavioral measures (observing and recording behavior), and physical measures (measurements of bodily activity).

REVIEW OF KEY TERMS

operational definition	absolute zero	ratio scale	tests
identity	nominal scale	discrete variables	behavioral measures
magnitude	ordinal scale	continuous variables	reactivity
equal unit size	interval scale	self-report measures	physical measures

MODULE EXERCISES

(Answers to odd-numbered exercises appear in Appendix A.)

1. Which of the following is an operational definition of depression?
   a. That low feeling you get sometimes.
   b. What happens when a relationship ends.
   c. Your score on a 50-item depression inventory.
   d. The number of boxes of tissues that you cry your way through.

2. Identify the type of measure used in each of the following situations:
   a. As you leave a restaurant, you are asked to answer a few questions regarding what you thought about the service.
   b. When you join a weight loss group, they ask that you keep a food journal noting everything that you eat each day.
   c. As part of a research study you are asked to complete a 30-item anxiety inventory.
   d. When you visit your career services office, they give you a test that indicates professions to which you are best suited.
   e. While eating in the dining hall one day, you notice that food services have people tallying the number of patrons selecting each entrée.
   f. As part of a research study your professor takes pulse and blood pressure measurements on students before and after completing a class exam.

CRITICAL THINKING CHECK ANSWERS

5.1

1. Nonverbal measures:

   - number of twitches per minute
   - number of fingernails chewed to the quick

   Physiological measures:

   - blood pressure
   - heart rate
   - respiration rate
   - galvanic skin response

   These definitions are quantifiable and based on measurable events. They are not conceptual as a dictionary definition would be.
2. a. nominal
   b. ordinal
   c. ratio
   d. interval
   e. ordinal
   f. nominal
   g. ratio

5.2

1. Self-report measures and behavioral measures are more subjective; tests and physical measures are more objective.
2. The machine may not be operating correctly, or the person operating the machine may not be using it correctly. Recommendations: proper training of individuals taking the measures; checks on equipment; multiple measuring instruments; multiple measures.

WEB RESOURCES

Check your knowledge of the content and key terms in this module with a practice quiz and interactive flashcards at **www.cengage.com/ psychology/jackson**, or for step-by-step practice and information, check out the Statistics and Research Methods Workshops at **www.cengage. com/psychology/workshops**.

Reliability and Validity

LEARNING OBJECTIVES

- Explain what reliability is and how it is measured.

- Identify and explain the four types of reliability discussed in the text.

- Explain what validity is and how it is measured.

- Identify and explain the four types of validity discussed in the text.

RELIABILITY

reliability: An indication of the consistency or stability of a measuring instrument.

One means of determining whether the measure you are using is effective is to assess its reliability. **Reliability** refers to the consistency or stability of a measuring instrument. In other words, the measuring instrument must measure exactly the same way every time it is used. This consistency means that individuals should receive a similar score each time they use the measuring instrument. For example, a bathroom scale needs to be reliable, that is, it needs to measure the same way every time an individual uses it, or otherwise it is useless as a measuring instrument.

Error in Measurement

Consider some of the problems with the four types of measures discussed in the previous module (i.e., self-report, tests, behavioral, and physical). Some problems, known as *method errors*, stem from the experimenter and the testing situation. Does the individual taking the measures know how to use the measuring instrument properly? Is the measuring equipment working correctly? Other problems, known as *trait errors*, stem from the participants. Were the participants being truthful? Did they feel well on the day of the test? Both types of problems can lead to measurement error.

In fact, a measurement is a combination of the true score and an error score. The true score is what the score on the measuring instrument would be if there were no error. The error score is any measurement error (method or trait) (Leary, 2001; Salkind, 1997). The following formula represents the *observed score* on a measure, that is, the score recorded for a participant on the measuring instrument used. The observed score is the sum of the true score and the measurement error.

$$\text{Observed score} = \text{True score} + \text{Measurement error}$$

The observed score becomes increasingly reliable (more consistent) as we minimize error and thus have a more accurate true score. True scores should not vary much over time, but error scores can vary tremendously from one testing session to another. How then can we minimize error in measurement? We can make sure that all the problems related to the four types of measures are minimized. These problems include those in recording or scoring data (method error) and those in understanding instructions, motivation, fatigue, and the testing environment (trait error). The conceptual formula for reliability is

$$\text{Reliability} = \frac{\text{True score}}{\text{True score} + \text{Error score}}$$

This conceptual formula indicates that a reduction in error leads to an increase in reliability. If there is no error, reliability is equal to 1.00, the highest possible reliability score. Also, as error increases, reliability drops below 1.00. The greater the error, the lower the reliability of a measure.

How to Measure Reliability: Correlation Coefficients

Reliability is measured using correlation coefficients. We briefly discuss them here; a more comprehensive discussion appears in Chapter Five.

correlation coefficient: A measure of the degree of relationship between two sets of scores. It can vary between −1.00 and +1.00.

A **correlation coefficient** measures the degree of relationship between two sets of scores and can vary between −1.00 and +1.00. The stronger the relationship between the variables, the closer the coefficient is to either −1.00 or +1.00. The weaker the relationship between the variables, the closer the coefficient is to 0. Suppose then that of individuals measured on two variables, the top-scoring individual on variable 1 was also top scoring on variable 2, the second-highest-scoring person on variable 1 was also the second highest on variable 2, and so on down to the lowest-scoring person. In this case there would be a perfect positive correlation (+1.00) between variables 1 and 2. In the case of a perfect negative correlation (−1.00), the person having the highest score on variable 1 would have the lowest score on variable 2, the person with the second-highest score on variable 1 would have the second-lowest score on variable 2, and so on. In reality variables are almost never perfectly correlated. Thus most correlation coefficients are less than 1.

A correlation of 0 between two variables indicates the absence of any relationship as might occur by chance. Suppose we drew a person's scores on variables 1 and 2 out of a hat containing random scores, and suppose we did the same for each person in the group. We would expect no relationship between individuals' scores on the two variables. It would be impossible to predict a person's performance on variable 2 based on the score on variable 1 because there would be no relationship (a correlation of 0) between the variables.

The sign preceding the correlation coefficient indicates whether the observed relationship is positive or negative. However, the terms "positive" and "negative" do not refer to good and bad relationships but rather to how the variables are related. A **positive correlation** indicates a direct relationship between variables: When we see high scores on one variable, we tend to see high scores on the other; when we see low or moderate scores on one variable, we see similar scores on the second. Variables that are positively correlated include height with weight and high school GPA with college GPA.

positive correlation: A direct relationship between two variables in which an increase in one is related to an increase in the other and a decrease in one is related to a decrease in the other.

negative correlation: An inverse relationship between two variables in which an increase in one variable is related to a decrease in the other and vice versa.

A **negative correlation** indicates an inverse, or negative, relationship: High scores on one variable go with low scores on the other and vice versa. Examples of negative relationships are sometimes more difficult for students to generate and to think about. In adults, however, many variables are negatively correlated with age: As age increases, variables such as sight, hearing ability, strength, and energy level tend to decrease.

Correlation coefficients can be weak, moderate, or strong. Table 6.1 gives guidelines for these categories. To establish the reliability (or consistency) of a measure, we expect a strong correlation coefficient—usually in the .80s or .90s—between the two variables or scores being measured (Anastasi & Urbina, 1997). We also expect the coefficient to be positive. A positive coefficient indicates consistency, that is, those who scored high at one time also scored high at another time, those who scored low at one point scored low again, and those with intermediate scores the first time scored similarly the

TABLE **6.1**
Values for Weak, Moderate, and Strong Correlation Coefficients

Correlation Coefficient	Strength of Relationship
±.70–1.00	Strong
±.30–.69	Moderate
±.00–.29	None (.00) to Weak

second time. A negative coefficient indicates an inverse relationship between the scores taken at two different times, and it is hardly consistent (i.e., reliable) for a person to score very high at one time and very low at another. Thus to establish that a measure is reliable, we need a positive correlation coefficient of around .80 or higher.

Types of Reliability

There are four types of reliability: test/retest reliability, alternate forms reliability, split-half reliability, and interrater reliability. Each type provides a measure of consistency, but they are used in different situations.

Test/Retest Reliability

test/retest reliability: A reliability coefficient determined by assessing the degree of relationship between scores on the same test administered on two different occasions.

One of the most often used and obvious ways of establishing reliability is to repeat the same test on a second occasion, a process known as **test/retest reliability**. The correlation coefficient obtained is between the two scores of an individual on the same test administered on two occasions. If the test is reliable, we expect the two scores for each individual to be similar, and thus the resulting correlation coefficient will be high (close to +1.00). This measure of reliability assesses the stability of a test over time. Naturally some error will be present in each measurement (for example, an individual may not feel well at one testing or may have problems during the testing session such as with a broken pencil). Therefore it is unusual for the correlation coefficient to be +1.00, but we expect it to be +.80 or higher. A problem related to test/retest measures is that on many tests there are *practice effects*, that is, some people get better at the second testing, and this "practice" lowers the observed correlation. A second problem may occur if the interval between test times is short: Individuals may remember how they answered previously, both correctly and incorrectly. In this case we may be testing their memories and not the reliability of the testing instrument, and we may observe a spuriously high correlation.

Alternate-Forms Reliability

alternate-forms reliability: A reliability coefficient determined by assessing the degree of relationship between scores on two equivalent tests.

One means of controlling for test/retest problems is to use **alternate-forms reliability**, that is, using alternate forms of the testing instrument and correlating the performance of individuals on the two different forms. In this case the tests taken at times 1 and 2 are different but equivalent or parallel (hence the terms *equivalent-forms reliability* and *parallel-forms reliability* are also used).

As with test/retest reliability alternate-forms reliability establishes the stability of the test over time. In addition, it also establishes the equivalency of the items from one test to another. One problem with alternate-forms reliability is making sure that the tests are truly parallel. To help ensure equivalency, the tests should have the same number of items, the items should be of the same difficulty level, and instructions, time limits, examples, and format should all be equal—often difficult, if not impossible, to accomplish. Further, if the tests are truly equivalent, there is the potential for practice, although not to the same extent as when exactly the same test is administered twice.

Split-Half Reliability

split-half reliability: A reliability coefficient determined by correlating scores on one half of a measure with scores on the other half of the measure.

A third means of establishing reliability is by splitting the items on the test into equivalent halves and correlating scores on one half of the items with scores on the other half. This **split-half reliability** gives a measure of the equivalence of the content of the test but not of its stability over time as test/retest and alternate-forms reliability do. The biggest problem with split-half reliability is determining how to divide the items so that the two halves are in fact equivalent. For example, it would not be advisable to correlate scores on multiple-choice questions with scores on short-answer or essay questions. What is typically recommended is to correlate scores on even-numbered items with scores on odd-numbered items. Thus if the items at the beginning of the test are easier or harder than those at the end of the test, the half scores are still equivalent.

Interrater Reliability

interrater reliability: A reliability coefficient that assesses the agreement of observations made by two or more raters or judges.

Finally, to measure the reliability of observers rather than tests, you can use **interrater reliability**, which is a measure of consistency that assesses the agreement of observations made by two or more raters or judges. Let's say that you are observing play behavior in children. Rather than simply making observations on your own, it is advisable to have several independent observers collect data. The observers all watch the children playing but independently count the number and types of play behaviors they observe. Once the data are collected, interrater reliability needs to be established by examining the percentage of agreement among the raters. If the raters' data are reliable, then the percentage of agreement should be high. If the raters are not paying close attention to what they are doing or if the measuring scale devised for the various play behaviors is unclear, the percentage of agreement among observers will not be high. Although interrater reliability is measured using a correlation coefficient, the following formula offers a quick means of estimating interrater reliability:

$$\text{Interrater reliability} = \frac{\text{Number of agreements}}{\text{Number of possible agreements}} \times 100$$

Thus, if your observers agree 45 times out of a possible 50, the interrater reliability is 90%—fairly high. However, if they agree only 20 times out of 50, then the interrater reliability is 40%—low. Such a low level of agreement indicates a problem with the measuring instrument or with the individuals using the instrument and should be of great concern to a researcher.

IN REVIEW	Features of Types of Reliability			
	Types of Reliability			
	Test/Retest	**Alternate-Forms**	**Split-Half**	**Interrater**
What it measures	Stability over time	Stability over time and equivalency of items	Equivalency of items	Agreement between raters
How it is accomplished	Administer the same test to the same people at two different times	Administer alternate but equivalent forms of the test to the same people at two different times	Correlate performance for a group of people on two equivalent halves of the same test	Have at least two people count or rate behaviors and determine the percentage of agreement among them

CRITICAL THINKING CHECK 6.1

1. Why does alternate-forms reliability provide a measure of both equivalency of items and stability over time?
2. Two people observe whether or not vehicles stop at a stop sign. They make 250 observations and disagree 38 times. What is the interrater reliability? Is this good, or should it be of concern to the researchers?

VALIDITY

validity: An indication of whether the instrument measures what it claims to measure.

In addition to being reliable, measures must also be valid. **Validity** refers to whether a measuring instrument measures what it claims to measure. There are several types of validity; we will discuss four. As with reliability, validity is measured by the use of correlation coefficients. For instance, if researchers developed a new test to measure depression, they might establish the validity of the test by correlating scores on the new test with scores on an already established measure of depression, and as with reliability we would expect the correlation to be positive. Unlike reliability coefficients, however, there is no established criterion for the strength of the validity coefficient. Coefficients as low as .20 or .30 may establish the validity of a measure (Anastasi & Urbina, 1997). What is important for validity coefficients is that they are *statistically significant* at the .05 or .01 level. We explain this term in a later module, but in brief it means that the results are most likely not due to chance.

Content Validity

content validity: The extent to which a measuring instrument covers a representative sample of the domain of behaviors to be measured.

A systematic examination of the test content to determine whether it covers a representative sample of the domain of behaviors to be measured assesses **content validity**. In other words, a test with content validity has items that satisfactorily assess the content being examined. To determine whether a test has content validity, researchers consult experts in the area being tested.

As an example, when designers of the GRE generate a subject exam for psychology, they ask professors of psychology to examine the questions to establish that they represent relevant information from the entire discipline of psychology as we know it today.

face validity: The extent to which a measuring instrument appears valid on its surface.

Sometimes face validity is confused with content validity. **Face validity** simply addresses whether or not a test looks valid on its surface. Does it appear to be an adequate measure of the conceptual variable? Face validity is not really validity in the technical sense because it refers not to what the test actually measures but to what it appears to measure. Face validity relates to whether the test looks valid to those who selected it and to those who take it. For instance, does the test selected by the school board to measure student achievement "appear" to be an actual measure of achievement? Face validity has more to do with rapport and public relations than with actual validity (Anastasi & Urbina, 1997).

Criterion Validity

criterion validity: The extent to which a measuring instrument accurately predicts behavior or ability in a given area.

The extent to which a measuring instrument accurately predicts behavior or ability in a given area establishes **criterion validity**. Two types of criterion validity may be used, depending on whether the test is used to estimate present performance (*concurrent validity*) or to predict future performance (*predictive validity*). The SAT and GRE are examples of tests that have predictive validity because performance on the tests correlates with later performance in college and graduate school, respectively. The tests can be used with some degree of accuracy to "predict" future behavior. A test used to determine whether someone qualifies as a pilot is a measure of concurrent validity. The test is estimating the person's ability at the present time, not attempting to predict future outcomes. Thus concurrent validation is used for the diagnosis of existing status rather than the prediction of future outcomes.

Construct Validity

construct validity: The degree to which a measuring instrument accurately measures a theoretical construct or trait that it is designed to measure.

Construct validity is considered by many to be the most important type of validity. The **construct validity** of a test assesses the extent to which a measuring instrument accurately measures a theoretical construct or trait that it is designed to measure. Some examples of theoretical constructs or traits are verbal fluency, neuroticism, depression, anxiety, intelligence, and scholastic aptitude. One means of establishing construct validity is by correlating performance on the test with performance on a test for which construct validity has already been determined. Thus performance on a newly developed intelligence test might be correlated with performance on an existing intelligence test for which construct validity has been previously established. Another means of establishing construct validity is to show that the scores on the new test differ across people with different levels of the trait being measured. For example, if a new test is designed to measure depression, you can compare scores on the test for those known to be suffering from depression with scores for those not suffering from depression. The new measure has construct validity if it measures the construct of depression accurately.

The Relationship between Reliability and Validity

Obviously a measure should be both reliable and valid. It is possible, however, to have a test or measure that meets one of these criteria and not the other. Think for a moment about how this situation might occur. Can a test be reliable without being valid? Can a test be valid without being reliable? To answer these questions, suppose we are going to measure intelligence in a group of individuals with a "new" intelligence test. The test is based on a rather ridiculous theory of intelligence, which states that the larger your brain is, the more intelligent you are. The assumption is that the larger your brain is, the larger your head is. Thus the test is going to measure intelligence by measuring head circumference; so we gather a sample of individuals and measure the circumference of each person's head.

Is this a reliable measure? Many people immediately say no because head circumference seems like such a laughable way to measure intelligence. But reliability is a measure of consistency, not truthfulness. Is this test going to consistently measure the same thing? Yes, it is consistently measuring head circumference, and this measurement is not likely to change over time. Thus each person's score at one time will be the same or very close to the same as the person's score at a later time. The test is therefore very reliable.

Is the test a valid measure of intelligence? No, it in no way measures the construct of intelligence. Thus we have established that a test can be reliable without being valid, and because the test lacks validity, it is not a good measure.

Can the reverse be true? That is, can a test be valid (it truly measures what it claims to measure) and not be reliable? If a test truly measures intelligence, individuals would score about the same each time they took it because intelligence does not vary much over time. Thus if the test is valid, it must be reliable. Therefore a test can be reliable and not valid, but if it is valid, it is necessarily reliable.

IN REVIEW Features of Types of Validity

		Types of Validity		
	Content	**Criterion/ Concurrent**	**Criterion/ Predictive**	**Construct**
What it measures	Whether the test covers a representative sample of the domain of behaviors to be measured	The ability of the test to estimate present performance	The ability of the test to predict future performance	The extent to which the test measures a theoretical construct or trait
How it is accomplished	Ask experts to assess the test to establish that the items are representative of the trait being measured	Correlate performance on the test with a concurrent behavior	Correlate performance on the test with a behavior in the future	Correlate performance on the test with performance on an established test or with people who have different levels of the trait the test claims to measure

<table>
<tr><td>CRITICAL THINKING CHECK 6.2</td><td>

1. You have just developed a new comprehensive test for introductory psychology that covers all aspects of the course. What type(s) of validity would you recommend establishing for this measure?
2. Why is face validity not considered a true measure of validity?
3. How is it possible for a test to be reliable but not valid?
4. If on your next psychology examination you find that all of the questions are about American history rather than psychology, would you be more concerned about the reliability or validity of the test?

</td></tr>
</table>

SUMMARY

We discussed various types of reliability (consistency) and validity (truthfulness) in measures. This discussion included an examination of error in measurement, correlation coefficients used to assess reliability and validity, and the relationship between reliability and validity as well as several types of reliability (test/retest, alternate-forms, split-half, and interrater) and validity (content, face, criterion, and construct).

REVIEW OF KEY TERMS

reliability	test/retest reliability	interrater reliability	criterion validity
correlation coefficient	alternate-forms reliability	validity	construct validity
positive correlation		content validity	
negative correlation	split-half reliability	face validity	

MODULE EXERCISES

(Answers to odd-numbered exercises appear in Appendix A.)

1. Which of the following correlation coefficients represents the highest (best) reliability score?
   a. +.10
   b. −.95
   c. +.83
   d. .00
2. When you arrive for your psychology exam, you are flabbergasted to find that all of the questions are on calculus and not psychology. The next day in class, students complain so much that the professor agrees to give you all a makeup exam the following day. When you arrive at class the next day, you find that, although the questions are different, they are once again on calculus. In this example there should be high reliability of what type? What type(s) of validity is the test lacking? Explain your answers.
3. The librarians are interested in how the computers in the library are being used. They have three observers watch the terminals to see if students do research on the Internet, use e-mail, browse the Internet, play games, or do schoolwork (write papers, type homework, and so on). The three observers disagree 32 out of 75 times. What is the interrater reliability? How would you recommend that the librarians use the data?

CRITICAL THINKING CHECK ANSWERS

6.1

1. Because different questions on the same topic are used, alternative-forms reliability tells us whether the questions measure the same concepts (equivalency). Whether individuals perform similarly on equivalent tests at different times indicates the stability of a test.
2. If they disagreed 38 times out of 250 times, then they agreed 212 times out of 250 times. Thus, $212/250 = 0.85 \times 100 = 85\%$, which is very high interrater agreement.

6.2

1. Content and construct validity should be established for the new test.
2. Face validity has to do only with whether a test looks valid, not with whether it truly is valid.
3. A test can consistently measure something other than what it claims to measure.
4. You should be more concerned about the validity of the test because it does not measure what it claims to measure.

WEB RESOURCES

Check your knowledge of the content and key terms in this module with a practice quiz and interactive flashcards at **www.cengage.com/psychology/jackson,** or for step-by-step practice and information, check out the Statistics and Research Methods Workshops at **www. cengage.com/psychology/workshops**.

CHAPTER THREE SUMMARY AND REVIEW: VARIABLES

In Module 5 several elements important in measuring and manipulating variables were introduced. We learned the importance of operationally defining both the independent and dependent variables in a study in terms of the activities involved in measuring or manipulating each variable. It is also important to determine the scale or level of measurement of a variable based on the properties (identity, magnitude, equal unit size, and absolute zero) of the particular variable. Once established, the level of measurement (nominal, ordinal, interval, or ratio) helps determine the appropriate statistics to be used with the data. Data can also be classified as discrete (whole number units) or continuous (allowing for fractional amounts). We next described several types of measures, including self-report measures (reporting on how you act, think, or feel), tests (ability or personality), behavioral measures (observing and recording behavior), and physical measures (measurements of bodily activity).

Finally, in Module 6 we examined various types of reliability (consistency) and validity (truthfulness) in measures. We discussed error in measurement, correlation coefficients used to assess reliability and validity, and the relationship between reliability and validity.

CHAPTER THREE REVIEW EXERCISES

(Answers to exercises appear in Appendix A.)

Fill-in Self-Test

Answer the following questions. If you have trouble answering any of the questions, restudy the relevant material before going on to the multiple-choice self-test.

1. A definition of a variable in terms of the activities a researcher uses to measure or manipulate it is an _____.
2. _____ is a property of measurement in which the ordering of numbers reflects the ordering of the variable.
3. A(n) _____ scale is a scale in which objects or individuals are broken into categories that have no numerical properties.
4. A(n) _____ scale is a scale in which the units of measurement between the numbers on the scale are all equal in size.
5. Questionnaires or interviews that measure how people report that they act, think, or feel are _____.

6. _____ occurs when participants act unnaturally because they know they are being observed.
7. When reliability is assessed by determining the degree of relationship between scores on the same test that is administered on two different occasions, _____ is being used.
8. _____ produces a reliability coefficient that assesses the agreement of observations made by two or more raters or judges.
9. _____ assesses the extent to which a measuring instrument covers a representative sample of the domain of behaviors to be measured.
10. The degree to which a measuring instrument accurately measures a theoretic construct or trait that it is designed to measure is assessed by _____.

Multiple-Choice Self-Test

Select the single best answer for each of the following questions. If you have trouble answering any of the questions, restudy the relevant material.

1. Gender is to the _____ property of measurement as time is to the _____ property of measurement.
   a. magnitude; identity
   b. equal unit size; magnitude
   c. absolute zero; equal unit size
   d. identity; absolute zero

2. Arranging a group of individuals from heaviest to lightest represents the _____ property of measurement.
   a. identity
   b. magnitude
   c. equal unit size
   d. absolute zero

3. The letter grade on a test is to the _____ scale of measurement as height is to the _____ scale of measurement.
   a. ordinal; ratio
   b. ordinal; nominal
   c. nominal; interval
   d. interval; ratio

4. Weight is to the _____ scale of measurement as political affiliation is to the _____ scale of measurement.
   a. ratio; ordinal
   b. ratio; nominal
   c. interval; nominal
   d. ordinal; ratio

5. Measuring in whole units is to _____ as measuring in whole units and/or fractional amounts is to _____.
   a. discrete variable; continuous variable
   b. continuous variable; discrete variable
   c. nominal scale; ordinal scale
   d. both a and c

6. An individual's potential to do something is to _____ as an individual's competence in an area is to _____.
   a. tests; self-report measures

   b. aptitude tests; achievement tests
   c. achievement tests; aptitude tests
   d. self-report measures; behavioral measures

7. Sue decided to have participants in her study of the relationship between amount of time spent studying and grades keep a journal of how much time they spent studying each day. The type of measurement that Sue is employing is known as a(n) _____.
   a. behavioral self-report measure
   b. cognitive self-report measure
   c. affective self-report measure
   d. aptitude test

8. Which of the following correlation coefficients represents the variables with the weakest degree of relationship?
   a. −.99
   b. −.49
   c. +.83
   d. +.01

9. Which of the following is true?
   a. Test/retest reliability is determined by assessing the degree of relationship between scores on one half of a test with scores on the other half of the test.
   b. Split-half reliability is determined by assessing the degree of relationship between scores on the same test that is administered on two different occasions.
   c. Alternate-forms reliability is determined by assessing the degree of relationship between scores on two different but equivalent tests.
   d. None of the above.

10. If observers disagree 20 times out of 80, then the interrater reliability is _____.
    a. 40%
    b. 75%
    c. 25%
    d. indeterminable

11. Which of the following is *not* a type of validity?
    a. criterion validity
    b. content validity

c. face validity

d. alternate-forms validity

12. Which of the following is true?
   a. Construct validity is the extent to which a measuring instrument covers a representative sample of the domain of behaviors to be measured.
   b. Criterion validity is the extent to which a measuring instrument accurately predicts behavior or ability in a given area.

c. Content validity is the degree to which a measuring instrument accurately measures a theoretic construct or trait that it is designed to measure.

d. Face validity is a measure of the truthfulness of a measuring instrument.

KEY TERMS

Here are the terms from the glossary for Modules 5–6. Go through the list and see if you can remember the definition of each.

Absolute zero	Criterion validity	Negative correlation	Reliability
Alternate-forms reliability	Discrete variables	Nominal scale	Self-report measures
	Equal unit size	Operational definition	Split-half reliability
Behavioral measures	Face validity	Ordinal scale	Test/retest reliability
Construct validity	Identity	Physical measures	Tests
Content validity	Interrater reliability	Positive correlation	Validity
Continuous variables	Interval scale	Ratio scale	
Correlation coefficient	Magnitude	Reactivity	

CHAPTER 4

Descriptive Methods

8 | SURVEY METHODS

Survey Construction
Writing the Questions
Arranging the Questions

Administering the Surveys
Mail Surveys
Telephone Surveys
Personal Interviews

Sampling Techniques
Probability Sampling
Nonprobability Sampling

SUMMARY
REVIEW OF KEY TERMS
MODULE EXERCISES
CRITICAL THINKING CHECK ANSWERS
WEB RESOURCES
LAB RESOURCES

CHAPTER FOUR SUMMARY AND REVIEW: DESCRIPTIVE METHODS

In the preceding chapters we discussed certain aspects of getting started with a research project. We now turn to a discussion of actual research methods—the nuts and bolts of conducting a research project—starting with the types of nonexperimental designs. In this chapter we discuss descriptive methods. These methods, as the name implies, allow us to describe a situation; however, they do not allow us to make accurate predictions or to establish a cause-and-effect relationship between variables. We examine three categories of descriptive methods, observational methods, qualitative methods, and surveys, and provide an overview and examples of each. In addition, we note any special considerations that apply when using these methods.

Observational and Qualitative Methods

LEARNING OBJECTIVES

- Explain the difference between naturalistic and laboratory observation.
- Explain the difference between participant and nonparticipant observation.
- Explain the difference between disguised and nondisguised observation.
- Describe how to use a checklist versus a narrative record.
- Describe an action item versus a static item.
- Describe the qualitative method.
- Describe the case study method.
- Describe the archival method.
- Describe the interview method.
- Describe the field study method.
- Describe what action research is.

As noted in Chapter One, the observational method in its most basic form is as simple as it sounds—making observations of human or other animal behavior. This method is not used as widely in psychology as in other disciplines such as sociology, ethology, and anthropology because most psychologists want to be able to do more than describe. However, this method is of great value in some situations. When we begin research in an area, it may be appropriate to start with an observational study before doing anything more complicated. In addition, certain behaviors that cannot be studied in experimental situations lend themselves nicely to observational research. We discuss two types of observational studies, naturalistic (or field) observation and laboratory (or systematic) observation, along with the advantages and disadvantages of each type. In addition, we discuss various qualitative methods.

NATURALISTIC OBSERVATION

ecological validity: The extent to which research can be generalized to real-life situations.

Naturalistic observation (sometimes referred to as *field observation*) involves watching people or animals in their natural habitats. The greatest advantage of this type of observation is the potential for observing natural or true behaviors. The idea is that animals or people in their natural habitat rather than in an artificial laboratory setting should display more realistic, natural behaviors. For this reason, naturalistic observation has greater ecological validity than most other research methods. **Ecological validity** refers to the extent to which research can be generalized to real-life situations (Aronson & Carlsmith, 1968). Both Jane Goodall and Dian Fossey engaged in naturalistic observation in their work with chimpanzees and gorillas, respectively. However, as we will see, they used the naturalistic method slightly differently.

OPTIONS WHEN USING OBSERVATION

undisguised observation: Studies in which the participants are aware that the researcher is observing their behavior.

nonparticipant observation: Studies in which the researcher does not participate in the situation in which the research participants are involved.

Both Goodall and Fossey used **undisguised observation**, that is, they made no attempt to disguise themselves while making observations. Goodall's initial approach was to observe the chimpanzees from a distance. Thus she attempted to engage in **nonparticipant observation**, a study in which the researcher does not take part (participate) in the situation in which the research participants are involved. Fossey, on the other hand, attempted to infiltrate the group of gorillas that she was studying. She tried to act as they did in the hopes of being accepted as a member of the group so that she could observe as an insider. In **participant observation** then the researcher actively participates in the situation in which the research participants are involved.

"SHE'S BEEN WATCHING US FOR YEARS. WHEN THE HELL IS SHE GOING TO WRITE HER BOOK?"

participant observation:
Studies in which the researcher actively participates in the situation in which the research participants are involved.

Take a moment to think about the issues involved in either of these methods. In nonparticipant observation there is the possibility of reactivity, participants reacting in an unnatural way to someone obviously watching them. Thus Goodall's sitting back and watching the chimpanzees may have caused them to "react" to her presence, and she therefore may not have observed their naturalistic or true behaviors. Fossey, on the other hand, claimed that the gorillas accepted her as a member of their group, thereby minimizing or eliminating reactivity. This claim is open to question, however, because no matter how much like a gorilla she acted, she was still human.

disguised observation:
Studies in which the participants are unaware that the researcher is observing their behavior.

Imagine how much more effective both participant and nonparticipant observation might be if researchers used **disguised observation,** that is, concealing the fact that they were observing and recording participants' behaviors. Disguised observation allows the researcher to make observations in a relatively unobtrusive manner. As a nonparticipant a researcher can make observations while hiding or by videotaping participants. Reactivity is not an issue because participants are unaware that anyone is observing their behavior. Hiding or videotaping, however, may raise ethical problems if the participants are humans. This concern is one reason that prior to beginning a study, all research, both human and animal, must be approved by an Institutional Review Board (IRB) or Animal Care and Use Committee, as described in Module 4.

Disguised observation may also be used when one is acting as a participant in the study. Rosenhan (1973) demonstrated this method in his classic study on the validity of psychiatric diagnoses. Rosenhan had 8 sane individuals seek admittance to 12 different mental hospitals. Each was asked to go to a hospital and complain of the same symptoms: hearing voices that said "empty," "hollow," and "thud." Once admitted to the mental ward, the individuals no longer reported hearing voices. If admitted, each individual was to make written recordings of patient-staff interactions. Rosenhan was interested in how long it would take a "sane" person to be released from the mental hospital. He found that the length of stay varied from 7 to 52 days, although the hospital staff never detected that the individuals were "sane" and part of a disguised participant study.

expectancy effects:
The influence of the researcher's expectations on the outcome of the study.

In addition to reactivity, researchers who use this method are concerned about **expectancy effects**, which are the effects of the researcher's expectations on the outcome of the study. For example, researchers may pay more attention to behaviors that they expect or that support their hypotheses while possibly ignoring behaviors that do not support their hypotheses. Because the only data in an observational study are the observations made by the researcher, expectancy effects can be a serious problem, leading to biased results.

Besides these potential problems, naturalistic observation can be costly, especially in studies like those conducted by Goodall and Fossey in which travel to another continent is required. Further, such observation is usually time-consuming because researchers are often open to studying many different behaviors when conducting this type of study. Thus anything of interest may be observed and recorded. This flexibility often means that the study can go on indefinitely and there is little control over what happens in it.

LABORATORY OBSERVATION

An observational method that is usually less costly and time-consuming and affords more control is laboratory, or systematic, observation. In contrast to naturalistic observation, systematic or laboratory observation involves observing behavior in a more contrived setting, usually a laboratory, and involves focusing on a small number of carefully defined behaviors. The participants are more likely to know that they are participating in a research study in which they are being observed. As with naturalistic observation, however, the researcher can be either a participant or a nonparticipant and either disguised or undisguised. For example, in the classic "strange situation" study by Ainsworth and Bell (1970), mothers brought their children to a laboratory playroom. The mothers and children were then observed through a two-way mirror in various situations such as when the child explored the room, was left alone in the room, was left with a stranger, and was reunited with the mother. This study used nonparticipant observation. In addition, it was conducted in an undisguised manner for the mothers (who were aware they were being observed) and disguised for the children (who were unaware they were being observed).

Laboratory observation may also be conducted with the researcher as a participant in the situation. For example, a developmental psychologist could observe play behavior in children as an undisguised participant by playing with the children or by posing as a teacher or day care worker in the laboratory setting. In other studies involving laboratory observation, the participant is disguised. Research on helping behavior (altruism) often uses this method. Thus researchers might stage what appears to be an emergency while participants are supposedly waiting for an experiment to begin. The researcher participates in a disguised manner in the "emergency situation" and observes how the "real" participants act. Do they offer help right away, and does offering help depend on the number of people present?

In laboratory observation, as with naturalistic observation, we are concerned with reactivity and expectancy effects. In fact, reactivity may be a greater concern because most people "react" simply to being in a laboratory. As noted, one way of attempting to control reactivity is by using a disguised type of design.

An advantage of systematic or laboratory settings is that they are contrived (not natural) and therefore offer the researcher more control. The situation has been manufactured to some extent to observe a specific behavior or set of behaviors. Because the situation is contrived, the likelihood that the participants will actually engage in the behavior of interest is far greater than it would be in a natural setting. Most researchers view this control as advantageous because it reduces the length of time needed for the study. Notice, however, that as we increase control, we decrease flexibility. We are not free to observe whatever behavior we find of interest on any given day, as we would be with a naturalistic study. Researchers have to decide what is of greatest importance to them and then choose either the naturalistic or laboratory method.

DATA COLLECTION

Another decision to be faced when conducting observational research is how to collect the data. In Module 5 we discussed several types of measures: self-report measures, tests, behavioral measures, and physical measures. Because observational research involves observing and recording behavior, data are most often collected through the use of behavioral measures. As noted in Module 5, behavioral measures can be taken in a direct manner (at the time the behavior occurs) or in an indirect manner (via audio- or videotape). In addition, researchers using the observational technique can collect data using narrative records or checklists.

Narrative Records

narrative records: Full narrative descriptions of a participant's behavior.

Narrative records are full narrative descriptions of a participant's behavior. These records may be created in a direct manner—by taking notes—or in an indirect manner—by audio- or videotaping the participants and then taking notes later. The purpose of narrative records is to capture completely everything the participant said or did during a specified period of time.

One of the best examples of the use of narrative records is the work of Jean Piaget. Piaget studied cognitive development in children and kept extensive narrative records concerning everything a child did during the specified time period. His records were a running account of exactly what the child said and did.

Although narrative records provide a complete account of what took place with each participant in a study, they are a very subjective means of collecting data. In addition, narrative records cannot be analyzed quantitatively. To be analyzed, the data must be coded in some way that reduces the huge volume of narrative information to a more manageable quantitative form such as the number of problems solved correctly by children in different age ranges. The data should be coded by more than one person to establish interrater reliability. You may recall from Module 6 that interrater reliability is a measure of reliability that assesses the agreement of observations made by two or more raters or judges.

Checklists

A more structured and objective method of collecting data involves using a **checklist,** a tally sheet on which the researcher records attributes of the participants and whether particular behaviors were observed. Checklists enable researchers to focus on a limited number of specific behaviors.

Researchers use two basic types of items on checklists. A **static item** is a means of collecting data on characteristics that do not change while the observations are being made. These static features may include how many people are present; the gender, race, and age of the participant; or what the weather is like (if relevant). Depending on the nature of the study, many different characteristics may be noted using static items. For instance, observations of hospital patients might include information on their general health, and observations of driving behavior might include the make and type of vehicle driven.

The second type of item used on a checklist, an **action item,** is used to record whether specific behaviors are present or absent during the observational time period. Action items could be used to record the type of stop made at a stop sign (complete, rolling, or none) or the type of play behavior observed in children (solitary, cooperative, or parallel). Typically action items provide a means of tallying the frequency of different categories of behavior.

As discussed in Module 5, it is important that researchers who use the checklists understand the operational definition of each characteristic being measured in order to increase the reliability and validity of the measures. As you may recall, an operational definition of a variable is a definition of the variable in terms of the operations (activities) a researcher uses to measure or manipulate it. Thus to use a checklist accurately, the person collecting the data must clearly understand what constitutes each category of behavior being observed.

The advantage of checklists over narrative records is that the data are already quantified and do not have to be reduced in any way. The disadvantage is that the behaviors and characteristics to be observed are determined when the checklist is devised. As a consequence, an interesting behavior that would have been included in a narrative record may be missed or not recorded because it is not part of the checklist.

checklist: A tally sheet on which the researcher records attributes of the participants and whether particular behaviors were observed.

static item: A type of item used on a checklist on which attributes that do not change are recorded.

action item: A type of item used on a checklist to note the presence or absence of behaviors.

IN REVIEW Features of Types of Observational Studies		
	Naturalistic	Laboratory
Description	Observing people or other animals in their natural habitats	Observing people or other animals in a contrived setting, usually a laboratory
Options	Participant versus nonparticipant	Participant versus nonparticipant
	Disguised versus undisguised	Disguised versus undisguised
Means of data collection	Narrative records	Narrative records
	Checklists	Checklists
Concerns	Reactivity	Reactivity
	Expectancy effects	Expectancy effects
	Time	Lack of flexibility
	Money	
	Lack of control	

CRITICAL THINKING CHECK 7.1

1. Explain the differences in terms of flexibility and control between naturalistic and laboratory observational research.
2. If reactivity were your greatest concern in an observational study, which method would you recommend using?
3. Why is data reduction of greater concern when using narrative records as opposed to checklists?

QUALITATIVE METHODS

qualitative research: A type of social research based on field observations that is analyzed without statistics.

Qualitative research focuses on phenomena that occur in natural settings, and the data are analyzed without the use of statistics. Qualitative research usually takes place in the field or wherever the participants normally conduct their activities. When using qualitative methods, however, researchers are typically not interested in simplifying, objectifying, or quantifying what they observe. Instead, when conducting qualitative studies, researchers are more interested in interpreting and making sense of what they have observed. Researchers using this approach may not necessarily believe that there is a single "truth" to be discovered but rather that there are multiple positions or opinions and that each have some degree of merit.

Qualitative research entails observation and/or unstructured interviewing in natural settings. The data are collected in a spontaneous and open-ended fashion. Consequently, these methods have far less structure and control than do quantitative methods. Researchers who prefer quantitative methods often regard this tendency toward flexibility and lack of control as a threat to the reliability and validity of a study. Those who espouse qualitative methods, however, see these characteristics as strengths. They believe that the participants eventually adjust to the researcher's presence (thus reducing reactivity) and that once they do, the researcher is able to acquire perceptions from different points of view. Please keep in mind that most of the methodologies used by qualitative researchers are also used by quantitative researchers. The difference is in the intent of the study. The quantitative researcher typically starts with a hypothesis for testing, observes and collects data, statistically analyzes the data, and draws conclusions. Qualitative researchers are far less structured and go more with the flow of the research setting and the participants. They may change what they are observing based on changes that occur in the field setting. Qualitative researchers typically make passive observations with no intent of manipulating a causal variable. Qualitative research has been more commonly used by other social researchers such as sociologists and anthropologists, but it is growing in applicability and popularity among psychologists.

Case Study Method

One of the oldest qualitative research methods is the *case study method*, an in-depth study of one or more individuals, groups, social settings, or events in the hope of revealing things that are true of all of us. For instance, Freud's theory of personality development was based on a small number of case studies. Piaget, whose research was used as an example of observational methods, began studying cognitive development by completing case studies on his own three children. This inquiry piqued his interest in cognitive development to such an extent that he then began to use observational methods to study hundreds of other children. As another example, much of the research on split-brain patients and hemispheric specialization was conducted using case studies of the few individuals whose corpus callosum had been severed.

One advantage of case study research is that it often suggests hypotheses for future studies, as in Piaget's case. It also provides a method to study rare phenomena such as rare brain disorders or diseases, as in the case of split-brain patients. Case studies may also offer tentative support for a psychological theory.

Case study research also has problems. The individual, group, setting, or event being observed may be atypical, and consequently, any generalizations made to the general population would be erroneous. For example, Freud formulated a theory of personality development that he believed applied to everyone based on case studies of a few atypical individuals. Another potential problem is expectancy effects: Researchers may be biased in their interpretations of their observations or data collection, paying more attention to data that support their theory and ignoring data that present problems for it. Because of these limitations, case study research should be used with caution, and the data should be interpreted for what they are—observations on one or a few possibly unrepresentative individuals, groups, settings, or events.

archival method: A descriptive research method that involves describing data that existed before the time of the study.

Archival Method

A second qualitative method is the **archival method**, which involves describing data that existed before the time of the study. In other words, the data were not generated as part of the study. One of the biggest advantages of archival research is that the problem of reactivity is somewhat minimized because the data have already been collected and the researcher does not have to interact with the participants in any way. As an example, let's assume that a researcher wants to study whether more babies are born when the moon is full. The researcher could use archival data from hospitals and count the number of babies born on days with full moons versus those with no full moons for as far back as he or she would like. You can see, based on this example, that another advantage of archival research is that it is usually less time-consuming than most other research methods because the data already exist. Thus researchers are not confronted with the problems of getting participants for their study and taking the time to observe them because these tasks have already been done for them.

There are many sources for archival data. The best-known is the U.S. Census Bureau. However, any organization that collects data is an archival source: the National Opinion Research Center, the Educational Testing Service, and local, state, and federal public records can all be sources of archival data. In addition to organizations that collect data, archival research may be conducted based on the content of newspapers or magazines, data in a library, police incident reports, hospital admittance records, or computer databases.

Some data sources might be considered better than others. For instance, reviewing letters to the editor at a local newspaper to gauge public sentiment on a topic might lead to biases in the data. In other words, there is a selection bias in who decided to write to the editor, and some opinions or viewpoints may be overlooked simply because the individuals who hold those viewpoints decided not to write to the editor. Moreover, in all archival research studies, researchers are basing conclusions on data collected by another person or organization. This second-hand collection means that the researchers can never be sure whether the data are reliable or valid. In addition, they cannot be sure that what is currently in the archive represents everything that was originally collected. Some of the data may have been purged at some time, and researchers will not know this. Nor will they know why any data were purged or why some data were purged and some left. Thus as a research method archival research typically provides a lot of flexibility in terms of what is studied but no control in terms of who was studied or how they were studied.

Interviews and Focus Group Interviews

Interviews can be thought of as the verbal equivalent of a pencil and paper survey. During an interview the researcher is having a conversation with the respondent and the conversation has a purpose. An **interview** typically involves asking questions in a face-to-face manner, and it may be conducted anywhere—at the individual's home, on the street, or in a shopping mall. There are three different types of interviews, the standardized interview, the semistandardized interview, and the unstandardized interview (Berg, 2009; Esterberg, 2002). The *standardized interview* is somewhat formal in structure, and the questions are typically asked in a specific order. There is little deviation of the wording of the questions. That is, questions are asked just as they are written, and there is no question clarification provided to respondents,

interview: A method that typically involves asking questions in a face-to-face manner that may be conducted anywhere.

nor are general questions about the interview answered or additional questions added on the spur of the moment.

The *semistandardized interview* has some structure to it, but the wording of the questions is flexible, the level of the language may be modified, and the interviewer may choose to answer questions and provide further explanation if requested. Respondents have a greater ability to express their opinions in their own words when using this type of interview structure. Lastly, there is more flexibility in terms of the interviewer adding or deleting questions.

The *unstandardized interview* is completely unstructured in that there is no set order to the questions, nor a set wording to the questions. The questions are more spontaneous and free flowing. This flexibility obviously means that the level of the language can be modified and that the interviewer may provide question clarification, answer questions the respondent may have, and add or delete questions.

When conducting an interview, no matter the type of interview, the researcher needs to think about the order of the questions. It is generally recommended that one begins with questions that the respondent should find easy and nonthreatening before moving on to the more important questions. Sensitive questions should come later in the interview when the respondent is more at ease with the situation. At some point there should be validation of the more sensitive questions, that is, questions that restate important or sensitive questions. These validation questions should be worded differently than the previous questions on the same topic. If your interview involves several topics, you should arrange the questions on each topic in the manner described above. In addition, when interviewing on more than one topic, there should be some sort of transition between the questions on each topic such as "The next series of questions will ask you about ..."

One advantage of interviews is that they allow the researcher to record not only verbal responses but also any facial or bodily expressions or movements, such as grins, grimaces, or shrugs. These nonverbal responses may give the researcher greater insight into the respondents' true opinions and beliefs.

focus group interview: A method that involves interviewing 6 to 10 individuals at the same time.

A variation on interviewing individuals is the **focus group interview**. Focus group interviews involve interviewing 6 to 10 individuals at the same time. Focus groups usually meet once for 1 to 2 hours. The questions asked of the participants are open ended and addressed to the whole group. This procedure allows participants to answer in any way they choose and to respond to each other. One concern with focus group interviews is that one or two of the participants may dominate the conversation. Consequently, it is important that the individual conducting the focus group is skilled at dealing with such problems.

Focus group interviews are a flexible methodology that permit the gathering of a large amount of information from many people in a fairly short amount of time. Because of their flexibility, focus group interviews allow the moderator to explore other topics that might arise based on the discussion of the group.

Field Studies

field studies: A method that involves observing everyday activities as they happen in a natural setting.

Earlier in the module we discussed a methodology that is very similar to field studies, naturalistic observation. **Field studies** involve observing everyday activities as they happen in a natural setting. In addition, the observer is directly involved with those that are being observed. In this sense field studies are similar to participant observation. The main difference is that when field studies are used, data are always collected in a narrative form and left in that form because the research is qualitative. The hope of the researcher conducting a field study is to acquire the perspective and point of view of an insider while also keeping an objective analytic perspective. The data produced are in the form of extensive written notes that provide detailed descriptions. Observers should take note of the ongoing social processes, but they should not interfere with these processes or attempt to impose their perspectives. This balancing act requires quite a bit of skill because the researcher is a participant in the situation but cannot influence those being observed. In other words, we want those being observed to act as they would if the researcher were not there, and we want the outcomes to be the same as they would have been if the researcher were not there. This method is unlike participant observation in which those being observed may not realize they are being observed. With field studies subjects realize they are being observed, meaning there is the issue of reactivity that we discussed earlier in the module. The goal of field studies is a holistic understanding of a culture, subculture, or group.

Action Research

action research: A method in which research is conducted by a group of people to identify a problem, attempt to resolve it, and then assess how successful their efforts were.

The final type of qualitative research we will discuss is **action research**, research conducted by a group of people to identify a problem, attempt to resolve it, and then assess how successful their efforts were. This research is highly applied in that it is typically conducted by those who have a problem in order to solve the problem. That is, action research follows the old adage "If you want something done right, do it yourself." So rather than hire someone to analyze a social program in order to assess its effectiveness, those who work in the program would identify a problem to be evaluated, explore the problem, and then define an agenda for action.

Action research has a wide range of applications, e.g., in schools, hospitals, social agencies, the justice system, and community contexts. The methodology uses a collaborative approach that as an end result gives people a course of action to fix a problem. It utilizes a participatory democratic style.

There are three basic phases to action research. The first process is *looking* in which the researchers gather information, identify a problem, and identify who the stakeholders are. The second process is *thinking*, which involves thinking about the problem, gathering the information to answer the questions posed, and analyzing and interpreting the data. Areas of success should be identified along with possible deficiencies. The final process is *action*—thus the name action research. After looking and thinking, action needs to be taken to improve the lives of the participants (i.e., the stakeholders). This last process also involves sharing the results not only with the stakeholders but with the larger community.

Unlike other methodologies, action research is typically not published in academic journals but instead might be presented in a newspaper article, on television, or in a magazine. These venues mean that the language and content of action research is easier to understand and typically does not include difficult-to-understand statistical techniques, that is, it is written at a level that a lay person can understand.

Qualitative Data Analysis

Let's begin our discussion of qualitative data analysis by identifying the similarities between it and quantitative data analysis. Both types of data analysis involve the researcher making some type of inference based on the data. In addition, both types of data analysis involve the researcher carefully examining the data that have been collected in order to reach a conclusion. Finally, researchers who use both types of analyses make their findings public so that they can be scrutinized and reviewed by others.

The main difference between qualitative and quantitative data analyses is that statistics and mathematical formulas are not used with qualitative analyses. Most of the data collected are nominal in scale and are collected via extensive note taking. Consequently, the data are verbal in nature rather than numerical and consist of very detailed notes on what was observed via the particular methodology used. Unlike quantitative analyses in which data analysis cannot take place until after all data have been collected, with qualitative analyses the results of early review of the data might guide what data are collected later in the study. Qualitative analyses usually involve reading through the notes taken and trying to conceptualize from the data. During this stage the researcher is looking for patterns in the data. Accordingly, researchers might code the data by organizing it into conceptual categories. They then would attempt to create themes or concepts. Computers or word processors can be used to help with the data analysis by searching through the notes to identify certain words or phrases that might help to develop themes and concepts.

IN REVIEW	Features of Types of Qualitative Studies
Type of Study	**Description**
Case Study	An in-depth study of one or more individuals, groups, social settings, or events in the hope of revealing things that are true of all of us
Archival Study	A method that involves describing data that existed before the time of the study
Interview	A method that involves asking questions in a face-to-face manner; it may be conducted anywhere
Focus Group Interview	A method that involves interviewing 6 to 10 individuals at the same time
Field Studies	A method that involves observing everyday activities as they happen in a natural setting.
Action Research	Research conducted by a group of people to identify a problem, attempt to resolve it, and then assess how successful their efforts were

SUMMARY

In this module we discussed various ways of conducting a descriptive study. The methods presented were observational method (naturalistic versus laboratory), the case study method, the archival method, the interview and focus group interview methods, field research, and action research. Several advantages and disadvantages of each method were discussed. For observational methods the important issues are reactivity, experimenter expectancies, time, cost, control, and flexibility. The case study method is limited because it describes only one or a few people and is very subjective in nature, but it is often a good means of beginning a research project. The archival method is limited by the fact that the data already exist and were collected by someone other than the researcher. The interview method may be limited by the quality of the interviewer, whereas field research is limited by the ability of the researcher to blend in and not affect the behaviors of those being observed. Finally, action research is a very applied type of research that can be limited because the very people who are conducting the research are also the participants in the research.

REVIEW OF KEY TERMS

ecological validity	participant observation	checklist	interview
undisguised observation	disguised observation	static item	focus group interview
nonparticipant observation	expectancy effects	action item	field studies
	narrative records	qualitative research	action research
		archival method	

MODULE EXERCISES

(Answers to odd-numbered exercises appear in Appendix A.)

1. Imagine that you want to study cell phone use by drivers. You decide to conduct an observational study of drivers by making observations at three locations—a busy intersection, an entrance/exit to a shopping mall parking lot, and a residential intersection. You are interested in the number of people who use cell phones while driving. How would you recommend conducting this study? How would you recommend collecting the data? What concerns do you need to take into consideration?

2. Explain the difference between participant and nonparticipant observation and disguised and undisguised observation.
3. How does using a narrative record differ from using a checklist?
4. Explain how qualitative research differs from quantitative research.
5. Explain the archival method.
6. Explain the difference between an interview and a focus group interview.
7. Why is action research considered an applied form of research?

CRITICAL THINKING CHECK ANSWERS

7.1

1. Naturalistic observation has more flexibility because researchers are free to observe any behavior they may find interesting. Laboratory observation has less flexibility because the behaviors to be observed are usually determined before the study begins. It is thus difficult to change what is being observed once the study has begun. Because naturalistic observation affords greater flexibility, it also has less control: the researcher does not control what happens during the study.

Laboratory observation, having less flexibility, also has more control: the researcher determines more of the research situation.

2. If reactivity were your greatest concern, you might try using disguised observation. In addition, you might opt for a more naturalistic setting.

3. Data reduction is of greater concern when using narrative records because the narrative records must be interpreted and reduced to a quantitative form, using multiple individuals to establish interrater reliability. Checklists do not involve interpretation or data reduction because the individual collecting the data simply records whether a behavior is present or how often a behavior occurs.

WEB RESOURCES

Check your knowledge of the content and key terms in this module with a practice quiz and interactive flashcards at **www.cengagecom/ psychology/jackson**, or for step-by-step practice and information, check out the Statistics and Research Methods Workshops at **www.cengage. com/psychology/workshops**.

LAB RESOURCES

For hands-on experience using the research methods described in this module, see Chapter One ("Naturalistic Observation") in *Research Methods Laboratory Manual for Psychology*, 3rd ed., by William Langston (Belmont, CA: Wadsworth, 2011).

MODULE 8

Survey Methods

LEARNING OBJECTIVES

- Differentiate open-ended, closed-ended, and partially open-ended questions.
- Explain the differences among loaded questions, leading questions, and double-barreled questions.
- Identify the three methods of surveying.
- Identify advantages and disadvantages of the three survey methods.
- Differentiate probability and nonprobability sampling.
- Differentiate random sampling, stratified random sampling, and cluster sampling.

Another means of collecting data for descriptive purposes is to use a survey. We discuss several elements to consider when using surveys, including constructing the survey, administering the survey, and choosing sampling techniques.

_____

SURVEY CONSTRUCTION

For the data collected in a survey to be both reliable and valid, the researcher must carefully plan the survey instrument. The type of questions used and the order in which they appear may vary depending on how the survey is ultimately administered (e.g., a mail survey versus a telephone survey).

Writing the Questions

The first task in designing a survey is to write the survey questions. Questions should be written in clear simple language to minimize confusion. Take a moment to think about surveys or exam questions you may have encountered on which because of poor wording, you misunderstood what was being asked of you. Consider the following questions:

How long have you lived in Harborside?
How many years have you lived in Harborside?

In both instances the researcher is interested in determining the number of years the individual has resided in the area. Notice, however, that the first question does not actually ask for this information. An individual might answer "Since I was 8 years old" (a meaningless response unless the survey also asks for current age) or "I moved to Harborside right after I got married." In either case the participant's interpretation of the question is different from the researcher's intent. It is therefore important to spend time thinking about the simplest wording that elicits the specific information of interest to the researcher.

Another consideration when writing survey questions is whether to use open-ended, closed-ended, partially open-ended, or rating-scale questions. Table 8.1 provides examples of these types of questions. **Open-ended questions** ask participants to formulate their own responses. On written surveys, researchers can control the length of the response to some extent by the amount of room they leave for the respondent to answer the question. A single line encourages a short answer, whereas several lines indicate that a longer response is expected. **Closed-ended questions** ask the respondent to choose from a limited number of alternatives. Participants may be asked to choose the one answer that best represents their beliefs or to check as many answers as apply to them. When writing closed-ended questions, researchers must make sure that the alternatives provided include all possible answers. For example, suppose a question asks how many hours of television the respondent watched the previous day and provides the following

open-ended questions: Questions for which participants formulate their own responses.

closed-ended questions: Questions for which participants choose from a limited number of alternatives.

TABLE **8.1**
Examples of types of survey questions

Open-ended

Has your college experience been satisfying thus far?

_____

_____

Closed-ended

Has your college experience been satisfying thus far?

Yes_____   No_____

Partially open-ended

With regard to your college experience, which of the following factors
do you find satisfying?

Academics_____

Relationships_____

Residence halls_____

Residence life_____

Social life_____

Food service_____

Other_____

Likert rating scale

I am very satisfied with my college experience.

1	2	3	4	5
Strongly Disagree	Disagree	Neutral	Agree	Strongly Agree

---

partially open-ended questions: Closed-ended questions with an open-ended "Other" option.

rating scale: A numerical scale on which survey respondents indicate the direction and strength of their response.

Likert rating scale: A type of numerical rating scale developed by Rensis Likert in 1932.

alternatives: 0–1 hour, 2–3 hours, 4–5 hours, or 6 or more hours. What if an individual watched 1.5 hours? Should the respondent select the first or second alternative? Each participant would have to decide which to choose. This inconsistent responding would compromise the data collected, that is, the data would be less reliable and valid. **Partially open-ended questions** are similar to closed-ended questions, but one alternative is "Other" with a blank space next to it. If none of the alternatives provided is appropriate, the respondent can mark "Other" and write a short explanation.

Finally, researchers may use some sort of **rating scale** that asks participants to choose a number representing the direction and strength of their response. One advantage of using a rating scale is that it is easy to convert the data to an ordinal or interval scale of measurement and proceed with statistical analysis. One popular version is the **Likert rating scale**, which is named after the researcher who developed the scale in 1932 and which presents a statement rather than a question. Respondents are asked to rate their level of agreement with the statement. The example in Table 8.1 uses a Likert scale with five alternatives. If you want to provide respondents with a neutral alternative, you should use a scale with an odd number of alternatives (the middle point on the scale reflecting the neutral response). However, if you want to force respondents to lean in one direction or another, you should use an even number of alternatives.

Each type of question has advantages and disadvantages. Open-ended questions allow for a greater variety of responses from participants but are difficult to analyze statistically because the data must be coded or reduced in some manner. Closed-ended questions are easy to analyze statistically, but they seriously limit the range of participant responses. Many researchers prefer to use a Likert-type scale because it is very easy to analyze statistically. Most psychologists view this scale as interval in nature, although there is some debate, and others see it as an ordinal scale. As we will see in later modules, a wide variety of statistical tests can be used with interval data.

When researchers write survey items, it is very important that their wording not mislead the respondent; several types of questions can do just that. A **loaded question** includes nonneutral or emotionally laden terms. Consider this question: "Do you believe radical extremists should be allowed to burn the American flag?" The phrase *radical extremists* loads the question emotionally, conveying the opinion of the person who wrote the question. A **leading question** sways the respondent to answer in a desired manner. Take for example "Most people agree that conserving energy is important—do you agree?" The phrase "Most people agree" encourages the respondent to agree also. Finally, a **double-barreled question** asks more than one thing. Double-barreled questions often include the word "and" or "or." For example, the following question is double-barreled: "Do you find using a cell phone to be convenient and time-saving?" This question should be divided into two separate items, one addressing the convenience of cell phones and one addressing whether they save time.

Lastly, when writing a survey, the researcher should also be concerned with participants who employ a particular response set or **response bias**, the tendency to consistently give the same answer to almost all the items on a survey. This bias is often referred to as "yea-saying" or "nay-saying." In other words, respondents might agree (or disagree) with one or two of the questions, but to make answering the survey easier on themselves, they simply respond yes (or no) to almost all of the questions. One way to minimize participants adopting a response bias is to word the questions so that a positive (or negative) response to every question would be unlikely. For instance, an instrument designed to assess depression might phrase some of the questions so that agreement means the respondent is depressed ("I frequently feel sad"), whereas other questions have the meaning reversed so that disagreement indicates depression ("I am happy almost all of the time"). Although some individuals might legitimately agree with both statements, a respondent who consistently agrees (or disagrees) with questions phrased in standard and reversed formats may raise suspicions of response bias.

loaded question: A question that includes nonneutral or emotionally laden terms.

leading question: A question that sways the respondent to answer in a desired manner.

double-barreled question: A question that asks more than one thing.

response bias: The tendency to consistently give the same answer to almost all of the items on a survey.

Arranging the Questions

Another consideration is how to arrange questions on the survey. Writers of surveys sometimes assume that the questions should be randomized, but randomization is not the best arrangement to use. Dillman (1978) and Dillman, Smyth, and Christian (2009) provide some tips for arranging questions on surveys. First, present related questions in subsets. This arrangement ensures that the general concept being investigated is made obvious to the respondents. It also helps respondents focus on one issue at a time. However, do not follow this suggestion if you do not want the general concept being investigated to be obvious to the respondents. Second, place questions that deal with sensitive topics such as drug use or sexual experiences at the end of the survey. Respondents are more likely to answer questions of a sensitive nature if they have already committed themselves to filling out the survey by answering questions of a less sensitive nature. Third, ask questions about events in the order the events occurred. If you are asking about past employment history, it will be easier for the respondent to answer questions on this topic if they start at the beginning and move on to the present time. Finally, to prevent participants from losing interest in the survey, place **demographic questions**—questions that ask for basic information such as age, gender, ethnicity, or income—at the end of the survey. Although this information is important for the researcher, many respondents view it as boring; so avoid beginning your survey with these items.

demographic questions: Questions that ask for basic information such as age, gender, ethnicity, or income.

ADMINISTERING THE SURVEY

In this section we examine three methods of surveying, mail surveys, telephone surveys, and personal interviews, along with the advantages and disadvantages of each.

Mail Surveys

mail survey: A written survey that is self-administered.

Mail surveys are written surveys that are self-administered. They can be sent through the traditional mail system or by e-mail. It is especially important that a mail survey be clearly written and self-explanatory because no one is available to answer questions regarding the survey once it has been mailed out.

Mail surveys have several advantages. Traditional mail surveys were generally considered to have less **sampling bias**, a tendency for one group to be overrepresented in a sample, than phone surveys or personal interviews. This trait was considered to be the case because almost everyone has a mailing address and thus can receive a survey, but not everyone has a phone or is available to spend time on a personal interview. However, one mechanism researchers used to employ to obtain mailing addresses was via phonebooks. This practice now presents a problem with respect to mail surveys because 25% of the U.S. has unlisted phone numbers and thus will not be included in phonebooks. In addition, many phonebooks no longer provide full mailing addresses. One way, however, to counter this problem is by using the U.S. Postal Service DSF, an electronic file containing all delivery point addresses

sampling bias: A tendency for one group to be overrepresented in a sample.

serviced by the U.S. Postal Service. It is estimated that the DSF provides up to 95% coverage rates (Dillman, Smyth, & Christian, 2009).

interviewer bias: The tendency for the person asking the questions to bias the participants' answers.

Mail surveys do eliminate the problem of **interviewer bias**, that is, the tendency for the person asking the questions (usually the researcher) to bias or influence the participants' answers. An interviewer might bias participants' answers by nodding and smiling more when they answer as expected or frowning when they give unexpected answers. Interviewer bias is another example of an expectancy effect (discussed in Module 7).

Mail surveys also have the advantage of allowing the researcher to collect data on more sensitive information. Participants who might be unwilling to discuss personal information with someone over the phone or face-to-face might be more willing to answer such questions on a written survey. A mail survey is also usually less expensive than a phone survey or personal interview in which the researcher has to pay workers to phone or canvas neighborhoods. Additionally, the answers provided on a mail survey are sometimes more complete because participants can take as much time as they need to think about the questions and to formulate their responses without feeling the pressure of someone waiting for an answer.

Mail surveys also have potential problems. One is that no one is available to answer questions. So if an item is unclear to the respondent, it may be left blank or misinterpreted; biasing the results. Another problem with mail surveys is a generally low return rate. Typically a single mailing produces a response rate of 25 to 30%, much lower than is usually achieved with phone surveys or personal interviews. However, follow-up mailings may produce a response rate as high as 50% (Bourque & Fielder, 2003; Erdos, 1983). A good response rate is important in order to maintain a representative sample. If only a small portion of the original sample returns the survey, the final sample may be biased. Online response rates tend to be as bad and sometimes worse than those for traditional mail survey, typically in the 10–20% range (Bourque & Fielder, 2003).

Shere Hite's (1987) work, based on surveys completed by 4,500 women, is a classic example of the problem of a biased survey sample. In her book *Women and Love* Hite claimed, based on her survey, that 70% of women married 5 or more years were having affairs, 84% of them were dissatisfied with their intimate relationships with men, and 95% felt emotionally harassed by the men they loved. These results were widely covered by news programs and magazines and were even used as a cover story in *Time* (Wallis, 1987). Although Hite's book became a best seller, largely because of the news coverage that her results received, researchers questioned her findings. It was discovered that the survey respondents came from one of two sources. Some surveys were mailed to women who were members of various women's organizations such as professional groups, political groups, and women's rights organizations. Other women were solicited through talk show interviews given by Hite in which she publicized an address women could write to in order to request a copy of the survey. Both of these methods of gathering participants for a study should set off warning bells for you. In the first situation women who are members of women's organizations are hardly representative of the average woman in the United States. The second situation represents a case of self-selection. Those who are interested in their relationships and who are possibly having problems in their relationships might be more likely to write for a copy of the survey and participate in it.

After beginning with a biased sample, Hite had a return rate of only 4.5%. That is, the 4,500 women who filled out the survey represented only 4.5% of those who received surveys. Hite sent out 100,000 surveys and got only 4,500 back. This percentage represents a very poor and unacceptable return rate. How does a low return rate further bias the results? Who is likely to take the time to return a long (127-question) survey on which the questions were of a personal nature and often pertained to problems in relationships with male partners? Most likely it would be women with strong opinions on the topic, possibly women who were having problems in their relationships and wanted to tell someone about them. Thus Hite's results were based on a specialized group of women, yet she attempted to generalize her results to all American women. The Hite survey has become a classic example of how a biased sample can lead to erroneous conclusions.

Telephone Surveys

telephone survey: A survey in which the questions are read to participants over the telephone.

Telephone surveys involve telephoning participants and reading questions to them. Years ago surveying via telephone was problematic because only wealthier individuals had telephones. We eventually reached a point where 95% of the population had a landline telephone, and at that time, this method typically provided a representative sample. In fact, researchers did not even have to worry about those with unlisted numbers (typically individuals who are better off financially) because of a technique known as random-digit dialing (RDD) in which random numbers are dialed—RDD obviously included unlisted numbers.

However, with technological advances came problems for surveying via telephone. First, increased telemarketing led many people to use answering machines, caller ID, or call blocking as a way to screen and/or avoid unwanted calls. Moreover, people became more willing to say "no" to unwanted callers. Individual homes also began to have more than one phone line, which is problematic when attempting to generate a representative sample of respondents. In addition, many homes also had fax lines installed which obviously would not be answered when RDD was used to call them. Finally, with the increase in use of cellular telephones, many people have begun to cancel their landline telephones in favor of cellular telephones. In 2003 almost 50% of the U.S. used cellular telephones and 3% substituted cellular telephones for landlines. However, by 2007 16% of the U.S. has substituted cellular telephones for landlines. This practice effectively means that a significant percentage of the U.S. population would be missed by RDD sampling. Consequently we have a situation in which the opposite of what was true 30 years ago is true now: mail surveys can now achieve a higher response rate than the typical telephone survey (Dillman, Smyth, & Christian, 2009).

Nevertheless, telephone surveys can help to alleviate one of the problems with mail surveys because respondents can ask that the questions be clarified. Moreover, the researchers can ask follow-up questions if needed in order to provide more reliable data.

On the other hand, telephone surveys do have other disadvantages than mail surveys. First, they are more time-consuming than a mail survey because the researchers must read each of the questions and record the responses. Second, they can be costly. The researchers must call the individuals themselves or pay others to do the calling. If the calls are long distance, then the cost is even greater. Third is the problem of interviewer bias. Finally, participants are more likely to give socially desirable responses over the phone than on a mail survey. A **socially desirable response** is a response that is given because participants believe it is deemed appropriate by society rather than because it truly reflects their own views or behaviors. For example, respondents may say that they attend church at least twice a month or read to their children several times a week because they believe these actions are what society expects of them, not because they actually perform them.

socially desirable response: A response that is given because a respondent believes it is deemed appropriate by society.

Personal Interviews

A **personal interview** in which the questions are asked face-to-face may be conducted anywhere—at the individual's home, on the street, or in a shopping mall. We discussed this interview method in Module 7 as a type of qualitative method, and thus you are familiar with the general concepts behind this methodology. We discuss it again in this module as a quantitative method.

personal interview: A survey in which the questions are asked face to face.

One advantage of personal interviews is that they allow the researcher to record not only verbal responses but also any facial or bodily expressions or movements such as grins, grimaces, or shrugs. These nonverbal responses may give the researcher greater insight into the respondents' true opinions and beliefs. A second advantage to personal interviews is that participants usually devote more time to answering the questions than they do in telephone surveys. As with telephone surveys, respondents can ask for question clarification.

Potential problems with personal interviews include many of those discussed in connection with telephone surveys: interviewer bias, socially desirable responses, and even greater time and expense than with telephone surveys. In addition, the lack of anonymity in a personal interview may affect the responses. Participants may not feel comfortable answering truthfully when someone is standing right there listening to them and writing down their responses. Finally, although personal interviews used to generate response rates that were fairly high (typically around 80%, Dillman, 1978; Erdos, 1983), they no longer do so. This decreased response rate is due to several reasons. One obstacle is that more people live in gated communities or locked apartment buildings to which interviewers cannot gain access. A second barrier is that people are very hesitant to open their door to a stranger for any reason (Dillman, Smyth, & Christian, 2009). Thus we have reached a point where using the personal interview as a type of quantitative survey technique is somewhat rare.

In summary the three traditional survey methods offer different advantages and disadvantages, and because of changes in society and technological advances, researchers have found it necessary to rethink traditional views on what might be the best way to conduct a survey. In fact, the recommended approach now it multimodal, with the preferred modes being mail, email/web-based, and telephone. This method is referred to as the total design method by Dillman, Smyth, and Christian (2009) and involves using multiple modes and multiple follow-up procedures. Using this method, respondents might be contacted via mail to let them know they can go online to complete a survey. They might be sent a postcard as a first reminder, an e-mail as a second reminder, and a telephone call as a third. If they do not answer the survey online after all of these reminders, they might be called and given the opportunity to respond to the survey via telephone and often times the telephone survey might be automated rather than given by a live person. Using this multimodal approach with varying follow-up procedures will often lead to response rates between 75–85% (Dillman, Smyth, & Christian, 2009; Greene, Speizer, & Wiitala, 2007). This multimodal approach also means that survey methodologists must now be competent in multiple modes of surveying rather than specializing in only one mode.

SAMPLING TECHNIQUES

Another concern for researchers using the survey method is who participates in the survey. For the results to be meaningful, the individuals who take the survey should be representative of the population under investigation. As discussed in Module 2, the population consists of all of the people about whom a study is meant to generalize and the sample represents the subset of people from the population who actually participate in the study. In almost all cases it is not feasible to survey the entire population. Instead, we select a subgroup or sample from the population and give the survey to them. If we are to draw reliable and valid conclusions concerning the population, it is imperative that the sample be "like" the population, that is, a **representative sample**. With a representative sample we can be fairly confident that the results we find based on the sample also hold for the population. In other words, we can generalize from the sample to the population. There are two ways to sample individuals from a population: probability and nonprobability sampling.

representative sample: A sample that is like the population.

Probability Sampling

When researchers use **probability sampling**, each member of the population has an equal likelihood of being selected to be part of the sample. We discuss three types of probability sampling: random sampling, stratified random sampling, and cluster sampling.

probability sampling: a sampling technique in which each member of the population has an equal likelihood of being selected to be part of the sample.

A random sample is achieved through **random selection** in which each member of the population is equally likely to be chosen as part of the sample. Let's say we start with a population of 300 students enrolled in introductory psychology classes at a university. How should we go about selecting a random sample of 30 students? We do not want simply to take one 30-person section of introductory psychology because depending on the instructor and the time of day of the class, there could be biases in who registered for this section. If it is an early morning class, it could represent students who like to get up early or those who registered for classes so late that nothing else was available. Thus these students would not be representative of all students in introductory psychology.

random selection: A method of generating a random sample in which each member of the population is equally likely to be chosen as part of the sample.

BIZARRE SEQUENCE OF COMPUTER-GENERATED RANDOM NUMBERS

Generating a random sample can be accomplished by using a table of random numbers such as that provided in Appendix B (Table B.1). When using a random numbers table, the researcher chooses a starting place arbitrarily. Once the starting point is determined, the researcher looks at the number—say, six—counts down six people in the population, and chooses the sixth person to be in the sample. The researcher continues in this manner by looking at the next number in the table, counting down through the population, and including the appropriately numbered person in the sample. For our sample we continue this process until we select a sample of 30 people. A random sample can be generated in other ways such as by computer or by pulling names randomly out of a hat. The point is that in random sampling each member of the population is equally likely to be chosen as part of the sample.

Sometimes a population is made up of members of different groups or categories. For instance, both men and women make up the 300 students enrolled in introductory psychology but maybe not in equal proportions. If we want to draw conclusions about the population of introductory psychology students based on our sample, then our sample must be representative of the strata within the population. So if the population consists of 70% women and 30% men, then we need to ensure that the sample is similarly proportioned.

One means of attaining such a sample is stratified random sampling. A **stratified random sample** allows us to take into account the different subgroups of people in the population and to guarantee that the sample accurately represents the population on specific characteristics. We begin by dividing the population into strata or subsamples. In our example the strata (men and women) are based on gender. We then randomly select 70% of our sample from the female stratum and 30% of our sample from the male stratum. In this manner we ensure that the characteristic of gender in the sample is representative of the population.

stratified random sampling: A sampling technique designed to ensure that subgroups or strata are fairly represented.

cluster sampling: A sampling technique in which clusters of participants that represent the population are used.

Often the population is too large for random sampling of any sort. In these cases it is common to use cluster sampling. As the name implies, **cluster sampling** involves using participants who are already part of a group, or "cluster." For example, if you were interested in surveying students at a large university where it might not be possible to use true random sampling, you might sample from classes that are required of all students at the university such as English composition. If the classes are required of all students, they should contain a good mix of students, and if you use several classes, the sample should represent the population.

Nonprobability Sampling

nonprobability sampling: A sampling technique in which the individual members of the population do not have an equal likelihood of being selected to be a member of the sample.

Nonprobability sampling is used when the individual members of the population do not have an equal likelihood of being selected to be a member of the sample. Nonprobability sampling is typically used because it tends to be less expensive and generating samples is easier. We discuss two types of nonprobability sampling: convenience sampling and quota sampling.

convenience sampling: A sampling technique in which participants are obtained wherever they can be found and typically wherever it is convenient for the researcher.

Convenience sampling involves getting participants wherever you can find them and normally wherever is convenient. This method is sometimes referred to as *haphazard sampling*. Say you wanted a sample of 100 college students. You could stand outside the library and ask people who pass by to participate, or you could ask students in some of your classes to participate. This approach might sound similar to cluster sampling, but there is a difference. With cluster sampling we try to identify clusters that are representative of the population. With convenience sampling, however, we simply use whoever is available as a participant in the study.

quota sampling: A sampling technique that involves ensuring that the sample is like the population on certain characteristics but uses convenience sampling to obtain the participants.

A second type of nonprobability sampling is quota sampling. Quota sampling is to nonprobability sampling what stratified random sampling is to probability sampling. In other words, **quota sampling** involves ensuring that the sample is like the population on certain characteristics. However, even though we try to ensure similarity with the population on certain characteristics, we do not sample from the population randomly. We simply take participants wherever we find them, through whatever means is convenient. Thus this method is slightly better than convenience sampling, but there is still not much effort devoted to creating a sample that is truly representative of the population nor one in which all members of the population have an equal chance of being selected for the sample.

IN REVIEW Survey Methods

Types of Survey Method

Mail survey	A written survey that is self-administered
Telephone survey	A survey conducted by telephone in which the questions are read to the respondents
Personal interview	A face-to-face interview of the respondent

(continued)

| IN REVIEW | Survey Methods |

Sampling Techniques

Random sampling	A sampling technique in which each member of the population is equally likely to be chosen as part of the sample
Stratified random sampling	A sampling technique intended to guarantee that the sample represents specific subgroups or strata
Cluster sampling	A sampling technique in which clusters of participants who represent the population are identified and included in the sample
Convenience sampling	A sampling technique in which participants are obtained wherever they can be found and normally wherever is convenient for the researcher
Quota sampling	A sampling technique that involves ensuring that the sample is like the population on certain characteristics but uses convenience sampling to obtain the participants

Question Types

Open-ended questions	Questions for which respondents formulate their own responses
Closed-ended questions	Questions on which respondents must choose from a limited number of alternatives
Partially open-ended questions	Closed-ended questions with an open-ended "Other" option
Rating scales (Likert scale)	Questions on which respondents must provide a rating on a numerical scale

Concerns

Sampling bias

Interviewer bias

Socially desirable responses

Return rate

Expense

CRITICAL THINKING CHECK 8.1

1. With which survey method(s) is interviewer bias of greatest concern?
2. Shere Hite had 4,500 surveys returned to her. This is a large sample, which is desirable, so what was the problem with using all of the surveys returned?
3. How is stratified random sampling different from random sampling?
4. What are the problems with the following survey questions?
   a. Do you agree that school systems should be given more money for computers and recreational activities?
   b. Do you favor eliminating the wasteful excesses in the city budget?
   c. Most people feel that teachers are underpaid. Do you agree?

SUMMARY

In this module we discussed various ways of conducting survey research. This discussion included a description of mail, telephone, and personal interviews as a means of conducting surveys. In addition, we covered advantages and disadvantages of these methods, including the problems of biased samples, poor return rates, interviewer biases, socially desirable responses, and expense. We also discussed various methods of sampling participants for surveys along with how best to write a survey and arrange the questions on the survey.

REVIEW OF KEY TERMS

open-ended questions
closed-ended questions
partially open-ended questions
rating scale
Likert rating scale
loaded question
leading question

double-barreled question
response bias
demographic questions
mail survey
sampling bias
interviewer bias

telephone survey
socially desirable response
personal interview
representative sample
probability sampling
random selection

stratified random sampling
cluster sampling
nonprobability sampling
convenience sampling
quota sampling

MODULE EXERCISES

(Answers to odd-numbered exercises appear in Appendix A.)

1. A student at your school wants to survey students regarding their credit card use. She decides to conduct the survey at the student center during lunch hour by surveying every fifth person leaving the center. What type of survey would you recommend she use? What type of sampling technique is being used? Can you identify a better way of sampling the student body?

2. Imagine that the following questions represent some of those from the survey described in Exercise 1. Can you identify any problems with these questions?

   a. Do you believe that capitalist bankers should charge such high interest rates on credit card balances?

   b. How much did you charge on your credit cards last month? $0–$400; $500–$900; $1,000–$1,400; $1,500–$1,900; $2,000 or more

   c. Most Americans believe that a credit card is a necessity. Do you agree?

CRITICAL THINKING CHECK ANSWERS

8.1

1. Interviewer bias is of greatest concern with personal interviews because the interviewer is physically present. It is also of some concern with telephone interviews. However, because the telephone interviewer is not actually with the respondent, it is not as great a concern as it is with personal interviews.

2. The problem with using all 4,500 returned surveys was that Hite sent out 100,000 surveys. Consequently 4,500 represented a very small return rate (4.5%). If the 100,000 individuals who were sent surveys were a representative sample, it is doubtful that the 4,500 who returned them were representative of the population.

3. Stratified random sampling involves randomly selecting individuals from strata, or groups. Using stratified random sampling ensures that subgroups, or strata, are fairly represented. This fair representation of subgroups does not always happen when simple random sampling is used.

4. a. This is a double-barreled question. It should be divided into two questions, one pertaining to money for computers and one pertaining to money for recreational activities.

   b. This is a loaded question. The phrase "wasteful excesses" loads the question emotionally.

   c. This is a leading question. Using the phrase "Most people feel" sways the respondent.

WEB RESOURCES

Check your knowledge of the content and key terms in this module with a practice quiz and interactive flashcards at **www.cengage.com/psychology/jackson**, or for step-by-step practice and information, check out the Statistics and Research Methods Workshops at **www.cengage.com/psychology/workshops**.

LAB RESOURCES

For hands-on experience using the research methods described in this module, see Chapter Two ("Survey Research") in *Research Methods* *Laboratory Manual for Psychology*, 2nd ed., by William Langston (Belmont, CA: Wadsworth, 2005).

CHAPTER FOUR SUMMARY AND REVIEW: DESCRIPTIVE METHODS

In this chapter we discussed various ways of conducting a descriptive study. The methods presented were the observational method (naturalistic versus laboratory), various qualitative methods (i.e., the case study method, the archival method, the interview method, and the field study method), and the survey method (mail, telephone, or personal interview). Several advantages and disadvantages of each method were discussed. For observational methods important issues include reactivity, experimenter expectancies, time, cost, control, and flexibility. The case study method is limited because it describes only one or a few people and is very subjective in nature, but it is often a good means of beginning a research project. The archival method is limited by the fact that the data already exist and were collected by someone other than the researcher. The interview method and the field study method can be limited by the quality of the interviewer/observer. The various survey methods may have problems of biased samples, poor return rates, interviewer biases, socially desirable responses, and expense. We discussed various methods of sampling participants for surveys along with how best to write a survey and arrange the questions on the survey.

Keep in mind that all of the methods presented here are descriptive in nature. They allow researchers to describe what has been observed in a group of people or other animals, but they do not allow us to make accurate predictions or to determine cause-and-effect relationships. In later sections we address methods that allow us to do more than simply describe—methods that allow us to make predictions and assess causality.

CHAPTER FOUR REVIEW EXERCISES

(Answers to exercises appear in Appendix A.)

Fill-in Self-Test

Answer the following questions. If you have trouble answering any of the questions, restudy the relevant material before going on to the multiple-choice self-test.

1. Observational studies in which the researcher does not participate in the situation with the research participants utilize _____ observation.
2. The extent to which an experimental situation can be generalized to natural settings and behaviors is known as _____.
3. Observational studies in which the participants are unaware that the researcher is observing their behavior utilize _____ observation.
4. _____ are full narrative descriptions of a participant's behavior.
5. A _____ item is used on a checklist to indicate attributes that will not change.
6. _____ involves a tendency for one group to be overrepresented in a study.
7. When participants give a response that they believe is deemed appropriate by society, they are giving a _____.
8. Using _____ involves generating a random sample in which each member of the population is equally likely to be chosen as part of the sample.

9. _____ is a sampling technique designed to ensure that subgroups are fairly represented.
10. Questions for which participants choose from a limited number of alternatives are known as _____.
11. A numerical scale on which survey respondents indicate the direction and strength of their responses is a _____.
12. A question that sways a respondent to answer in a desired manner is a _____.

Multiple-Choice Self-Test

Select the single best answer for each of the following questions. If you have trouble answering any of the questions, restudy the relevant material.

1. _____ observation has greater _____ validity than _____ observation.
   a. Laboratory; construct; naturalistic
   b. Laboratory; ecological; naturalistic
   c. Naturalistic; ecological; laboratory
   d. Naturalistic; content; laboratory
2. Which of the following is true?
   a. Naturalistic observation involves observing how humans or other animals behave in their natural setting.
   b. Naturalistic observation decreases the ecological validity of a study.
   c. Laboratory observation increases the ecological validity of a study.
   d. All of the above.
3. _____ is (are) a greater concern when using _____ observation because the observations are made in an _____ manner.
   a. Reactivity; undisguised; obtrusive
   b. Expectancy effects; disguised; unobtrusive
   c. Reactivity; disguised; unobtrusive
   d. Expectancy effects; disguised; obtrusive
4. Naturalistic observation is to _____ as laboratory observation is to _____.

   a. more control; more flexibility
   b. more control; less control
   c. more flexibility; more control
   d. more flexibility; less control
5. Checklists are to _____ as narrative records are to _____.
   a. more subjective; less subjective
   b. less subjective; more subjective
   c. less objective; more objective
   d. both b and c
6. A tally sheet for recording attributes that do not change contains _____ items.
   a. static
   b. action
   c. narrative
   d. nonnarrative
7. Personal interview surveys have the concern of _____ but have the advantage of _____.
   a. low return rate; eliminating interviewer bias
   b. interviewer bias; question clarification
   c. sampling bias; eliminating interviewer bias
   d. both b and c
8. Rich is conducting a survey of student opinion of the dining hall at his university. Rich decides to conduct his survey by using every 10th name on the registrar's alphabetical list of all students at his school. The type of sampling technique that Rich is using is _____.
   a. representative cluster sampling
   b. cluster sampling
   c. stratified random sampling
   d. random sampling
9. Imagine that you wanted to assess student opinion of the dining hall by surveying a subgroup of 100 students at your school. In this situation the subgroup of students represents the _____ and all of the students at your school represent the _____.
   a. sample; random sample
   b. population; sample
   c. sample; population
   d. cluster sample; sample

10. A question including nonneutral or emotionally laden terms is a _____ question.
    a. loaded
    b. leading
    c. double-barreled
    d. open-ended

11. Open-ended question is to _____ question as a closed-ended question is to _____ question.
    a. multiple choice; short answer
    b. short answer; multiple choice
    c. short answer; essay
    d. multiple choice; essay

12. Consider the following survey question: "Most Americans consider a computer to be a necessity. Do you agree?" This is an example of a _____ question.
    a. leading
    b. loaded
    c. rating scale
    d. double-barreled

KEY TERMS

Here are the terms from the glossary presented in Modules 7–8. Go through the list and see if you can remember the definition of each.

Action item
Action research
Archival method
Checklist
Closed-ended questions
Cluster sampling
Convenience sampling
Demographic questions
Disguised observation
Double-barreled question
Ecological validity

Expectancy effects
Field studies
Focus group interview
Interview
Interviewer bias
Leading question
Likert rating scale
Loaded question
Mail survey
Narrative records
Nonparticipant observation

Nonprobability sampling
Open-ended questions
Partially open-ended questions
Participant observation
Personal interview
Probability sampling
Qualitative research
Quota sampling
Random selection
Rating scale

Representative sample
Response bias
Sampling bias
Socially desirable response
Static item
Stratified random sampling
Telephone survey
Undisguised observation

Predictive (Relational) Methods

10 | QUASI-EXPERIMENTAL DESIGNS

Nonmanipulated Independent Variables

An Example: Snow and Cholera

Types of Quasi-Experimental Designs
Single-Group Posttest-Only Design
Single-Group Pretest/Posttest Design
Single-Group Time-Series Design
Nonequivalent Control Group Posttest-Only Design
Nonequivalent Control Group Pretest/Posttest Design
Multiple-Group Time-Series Design

Internal Validity and Confounds in Quasi-Experimental Designs

SUMMARY
REVIEW OF KEY TERMS
MODULE EXERCISES
CRITICAL THINKING CHECK ANSWERS
WEB RESOURCES
LAB RESOURCES

11 | CONDUCTING SINGLE-CASE RESEARCH

Types of Single-Case Designs
Reversal Designs
   ABA Reversal Designs
   ABAB Reversal Designs
Multiple-Baseline Designs
   Multiple Baselines across Participants
   Multiple Baselines across Behaviors
   Multiple Baselines across Situations

SUMMARY
REVIEW OF KEY TERMS
MODULE EXERCISES
CRITICAL THINKING CHECK ANSWERS
WEB RESOURCES
LAB RESOURCES

CHAPTER FIVE SUMMARY AND REVIEW: PREDICTIVE (RELATIONAL) METHODS

n this chapter we discuss correlational research methods, quasi-experimental methods, and single-case and small-*n* designs. As a research method correlational designs allow researchers to describe the relationship between two measured variables. We begin with a discussion of how to conduct correlational research, the magnitude and the direction of correlations, and graphical representations of correlations. We then turn to special considerations when interpreting correlations and how to use correlations for predictive purposes.

We next explain various quasi-experimental methods. Quasi-experimental research can be thought of as an intermediate point between correlational and true experimental research. As such, it allows us to draw slightly stronger conclusions than we might with correlational research. We can say there is more than a simple relationship between variables, but we cannot draw as strong a conclusion as we can with true experimental research. We cannot say that we have observed a causal relationship between variables. Quasi-experimental research frequently fits into the category of field research; that is, it often involves conducting research in naturalistic settings.

Our discussion of quasi-experimental research will begin with a brief discussion of what it is and how it differs from correlational and experimental research. We then describe various types of quasi-experimental research designs and discuss how the method limits internal validity in a study. Finally, we move on to another type of field research, single-case research. As with quasi-experimental designs we discuss the value of single-case research and describe various types of single-case designs.

Conducting Correlational Research

LEARNING OBJECTIVES

- Describe the difference between strong, moderate, and weak correlation coefficients.

- Draw and interpret scatterplots.

- Explain negative, positive, curvilinear, and no relationship between variables.

- Explain how assuming causality and directionality, the third-variable problem, restrictive ranges, and curvilinear relationships can be problematic when interpreting correlation coefficients.

- Explain how correlations allow us to make predictions.

When conducting correlational studies, researchers determine whether two naturally occurring variables (for example, height and weight or smoking and cancer) are related to each other. Such studies assess whether the variables are "co-related" in some way: Do tall people tend to weigh more than people of average height, or do those who smoke tend to have a higher-than-normal incidence of cancer? As we saw in Module 2, the correlational method is a type of nonexperimental method that describes the relationship between two measured variables. In addition to describing a relationship, correlations allow us to make predictions from one variable to another. If two variables are correlated, we can predict from one variable to the other with a certain degree of accuracy. Thus knowing that height and weight are correlated allows us to estimate, within a certain range, an individual's weight based on knowing the person's height.

Correlational studies are conducted for a variety of reasons. Sometimes it is impractical or ethically impossible to do an experimental study. For instance, it would be ethically impossible to manipulate smoking and assess whether it causes cancer in humans. How would you as a participant in an experiment like to be randomly assigned to the smoking condition and be told that you have to smoke a pack of cigarettes a day? Obviously this approach is not a viable experiment; however, one means of assessing the relationship between smoking and cancer is through correlational studies. In this type of study we can examine people who have already chosen to smoke and assess the degree of relationship between smoking and cancer.

Sometimes researchers choose to conduct correlational research because they are interested in measuring many variables and assessing the relationships between them. For example, they might measure various aspects of personality and assess the relationship between dimensions of personality.

―――――――

MAGNITUDE, SCATTERPLOTS, AND TYPES OF RELATIONSHIPS

magnitude: An indication of the strength of the relationship between two variables.

Correlations vary in their **magnitude**, the strength of the relationship. Sometimes there is no relationship between variables, or the relationship may be weak; other relationships are moderate or strong. Correlations can also be represented graphically in a scatterplot or scattergram. In addition, relationships are of different types: positive, negative, none, or curvilinear.

Magnitude

The magnitude, or strength, of a relationship is determined by the correlation coefficient describing the relationship. As we saw in Module 6, a correlation coefficient is a measure of the degree of relationship between two variables; it can vary between −1.00 and +1.00. The stronger the relationship between the variables, the closer the coefficient is to either −1.00 or +1.00. The weaker the relationship between the variables, the closer the coefficient is to 0. You may recall from Module 6 that we typically discuss correlation coefficients as assessing a strong, moderate, or weak relationship, or no relationship at all. Table 9.1 provides general guidelines for assessing the magnitude of a relationship, but these ranges do not necessarily hold for all variables and all relationships.

A correlation coefficient of either −1.00 or +1.00 indicates a perfect correlation—the strongest relationship possible. For example, if height and weight were perfectly correlated (+1.00) in a group of 20 people, this coefficient would mean that the person with the highest weight was also the tallest person, the person with the second-highest weight was the second-tallest person, and so on down the line. In addition, in a perfect relationship each individual's score on one variable goes perfectly with his or her score on the other variable. For instance, this might mean that for every increase (decrease) in height of 1 inch, there is a corresponding increase (decrease) in weight of 10 pounds. If height and weight had a perfect negative correlation (−1.00), this coefficient would mean that the person with the highest weight was the shortest, the person with the second-highest weight was the second shortest, and so on, and that height and weight increased (decreased) by a set amount for each individual. It is very unlikely that you will ever observe a perfect correlation between two variables, but you may observe some very strong relationships between variables (±.70−.99). To sum up, whereas a correlation coefficient of ±1.00 represents a perfect relationship, a coefficient of 0 indicates no relationship between the variables.

Scatterplots

scatterplot: A figure that graphically represents the relationship between two variables.

A **scatterplot,** or scattergram, is a figure showing the relationship between two variables that graphically represents a correlation coefficient. Figure 9.1 presents a scatterplot of the height and weight relationship for 20 adults.

TABLE **9.1**

Estimates for Weak, Moderate, and Strong Correlation Coefficients

Correlation Coefficient	Strength of Relationship
±.70−1.00	Strong
±.30−.69	Moderate
±.00−.29	None (.00) to weak

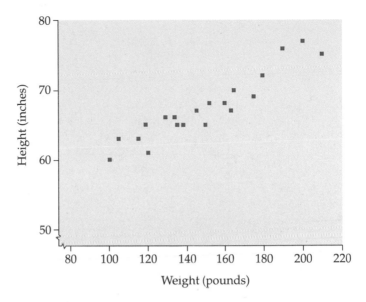

FIGURE **9.1** Scatterplot for height and weight

In a scatterplot two measurements are represented for each participant by the placement of a marker. In Figure 9.1 the horizontal x-axis shows the participant's weight, and the vertical y-axis shows height. The two variables could be reversed on the axes, and it would make no difference in the scatterplot. This scatterplot shows an upward trend, and the points cluster in a linear fashion. The stronger the correlation is, the more tightly the data points cluster around an imaginary line through their center. When there is a perfect correlation (±1.00), the data points all fall on a straight line. In general, a scatterplot may show four basic patterns: a positive relationship, a negative relationship, no relationship, or a curvilinear relationship.

Positive Relationships

The relationship represented in Figure 9.2a shows a positive correlation, one in which there is a direct relationship between the two variables: An increase in one variable is related to an increase in the other, and a decrease in one is related to a decrease in the other. Notice that this scatterplot is similar to the one in Figure 9.1. The majority of the data points fall along an upward angle (from the lower left corner to the upper right corner). In this example a person who scored low on one variable also scored low on the other, an individual with a mediocre score on one variable had a mediocre score on the other, and anyone who scored high on one variable also scored high on the other. In other words, an increase (decrease) in one variable is accompanied by an increase (decrease) in the other; as variable x increases (or decreases), variable y does the same. If the data in Figure 9.2a represented height and weight measurements, we could say that those who are taller tend to weigh more, whereas

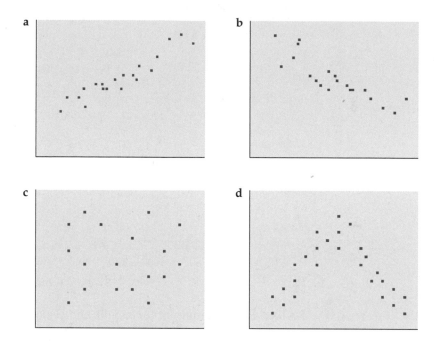

FIGURE **9.2** Possible types of Correlational relationships: (a) positive; (b) negative; (c) none; (d) curvilinear

those who are shorter tend to weigh less. Notice also that the relationship is linear: We could draw a straight line representing the relationship between the variables, and the data points would all fall fairly close to that line.

Negative Relationships

Figure 9.2b represents a negative relationship between two variables. Notice that in this scatterplot the data points extend from the upper left to the lower right. This negative correlation indicates that an increase in one variable is accompanied by a *decrease* in the other variable. This correlation represents an inverse relationship: The more of variable *x* that we have, the less we have of variable *y*. Assume that this scatterplot represents the relationship between age and eyesight. As age increases, the ability to see clearly tends to decrease—a negative relationship.

No Relationship

As shown in Figure 9.2c, it is also possible to observe no meaningful relationship between two variables. In this scatterplot the data points are scattered randomly. As you would expect, the correlation coefficient for these data is very close to 0 (−.09).

Curvilinear Relationships

A correlation coefficient of 0 indicates no meaningful relationship between two variables. However, it is also possible for a correlation coefficient of 0 to indicate a curvilinear relationship, as illustrated in Figure 9.2d. Imagine that this graph represents the relationship between psychological arousal (the *x*-axis) and performance (the *y*-axis). Individuals perform better when they are moderately aroused than when arousal is either very low or very high. The correlation coefficient for these data is also very close to 0 (−.05). Think about why this strong curvilinear relationship leads to a correlation coefficient close to 0. The strong positive relationship depicted in the left half of the graph essentially cancels out the strong negative relationship in the right half of the graph. Although the correlation coefficient is very low, we would not conclude that there is no relationship between the two variables. As the figure shows, the variables are very strongly related to each other in a curvilinear manner, with the points being tightly clustered in an inverted U shape.

Correlation coefficients only tell us about linear relationships. Thus even though there is a strong relationship between the two variables in Figure 9.2d, the correlation coefficient does not indicate this relationship because it is curvilinear. For this reason it is important to examine a scatterplot of the data in addition to calculating a correlation coefficient. Alternative statistics (beyond the scope of this text) can be used to assess the degree of curvilinear relationship between two variables.

IN REVIEW Relationships Between Variables

	Type of Relationships			
	Positive	Negative	None	Curvilinear
Description of Relationship	Variables increase and decrease together	As one variable increases, the other decreases in an inverse relationship	Variables are unrelated and do not move together in any way	Variables increase together up to a point and then as one continues to increase, the other decreases
Description of scatterplot	Data points are clustered in a linear pattern extending from lower left to upper right	Data points are clustered in a linear pattern extending from upper left to lower right	There is no pattern to the data points they are scattered all over the graph	Data points are clustered in a curved linear pattern forming a U shape or an inverted U shape
Example of variables related in this manner	Smoking and cancer	Mountain elevation and temperature	Intelligence and weight	Memory and age

CRITICAL THINKING CHECK 9.1

1. Which of the following correlation coefficients represents the weakest relationship between two variables?
−.59 +.10 −1.00 +.76
2. Explain why a correlation coefficient of 0 or close to 0 may not mean that there is no relationship between the variables.
3. Draw a scatterplot representing a strong negative correlation between depression and self-esteem. Make sure you label the axes correctly.

MISINTERPRETING CORRELATIONS

Correlational data are frequently misinterpreted, especially when presented by newspaper reporters, talk show hosts, and television newscasters. Here we discuss some of the most common problems in interpreting correlations. Remember, a correlation simply indicates that there is a weak, moderate, or strong relationship (either positive or negative) or no relationship between two variables.

The Assumptions of Causality and Directionality

The most common error made when interpreting correlations is assuming that the relationship observed is causal in nature: that a change in variable A *causes* a change in variable B. Correlations simply identify relationships; they do not indicate causality. For example, a commercial recently appeared on television sponsored by an organization promoting literacy. The statement was made at the beginning of the commercial that a strong positive correlation had been observed between illiteracy and drug use in high school students (those high on the illiteracy variable also tended to be high on the drug use variable). The commercial concluded with a statement along the lines of "Let's stop drug use in high school students by making sure they can all read." Can you see the flaw in this conclusion? The commercial did not air for very long, probably because someone pointed out the error.

This commercial made the twin errors of assuming causality and directionality. **Causality** refers to the assumption that the correlation between two variables indicates a causal relationship, and **directionality** refers to the inference made with respect to the direction of a causal relationship between two variables. The commercial assumed that illiteracy was causing drug use; it claimed that if illiteracy were lowered, then drug use would also be lowered. As we know, a correlation between two variables indicates only that they are related, that is, they vary together. Although it is possible that one variable causes changes in the other, we cannot draw this conclusion from correlational data.

Research on smoking and cancer illustrates this limitation of correlational data. For research with humans we have only correlational data indicating a positive correlation between smoking and cancer. Because the data are correlational, we cannot conclude that there is a causal relationship. In this situation it is probable that the relationship is causal. However, based solely on correlational data, we cannot draw that conclusion, nor can we assume the direction of the relationship. Thus the tobacco industry could argue that, yes, there is a correlation between smoking and cancer, but maybe cancer causes smoking, or maybe individuals predisposed to cancer are more attracted to smoking cigarettes. Even though experimental data based on research with laboratory animals indicate that smoking causes cancer, the tobacco industry questions whether the research is applicable to humans and for years continued to state that no research had produced evidence of a causal link between smoking and cancer in humans.

A classic example of the assumption of causality and directionality with correlational data occurred when researchers observed a strong negative correlation between eye movement patterns and reading ability in children. Poor

causality: The assumption that a correlation indicates a causal relationship between two variables.

directionality: The inference made with respect to the direction of a causal relationship between two variables.

readers tended to make more erratic eye movements than normal, more movements from right to left, and more stops per line of text. Based on this correlation, some researchers assumed causality and directionality: They presumed that poor oculomotor skills caused poor reading and proposed programs for "eye movement training." Many elementary school students who were poor readers spent time in such training, supposedly developing oculomotor skills in the hope that these skills would improve their reading ability. Experimental research later provided evidence that the relationship between eye movement patterns and reading ability is indeed causal, but that the direction of the relationship is the reverse: poor reading causes more erratic eye movements! Children who are having trouble reading need to go back over the information more and stop and think about it more. When children improve their reading skills (i.e., improve recognition and comprehension), their eye movements become smoother (Olson & Forsberg, 1993). Because of the errors of assuming causality and directionality, many children never received the appropriate training to improve their reading ability.

The Third-Variable Problem

When we interpret a correlation, it is important to remember that although the correlation between the variables may be very strong, the relationship may be the result of a third variable that influences both of the measured variables. The **third-variable problem** results when a correlation between two variables is dependent on another (third) variable.

third-variable problem: The problem of a correlation between two variables being dependent on another (third) variable.

A good example of the third-variable problem is a well-cited study conducted by social scientists and physicians in Taiwan (Li, 1975). The researchers attempted to identify the variables that best predicted the use of birth control; a question of interest to the researchers because of overpopulation problems in Taiwan. They collected data on various behavioral and environmental variables and found that the variable most strongly correlated with contraceptive use was the number of electrical appliances (yes, electrical appliances—stereos, toasters, televisions, and so on) in the home. If we take this correlation at face value, it means that individuals who use many electrical appliances tend also to use contraceptives, whereas those with fewer electrical appliances tend to use contraceptives less.

It should be obvious that this relationship is not causal (buying electrical appliances does not cause individuals to use birth control, nor does using birth control cause individuals to buy electrical appliances). Thus we probably do not have to worry about people assuming either causality or directionality when interpreting this correlation. The problem is a third variable. In other words, the relationship between electrical appliances and contraceptive use is not really a meaningful relationship; other variables are tying them together. Can you think of other ways in which individuals who use contraceptives and who have a large number of appliances might be similar? Education is a possible third variable. Individuals with a higher education level tend to be better informed about contraceptives and also tend to have a higher socioeconomic status (they get better paying jobs). Their higher socioeconomic status allows them to buy more "things," including electrical appliances.

partial correlation: A correlational technique that involves measuring three variables and then statistically removing the effect of the third variable from the correlation of the remaining two.

It is possible statistically to determine the effects of a third variable by using a correlational procedure known as **partial correlation**, which involves measuring all three variables and then statistically removing the effect of the third variable from the correlation of the remaining two. If the third variable (in this case, education) is responsible for the relationship between electrical appliances and contraceptive use, then the correlation should disappear when the effect of education is removed, or partialed out.

Restrictive Range

restrictive range: A variable that is truncated and has limited variability.

The idea behind measuring a correlation is that we assess the degree of relationship between two variables. Variables by definition must vary. When a variable is truncated, we say that it has a **restrictive range**, that is, the variable does not vary enough. Look at Figure 9.3a, which represents a scatterplot of SAT scores and college GPAs for a group of students. SAT scores and GPAs are positively correlated. Neither of these variables is restricted in range (for this group of students, SAT scores vary from 400 to 1600 and GPAs vary from 1.5 to 4.0), so we have the opportunity to observe a relationship between the variables. Now look at Figure 9.3b, which represents the correlation between the same two variables, except the range on the SAT variable is restricted to those who scored between 1000 and 1150. The SAT variable has been restricted, or truncated, and does not "vary" very much. As a result the opportunity to observe a correlation has been diminished. Even if there were a strong relationship between these variables, we could not observe it because of the restricted range of one of the variables. Thus when interpreting and using correlations, beware of variables with restricted ranges.

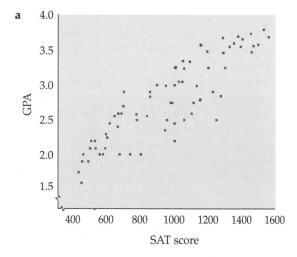
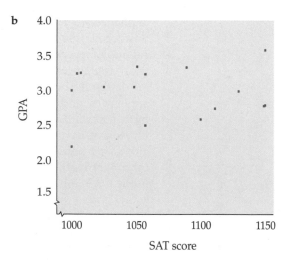

FIGURE **9.3** Restrictive range and correlation

Curvilinear Relationships

Curvilinear relationships and the caution in interpreting them were discussed earlier in the module. Because correlations are a measure of linear relationships, when a relationship is curvilinear, a correlation coefficient does not adequately indicate the degree of relationship between the variables. If necessary, look back over the previous section on curvilinear relationships in order to refresh your memory concerning them.

IN REVIEW Misinterpreting Correlations

	\multicolumn{4}{c}{Types of Misinterpretations}			
	Causality and Directionality	Third Variable	Restrictive Range	Curvilinear Relationship
Description of Misinterpretation	We assume that the correlation is causal and that one variable causes changes in the other.	Other variables are responsible for the observed correlation.	One or more of the variables is truncated or restricted, and the opportunity to observe a relationship is minimized.	The curved nature of the relationship decreases the observed correlation coefficient.
Examples	We assume that smoking causes cancer or that illiteracy causes drug abuse because a correlation has been observed.	We find a strong positive relationship between birth control and the number of electrical appliances.	If SAT scores are restricted (limited in range), the correlation between SAT and GPA appears to decrease.	As arousal increases, performance increases up to a point; as arousal continues to increase, performance decreases.

CRITICAL THINKING CHECK 9.2

1. "I have recently observed a strong negative correlation between depression and self-esteem." Explain what this statement means. Make sure you avoid the misinterpretations described in the text.
2. General State University officials recently investigated the relationship between SAT scores and GPAs (at graduation) for its senior class. They were surprised to find a weak correlation between these two variables. They know they have a grade inflation problem (the whole senior class graduated with GPAs of 3.0 or higher), but they are unsure how this might help account for the low correlation observed. Can you explain?

Prediction and Correlation

Correlation coefficients not only describe the relationship between variables, but they also allow us to make predictions from one variable to another. Correlations between variables indicate that when one variable is present at a certain level, the other also tends to be present at a certain level. Notice the wording. The statement is qualified by the phrase "tends to." We are not saying that a prediction is guaranteed or that the relationship is causal but simply that the variables seem to occur together at specific levels. Think about some of the examples used in this module. Height and weight are positively correlated. One is not causing the other; nor can we predict an individual's weight exactly based on height (or vice versa). But because the two variables are correlated, we can predict with a certain degree of accuracy what an individual's approximate weight might be if we know the person's height.

Let's take another example. We have noted a correlation between SAT scores and college freshman GPAs. Think about the purpose of the SAT. College admissions committees use the test as part of the admissions procedure because there is a positive correlation between SAT scores and college freshman GPAs. Individuals who score high on the SAT tend to have higher college freshman GPAs; those who score lower on the SAT tend to have lower college freshman GPAs. Therefore knowing students' SAT scores can help predict, with a certain degree of accuracy, their freshman GPAs and their potential for success in college. At this point some of you are probably saying, "But that isn't true for me. I scored poorly (or very well) on the SAT, and my GPA is great (or not so good)." Statistics tell us only the trend for most people in the population or sample. There are always outliers—the few individuals who do not fit the trend. Most people, however, are going to fit the pattern.

Think about another example. There is a strong positive correlation between smoking and cancer, but you may know someone who has smoked for 30 or 40 years and does not have cancer or any other health problems. Does this one individual negate the fact that there is a strong relationship between smoking and cancer? No. To claim that it does would be a classic **person-who argument**, that is, arguing that a well established statistical trend is invalid because we know a "person who" went against the trend (Stanovich, 2007). A counterexample does not change the existence of a strong statistical relationship between the variables nor that you are increasing your chance of getting cancer if you smoke. Because of the correlation between the variables, we can predict (with a fairly high degree of accuracy) who might get cancer based on knowing a person's smoking history.

person-who argument: Arguing that a well-established statistical trend is invalid because we know a "person who" went against the trend.

SUMMARY

After reading this module, you should have an understanding of the correlational research method, which allows researchers to observe relationships between variables, and of correlation coefficients, the statistics that assess the relationship. Correlations vary in type (positive, negative, none, or curvilinear) and magnitude (weak, moderate, or strong). The pictorial representation of a correlation is a scatterplot. A scatterplot allows us to see the relationship, facilitating its interpretation.

Several errors are commonly made when interpreting correlations, including assuming causality and directionality, overlooking a third variable, having a restrictive range on one or both variables, and assessing a curvilinear relationship. Knowing that two variables are correlated allows researchers to make predictions from one variable to the other.

REVIEW OF KEY TERMS

magnitude	causality	third-variable problem	restrictive range
scatterplot	directionality	partial correlation	person-who argument

MODULE EXERCISES

(Answers to odd-numbered exercises appear in Appendix A.)

1. A health club recently conducted a study of its members and found a positive relationship between exercise and health. It was claimed that the correlation coefficient between the variables of exercise and health was +1.25. What is wrong with this statement? In addition, it was stated that this finding proved that an increase in exercise increases health. What is wrong with this statement?

2. Draw a scatterplot indicating a strong negative relationship between the variables of income and mental illness. Be sure to label the axes correctly.

3. We have mentioned several times that there is a fairly strong positive correlation between SAT scores and freshman GPAs. The admissions process for graduate school is based on a similar test, the GRE, which like the SAT has a total point range of 400 to 1,600. Let's assume that graduate schools do not accept anyone who scores below 1,000 and that a GPA below 3.00 represents failing work in graduate school. What would we expect the correlation between GRE scores and graduate school GPAs to be like in comparison to the correlation between SAT scores and college GPAs? Why would we expect this?

CRITICAL THINKING CHECK ANSWERS

9.1

1. +.10
2. A correlation coefficient of 0 or close to 0 may indicate no relationship or a weak relationship. However, if the relationship is curvilinear, the correlation coefficient could also be 0 or close to this. In this latter case there is a relationship between the two variables, but because the relationship is curvilinear, the correlation coefficient does not truly represent the strength of the relationship.

3.

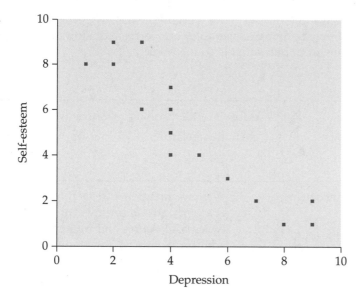

9.2

1. A strong negative correlation between depression and self-esteem means that as individuals become more depressed, their self-esteem tends to decrease, whereas when individuals become less depressed, their self-esteem tends to increase. It does not mean that one variable causes changes in the other but simply that the variables tend to move together in a certain manner.

2. General State University officials observed such a weak correlation between GPAs and SAT scores because of a restrictive range on the GPA variable. Because of grade inflation, the whole senior class graduated with a GPA of 3.0 or higher. This restriction on one of the variables lessens the opportunity to observe a correlation.

WEB RESOURCES

Check your knowledge of the content and key terms in this module with a practice quiz and interactive flashcards at **www.cengage.com/psychology/jackson**, or for step-by-step practice and information, check out the Statistics and Research Methods Workshops at **www.cengage.com/psychology/workshops**.

LAB RESOURCES

For hands-on experience using the research methods described in this module, see Chapter 3 ("Correlation Research") in *Research Methods* *Laboratory Manual for Psychology*, 2nd ed., by William Langston (Belmont, CA: Wadsworth, 2005).

Quasi-Experimental Designs

LEARNING OBJECTIVES

- Describe how quasi-experimental designs differ from correlational and experimental designs.

- Explain what a subject (participant) variable is.

- Differentiate single group designs and nonequivalent control group designs.

- Describe advantages and disadvantages of posttest-only designs and pretest/posttest designs.

- Explain a time-series design.

The term "quasi" (meaning "having some but not all of the features") preceding the term "experimental" indicates that we are dealing with a design that resembles an experiment but is not exactly an experiment. How does a quasi-experimental design differ from an experimental design? Sometimes the difference is the lack of a control group or a comparison group, that is, only one group is given a treatment and then assessed. At other times the independent variable is not a true manipulated independent variable; instead, it is a participant variable or a nonmanipulated independent variable. And finally, some designs may be considered quasi-experimental because participants were not randomly assigned to conditions, that is, they were already part of a group and the researcher attempted to manipulate a variable between preexisting groups.

NONMANIPULATED INDEPENDENT VARIABLES

In some quasi-experiments the researcher is interested in comparing groups of individuals (as is done in an experiment), but the groups occur naturally. In other words, participants are not assigned randomly to the groups. Notice the difference between this type of quasi-experimental design and correlational research. We are not simply looking for relationships between variables such as between smoking and cancer. In quasi-experimental research we are testing a hypothesis. An example is that individuals who have smoked for 20 years have a higher incidence of respiratory illness than nonsmokers. We would randomly select a group of individuals who had smoked for 20 years and a group of individuals who had never smoked to serve as a control. Thus rather than simply looking for a relationship between smoking and cancer or illness, we are comparing two groups to test a hypothesis.

nonmanipulated independent variable: The independent variable in a quasi-experimental design in which participants are not randomly assigned to conditions but rather come to the study as members of each condition.

The independent variable is referred to as a **nonmanipulated independent variable** because participants are not randomly assigned to the two groups. We are not truly manipulating smoking; participants come to the study as either smokers or nonsmokers. However, we do make comparisons between the groups. Consequently the study has the intent and "flavor" of an experiment without being a true experiment. Nonmanipulated independent variables are also known as *subject (participant) variables*. A subject variable, you may recall from Module 2, is a characteristic of the participant that cannot be changed such as ethnicity, gender, age, or political affiliation. If a study is designed to assess differences in individuals on some participant variable, by default it is a quasi-experiment and not a true experiment because it uses a nonmanipulated independent variable, that is, participants are not randomly assigned to conditions.

AN EXAMPLE: SNOW AND CHOLERA

In the 1850s in London, England, there were frequent outbreaks of cholera, an infection of the small intestine. The cause at the time was unknown, but the common theory was that cholera was somehow spread as people came in contact with cholera victims and shared or breathed the same air. This hypothesis was known as the effluvia theory. John Snow in his quest for the cause of cholera had an alternative hypothesis (Goldstein & Goldstein, 1978). Snow thought that people contracted cholera by drinking contaminated water. He based his hypothesis on the observation that of the several different water companies serving London, some provided water from upstream (it had not yet passed through the city and possibly become contaminated), whereas others used water from downstream (after it had passed through the city and possibly become contaminated).

To test this hypothesis, Snow used a quasi experimental design. Obviously it was not feasible to use a true experimental design because it would have been impossible to randomly assign different houses to contract with a specific water company. Snow therefore had to look at houses that already received their water from a downstream company versus houses that received water from upstream. You should begin to see some of the problems inherent in quasi-experimental research. If people chose their water company, then there was most likely a reason for the choice. In most cases the reason was socioeconomic: The wealthy neighborhoods used upstream (more costly) companies, whereas the poor neighborhoods used downstream (less costly) companies. This socioeconomic distinction obviously presented a problem for Snow because he had no way of knowing whether differences in cholera incidence were due to the different water companies or to something else related to socioeconomic level such as diet, living conditions, or medical care.

Luckily for Snow, he was able to find one neighborhood in which socioeconomic status was stable but different houses received water from two different companies in an unsystematic manner. Hence the choice of water companies in this neighborhood appeared to be random. It was so random in fact that in some cases the choice of water company varied from house to house on a single street. Here was a naturally occurring situation in which socioeconomic level was controlled and the choice of water company varied. It was important, however, to ensure that not only the water company but also the contamination level of the water varied. Snow was lucky in this respect, too, because one company had moved upstream after a previous cholera epidemic, and the other company had stayed downstream. Snow calculated the number of deaths by cholera for individuals receiving water from upstream versus those receiving water from downstream. He found that there were 37 deaths per 10,000 households for the upstream company and 315 deaths per 10,000 households for the downstream company. Therefore it appeared that water contamination was responsible for the spread of cholera.

As a review the nonmanipulated independent variable in Snow's study was water company. This was a participant variable because individuals came to the study with their choice of water company already established. The dependent variable was the number of deaths by cholera. Snow observed a difference in death rates between the two companies and concluded that the type of water (more contaminated versus less contaminated) appeared to be the cause. Snow was particularly lucky because of the naturally occurring situation in which socioeconomic level was controlled but water company varied. This type of control is often lacking in quasi-experimental research. Still, even with such control, there is not as much control as in an experiment because participants are not randomly assigned to conditions. Consequently it is still possible for uncontrolled differences between the groups to affect the outcome of the study.

IN REVIEW	Quasi-Experimental Versus Correlational Methods		
	Variables	**Conclusions**	**Cautions**
Correlational method	Two measured variables	The variables may be related in some way.	We cannot conclude that the relationship is causal.
Quasi-experimental method	Typically one nonmanipulated independent variable and one measured dependent variable	Systematic differences have been observed between two or more groups, but we cannot say that the nonmanipulated independent variable definitely caused the differences.	Due to confounds inherent in the use of nonmanipulated independent variables, there may be alternative explanations for the results.

CRITICAL THINKING CHECK 10.1

1. Which of the following variables would be a participant variable if used as a nonmanipulated independent variable in a quasi-experiment?

   gender   ethnicity
   religious affiliation   visual acuity
   amount of time spent studying   amount of alcohol consumed

2. How does the quasi-experimental method allow us to draw slightly stronger conclusions than the correlational method? Why is it that the conclusions drawn from quasi-experimental studies cannot be stated in as strong a manner as those from a true experiment?

TYPES OF QUASI-EXPERIMENTAL DESIGNS

The quasi-experimental design has several possible variations (Campbell & Stanley, 1963; Cook & Campbell, 1979; and Shadish, Cook, & Campbell, 2002). One distinction is whether there are one or two groups of participants. A second distinction has to do with how often measurements are taken. We begin by discussing quasi-experimental designs in which only one group of participants is observed. These designs include the single-group posttest-only design, the single-group pretest/posttest design, and the single-group time-series design. We then consider designs that use two groups, which are referred to as *nonequivalent control group designs* and which include the nonequivalent control group posttest-only design, the nonequivalent control group pretest/posttest design, and the multiple-group time-series design.

Single-Group Posttest-Only Design

single-group posttest-only design: A design in which a single group of participants is given a treatment and then tested.

The **single-group posttest-only design** is the simplest quasi-experimental design. As the name implies, it involves the use of a single group of participants to whom some treatment is given. The participants are then assessed on the dependent variable. Research in education is frequently of this type. For example, a new educational technique—such as interactive learning, outcomes learning, or computer-assisted learning—is proposed, and school systems begin to adopt it. Posttest measures are then taken to determine the amount learned by students. However, there is neither a comparison group nor a comparison of the results to any previous measurements (usually because what is learned via the new method is so "different" from the old method that the claim is made that comparisons are not valid). This lack of comparison is the problem with this type of design: How can we claim a method is better when we cannot compare the results for the group who participated with the results for any other group or standard? This design is open to so many criticisms and potential flaws that results based on this type of study should always be interpreted with caution.

Single-group posttest-only designs are frequently reported in popular literature in which they are also frequently misinterpreted by those who read them. How many times have you read about people who lived through a certain experience or joined a particular group claiming that the experience or the group had an effect on their lives? These are examples of single-group posttest-only designs, and such designs cannot be used to draw conclusions about how an experience has affected the individuals involved. The change in their lives could be due to any number of variables other than the experience or the program.

Single-Group Pretest/Posttest Design

single-group pretest/posttest design: A design in which a single group of participants takes a pretest, then receives some treatment, and finally takes a posttest.

The **single-group pretest/posttest design** is an improvement over the posttest-only design in that measures are taken twice: before the treatment and after the treatment. The two measures can then be compared, and differences in the measures are assumed to be the result of the treatment. For instance, if a single group of depressed individuals wanted to receive treatment (counseling) for their depression, we would measure their level of depression before the treatment, we would then have them participate in the counseling, and finally, we would measure their level of depression after the treatment. Can you think of possible problems with this design? The greatest is the lack of a comparison group. With no comparison group, we do not know whether any observed change in depression is due to the treatment or to something else that may have happened during the time of the study. Maybe the pretest depression measure was taken right after the holidays when depression is higher than during the rest of the year for many people. Consequently the participants might have scored lower on the posttest depression measure regardless of the counseling.

Single-Group Time-Series Design

The **single-group time-series design** involves using a single group of participants, taking multiple measures over a period of time before introducing the treatment, and then continuing to take several measures after the treatment. The advantage of this design is that the multiple measures allow us to see whether the behavior is stable before treatment and how, or if, it changes at the points in time at which measures are taken after treatment.

An oft-cited good example of a time-series design, discussed by Campbell (1969), was used to evaluate the 1955 crackdown on speeding in Connecticut. The state found it necessary to institute the crackdown after a record-high number of traffic fatalities occurred in 1955. A pretest/posttest design would simply have compared the number of fatalities before the crackdown with the number afterward. The number of deaths fell from 324 in 1955 to 284 in 1956. However, alternative hypotheses other than the crackdown could have been offered to explain the drop. Perhaps the number of deaths in 1955 was unusually high based on chance, that is, the number was just a "fluke." Campbell recommended a time-series design, examining traffic fatalities over an extended period. Figure 10.1 illustrates the results of this design, which includes traffic fatalities for the years 1951 through 1959. As can be seen in the figure, 1955 was a record-high year; after the crackdown the

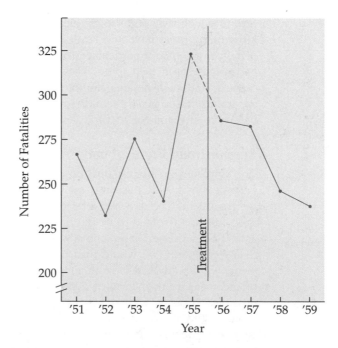

FIGURE **10.1** Connecticut traffic fatalities: 1951–1959

Source: D. T. Campbell, (1969). Reforms as experiments. *American Psychologist*, 24, 409–429. Copyright 1969 by the American Psychological Association. Reprinted with permission.

number of fatalities declined not only in 1956 but also in the 3 following years. Using the time-series design then allowed for a clearer interpretation than was possible with data from only 1955 and 1956.

Campbell still saw a problem with attributing the decline to the crackdown. The problem is statistical regression, or regression to the mean. Statistical regression occurs when individuals are selected for a study because their scores on some measure are extreme—either extremely high or extremely low. If we were studying students who scored in the top 10% on the SAT and we retested them on the SAT, we would expect them to do well again. Not all students, however, would score as well as they did originally because of *statistical regression*, often referred to as **regression to the mean**. Regression to the mean is a threat to internal validity in which extreme scores, upon retesting, tend to be less extreme, moving toward the mean. In other words, some of the students did well the first time due to chance or luck. What happens when they take the test a second time? They are not as lucky, and their scores regress toward the mean.

Regression to the mean occurs in many situations other than in research studies. Many people think that a hex is associated with being on the cover of *Sports Illustrated* and that an athlete's performance declines after appearing on the cover. This decline can be explained by regression to the mean. Athletes are most likely to appear on the cover of *Sports Illustrated* after a very successful season or at the peak of their careers. What is most likely to happen after they have been performing exceptionally well over a period of time? They are likely to regress toward the mean and perform in a more average manner (Cozby, 2001). In a research study, having an equivalent control group of participants with extreme scores indicates whether changes in the dependent measure are due to regression to the mean or to the effects of the treatment variable.

Because of regression to the mean, with the very high death rate in 1955, we would expect a drop in the death rate for several years, whether there was a speeding crackdown or not, because the average death rate (calculated over several years) would remain the same. We will discuss Campbell's recommendation for an improved design shortly when we cover the multiple-group time-series design.

Nonequivalent Control Group Posttest-Only Design

The **nonequivalent control group posttest-only design** is similar to the single-group posttest-only design, but a nonequivalent control group is added as a comparison group. Notice that the control group is nonequivalent, meaning that participants are not assigned to either the experimental or the control group in a random manner. Instead, they are members of each group because of something that they chose or did, that is, they come to the study already a member of one of the groups. This design is similar to the quasi-experimental study conducted by Snow on cholera and discussed earlier in this module. Participants selected either the upstream or the downstream water company, and Snow took posttest measures on death rates by cholera. As noted earlier, Snow had some evidence that the two groups were somewhat equivalent on income level because they all lived in the same neighborhood. In many situations, however, there is no assurance that the two groups are at all equivalent on any

regression to the mean: A threat to internal validity in which extreme scores upon retesting tend to be less extreme, moving toward the mean.

nonequivalent control group posttest-only design: A design in which at least two nonequivalent groups are given a treatment and then a posttest measure.

variable prior to the study. For this reason we cannot say definitively that the treatment is responsible for any observed changes in the groups. It could be that the groups were not equivalent at the beginning of the study, and hence the differences observed between the two groups on the dependent variable may be due to the nonequivalence of the groups and not to the treatment.

Nonequivalent Control Group Pretest/Posttest Design

nonequivalent control group pretest/posttest design: A design in which at least two nonequivalent groups are given a pretest, then a treatment, and finally a posttest.

An improvement over the previous design involves the addition of a pretest measure, making it a **nonequivalent control group pretest/posttest design**. This design is still not a true experimental one because as with the previous designs participants are not randomly assigned to the two conditions. However, a pretest allows us to assess whether the groups are equivalent on the dependent measure before the treatment is given to the experimental group. In addition, we can assess any changes that may have occurred in either group after treatment by comparing the pretest measures for each group with their posttest measures. Thus not only can we compare the performances of the two groups on both pretest and posttest measures, but we can compare performance within each group from the pretest to the posttest. If the treatment has some effect, then there should be a greater change from pretest to posttest for the experimental group than for the control group.

Williams (1986) and her colleagues used this design in a series of studies to assess the effects of television on communities. The researchers found a small Canadian town that had no television reception until 1973; they designated this town the Notel group. Life in Notel was then compared to life in two other communities: Unitel, which received only one station at the beginning of the study, and Multitel, which received four channels at the beginning of the study. A single channel was introduced to Notel at the beginning of the study. During the 2 years of the study Unitel began receiving three additional stations. The researchers measured such factors as participation in community activities and aggressive behavior in children in all three groups, both before and after the introduction of television in Notel. Results showed that after the introduction of television in Notel, there was a significant decline in participation in community activities and a significant increase in aggressive behavior in children.

Multiple-Group Time-Series Design

multiple-group time-series design: A design in which a series of measures are taken on two or more groups both before and after a treatment.

The logical extension of the previous design is to take more than one pretest and posttest. In a **multiple-group time-series design** several measures are taken on nonequivalent groups before and after treatment. Refer to the study of the crackdown on speeding in Connecticut following a high number of traffic fatalities in 1955. Converting that single-group time-series design to a multiple-group time-series design would involve finding a comparison group—a state that did not crack down on speeding—during the same time period. Campbell (1969) found four other states that did not crack down on speeding at the same time as Connecticut. Figure 10.2 presents the data from this design. As can be seen, the fatality rates in the states used as the control group remained fairly stable, while the fatality rates in Connecticut decreased. Based on these data, Campbell concluded that the crackdown had the desired effect on fatality rates.

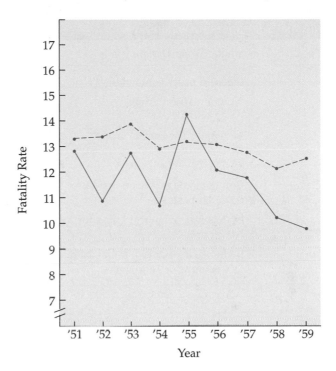

FIGURE **10.2** Multiple-group time-series design comparing Connecticut fatality rates (solid line) with the fatality rates of four other states (dashed line) used as a control group

Source: D. T. Campbell, (1969). Reforms as experiments. *American Psychologist*, 24, 409–429. Copyright 1969 by the American Psychological Association. Reprinted with permission.

INTERNAL VALIDITY AND CONFOUNDS IN QUASI-EXPERIMENTAL DESIGNS

confound: An uncontrolled extraneous variable or flaw in an experiment.

internal validity: The extent to which the results of an experiment can be attributed to the manipulation of the independent variable rather than to some confounding variable.

As we have pointed out several times, the results of quasi-experimental research need to be interpreted with caution because the design includes only one group or a nonequivalent control group. These results are always open to alternative explanations, or **confounds**, uncontrolled extraneous variables or flaws in an experiment. Because of the weaknesses in quasi-experimental designs, we can never conclude that the independent variable definitely caused any of the observed changes in the dependent variable. **Internal validity** is the extent to which the results of an experiment can be attributed to the manipulation of the independent variable rather than to some confounding variable. Quasi-experimental designs lack internal validity. We will continue to discuss internal validity and confounds when we cover true experimental designs in Module 12 as well as discussing how a true experiment helps to control for these confounds.

IN REVIEW	Quasi-Experimental Designs	
	Single Group Designs	**Nonequivalent Control Group Designs**
Posttest-only	Open to many confounds	Control group is nonequivalent
	No comparison group	No pretest measures to establish equivalence of groups
	No equivalent control group	Can compare groups on posttest measures, but differences may be due to treatment or confounds
Pretest/posttest	Can compare scores on pretest to those on posttest	Can compare between groups on pretest and posttest
	No equivalent control group for comparison	Can compare within groups from pretest to posttest
	If change is observed, it may be due to treatment or confounds	Because participants are not randomly assigned to groups, cannot say that they are equivalent
		If change is observed, may be due to treatment or confounds
Time series	Because many measures are taken, can see effect of treatment over time	Because many measures are taken, can see effect of treatment over time
	No control group for comparison	Nonequivalent control group available for comparison
	If change is observed, it may be due to treatment or confounds	Because participants are not randomly assigned to groups, cannot say that they are equivalent

CRITICAL THINKING CHECK 10.2

1. A researcher randomly selects a group of smokers and a group of non-smokers and then measures lung disease in each group. What type of design is this? If the researcher observes a difference between the groups in the rate of lung disease, why can he or she not conclude that the difference is caused by smoking?
2. How are pretest/posttest designs an improvement over posttest-only designs?

SUMMARY

In this module you were introduced to quasi-experimental designs, a type of design that falls somewhere between a correlational design and a true experimental design. Important concepts related to quasi-experimental designs include nonmanipulated independent variables (participant variables), internal validity, and confounds. Quasi-experimental designs include both single-group designs and nonequivalent control group designs.

REVIEW OF KEY TERMS

nonmanipulated independent variable	single-group pretest/ posttest design	nonequivalent control group posttest-only design	multiple-group time-series design
single-group posttest-only design	single-group time-series design	nonequivalent control group pretest/ posttest design	confound
	regression to the mean		internal validity

MODULE EXERCISES

(Answers to odd-numbered exercises appear in Appendix A.)

1. What is the difference between a true experimental design and a quasi-experimental design?
2. A psychology professor is interested in whether implementing weekly quizzes improves student learning. She decides to use the weekly quizzes in one section of her introductory psychology class and not to use them in another section of the same course.

Which type of quasi-experimental design do you recommend for this study?

3. If the psychology professor in Exercise 2 had access to only one section of introductory psychology, describe how she might use a single-group design to assess the effectiveness of weekly quizzes. Which of the three single-group designs would you recommend?
4. Identify some possible confounds in each of the studies you outlined in your answers to Exercises 2 and 3.

CRITICAL THINKING CHECK ANSWERS

10.1

1. Gender, religious affiliation, ethnicity, and visual acuity would all be participant variables.
2. There is slightly more control in a quasi-experimental study than in a correlational study because typically some sort of treatment is introduced. However, because participants are already members of either the control or the "experimental" group, we cannot conclude that the independent variable definitely caused changes in the dependent variable as we can when using a true experimental design.

10.2

1. This is a nonequivalent control group posttest-only design. The participants come

to the study as either smokers or nonsmokers. The researcher then takes posttest measures on them. We cannot conclude that any observed differences in lung disease are due to smoking because variables other than smoking may differ between the two groups.

2. Pretest/posttest designs are an improvement because they allow assessment of whether the groups are similar or different before we introduce the treatment and how much they change after the treatment is introduced. By this means we can determine whether the groups are in fact equivalent before the treatment.

WEB RESOURCES

Check your knowledge of the content and key terms in this module with a practice quiz and interactive flashcards at **www.cengage.com/ psychology/jackson,** or for step-by-step practice and information, check out the Statistics and Research Methods Workshops at **www.cengage. com/psychology/workshops.**

LAB RESOURCES

For hands-on experience using the research methods described in this module, see Chapter 9 ("Field Experiments") in *Research Methods* *Laboratory Manual for Psychology,* 2nd ed., by William Langston (Belmont, CA: Wadsworth, 2005).

Conducting Single-Case Research

LEARNING OBJECTIVES

- Describe advantages and disadvantages of ABA versus ABAB reversal designs.

- Differentiate multiple-baseline designs (i.e., across participants, across behaviors, and across situations).

U p to this point the quasi-experiments discussed have all involved studying groups of people. In certain types of research researchers use methods that minimize the number of participants in a study. This procedure may sound contrary to the basic principles of design discussed so far. However, in these methods often referred to as **single-case designs**, only one person is measured repeatedly. Frequently the research is replicated on one or two other participants. Thus we sometimes refer to these studies as **small-*n* designs**. Such studies can also be thought of as a variation of the pretest/posttest quasi-experimental design described in Module 10. But in this case pre- and posttest measures are taken on the single participant in the study.

Researchers may choose a single-case design for several reasons. They may want information on only the single participant being studied. They may not be interested in trying to generalize the results to a population, but rather they may only be interested in how the one participant reacts to the manipulation. Single-case research is often used in clinical settings. In clinical studies many researchers believe that it is unethical to use traditional experimental methods in which one group of participants receives the treatment and the other group serves as a control. They believe it is unethical to withhold treatment from one group, particularly when the participants may really need the treatment. In such instances single-case or small-*n* designs are more ethically appealing because they involve providing treatment to all who participate in the study.

Sidman (1960) argues that of the several reasons for conducting single-case studies, each is based on a flaw in designs that use many participants (group designs). One problem with group designs, according to Sidman, is that they do not allow for adequate replication of results whereas single-case designs do. Consequently single-case designs are better at demonstrating a reliable effect of an independent variable.

A second problem is that group designs contribute to error variance in a study. Error variance is the random differences in scores found within the conditions of an experiment. Using many people in a group design increases error variance resulting from individual differences. The increase in error variance may make it difficult to identify a relationship between the variables in the study.

single-case design: A design in which only one participant is used.

small-*n* design: A design in which only a few participants are studied.

A third problem that Sidman notes is that when using group designs, we typically look at the mean performance in each group. However, a mean score for a given condition may not accurately represent the performance of all the participants in that condition. Once we have drawn conclusions based on the mean performance within a group, we then attempt to generalize the results to individuals. Psychologists thus draw conclusions about individual behavior based on studying the average performance of a group of people.

Single-case and small-*n* designs address each of these problems. To determine the reliability of the effect, we can either repeatedly manipulate the independent variable with the same participant or perform replications with a few other participants. Further, error variance resulting from individual differences is eliminated because only one participant is used. Finally, rather than looking at group means and conducting the appropriate statistical analyses, we look at only the performance of the single participant in the study to determine the relationship between the independent and dependent variables. Most commonly we graph the performance of the single participant and examine the resulting graph. The effect of the independent variable is determined by how much the participant's behavior changes from one condition to another. Also because the findings are based on an individual's performance, it makes sense to generalize the results to other individuals.

TYPES OF SINGLE-CASE DESIGNS

Single-case designs are of several types. The basic distinction is between a reversal design and a multiple-baseline design. In the reversal design the researcher typically studies a single behavior in a single participant in a single situation, whereas in the multiple-baseline design the researcher may study multiple people, behaviors, or situations.

Reversal Designs

reversal design: A single-case design in which the independent variable is introduced and removed one or more times.

A **reversal design** is a design with only one participant; the independent variable is introduced and removed one or more times. We typically begin the study by taking baseline measures, equivalent to a control condition in a group design. In other words we need to assess how the participant performs before we introduce the independent variable. Once baseline measures are taken, we can introduce the independent variable. At this point we have a simple AB design, with A representing baseline performance and B the introduction of the independent variable. The problem with this simple pretest/posttest design is that if a change in behavior is observed, we do not know whether it is due to the introduction of the independent variable or to an extraneous variable (a confound) that happened to occur at the same time. In order to improve on this design, typically some type of reversal is introduced.

ABA Reversal Designs

ABA reversal design: A single-case design in which baseline measures are taken, the independent variable is introduced and behavior is measured, and the independent variable is then removed (a return to baseline condition) and measures are taken again.

An **ABA reversal design** involves taking baseline measures (A), introducing the independent variable (B) and measuring behavior again, and then removing the independent variable and taking new measures (A) after returning to the baseline condition. In this manner we can see whether the behavior changes with the introduction of the independent variable and then whether it changes back to baseline performance once the independent variable is removed. This combination of changes gives us a better indication of the effectiveness of the treatment.

The problem with this design is an ethical one. If the treatment helped to improve the participant's life in some way, it is not ethical to end the experiment by removing the treatment and possibly returning the participant to his or her original state. Thus a further improvement over the ABA design is the ABAB design.

ABAB Reversal Designs

ABAB reversal design: A design in which baseline and independent variable conditions are reversed twice.

The **ABAB reversal design** involves reintroducing the independent variable after the second baseline condition. The experiment thus ends with the treatment, making it ethically more desirable. In addition, it allows us to further assess the effectiveness of the independent variable by introducing it a second time. A study by Hall, Axelrod, Foundopoulos, Shellman, Campbell, and Cranston (1971), which assessed the effectiveness of punishment in reducing the aggressive behavior of a 7-year-old deaf girl, illustrates this design. The participant pinched and bit both herself and anyone else with whom she came in contact. The frequency of these behaviors averaged 72 occurrences per day, preventing normal classroom instruction. As can be seen in Figure 11.1, after a baseline measurement for five days, the experimenters introduced the treatment, in which the teacher pointed at the participant and shouted "No!" after each bite or pinch. The change in the participant's behavior with the introduction of the treatment was dramatic, even on the first day. Even though the participant was deaf, the treatment was still very effective. The number of bites and pinches per day dropped to zero by the end of the first treatment period. The researchers then returned to baseline for a few days to eliminate the possibility of an alternative explanation for the behavior change. As can be seen in the figure, the number of bites and pinches increased during this time. The treatment was then reintroduced on day 26, and once again the number of bites and pinches per day declined dramatically. Thus the ABAB reversal design has the advantage of being more ethical than the ABA design and of offering two baseline measures and two treatment measures to eliminate alternative explanations of

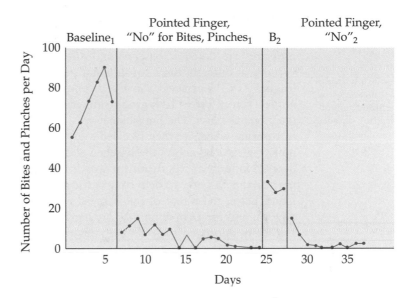

FIGURE **11.1** Number of bites and pinches during the school day

Source: From "The Effective Use of Punishment to Modify Behavior in the Classroom" by R. V. Hall, S. Axelrod, M. Foundopoulos, J. Shellman, R. A. Campbell, & S. S. Cranston, 1971, in K. D. O'Leary & S. O'Leary (Eds.), *Classroom Management: The Successful Use of Behavior Modification*, p. 175. Copyright 1972 by Allyn & Bacon. Reprinted with permission of Pearson Education.

behavior change. This design can be further extended to an ABABA design or an ABABAB design.

Multiple-Baseline Designs

One concern with single-case designs is *carryover effects*, that is, participants "carry" something with them from one condition to another. As a result of participating in one condition, they experience a change that they now carry with them to the second condition. For example, if the treatment in a reversal design permanently changes the participant, then he or she cannot revert to a baseline condition after treatment is introduced. In such cases it is not possible to use a reversal design. In addition, sometimes it is unethical to treat people (improve their condition) and then remove the treatment to assess a baseline condition.

In these situations a multiple-baseline design is recommended. In a **multiple-baseline design** rather than reversing the treatment and baseline conditions numerous times, we assess the effect of introducing the treatment over multiple participants, behaviors, or situations. We control for confounds not by reverting to baseline after each treatment as in a reversal design but by introducing the treatment at different times across different people, behaviors, or situations.

multiple-baseline design: A single-case or small-*n* design in which the effect of introducing the independent variable is assessed over multiple participants, behaviors, or situations.

Multiple Baselines across Participants

multiple-baseline design across participants: A small-*n* design in which measures are taken at baseline and after the introduction of the independent variable at different times across multiple participants.

A **multiple-baseline design across participants** is a small-*n* design in which measures are taken at baseline and after the introduction of the independent variable at different times for different people. As an example, Hall and his colleagues (1971) assessed the effectiveness of threatened punishment for low grades across three 10th-grade students. The three students were all failing their French class. The punishment was being kept after school for a half-hour of tutoring whenever they received a grade lower than C on their daily French quiz. Figure 11.2 shows the baseline and treatment results across the three students. Notice that the treatment was introduced at staggered times across the participants in order to help control for possible confounds. For the first participant, Dave, the threat of punishment was introduced on day 11, for Roy on day 16, and for Debbie on day 21. As shown in the graph, all participants immediately improved their quiz grades once the treatment was introduced. In fact, none of the three participants ever actually received extra tutoring because

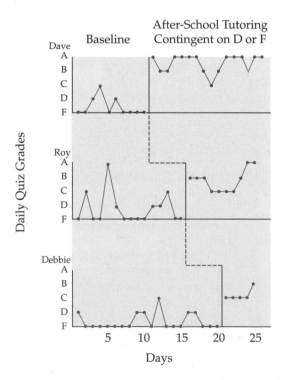

FIGURE **11.2** Quiz grades for three high school French students

Source: From "The Effective Use of Punishment to Modify Behavior in the Classroom" by R. V. Hall, S. Axelrod, M. Foundopoulos, J. Shellman, R. A. Campbell, & S. S. Cranston, 1971, in K. D. O'Leary & S. O'Leary (Eds.), *Classroom Management: The Successful Use of Behavior Modification*, p. 177. Copyright 1972 by Allyn & Bacon. Reprinted with permission of Pearson Education.

their grades improved immediately after the threat of punishment was introduced. By altering when the treatment is introduced to each participant, we minimize the possibility that some other extraneous variable produced the results. That is, because behavior changed for each participant right after the treatment was introduced and because the treatment was introduced at different times to each participant, we can feel fairly confident that it was the treatment and not an extraneous variable that caused the behavior change.

Multiple Baselines across Behaviors

multiple-baseline design across behaviors: A single-case design in which measures are taken at baseline and after the introduction of the independent variable at different times across multiple behaviors.

An alternative multiple-baseline design uses only one participant and assesses the effects of introducing a treatment over several behaviors. This design is referred to as a **multiple-baseline design across behaviors**. Imagine that a teacher wanted to minimize the number of problem behaviors emitted by a student during the school day. The teacher might begin by taking baseline measures on all of the problem behaviors (for example, aggressive behaviors, talking out of turn, and temper tantrums). The treatment might be introduced first for only aggressive behaviors. Several days after introducing that treatment, the teacher might introduce the treatment for talking out of turn and then several days later the treatment for temper tantrums. By introducing the treatments for different behaviors at different times, we can eliminate potential confounds. In other words, if all of the treatments were introduced at the same time and behavior changed, we would not know whether the change was due to the treatments or to extraneous variables that also changed at the same time. If we see a systematic improvement across behaviors when the treatment is introduced at different times, we can feel fairly certain that the treatment brought about the change.

Multiple Baselines across Situations

multiple-baseline design across situations: A single-case design in which measures are taken at baseline and after the introduction of the independent variable at different times across multiple situations.

A third way to use the multiple-baseline design is to assess the introduction of treatment across different situations: a **multiple-baseline design across situations**. For instance, Hall and his colleagues (1971) assessed the effectiveness of punishment on a young boy's crying, whining, and complaining behavior during school. The child emitted these behaviors only during reading and math classes each day. Hall devised a system in which the child was given five slips of colored paper bearing his name at the beginning of reading and arithmetic periods each day. One slip of paper was taken away each time he cried, whined, or complained. As can be seen in Figure 11.3, baseline performance was established for the number of cries, whines, and complaints in each class. Then the treatment was introduced on day 6 in the reading class and on day 11 in the math class. In both situations, the number of cries, whines, and complaints declined. Introducing the treatment at different times in the two classes minimizes the possibility that a confounding variable is responsible for the behavior change. Hall then reversed the treatment and went back to baseline. Reversal was possible in this situation because the treatment did not have any carryover effects and because reversing the treatment had no ethical ramifications. The treatment was then reintroduced on day 21 in both classes. Thus, this design is really a multiple-baseline reversal design across situations.

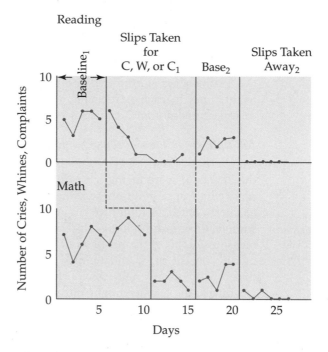

FIGURE **11.3** Frequency of cries (C), whines (W), and complaints (C_1) during reading and math classes

Source: From "The Effective Use of Punishment to Modify Behavior in the Classroom" by R. V. Hall, S. Axelrod, M. Foundopoulos, J. Shellman, R. A. Campbell, & S. S. Cranston, 1971, in K. D. O'Leary & S. O'Leary (Eds.), *Classroom Management: The Successful Use of Behavior Modification*, p. 180. Copyright 1972 by Allyn & Bacon. Reprinted with permission of Pearson Education.

IN REVIEW Single-Case Designs

Reversal Designs	Multiple-baseline Designs
ABA design: measures taken at baseline, after introduction of independent variable at baseline again	**Across participants:** measures taken at baseline and after introduction of independent variable at different times across multiple participants
ABAB design: measures taken at baseline, after introduction of independent variable at baseline again, and after introduction of independent variable again	**Across behaviors:** measures taken at baseline and after introduction of independent variable at different times across multiple behaviors
	Across situations: measures taken at baseline and after introduction of independent variable at different times across multiple situations

CRITICAL THINKING CHECK 11.1	1. Explain why single-case research is considered a variation of a quasi-experimental design.
	2. Why is an ABAB design considered more ethical than an ABA design?
	3. How do reversal designs attempt to control for confounds?
	4. How do multiple-baseline designs attempt to control for confounds?

SUMMARY

In this module you were introduced to single-case designs. Single-case or small-n designs include reversal designs and multiple-baseline designs. In a reversal design the independent variable is introduced and then removed (possibly several times) to assess its effect on the single participant in the study. In a multiple-baseline design the independent variable is introduced at different times across a few participants, behaviors, or situations.

REVIEW OF KEY TERMS

single-case design
small-n design
reversal design
ABA reversal design
ABAB reversal design

multiple-baseline design
multiple-baseline design across participants

multiple-baseline design across behaviors

multiple-baseline design across situations

MODULE EXERCISES

(Answers to odd-numbered exercises appear in Appendix A.)

1. Give three reasons for a researcher to use a single-case design.
2. Explain what a reversal design is. Identify advantages and disadvantages to using reversal designs.

3. How does a multiple-baseline design differ from a reversal design?
4. When conducting single-case research, why do we look at graphs of data rather than statistically analyzing the data as with other designs?

CRITICAL THINKING CHECK ANSWERS

11.1

1. Single-case research is considered a variation of a quasi-experimental design because it is similar to the single-group pretest/posttest quasi-experimental design in that it involves taking pretest and posttest measures on a single participant rather than on a group of participants.

2. An ABAB design is considered more ethical than an ABA design because the final condition involves administering the treatment to the participant rather than leaving the participant with no treatment (baseline).
3. Reversal designs attempt to control for confounds by reversing the baseline and treatment conditions one or more times to

assess the impact of the treatment on behavior.

4. Multiple-baseline designs attempt to control for confounds by introducing the treatment at differing time intervals to a few different people, to the same person in different situations, or to the same person across different behaviors.

WEB RESOURCES

Check your knowledge of the content and key terms in this module with a practice quiz and interactive flashcards at **www.cengage.com/ psychology/jackson**, or for step-by-step practice and information, check out the Statistics and Research Methods Workshops at **www.cengage. com/psychology/workshops**.

LAB RESOURCES

For hands-on experience using the research methods described in this module, see Chapter 9 ("Field Experiments") in *Research Methods* *Laboratory Manual for Psychology*, 2nd ed., by William Langston (Belmont, CA: Wadsworth, 2005).

CHAPTER FIVE SUMMARY AND REVIEW: PREDICTIVE (RELATIONAL) METHODS

After reading this chapter, you should have an understanding of the correlational research method, which allows researchers to observe relationships between variables. Correlations vary in type (positive, negative, none, or curvilinear) and magnitude (weak, moderate, or strong). The pictorial representation of a correlation is a scatterplot, which allows us to see the relationship, thus facilitating its interpretation.

Common errors made when interpreting correlations are assuming causality and directionality, overlooking a third variable, having a restrictive range on one or both variables, and assessing a curvilinear relationship. Knowing that two variables are correlated allows researchers to make predictions from one variable to the other.

You were also introduced to quasi-experimental designs, a type of design that falls somewhere between a correlational design and a true experimental design, and single-case designs. Important concepts related to quasi-experimental designs include nonmanipulated independent variables (participant variables), internal validity, and confounds. Quasi-experimental designs include both single-group designs and nonequivalent control group designs. Single-case or small-n designs include reversal designs and multiple-baseline designs. In a reversal design the independent variable is introduced and then removed (possibly several times) in order to assess its effect on the single participant in the study. In a multiple-baseline design the independent variable is introduced at different times across a few participants, behaviors, or situations.

CHAPTER FIVE REVIEW EXERCISES

(Answers to exercises appear in Appendix A.)

Fill-in Self-Test

Answer the following questions. If you have trouble answering any of the questions, restudy the relevant material before going on to the multiple-choice self-test.

1. A _____ is a figure showing the relationship between two variables graphically.
2. When an increase in one variable is related to a decrease in the other variable and vice versa, we have observed an inverse or _____ relationship.
3. When we assume that because we have observed a correlation between two variables, one variable must be causing changes in the other variable, we have made the errors of _____ and _____.
4. A variable that is truncated and does not vary enough is said to have a _____.
5. _____ is a procedure that allows us to predict an individual's score on one variable based on knowing his or her score on a second variable.
6. A _____ variable is a characteristic inherent in the participants that cannot be changed.
7. The _____ design involves giving a treatment to a single group of participants and then testing them.

8. A design in which a single group of participants is measured repeatedly before and after a treatment is a _____ design.

9. A design in which at least two nonequivalent groups are given a pretest, then a treatment, and finally a posttest is a _____ design.

10. A design in which only one participant is used is called a _____ design.

11. A design in which a few participants are studied is called a _____ design.

12. A single-case design in which baseline measures are taken, the independent variable is introduced and behavior is measured, and the independent variable is then removed and baseline measures taken again is a(n) _____ design.

13. A small-*n* design in which measures are taken at baseline and after the introduction of the independent variable at different times across multiple participants is a _____ design.

Multiple-Choice Self-Test

Select the single best answer for each of the following questions. If you have trouble answering any of the questions, restudy the relevant material.

1. The magnitude of a correlation coefficient is to _____ as the type of correlation is to _____.
   a. slope; absolute value
   b. sign; absolute value
   c. absolute value; sign
   d. none of the above

2. Strong correlation coefficient is to weak correlation coefficient as _____ is to _____.
   a. −1.00; +1.00
   b. −1.00; +.10
   c. +1.00; −1.00
   d. +.10; −1.00

3. Which of the following correlation coefficients represents the variables with the weakest degree of relationship?
   a. +.89
   b. −1.00
   c. +.10
   d. −.47

4. A correlation coefficient of +1.00 is to _____ as a correlation coefficient of −1.00 is to _____.
   a. no relationship; weak relationship
   b. weak relationship; perfect relationship
   c. perfect relationship; perfect relationship
   d. perfect relationship; no relationship

5. The clustering of points on a scatterplot in a pattern that extends from the upper left to the lower right suggests that the two variables depicted are _____.
   a. normally distributed
   b. positively correlated
   c. regressing toward the average
   d. negatively correlated

6. We would expect the correlation between height and weight to be _____, whereas we would expect the correlation between age in adults and hearing ability to be _____.
   a. curvilinear; negative
   b. positive; negative
   c. negative; positive
   d. positive; curvilinear

7. When we argue against a statistical trend based on one case, we are using a _____.
   a. third-variable
   b. regression analysis
   c. partial correlation
   d. person-who argument

8. If a relationship is curvilinear, we would expect the correlation coefficient to be _____.
   a. close to .00
   b. close to +1.00
   c. close to −1.00
   d. an accurate representation of the strength of the relationship

9. When using a _____ variable, participants are _____ assigned to groups.
   a. nonmanipulated independent; randomly
   b. nonmanipulated independent; not randomly
   c. participant; not randomly
   d. both b and c

10. Which of the following is a subject (participant) variable?
    a. ethnicity
    b. gender
    c. age
    d. all of the above

11. How does correlational research differ from quasi-experimental research?
    a. With correlational research we measure two variables.
    b. With quasi-experimental research there is one nonmanipulated independent variable and one measured variable.
    c. With quasi-experimental research there is one manipulated independent variable and one measured variable.
    d. Both a and b.

12. Students in one of Mr. Kirk's classes participate in new interactive history learning modules. Students in another class learn history using the traditional lecture method. After three months, all students take a test to assess their knowledge of history. What kind of design did Mr. Kirk use?
    a. nonequivalent control group posttest only design
    b. nonequivalent control group pretest-posttest design

    c. multiple-group time-series design
    d. single-group time-series design

13. Which of the following is a problem with nonequivalent control group designs?
    a. They are open to many confounds.
    b. There is no comparison group.
    c. There is no equivalent control group.
    d. Both a and c.

14. The difference between pretest/posttest designs and time-series design is that a time-series design takes _____ measures.
    a. fewer
    b. more
    c. the same number of
    d. more reliable

15. Which of the following is a type of single-case design?
    a. ABA reversal designs
    b. multiple baseline across participants
    c. time-series design
    d. single-group posttest only design

16. The ABA design is generally considered _____ than the ABAB design because participants _____.
    a. more desirable; are left with the effects of the treatment
    b. less desirable; are not left with the effects of the treatment
    c. more desirable; are not left with the effects of the treatment
    d. less desirable; are left with the effects of the treatment

KEY TERMS

Here are the terms from the glossary presented in Modules 9–11. Go through the list and see if you can remember the definition of each.

ABA reversal design	Directionality	Multiple-baseline design across behaviors	Multiple-baseline design across participants
ABAB reversal design	Internal validity		
Causality	Magnitude		
Confound			

Multiple-baseline design across situations

Multiple-baseline design

Multiple-group time-series design

Nonequivalent control group posttest-only design

Nonequivalent control group pretest/posttest design

Nonmanipulated independent variable

Partial correlation

Person-who argument

Regression to the mean

Restrictive range

Reversal design

Scatterplot

Single-case design

Single-group posttest-only design

Single-group time-series design

Single-group pretest-posttest design

Small-n design

Third-variable problem

CHAPTER 6

Explanatory Methods

13 | CORRELATED-GROUPS AND DEVELOPMENTAL DESIGNS

Within-Participants Experimental Designs

Matched-Participants Experimental Designs

Developmental Designs
Cross-Sectional Designs
Longitudinal Designs
Sequential Designs

SUMMARY
REVIEW OF KEY TERMS
MODULE EXERCISES
CRITICAL THINKING CHECK ANSWERS
WEB RESOURCES
LAB RESOURCES

14 | ADVANCED EXPERIMENTAL DESIGNS

Using Designs with More Than Two Levels of an Independent Variable
Comparing More Than Two Kinds of Treatment in One Study
Comparing Two or More Kinds of Treatment with the Control Group (No Treatment)
Comparing a Placebo Group with the Control and Experimental Groups

Using Designs with More Than One Independent Variable
Factorial Notation and Factorial Designs
Main Effects and Interaction Effects
Possible Outcomes of a 2 × 2 Factorial Design

SUMMARY
REVIEW OF KEY TERMS
MODULE EXERCISES
CRITICAL THINKING CHECK ANSWERS
WEB RESOURCES
LAB RESOURCES

CHAPTER SIX SUMMARY AND REVIEW: EXPLANATORY METHODS

In this chapter we explain the logic of the simple well-designed experiment. Pick up any newspaper or watch any news program, and you are confronted with results and claims based on scientific research. Some people dismiss or ignore many of the claims because they do not understand how a study or a series of studies can lead to a single conclusion. In other words, they do not understand the concept of control in experiments and that when control is maximized, the conclusion is most likely reliable and valid. Other people accept everything they read, assuming that whatever is presented in a newspaper must be true. They too are not able to assess whether the research was conducted in a reliable and valid manner. This chapter enables you to understand how to better assess experimental research studies.

In previous chapters we looked at nonexperimental designs. In Chapter Five we discussed correlational and quasi-experimental designs and their associated problems and limitations. We now turn to experimental designs and note the advantages of the true experimental design over the methods discussed previously.

Between-Participants Experimental Designs

LEARNING OBJECTIVES

- Explain a between-participants design.

- Differentiate independent variable and dependent variable.

- Differentiate control group and experimental group.

- Explain random assignment.

- Explain the relationship between confounds and internal validity.

- Describe the confounds of history, maturation, testing, regression to the mean, instrumentation, mortality, and diffusion of treatment.

- Explain what experimenter effects and participant effects are and how double-blind and single-blind experiments relate to these concepts.

- Differentiate floor and ceiling effects.

- Explain external validity.

between-participants design: An experiment in which different participants are assigned to each group.

In a **between-participants design** the participants in each group are different, that is, different people serve in the control and experimental groups. The idea behind experimentation, as explained in Module 2, is that the researcher manipulates at least one variable (the *independent variable*) and measures at least one variable (the *dependent variable*). The independent variable has at least two groups or conditions. In other words, one of the most basic ideas behind an experiment is that there are at least two groups to compare. We typically refer to these two groups, or conditions, as the control group and the experimental group. The *control group* serves as the baseline, or "standard," condition. The *experimental group* receives some level of the independent variable. Although we begin by describing the two groups in an experiment as the experimental and control groups, an experiment may involve the use of two experimental groups with no control group. An experiment can also have more than two groups, that is, multiple experimental groups.

Experimentation requires control. We first have to control who is in the study. The sample must be representative of the population about whom we are trying to generalize. Ideally we accomplish this representation through the use of random sampling. We also need to control who participates in each condition, so we should use random assignment of participants to the two conditions. By randomly assigning participants, we are trying to make the two groups as equivalent as possible. In addition to controlling who serves in the study and in each condition, we need to control what happens during the experiment so that the only difference between conditions is between the levels of the independent variable. If, after controlling for all of these factors, we observe changes when the independent variable is manipulated, we can then conclude that the independent variable caused the changes in the dependent variable.

Let's revisit the example in Modules 9 and 10 on smoking and cancer in order to examine the difference between correlational research and experimental research. In those modules we said that there was a positive correlation between smoking and cancer. We also noted that no experimental evidence with humans supported a causal relationship between smoking and cancer. Why is this the case? Think about actually trying to design an experiment to determine whether smoking causes cancer in humans, keeping in mind the potential ethical problems with such an experiment.

Let's first determine what the independent variable is. If you identified smoking behavior, you are correct. The control group would consist of people who do not smoke, and the experimental group would be the group who does smoke. To prevent confounding our study by previous smoking behavior, we would have to use only nonsmokers (those who had never smoked) in both the experimental and control groups. We would then randomly assign them to the smoking or nonsmoking groups. In addition to assigning participants to one of the two conditions, we would control all other aspects of their lives. This control means that all participants in the study must be treated exactly the same for the duration of the study except that half of them would smoke on a regular basis (we would decide when and how much) and half of them would not smoke at all. We would then determine the length of time the study should run. In this case participants would have to smoke for many years for us to assess any potential differences between groups. During this time all aspects of their lives that might contribute to cancer would have to be controlled, that is, held constant between the groups.

What would be the dependent variable? After several years had passed, we would begin to take measures on the two groups to determine whether there were any differences in cancer rates. Thus the cancer rate would be the dependent variable. If control was maximized and the experimental and control groups were treated exactly the same except for the level of the independent variable received, then any difference in cancer rate observed between the groups would have to be due to the only difference between them: the independent variable of smoking. This experimental study is illustrated in Figure 12.1.

You should be able to appreciate the problems associated with designing a true experiment to test whether smoking causes cancer in humans. First, it is not ethical for anyone to determine whether people should smoke or not. Second, it is not feasible to control all aspects of these individuals' lives for the period of time needed to conduct the study. It is for these reasons that there is no experimental study indicating that smoking causes cancer in humans.

It is perfectly feasible, however, to conduct experimental studies on other topics. For example, to study the effects of a mnemonic device (a study strategy) on memory, we could have one group use the device

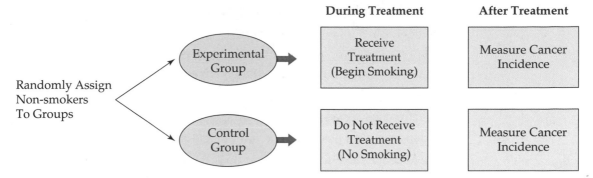

	During Treatment	**After Treatment**

Randomly Assign Non-smokers To Groups → Experimental Group → Receive Treatment (Begin Smoking) → Measure Cancer Incidence

Control Group → Do Not Receive Treatment (No Smoking) → Measure Cancer Incidence

FIGURE **12.1** Experimental study of the effects of smoking on cancer rates

while studying and another group not use it. We could then give each participant a memory test and look for a difference in performance between the two groups. Assuming that everything else was held constant (controlled), any difference observed would have to be due to the independent variable. If the mnemonic-using group performed better, we could conclude that the mnemonic device caused memory to improve.

posttest-only control group design: An experimental design in which the dependent variable is measured after the manipulation of the independent variable.

This memory study is what is known as a simple **posttest-only control group design**. We start with a control group and an experimental group made up of equivalent participants. We administer the treatment (mnemonic or no mnemonic), and we take a posttest (after-treatment) measure. It is very important that the experimental and control groups are equivalent because we want to be able to conclude that any differences observed between the two groups are due to the independent variable, not to some other difference between them. We help to ensure equivalency of groups by using random assignment.

When we manipulate the independent variable, we must also ensure that the manipulation is valid, that is, that there really is a difference in the manner in which the two groups are treated. This determination appears fairly easy for the mnemonic device study; either the participants use the prescribed mnemonic device, or they do not. However, how do we actually know that those in the mnemonic group truly are using the device and that those in the control group are not using *any* type of mnemonic device? These are questions the researcher needs to address before beginning the study so that the instructions leave no doubt as to what the participants in each condition should be doing during the study.

Finally, the researcher must measure the dependent variable (memory) to assess any effects of the independent variable. To be able to compare performance across the two groups, the same measurement device must be used for both groups. If the groups are equivalent at the beginning of the study and if the independent variable is adequately manipulated and the only difference between the two groups, then any differences observed on the dependent variable must be attributable to the independent variable.

pretest/posttest control group design: An experimental design in which the dependent variable is measured both before and after manipulation of the independent variable.

We could make the mnemonic device design slightly more sophisticated by using a **pretest/posttest control group design**, which involves adding a pretest to the design. This new design has the added advantage of ensuring that the participants are equivalent at the beginning of the study. This precaution is usually not considered necessary if participants are randomly assigned and if the researcher uses a sufficiently large sample of participants; as a general rule, having 20 to 30 participants per condition is considered adequate. There are disadvantages to pretest/posttest control group designs, including the possibility of increasing demand characteristics and experimenter effects (both discussed later in the module). The participants might guess before the posttest what is being measured in the study. If the participants make an assumption (either correct or incorrect) about the intent of the study, their behavior during the study may be changed from what would "normally" happen. With multiple testings there is also more opportunity for an experimenter to influence the participants. It is up to the researchers to decide which of these designs best suits their needs.

CONTROL AND CONFOUNDS

Obviously one of the most critical elements of an experiment is control, which must be maximized. If a researcher fails to control for something, then the study is open to confounds, that is, uncontrolled extraneous variables or flaws in an experiment (discussed in Module 10). If a study is confounded, then it is impossible to say whether changes in the dependent variable are caused by the independent variable or by the uncontrolled variable.

The problem for most psychologists is that maximizing control with human participants can be very difficult. In other disciplines control is not as difficult. For instance, marine biologists do not need to be as concerned about preexisting differences between sea snails because sea snails do not vary on as many dimensions as do humans (personality, intelligence, and rearing issues, among others, are not relevant as they are for humans). Because of the great variability among humans on all dimensions, psychologists need to be very concerned about preexisting differences. Consider the study on memory and mnemonic devices. A problem could occur if the differences in performance on the memory test resulted from the fact that based on chance, the more educated participants made up the experimental group and the less educated participants were in the control group. In this case we might have observed a difference between memory performance even if the experimental group had not used the mnemonic.

Even when we use random assignment as a means of minimizing differences between the experimental and control groups, we still need to think about control. So if conducting the study on memory and mnemonic devices, we should consider administering pretests as a means of assuring that the participants in the two groups are equivalent on any dimension (variable) that might affect memory performance. It is imperative that psychologists working with humans understand control and potential confounds due to human variability. If the basis of experimentation is that the control group and the experimental group (or the two experimental groups being compared) are as similar as possible except for differences in the independent variable, then it is up to the researcher to make sure that this situation is indeed the case. In short, the researcher needs to maximize the *internal validity* of the study, that is, the extent to which the results can be attributed to the manipulation of the independent variable rather than to some confounding variable. A study with good internal validity has no confounds and offers only one explanation for the results.

THREATS TO INTERNAL VALIDITY

There are several potential threats to the internal validity of a study. The confounds discussed below provide an overview of some potential problems and an opportunity to begin developing the critical thinking skills involved in designing a sound study. These confounds are most problematic for nonexperimental designs such as the quasi-experimental designs discussed in the previous chapter, but they may also pose a threat to experimental designs. Taking the precautions outlined here should indicate whether the confound is present in a study.

Nonequivalent Control Group

One of the most basic concerns in an experiment is that the participants in the control and experimental groups are equivalent at the beginning of the study. Using random sampling and random assignment is typically considered sufficient to address the potential problem of a nonequivalent control group. When random sampling and random assignment are not used, participant selection or assignment problems may result. In this case we would have a quasi-experimental design (discussed in Module 10), not a true experiment.

History

history effect: A threat to internal validity in which an outside event that is not a part of the manipulation of the experiment could be responsible for the results.

Changes in the dependent variable may be due to historical events that occur outside the study, leading to the confound known as a **history effect**. These events are most likely unrelated to the study but may nonetheless affect the dependent variable. Imagine that you are conducting a study on the effects of a certain program on stress reduction in college students. The study covers a 2-month period, during which students participate in your stress reduction program. If your posttest measure is taken during midterm or final exams, you might notice an increase in stress even though the participants are involved in a program intended to reduce stress. Not taking into account the historical point in the semester might lead you to an erroneous conclusion concerning the effectiveness of the stress reduction program. Notice also that a control group of equivalent participants would help reveal the confound in this study.

Maturation

maturation effect: A threat to internal validity in which participants' naturally occurring changes could be responsible for the observed results.

In research in which participants are studied over a period of time, a **maturation effect** can frequently be a problem. Participants mature physically, socially, and cognitively during the course of the study. Any changes in the dependent variable that occur over the course of the study therefore may be due to maturation and not to the independent variable of the study. Using a control group with equivalent participants indicates whether changes in the dependent variable are due to maturation; if they are, the participants in the control group change on the dependent variable during the course of the study even though they do not receive the treatment.

Testing

testing effect: A threat to internal validity in which repeated testing leads to better or worse scores.

In studies in which participants are measured numerous times, a **testing effect** may be a problem: repeated testing may lead to better or worse performance. Whereas many studies involve only pretest and posttest measures, others involve taking measures on an hourly, daily, weekly, or monthly basis. In these cases participants are exposed to the same or similar "tests" numerous times. As a result changes in performance on the test may be due to prior experience with it, not to the independent variable. As an example, if participants took the same math test before and after participating in a special math course, the improvement observed in scores might be due to participants' familiarity with and practice on the test items. This type of testing confound is sometimes referred to as a *practice effect*. Testing can also result in the opposite effect, a *fatigue effect* (sometimes referred to as a *negative practice effect*). Repeated testing fatigues the participants, and their performance declines as a result. Once again, having a control group of equivalent participants helps to control for testing confounds because researchers can see practice or fatigue effects in the control group.

Regression to the Mean

Statistical regression occurs when individuals are selected for a study because their scores on some measure were extreme, either extremely high or extremely low. *Regression to the mean* is a threat to internal validity in which extreme scores upon retesting tend to be less extreme, moving toward the mean. (To review this concept in more detail, refer to Module 10.)

Instrumentation

instrumentation effect: A threat to internal validity in which changes in the dependent variable may be due to changes in the measuring device.

An **instrumentation effect** occurs when the measuring device is faulty. Problems of consistency in measuring the dependent variable are most likely to occur when the measuring instrument is a human observer. The observer may become better at taking measures during the course of the study or may become fatigued. If the measures taken during the study are not taken consistently, then any change in the dependent variable may be due to measurement changes, not to the independent variable. Once again, having a control group of equivalent participants helps to identify this confound.

Mortality or Attrition

mortality (attrition): A threat to internal validity in which differential dropout rates may be observed in the experimental and control groups, leading to inequality between the groups.

Most research studies have a certain amount of **mortality**, or **attrition** (dropout). Most of the time the attrition is equal across experimental and control groups. It is of concern to researchers, however, when attrition is not equal across the groups. Assume that we begin a study with two equivalent groups of participants. If more participants leave one group than the other, then the two groups of participants are probably no longer equivalent, meaning that comparisons cannot be made between them.

What might cause differential attrition between groups? Imagine a study to test the effects of a program aimed at reducing smoking. We randomly select a group of smokers and then randomly assign half to the control group and half to the experimental group. The experimental group participates in the program to reduce smoking, but the heaviest smokers just cannot take its demands and quit. When we take a posttest measure on smoking, only the originally light to moderate smokers are left in the experimental group. Comparing them to the control group is pointless because the groups are no longer equivalent. Having a control group allows us to determine whether there is differential attrition across groups.

Diffusion of Treatment

diffusion of treatment: A threat to internal validity in which observed changes in the behaviors or responses of participants may be due to information received from other participants in the study.

When participants in a study are in close proximity to one another, a potential threat to internal validity is **diffusion of treatment**, that is, observed changes in the behaviors of participants may be due to information received from other participants. For instance, college students are frequently used as participants in research studies. Because many students live near one another and share classes, some may discuss an experiment in which they participated. If other students are planning to participate in the study in the future, the treatment has now been compromised because they know how some of the participants were treated. They know what is involved in one or more of the conditions in the study, and this knowledge may affect how they respond, regardless of the condition to which they are assigned. To control for this confound, researchers might try to run the participants in a study in large groups or within a short time span so that they do not have time to communicate with one another. In addition, researchers should stress to participants the importance of not discussing the experiment with anyone until it has ended.

Experimenter and Subject (Participant) Effects

experimenter effect: A threat to internal validity in which the experimenter, consciously or unconsciously, affects the results of the study.

Researchers invest considerable time and effort in designing experiments. Often this investment leads the researcher to consciously or unconsciously affect or bias the results of the study. Thus a researcher may unknowingly smile more when participants are behaving in the predicted manner and frown or grimace when participants are behaving in an undesirable manner. This type of **experimenter effect** is also referred to as *experimenter bias* because the results of the study are biased by the experimenter's expectations.

One of the most famous cases of experimenter effects is Clever Hans. Clever Hans was a horse that was purported to be able to do mathematical computations. Pfungst (1911) demonstrated that Hans's answers were based on experimenter effects. Hans supposedly solved mathematical problems by tapping out the answers with his hoof. A committee of experts who claimed Hans was receiving no cues from his questioners verified Hans's abilities. Pfungst later demonstrated that Hans in fact had no mathematical abilities and that tiny head and eye movements were Hans's signals to begin and end his tapping. When questioners asked Hans a question, they looked at Hans's hoof as he tapped out the answer. When Hans approached the correct number of taps, the questioners would unknowingly make a subtle head or eye movement in an upward direction. This movement was a cue to Hans to stop tapping.

If a horse was clever enough to pick up on cues as subtle as these, imagine how human participants might respond to similar subtle cues provided by an experimenter. For this reason many researchers choose to combat experimenter effects by conducting blind experiments. There are two types of blind experiments: a single-blind experiment and a double-blind experiment. In a **single-blind experiment** either the experimenter or the participants are blind to the manipulation being made. The experimenter being blind in a single-blind experiment helps to combat experimenter effects. In a **double-blind experiment** neither the experimenter nor the participant knows the condition in which the participant is serving; both parties are blind. Obviously, the coordinator of the study has this information; however, the researcher responsible for interacting with the participants does not know and therefore cannot provide cues.

single-blind experiment: An experimental procedure in which either the participants or the experimenter are blind to the manipulation being made.

double-blind experiment: An experimental procedure in which neither the experimenter nor the participant knows the condition to which each participant has been assigned; both parties are blind to the manipulation.

"IT WAS MORE OF A 'TRIPLE-BLIND' TEST. THE PATIENTS DIDN'T KNOW WHICH ONES WERE GETTING THE REAL DRUG, THE DOCTORS DIDN'T KNOW, AND, I'M AFRAID, NOBODY KNEW."

subject (participant) effect: A threat to internal validity in which the participant, consciously or unconsciously, affects the results of the study.

Sometimes participants in a study bias the results based on their own expectations. They know they are being observed and hence may not behave naturally, or they may simply behave differently than when they are in more familiar situations. This type of confound is referred to as a **subject (participant) effect**. Sometimes subject effects are of a specific type. For instance, many participants try to be "good subjects," meaning that they try to determine what the researcher wants and to adjust their behavior accordingly. Such participants may be very sensitive to real or imagined cues from the researcher, referred to as *demand characteristics*. The subjects are trying to guess what characteristics the experimenter is in effect "demanding." Using either a single-blind experiment in which the participants are blind or a double-blind experiment helps to combat subject effects.

placebo group: A group or condition in which participants believe they are receiving treatment but are not.

placebo: An inert substance that participants believe is a treatment.

A special type of subject effect is often present in research on the effects of drugs and medical treatments. Most people report improvement when they are receiving a drug or other medical treatment. Some of this improvement may be caused by a *placebo effect*, that is, the improvement may be due not to the effects of the treatment but to the participant's expectation that the treatment will have an effect. For this reason drug and medical research must use a special placebo condition, or **placebo group**, a group of subjects who believe they are receiving treatment but in reality are not. Instead, they are given an inert pill or substance called a **placebo**. The placebo condition helps to distinguish between the actual effects of the drug and placebo effects. As an example, in a study on the effects of "ionized" wrist bracelets on musculoskeletal pain, researchers at the Mayo Clinic used a double-blind procedure in which half of the participants wore a so-called ionized bracelet and half of the participants wore a placebo bracelet. Both groups were told that they were wearing ionized bracelets intended to help with musculoskeletal pain. At the end of 4 weeks of treatment, both groups showed significant improvement in pain scores in comparison to baseline scores. No significant differences were observed between the groups. In other words, those wearing the placebo bracelet reported as much relief from pain as those wearing the ionized bracelet (Bratton et al., 2002).

Floor and Ceiling Effects

floor effect: A limitation of the measuring instrument that decreases its ability to differentiate between scores at the bottom of the scale.

ceiling effect: A limitation of the measuring instrument that decreases its ability to differentiate between scores at the top of the scale.

When conducting research, researchers must choose a measure for the dependent variable that is sensitive enough to detect differences between groups. If the measure is not sensitive enough, real differences may be missed. Although this confound does not result from an uncontrolled extraneous variable, it does represent a flaw in the experiment. For instance, measuring the weights of rats in pounds rather than ounces or grams is not advisable because no differences will be found. In this instance the insensitivity of the dependent variable is called a **floor effect**. All of the rats would be at the bottom of the measurement scale because the measurement scale is not sensitive enough to differentiate between such low scores. Similarly, attempting to weigh elephants on a bathroom scale would also lead to sensitivity problems; however, this is a **ceiling effect**. All of the elephants would weigh at the top of the scale (300 or 350 pounds, depending on the scale used), and any changes that might occur in weight as a result of the treatment variable would not be reflected in the dependent variable. A pretest can help to identify whether a measurement scale is sensitive enough. Participants should receive different scores on the dependent measure on the pretest. If all participants are scoring about the same (either very low or very high), then a floor or ceiling effect may be present.

IN REVIEW	Threats to Internal Validity

Major Confounding Variables

Type of Confounding Variable	Description	Means of Controlling/ Minimizing
Nonequivalent control group	Problems in participant selection or assignment may lead to important differences between the participants assigned to the experimental and control groups	Use random sampling and random assignment of participants
History effect	Changes in the dependent variable may be due to outside events that take place during the course of the study	Use an equivalent control group
Maturation effect	Changes in the dependent variable may be due to participants maturing (growing older) during the course of the study	Use an equivalent control group
Testing effect	Changes in the dependent variable may be due to participants being tested repeatedly and getting either better or worse because of the repeated testings	Use an equivalent control group
Regression to the mean	Participants who are selected for a study because they are extreme (either high or low) on some variable may regress toward the mean and be less extreme at a later testing	Use an equivalent group of participants with extreme scores
Instrumentation effect	Changes in the dependent variable may be due to changes in the measuring device, either human or machine	Use an equivalent control group
Mortality (attrition)	Differential attrition or dropout in the experimental and control groups may lead to inequality between the groups	Monitor for differential loss of participants in experimental and control groups
Diffusion of treatment	Changes in the behaviors or responses of participants may be due to information they have received from others participating in the study	Attempt to minimize by testing participants all at once or as close together in time as possible
Experimenter and subject (participant) effects	Either experimenters or participants consciously or unconsciously affect the results of the study	Use a double-blind or single-blind procedure
Floor and ceiling effects	The measuring instrument used is not sensitive enough to detect differences	Ensure that the measuring instrument is reliable and valid before beginning the study

CRITICAL THINKING CHECK 12.1	1. We discussed the history effect with respect to a study on stress reduction. Review that section and explain how having a control group of equivalent participants would help to reveal the confound of history. 2. Imagine that a husband and wife who are very tall (well above the mean for their respective height distributions) have a son. Would you expect the child to be as tall as his father? Why or why not? 3. While grading a large stack of essay exams, Professor Hyatt becomes tired and hence more lax in her grading standards. Which confound is relevant in this example? Why?

THREATS TO EXTERNAL VALIDITY

external validity: The extent to which the results of an experiment can be generalized.

In addition to internal validity, a study must have external validity for the results to be meaningful. **External validity** is the extent to which the results can be generalized beyond the participants used in the experiment and beyond the laboratory in which the experiment was conducted.

Generalization to Populations

Generalization to the population being studied can be accomplished by randomly sampling participants from the population. Generalization to other populations, however, is problematic because most psychology research is conducted on college students, especially freshmen and sophomores; hardly a representative sample from the population at large. This problem—sometimes referred to as the **college sophomore problem** (Stanovich, 2007)—means that most conclusions are based on studies of young people with a late adolescent mentality who are still developing their own identities and attitudes (Cozby, 2001).

college sophomore problem: An external validity problem that results from using mainly college sophomores as participants in research studies.

Does using college students as subjects in most research compromise research ideals? There are three responses to the college sophomore criticism (Stanovich, 2007). First, using college sophomores does not negate the findings of the study; it simply means that the study needs to be replicated with participants from other populations in order to aid in overcoming this problem. Second, in the research conducted in many areas of psychology such as sensory research, the college sophomore problem is not an issue. The auditory and visual systems of college sophomores function in the same manner as do those of the rest of the population. Third, the population of college students today is varied. They come from different socioeconomic backgrounds and geographic areas. They have varied family histories and educational experiences. Hence it is likely that college sophomores may be fairly representative of the general population.

Generalization from Laboratory Settings

Conducting research in a laboratory setting enables us to maximize control. We have discussed at several points the advantages of maximizing control, but control also has the potential disadvantage of creating an artificial

exact replication: Repeating a study using the same means of manipulating and measuring the variables as in the original study.

conceptual replication: A study based on another study that uses different methods, a different manipulation, or a different measure.

systematic replication: A study that varies from an original study in one systematic way—for example, by using a different number or type of participants, a different setting, or more levels of the independent variable.

environment. So we need to exercise caution when generalizing from the laboratory setting to the real world. This problem is often referred to in psychology as the *artificiality criticism* (Stanovich, 2007). Keep in mind, however, that the whole point of experimentation is to create a situation in which control is maximized in order to determine cause-and-effect relationships. Obviously we cannot relax our control in an experiment just to counter this criticism.

How then can we address the artificiality criticism and the generalization issue? One way is through replication of the experiment so as to demonstrate that the result is reliable. A researcher might begin with an **exact replication**, that is, repeating the study in exactly the same manner. However, to more adequately address a problem such as the artificiality criticism, the researcher should consider a conceptual or systematic replication (Mitchell & Jolley, 2004). A **conceptual replication** tests the same concepts in a different way. Therefore we could use a different manipulation to assess its effect on the same dependent variable, or we could use the same manipulation and a different measure (dependent variable). A conceptual replication might also involve using other research methods to test the result. Accordingly, we might conduct an observational study (see Module 7) in addition to a true experiment to assess the generalizability of a finding. A **systematic replication** systematically changes one thing at a time and observes the effect, if any, on the results. For example, a study could be replicated with more or different participants, in a more realistic setting, or with more levels of the independent variable.

SUMMARY

Researchers should consider several factors when designing and evaluating a true experiment. First, they need to address the issues of control and possible confounds. The study needs to be designed with strong control and no confounds to maximize internal validity. Second, researchers should consider external validity in order to ensure that the study is as generalizable as possible while maintaining control. In addition, they should use the design most appropriate for the type of research they are conducting.

REVIEW OF KEY TERMS

between-participants design

posttest-only control group design

pretest/posttest control group design

history effect

maturation effect

testing effect

instrumentation effect

mortality (attrition)

diffusion of treatment

experimenter effect

single-blind experiment

double-blind experiment

subject (participant) effect

placebo group

placebo

floor effect

ceiling effect

external validity

college sophomore problem

exact replication

conceptual replication

systematic replication

MODULE EXERCISES

(Answers to odd-numbered exercises appear in Appendix A.)

1. A researcher is interested in whether listening to classical music improves spatial ability. She randomly assigns participants to either a classical music condition or a no-music condition. Participants serve in the music or no music conditions for the specified time period and then are tested on their spatial ability. What type of design is this?

2. You read in a health magazine about a study in which a new therapy technique for depression was examined. A group of depressed individuals volunteered to participate in the study, which lasted 9 months. There were 50 participants at the beginning of the study and 29 at the end of the 9 months. The researchers claimed that of those who completed the program, 85% improved. What possible confounds can you identify in this study?

3. On the most recent exam in your biology class, every student made an A. The professor claims that he must really be a good teacher for all of the students to have done so well. Given the confounds discussed in this module, what alternative explanation can you offer for this result?

4. What are internal validity and external validity? Why are they so important to researchers?

CRITICAL THINKING CHECK ANSWERS

12.1

1. Having a control group in the stress-reduction study would help to reveal the confound of history because if this confound is present, we would expect the control group also to increase in stress level, possibly more so than the experimental group. Having a control group informs a researcher about the effects of treatment versus no treatment and about the effects of historical events.

2. Based on what we have learned about regression to the mean, the son would probably not be as tall as his father. Because the father represents an extreme score on height, the son would most likely regress toward the mean and not be as tall as his father. However, because his mother is also extremely tall, there is the possibility that genetics may overcome regression to the mean.

3. This is an example of an instrumentation effect. The way the measuring device is used has changed over the course of the "study."

WEB RESOURCES

Check your knowledge of the content and key terms in this module with a practice quiz and interactive flashcards at **www.cengage.com/psychology/jackson**, or for step-by-step practice and information, check out the Statistics and Research Methods Workshops at **www.cengage.com/psychology/workshops**.

LAB RESOURCES

For hands-on experience using the research methods described in this module, see Chapter 4 ("Two-Group Experiments") in *Research Methods Laboratory Manual for Psychology*, 2nd ed., by William Langston (Belmont, CA: Wadsworth, 2005).

Correlated-Groups and Developmental Designs

LEARNING OBJECTIVES

- Explain correlated-groups designs.
- Describe order effects and how counterbalancing is related to this concept.
- Explain what a Latin square design is.
- Describe the differences among cross-sectional, longitudinal, and sequential developmental designs.

The designs described so far have all been between-participants designs, that is, the participants in each condition were different. We now consider the use of **correlated-groups designs**, designs in which the participants in the experimental and control groups are related. There are two types of correlated-groups designs: within-participants designs and matched-participants designs. In addition, we will consider developmental designs, most commonly used by developmental psychologists. These designs differ from those already described in that they use age as a variable.

correlated-groups design: An experimental design in which the participants in the experimental and control groups are related in some way.

WITHIN-PARTICIPANTS EXPERIMENTAL DESIGNS

within-participants design: A type of correlated-groups design in which the same participants are used in each condition.

In a **within-participants design** the same participants are used in all conditions. Within-participants designs are often referred to as *repeated-measures designs* because we are repeatedly measuring the same individuals. A random sample of participants is selected, but random assignment is not relevant or necessary because all participants serve in all conditions. Within-participants designs are popular in psychological research for several reasons.

First, within-participants designs typically require fewer participants than between-participants designs. For example, we could conduct the mnemonic devices study using a between-participants design and randomly assign different people to the control condition (no mnemonic device) and the experimental condition (those using a mnemonic device). If we wanted 20 participants in each condition, we would need a minimum of 20 people to serve in the control condition and 20 to serve in the experimental condition for a total of 40 participants. If we conducted the experiment using a within-participants design, we would need only 20 participants who would serve in both the control and experimental conditions. Because participants for research studies are difficult to recruit, using a within-participants design to minimize the number of participants needed is advantageous.

Second, within-participants designs usually require less time to conduct than between-participants designs. The study is conducted more quickly because participants can usually take part in all conditions in one session; the experimenter does not use a participant in one condition and then wait around for the next person to participate in the next condition. Further, the instructions need to be given to each participant only once. If there are 10 participants in a within-participants design and participants are run individually, the experiment need only be explained 10 times. If there are 10 participants in each condition in a between-participants design in which participants are run individually, the experiment needs to be explained 20 times.

Third, and most important, within-participants designs increase statistical power. When the same individuals participate in multiple conditions, individual differences between the conditions are minimized. This minimization of differences in turn reduces variability and increases the chances of achieving statistical significance. Think about it this way. In a between-participants design the differences between the groups or conditions may be mainly due to the independent variable. Some of the difference between the performances of the two groups, however, is due to the fact that the individuals in one group are different from the individuals in the other group. This difference is referred to as *variability due to individual differences*. In a within-participants design, however, most variability between the two conditions (groups) must come from the manipulation of the independent variable because both groups of scores are produced by the same participants. The differences between the groups cannot be caused by individual differences because the scores in both conditions come from the same person. Because of the reduction in individual differences (variability), a within-participants design has greater statistical power than a between-participants design—it provides a purer measure of the true effects of the independent variable.

Although the within-participants design has advantages, it also has weaknesses. First, within-participants designs are open to many types of confounds. As with between-participants designs internal validity is a concern for within-participants designs. In fact, several of the confounds described in the previous module are especially troublesome for within-participants designs. For instance, testing effects, called **order effects** in a within-participants design, are more problematic because all participants are measured at least twice: in the control condition and in the experimental condition. Because of the multiple testing both practice and fatigue effects are common.

order effects: A problem for within-participants designs in which the order of the conditions has an effect on the dependent variable.

Still, the effects can be equalized across conditions in a within-participants design by **counterbalancing**, that is, systematically varying the order of conditions for participants in a within-participants experiment. So if our memory experiment were counterbalanced, half of the people would participate in the control condition first, and the other half would participate in the experimental condition first. In this manner practice and fatigue effects would be evenly distributed across conditions.

counterbalancing: A mechanism for controlling order effects either by including all orders of treatment presentation or by randomly determining the order for each participant.

When experimental designs are more complicated (i.e., they have three, four, or more conditions), counterbalancing can become more cumbersome. For example, a design with three conditions has 6 possible orders ($3! = 3 \times 2 \times 1$) in which to present the conditions, a design with four conditions has 24 ($4! = 4 \times 3 \times 2 \times 1$) possible orderings for the conditions, and a design with five conditions has 120 possible orderings ($5! = 5 \times 4 \times 3 \times 2 \times 1$). Given that most research studies use a limited number of participants in each condition (usually 20 to 30), it is not possible to use all of the orderings of conditions (called *complete counterbalancing*) in studies with four or more conditions. Luckily there are alternatives to complete counterbalancing, known as partial counterbalancing. One partial counterbalancing alternative is to randomize the order of presentation of conditions for each participant. Another is to randomly select the number of orders that matches the number of participants. For instance, in a study with four conditions and 24 possible orderings, if we had 15 participants, we could randomly select 15 of the 24 possible orderings.

Latin square: A counter-balancing technique to control for order effects without using all possible orders.

A more formal way to use partial counterbalancing is to construct a **Latin square**, which utilizes a limited number of orders. When using a Latin square, we have the same number of orders as we have conditions. Thus a Latin square for a design with four conditions uses 4 orders rather than the 24 orders necessary to completely counterbalance a design with four conditions. Another criterion that must be met when constructing a Latin square is that each condition should be presented at each order. In other words, for a study with four conditions each condition should appear once in each ordinal position. In addition, in a Latin square, each condition should precede and follow every other condition once. A Latin square for a study with four conditions appears in Table 13.1. The conditions are designated A, B, C, and D so that you can see how the order of conditions changes in each of the four orders used; however, once the Latin square is constructed using the letter symbols, each of the four conditions is randomly assigned to one of the letters to determine which condition will be A, B, and so on. A more complete discussion of Latin square designs can be found in Keppel (1991).

Another type of testing effect often present in within-participants designs is known as a *carryover effect*; that is, participants "carry" something with them from one condition to another. As a result of participating in one condition, they experience a change that they now carry with them to the second condition. Some drug research may involve carryover effects. The effects of the drug received in one condition are present for a while and may be carried to the next condition. Our memory experiment would probably also involve a carryover effect. If individuals participate in the control condition first (no mnemonic) and then the experimental condition (using a mnemonic device), there probably would not be a carryover effect. If some individuals participate in the experimental condition first, however, it would be difficult not to continue using the mnemonic device once they have learned it. What they learned in one condition is carried with them to the next condition and alters their performance in it. Counterbalancing enables the experimenter to assess the extent of carryover effects by comparing performance in the experimental condition when presented first versus second. Using a matched-participants design (to be discussed next) eliminates carryover effects.

Finally, within-participants designs are more open to demand characteristics, the information the participant infers about what the researcher wants.

TABLE **13.1**
A Latin Square for a Design with Four Conditions

Order of Conditions			
A	B	D	C
B	C	A	D
C	D	B	A
D	A	C	B

Note: The four conditions in this experiment are randomly given the letter designations A, B, C, and D.

Because individuals participate in all conditions, they know how the instructions vary by condition and how each condition differs from the previous ones. This knowledge gives them information about the study that a participant in a between-participants design does not have. This information in turn may enable them to determine the purpose of the investigation and could lead to a change in their performance.

Not all research can be conducted using a within-participants design. Most drug research is conducted using different participants in each condition because drugs often permanently affect or change an individual. Consequently participants cannot serve in more than one condition. In addition, researchers who study reasoning and problem solving often cannot use within-participants designs because, once a participant has solved a problem, they cannot serve in another condition that requires them to solve the same problem again. Where possible, however, many psychologists choose to use within-participants designs because they believe the added strengths of the design outweigh the weaknesses.

MATCHED-PARTICIPANTS EXPERIMENTAL DESIGNS

matched-participants design: A type of correlated-groups design in which participants are matched between conditions on variable(s) that the researcher believes is (are) relevant to the study.

The second type of correlated-groups design is a **matched-participants design,** which shares certain characteristics with both between- and within-participants designs. As in a between-participants design different participants are used in each condition. Yet for each participant in one condition, there is a participant in the other condition(s) who matches him or her on some relevant variable or variables. For example, if weight is a concern in a study and the researchers want to ensure that for each participant in the control condition there is a participant of the same weight in the experimental condition, they match participants on weight. Matching the participants on one or more variables makes the matched-participants design similar to the within-participants design. A within-participants design has perfect matching because the same people serve in each condition, whereas with the matched-participants design we are attempting to achieve as much equivalence between groups of different participants as we can.

Why then do we not simply use a within-participants design? The answer is usually carryover effects. Taking part in one condition changes the participants in such a way that they cannot take part in the second condition. For instance, drug research usually utilizes between-participants designs or matched-participants designs but rarely within-participants designs. Participants cannot take both the placebo and the real drug as part of an experiment; hence, this type of research requires that different people serve in each condition. But to ensure equivalency between groups, the researcher may choose to use a matched-participants design.

The matched-participants design has advantages over both between-participants and within-participants designs. First, because there are different people in each group, testing effects and demand characteristics are minimized in comparison to a within-participants design. Second, the groups are more equivalent than those in a between-participants design and almost as equivalent as those in a within-participants design. Third, because participants have been matched on variables of importance to the study, the same types of statistics used for the within-participants designs are used for the matched-participants designs. In other words, data from a matched participants design are treated like data from a within-participants design. This similarity in data analysis means that a matched-participants design is as powerful as a within-participants design because individual differences have been minimized.

Of course, matched-participants designs also have weaknesses. First, more participants are needed than in a within-participants design. Second, if one participant in a matched-participants design drops out, the entire pair is lost. Thus mortality is even more of an issue in matched-participants designs than in other designs. Finally, the biggest weakness of the matched-participants design is the matching itself. Finding an individual willing to participate in an experiment who exactly (or very closely) matches another participant on a specific variable can be difficult. If the researcher is matching participants on more than one variable (say, height and weight), it becomes even more difficult. Because participants are hard to find, it is very difficult to find enough matched participants to take part in a matched-participants study.

IN REVIEW Comparison of Designs

	Within-Participants Design	Matched-Participants Design
Description	The same participants are used in all conditions	Participants are randomly assigned to each condition after being matched on relevant variables
Strengths	Fewer participants needed	Testing effects minimized
	Less time-consuming	Demand characteristics minimized
	Equivalency of groups ensured	Groups are fairly equivalent
	More powerful statistically	More powerful statistically
Weaknesses	Probability of testing effects is high	Matching is very difficult
	Probability of demand characteristics is high	More participants are needed

CRITICAL THINKING CHECK 13.1

1. If a researcher wants to conduct a study with four conditions and 15 participants in each condition, how many participants are needed for a between-participants design? For a within-participants design? For a matched participants design?
2. People with anxiety disorders are selected to participate in a study on a new drug for the treatment of these disorders. The researchers know that the drug is effective in treating them, but they are concerned with possible side effects. In particular, they are concerned with the effects of the drug on cognitive abilities. Therefore they ask each participant in the experiment to identify a family member or friend of the same

(continues)

gender as the participant and of a similar age (within 5 years) who does not have an anxiety disorder. The researchers then administer the drug to those with the disorder and measure cognitive functioning in both groups. What type of design is this? Would you suggest measuring cognitive functioning more than once? When and why?

DEVELOPMENTAL DESIGNS

Developmental psychologists typically use a special group of designs known as *developmental designs*. These designs differ from those already described in that they use age as a variable. There are two basic developmental designs: the cross-sectional design and the longitudinal design. The cross-sectional design shares some characteristics with between-participants designs in that individuals of different ages are studied. The longitudinal design shares some characteristics with within-participants designs in that the same individuals are studied over time as they mature.

Cross-Sectional Designs

cross-sectional design: A type of developmental design in which participants of different ages are studied at the same time.

When using the **cross-sectional design**, researchers study individuals of different ages at the same time. Thus a researcher interested in differences across ages in cognitive abilities might study groups of 5-year-olds, 8-year-olds, 11-year-olds, and so on. The advantage of this design is that a wide variety of ages can be studied in a short period. In fact, in some studies it is possible to collect all of the data in one day.

cohort: A group of individuals born at about the same time.

cohort effect: A generational effect in a study that occurs when the eras in which individuals are born affect how they respond in the study.

Even though ease of data collection is a great advantage, the cross-sectional method has its disadvantages. The main one is that although the researcher typically attempts to determine whether there are differences across different ages, the reality is that the researcher tests not only individuals of different ages but also individuals who were born at different times and raised in different generations, or cohorts. A **cohort** is a group of individuals born at about the same time. In a cross-sectional study the researcher wants to be able to conclude that any difference observed in the dependent variable (for example, cognitive abilities) is due to age, but because these individuals were raised at different times, some or all of the observed differences in cognitive ability could be due to a **cohort effect**, a generational effect. In a cross-sectional study a cohort effect might influence cognitive abilities because individuals born in successive generations go through different educational systems and have varying opportunities for education—for example, those born earlier might have had less access to education.

Longitudinal Designs

longitudinal design: A type of developmental design in which the same participants are studied repeatedly over time as they age.

An alternative to a cross-sectional design is a longitudinal design. With a **longitudinal design** the same participants are studied over a period of time.

Depending on the age range the researcher wants to study, a longitudinal design may span from a few years or months to decades. If the cognitive study just described were conducted longitudinally, the same participants would periodically be tested on cognitive abilities (say, every 3 years). This type of study eliminates any cohort effects because the same participants are studied over a period of time. Thus we do not have the confound of using participants who were born in different generations.

However, longitudinal designs introduce their own problems into a research study. First, they are more expensive and time-consuming than cross-sectional studies. Second, researchers using longitudinal studies need to be particularly cognizant of attrition problems over time because those who drop out of the study likely differ in some possibly meaningful way from those who remain. For instance, those who drop out may be healthier, wealthier, or more conscientious, and in general they may have more stable lives.

Sequential Designs

One way to overcome many of the problems with both cross-sectional and longitudinal designs is to use a design that is a combination of the two. The **sequential design** is a combined cross-sectional and longitudinal design in that a researcher begins with participants of different ages (as in a cross-sectional design) and tests or measures them. Then, either a number of months or years later, the researcher retests or measures the same individuals (as in a longitudinal design). A researcher could therefore measure cognitive abilities in a group of 5-, 8-, and 11-year-olds, then 3 years later measure the same individuals when they are 8, 11, and 14 years old, and finally measure them again when they are 11, 14, and 17 years old. Sequential designs are more expensive and time-consuming than the previous two types, but they have the advantage of allowing researchers to examine cohort effects, usually without taking as much time as a longitudinal design alone.

sequential design: A developmental design that is a combination of the cross-sectional and longitudinal designs.

SUMMARY

Researchers should use the design most appropriate for the type of research they are conducting. This decision means considering the strengths and weaknesses of the between-, within-, and matched-participants designs when determining which would be best for their study. Further, when conducting developmental studies, researchers have three designs from which to choose: a cross-sectional design, a longitudinal design, or a combination of the two, called a sequential design.

REVIEW OF KEY TERMS

correlated-groups design	order effects	matched-participants design	cohort effect
within-participants design	counterbalancing	cross-sectional design	longitudinal design
	Latin square	cohort	sequential design

MODULE EXERCISES

(Answers to odd-numbered exercises appear in Appendix A.)

1. How does using a Latin square aid a researcher in counterbalancing a study?

2. What are the similarities and differences between within-participants and matched-participants designs?

3. What are the similarities and differences between cross-sectional, longitudinal, and sequential designs?

CRITICAL THINKING CHECK ANSWERS

13.1

1. The researcher needs 60 participants for a between-participants design, 15 participants for a within-participants design, and 60 participants for a matched-participants design.

2. This is a matched-participants design. The researcher might consider measuring cognitive functioning before the study begins to ensure that there are no differences between the two groups of participants before the treatment. Obviously the researchers would also measure cognitive functioning at the end of the study.

WEB RESOURCES

Check your knowledge of the content and key terms in this module with a practice quiz and interactive flashcards at **www.cengage.com/psychology/jackson,** or for step-by-step practice and information, check out the Statistics and Research Methods Workshops at **www.cengage.com/psychology/workshops.**

LAB RESOURCES

For hands-on experience using the research methods described in this module, see Chapter 4 ("Two-Group Experiments") in *Research Methods Laboratory Manual for Psychology,* 2nd ed., by William Langston (Belmont, CA: Wadsworth, 2005).

Advanced Experimental Designs

LEARNING OBJECTIVES

- Explain what additional information can be gained by using designs with more than two levels of an independent variable.

- Explain factorial notation and the advantages of factorial designs.

- Identify main effects and interaction effects based on looking at graphs.

- Draw graphs for factorial designs based on matrices of means

The experiments described in the previous two modules typically involve manipulating one independent variable with only two levels, either a control group and an experimental group or two experimental groups. In this module we discuss experimental designs that involve one independent variable with more than two levels. Examining more levels of an independent variable allows us to address more complicated and interesting questions. Often experiments begin as two-group designs and then develop into more complex designs as the questions asked become more elaborate and sophisticated. The same design principles presented in Modules 12 and 13 apply to these more complex designs; that is, we still need to be concerned about control, internal validity, and external validity.

In addition, we discuss designs with more than one independent variable. These are usually referred to as **factorial designs**, indicating that more than one *factor*, or independent variable, is manipulated in the study (an independent variable is often referred to as a factor). We discuss the advantages of such designs over simpler designs. Further, we explain how to interpret the findings (called main effects and interaction effects) from such designs.

factorial design: A design with more than one independent variable.

USING DESIGNS WITH MORE THAN TWO LEVELS OF AN INDEPENDENT VARIABLE

Researchers may decide to use a design with more than two levels of an independent variable for three reasons. First, it allows them to compare multiple treatments. Second, it enables them to compare multiple treatments with no treatment (the control group). Third, more complex designs allow researchers to compare a placebo group with control and experimental groups (Mitchell & Jolley, 2004).

Comparing More Than Two Kinds of Treatment in One Study

To illustrate this advantage of more complex experimental designs, imagine that we want to compare the effects of various types of rehearsal on memory. We have participants study a list of 10 words using either rote rehearsal (repetition) or some form of elaborative rehearsal. Additionally, we specify the type of elaborative rehearsal to be used in the different experimental groups. Group 1 (the control group) uses rote rehearsal, group 2 uses an imagery mnemonic technique, and group 3 uses a story mnemonic device.

Notice that we do not simply conduct three studies or comparisons of group 1 to group 2, group 2 to group 3, and group 1 to group 3. Doing so is not recommended for several reasons. One reason has to do with the statistical analysis of the data. Although statistical concepts appear later in this text, you may be familiar with some statistical concepts and see the problem with making multiple comparisons. Each comparison must be statistically analyzed on its own, and this process can lead to an erroneous conclusion. The most likely error when making multiple comparisons is that they can lead us to conclude that there is an effect when in reality there is not.

Another advantage of comparing more than two kinds of treatment in one experiment is that it reduces both the number of experiments conducted and the number of participants needed. Once again, refer to the three-group memory experiment. If we do one comparison with three groups, we can conduct only one experiment, and we need participants for only three groups. However, if we conduct three comparisons, each with two groups, then we need to perform three experiments, and we need participants for six groups or conditions.

Comparing Two or More Kinds of Treatment with the Control Group (No Treatment)

Using more than two groups in an experiment also allows researchers to determine whether each treatment is more or less effective than no treatment (the control group). Suppose we are interested in the effects of aerobic exercise on anxiety. We hypothesize that the more aerobic activity one engages in, the more anxiety is reduced. We use a control group who does not engage in any aerobic activity and a high aerobic activity group who engages in 50 minutes per day of aerobic activity—a simple two-group design.

Now assume that when using this design, we find that both those in the control group and those in the experimental group have high levels of anxiety at the end of the study—not what we expected to find. A design with more than two groups might provide more information. Suppose we add another group to this study, a moderate aerobic activity group (25 minutes per day), and get the following results:

Control group	High anxiety
Moderate aerobic activity	Low anxiety
High aerobic activity	High anxiety

Based on these data, we have a V-shaped function. Up to a certain point, aerobic activity reduces anxiety. Yet when the aerobic activity exceeds a certain level, anxiety increases again. By conducting the study with only two groups, we miss this relationship and erroneously conclude that there is no relationship between aerobic activity and anxiety. Using a design with multiple groups allows us to see more of the relationship between the variables.

Figure 14.1 illustrates the difference between the results obtained with the three-group and with the two-group design in this hypothetical study. It also shows the other two-group comparisons: control compared to moderate aerobic activity and moderate aerobic activity compared to high aerobic activity. This set of graphs illustrates how two-group designs limit our ability to see the complete relationship between variables.

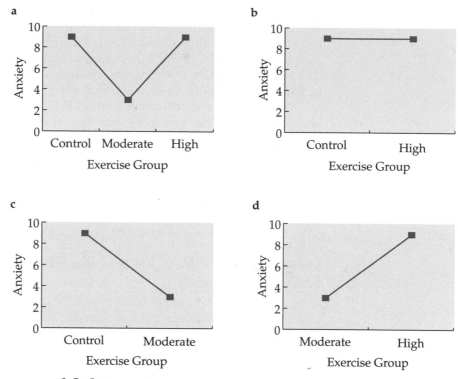

FIGURE **14.1** Determining relationships with three-group versus two-group designs: (a) three-groups design; (b) two-group comparison of control to high aerobic activity; (c) two-group comparison of control to moderate aerobic activity; (d) two-group comparison of moderate aerobic activity to high aerobic activity

Figure 14.1a shows clearly how the three-group design allows us to assess more fully the relationship between the variables. If we conduct only a two-group study such as those illustrated in Figure 14.1b, c, or d, we will draw a much different conclusion than that drawn from the three-group design. Comparing only the control to the high aerobic activity group (Figure 14.1b) leads us to conclude that aerobic activity does not affect anxiety. Comparing only the control and the moderate aerobic activity group (Figure 14.1c) leads us to believe that increasing aerobic activity reduces anxiety. Comparing only the moderate aerobic activity group and the high aerobic activity group (Figure 14.1d) lends itself to the conclusion that increasing aerobic activity increases anxiety.

Being able to assess the relationship between the variables means that we can determine the type of relationship. In the preceding example the variables produced a V-shaped function. Other variables may be related in a straight linear manner or in an alternative curvilinear manner (for example, a J- or

S-shaped function). In summary adding levels to the independent variable allows us to determine more accurately the type of relationship between variables.

Comparing a Placebo Group with the Control and Experimental Groups

A final advantage of designs with more than two groups is that they allow for the use of a *placebo group*, which improves an experiment. Consider an often-cited study by Paul (1966, 1967) involving children who suffered from maladaptive anxiety in public speaking situations. Paul used a control group, which received no treatment; a placebo group, which received a placebo that they were told was a potent tranquilizer; and an experimental group, which received desensitization therapy. Of those in the experimental group 85% showed improvement compared with only 22% in the control condition. If the placebo group had not been included, the difference between the therapy and control groups (85% − 22% = 63%) would have led to an overestimation of the effectiveness of the desensitization program. The placebo group showed 50% improvement, indicating that the therapy's true effectiveness is much less (85% − 50% = 35%). Thus a placebo group allows for a more accurate assessment of a therapy's effectiveness because in addition to spontaneous remission, it controls for participant expectation effects.

IN REVIEW Designs with More Than Two Levels of an Independent Variable	
Advantages	**Considerations**
Allows comparisons of more than two types of treatment	Making multiple comparisons may lead us to draw an erroneous conclusion
Requires fewer participants	
Allows comparisons of all treatments with control condition	
Allows for use of a placebo group with control and experimental groups	

USING DESIGNS WITH MORE THAN ONE INDEPENDENT VARIABLE

We now turn to a discussion of more complex designs: those with more than one independent variable, or factor. As discussed above, these designs are usually referred to as factorial designs, indicating that more than one factor, or variable, is manipulated in the study. In the study of the effects of rehearsal on memory, participants used one of three types of rehearsal (rote, imagery, or story) to determine their effects on the number of words recalled. Imagine that, upon further analysis of the data, we discovered that participants recalled concrete words such as desk, bike, and tree better than abstract words such as love, truth, and honesty in one rehearsal condition but not in another. Such a result is called an *interaction* between variables (a concept discussed in more detail later in the module). One advantage of using factorial designs is that they allow us to assess how variables interact. In the real world it is unusual to find that a certain behavior is produced by only one variable; behavior is usually contingent on many variables operating together in an interactive way. Designing experiments with more than one independent variable allows researchers to assess how multiple variables may affect behavior.

Factorial Notation and Factorial Designs

A factorial design then is one with more than one factor, or independent variable. A *complete factorial design* is one in which all levels of each independent variable are paired with all levels of every other independent variable. An *incomplete factorial design* also has more than one independent variable, but all levels of each variable are not paired with all levels of every other variable. The design illustrated in this module is a complete factorial design.

An independent variable must have at least two levels because if it does not vary, it is not a variable. Consequently the simplest complete factorial design is one with two independent variables, each with two levels. Let's consider an example. Suppose we manipulate two independent variables: word type (concrete versus abstract words) and rehearsal type (rote versus imagery). The independent variable Word Type has two levels, abstract and concrete; the independent variable Rehearsal Type also has two levels, rote and imagery. This design is known as a 2 × 2 factorial design.

The factorial notation for a factorial design is determined as follows:

Number of levels of independent variable 1 × Number of levels of independent variable 2 × Number of levels of independent variable 3 and so on ...

factorial notation: The notation that indicates how many independent variables are used in a study and how many levels are used for each variable.

Thus the **factorial notation** indicates how many independent variables are used in the study and how many levels are used for each of them. This concept is often confusing for students, who frequently think that in the factorial notation 2 × 2 the first number (2) indicates that there are two independent variables and the second number (2) indicates that each has two levels. This is *not* how to interpret factorial notation. Rather each number in the notation specifies the number of levels of a single independent variable. So a 3 × 6 factorial design is one with two independent variables; each of the two numbers in the factorial notation represents a single independent variable. In a 3 × 6 factorial design one independent variable has three levels whereas the other has six levels.

Referring to our 2 × 2 factorial design, we see that there are two independent variables, each with two levels. This factorial design has four conditions (2 × 2 = 4): abstract words with rote rehearsal, abstract words with imagery rehearsal, concrete words with rote rehearsal, and concrete words with imagery rehearsal. How many conditions would there be in a 3 × 6 factorial design? If you answer 18, you are correct. Is it possible to have a 1 × 3 factorial design? If you answer no, you are correct because it is not possible to have a factor (variable) with one level because then it does not vary.

Main Effects and Interaction Effects

main effect: An effect of a single independent variable.

interaction effect: The effect of each independent variable across the levels of the other independent variable.

Two kinds of information can be gleaned from a factorial design. The first is whether there are any main effects. A **main effect** is an effect of a single independent variable. In our design with two independent variables, two main effects are possible: an effect of word type and an effect of rehearsal type. In other words, there can be as many main effects as there are independent variables. The second type of information is whether there is an interaction effect, which as the name implies, is information regarding how the variables or factors interact. Specifically an **interaction effect** is the effect of each independent variable across the levels of the other independent variable. When there is an interaction between two independent variables, the effect of one independent variable depends on the level of the other independent variable. An example will make this point clearer.

Let's look at the data from the study on the effects of word type and rehearsal type on memory. Table 14.1 presents the mean performance for participants in each condition. This design was completely between-participants, with different participants serving in each of the four conditions. There were 8 participants in each condition, for a total of 32 participants in the study. Each participant in each condition was given a list of 10 words (either abstract or concrete) to learn using the specified rehearsal technique (rote or imagery).

Typically researchers begin by assessing whether there is an interaction effect because such an effect indicates that the effect of one independent variable depends on the level of the other. However, when first interpreting the results of two-way designs, students usually find it easier to look at the main effects and then move on to the interaction effect. Keep in mind that if we later find an interaction effect, then any main effects have to be qualified. Because we have two independent variables, there is the possibility of two main effects: one for word type (variable A in the table) and one for rehearsal type

TABLE **14.1**

Results of the 2 × 2 Factorial Design: Effects of Word Type and Rehearsal Type on Memory

Rehearsal Type (Independent Variable B)	Word Type (Independent Variable A)		Row Means (Main Effect of B)
	Concrete	Abstract	
Rote rehearsal	5	5	5
Imagery rehearsal	10	5	7.5
Column means (Main Effect of A)	7.5	5	

(variable B). The main effect of each independent variable tells us about the relationship between that single independent variable and the dependent variable. That is, do different levels of one independent variable bring about changes in the dependent variable?

We can find the answer to this question by looking at the row and column means in Table 14.1. The column means tell us about the overall effect of variable A (word type). They indicate that there is a difference in the numbers of words recalled between the concrete and abstract word conditions. More concrete words were recalled (7.5) than abstract words (5). The column means represent the average performance for the concrete and abstract word conditions summarized across the rehearsal conditions. In other words, we obtained the column mean of 7.5 for the concrete word conditions by averaging the numbers of words recalled in the concrete word/rote rehearsal condition and the concrete word/imagery rehearsal condition [(5 + 10)/2 = 7.5]. Similarly, the column mean for the abstract word conditions (5) was obtained by averaging the data from the two abstract word conditions [(5 + 5)/2 = 5]. (Note that determining the row and column means in this manner is possible only when the numbers of participants in each of the conditions are the same. If the numbers of participants in the conditions are unequal, then all individual scores in the single row or column must be used in the calculation of the row or column mean.)

The main effect for variable B (rehearsal type) can be assessed by looking at the row means. The row means indicate that there is a difference in the numbers of words recalled between the rote rehearsal and the imagery rehearsal conditions. More words were recalled when participants used the imagery rehearsal technique (7.5) than when they used the rote rehearsal technique (5). As with the column means the row means represent the average performance in the rote and imagery rehearsal conditions summarized across the word type conditions.

At face value the main effects tell us that overall participants recall more words when they are concrete and when imagery rehearsal is used. However, we now need to assess whether there is an interaction between the variables. If so, the main effects noted previously have to be qualified because an interaction indicates that the effect of one independent variable depends on the level of the other. That is, an interaction effect indicates that the effect of one independent variable varies at different levels of the other independent variable.

Look again at the data in Table 14.1. There appears to be an interaction in these results because when rote rehearsal is used, word type makes no difference (the means are the same—5 words recalled). Yet when imagery rehearsal is used, word type makes a big difference. Specifically then, when imagery is used with concrete words, participants do very well (recall an average of 10 words), yet when imagery is used with abstract words, participants perform the same as they did in both of the rote rehearsal conditions (they recall an average of only 5 words). Think about what this result means. When there is an interaction between the two variables, the effect of one independent variable differs at different levels of the other independent variable—there

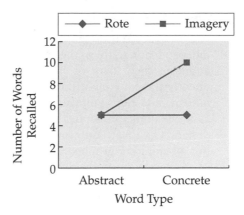

FIGURE **14.2** Line graph representing interaction between rehearsal type and word type

is a contrast or a difference in the way participants perform across the levels of the independent variables.

Another way to assess whether there is an interaction effect in a study is to graph the means. Figure 14.2 shows a line graph of the data presented in Table 14.1. The interaction may be easier for you to see here. First, when there is an interaction between variables, the lines are not parallel; they have different slopes. You can see in the figure that one line is flat (representing the data from the rote rehearsal conditions), whereas the other line has a positive slope (representing the data from the imagery rehearsal conditions). Look at the figure and think about the interaction. The flat line indicates that when rote rehearsal was used, word type had no effect; the line is flat because the means are the same. The line with the positive slope indicates that when imagery rehearsal was used, word type had a big effect; participants remembered more concrete words than abstract words.

Although the concept of interaction may seem difficult to understand, interactions often occur in our own lives. When we say "It depends," we are indicating that what we do in one situation depends on some other variable, that is, there is an interaction. For instance, whether you go to a party depends on whether you have to work and who is going to be at the party. If you have to work, you will not go to the party under any circumstance. However, if you do not have to work, you might go if a "certain person" is going to be there. If that person is not going to be there, you will not go. See if you can graph this interaction. The dependent variable, which always goes on the *y*-axis, is the likelihood of going to the party. One independent variable is placed on the *x*-axis (whether or not you have to work), and the levels of the other independent variable are captioned in the graph (whether the certain person is or is not present at the party).

To determine whether main effects or an interaction effect are meaningful, we need to conduct statistical analyses. We briefly discuss the appropriate analysis later in the text, but a more thorough discussion can be found in a statistics text.

Possible Outcomes of a 2 × 2 Factorial Design

A 2 × 2 factorial design has several possible outcomes. Because there are two independent variables, there may or may not be a significant effect of each. In addition, there may or may not be a significant interaction effect. Consequently there are eight possible outcomes in all (possible combinations of significant and nonsignificant effects). Figure 14.3, using the word recall study as an example, illustrates these eight possible outcomes for a 2 × 2 factorial design. Obviously only one of these outcomes is possible in a single study, but all eight are graphed to give a concrete illustration of each possibility.

For each graph the dependent variable (number of words recalled) is placed on the y-axis, and independent variable A (word type) is placed on the x-axis. The two means for one level of independent variable B (rehearsal type) are plotted, and a line is drawn to represent this level of independent variable B. In the same fashion the means for the second level of independent variable B are plotted, and a second line is drawn to represent this level of independent variable B. Next to each graph is a matrix showing the means from the four conditions in the study. The graphs are derived by plotting the four means from each matrix. In addition, whether there are main effects and an interaction effect is indicated.

Can you tell by looking at the graphs which ones represent interaction effects? Graphs a, b, c, and d do not have interaction effects, and graphs e, f, g, and h do. You should have a greater appreciation for interaction after looking at these graphs. Notice that in graphs a–d there is no interaction because each level of independent variable A (word type) affects the levels of independent variable B (rehearsal type) in the same way. Look at graphs c and d. In graph c the lines are parallel with no slope. This result indicates that for both rote and imagery rehearsal, word type makes no difference. In graph d the lines are parallel and sloped. This result indicates that for both rote and imagery rehearsal, word type has the same effect: Performance is poorer for abstract words and then increases by the same amount for concrete words.

Now look at graphs e–h, which represent interaction effects. Sometimes there is an interaction because even though there is no relationship between the independent variable and the dependent variable at one level of the second independent variable, there is a strong relationship at the other level of the second independent variable. Graphs e and f show this. In graph e when rote rehearsal is used, word type makes no difference, whereas when imagery rehearsal is used, word type makes a big difference. In graph f the interaction is due to a similar result. Sometimes, however, an interaction may indicate that an independent variable has an opposite effect on the dependent variable at different levels of the second independent variable. Graphs g and h illustrate this. In graph g when rote rehearsal is used, performance improves for concrete words versus abstract words (a positive relationship). However, when imagery rehearsal is used, performance decreases for concrete words versus abstract words (a negative relationship). Finally, graph h shows similar but more dramatic results. Here there is a complete crossover interaction in which exactly the opposite result is occurring for independent variable B at the levels of independent variable A. Notice also in this graph that although there is a large crossover interaction, there are no main effects.

| Rote | Imagery |

a. No Main Effects; No Interaction Effect

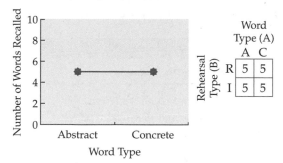

b. Main Effect of A; No Main Effect of B; No Interaction Effect

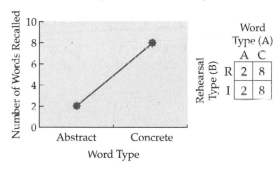

c. No Main Effect of A; Main Effect of B; No Interaction Effect

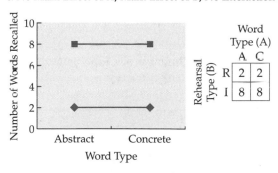

d. Main Effect of A; Main Effect of B; No Interaction Effect

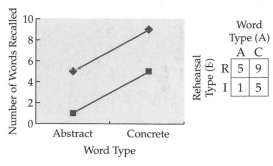

e. Main Effect of A; Main Effect of B; Interaction Effect

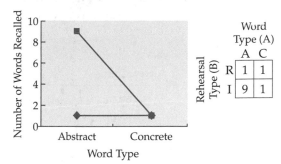

f. Main Effect of A; No Main Effect of B; Interaction Effect

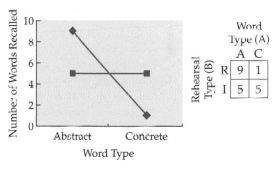

g. No Main Effect of A; Main Effect of B; Interaction Effect

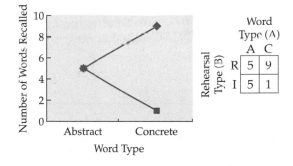

h. No Main Effects; Interaction Effect

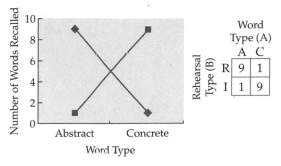

FIGURE **14.3** Possible outcomes of a 2 × 2 factorial design with rehearsal type and word type as independent variables

To make sure you completely understand interpreting main effects and interaction effects, cover the titles in each part of Figure 14.3 and quiz yourself on whether there are main effects and/or an interaction effect in each graph.

IN REVIEW	Complex Designs	
	Description	Advantage or Example
Factorial design	Any design with more than one independent variable	In the word recall study example, word type and rehearsal type were both manipulated to assess main effects and an interaction effect. The advantage is that the study more closely resembles the real world because the results are due to more than one factor (or variable).
Factorial notation	The numerical notation corresponding to a factorial design, indicating, in brief form, the number of independent variables and the number of levels of each variable	A 3 × 4 design has two independent variables, one with three levels and one with four levels.
Main effect	An effect of a single variable. A main effect describes the effect of a single variable as if there were no other variables in the study	In a study with two independent variables, two main effects are possible, one for each variable.
Interaction effect	The effect of each independent variable at the levels of the other independent variable	Interaction effects allow us to assess whether the effect of one variable depends on the level of the other variable. In this way we can more closely simulate the real world, where multiple variables often interact.

CRITICAL
THINKING
CHECK 14.1

1. What is the factorial notation for the following design? A pizza parlor owner is interested in which type of pizza his customers most prefer. He manipulates the type of crust for the pizzas by using thin, thick, and hand-tossed crusts. In addition, he manipulates the topping for the pizzas by offering cheese, pepperoni, sausage, veggie, and everything. He then has his customers sample the various pizzas and rate them. After you have determined the factorial notation, indicate how many conditions are in this study.
2. How many main effect(s) and interaction effect(s) are possible in a 4 × 6 factorial design?
3. Draw a graph representing the following data from a study using the same independent variables as in the module example.

(continues)

Determine whether there are any main effects or an interaction effect.

Rote rehearsal/Concrete words: $\overline{\overline{X}} = 10$
Rote rehearsal/Abstract words: $\overline{X} = 1$
Imagery rehearsal/Concrete words: $\overline{\overline{X}} = 9$
Imagery rehearsal/Abstract words: $\overline{\overline{X}} = 9$

SUMMARY

In this module we discussed designs that use more than two levels of an independent variable. Advantages to such designs include being able to compare more than two kinds of treatment, to use fewer participants, to compare all treatments with a control group, and to use placebo groups. In addition, we described experimental designs that use more than one independent variable. We discussed several advantages of using such designs and introduced the concepts of factorial notation, main effects, and interaction effects. After reading the sections on main and interaction effects, you should be able to create a graph with data from a factorial design and interpret it.

REVIEW OF KEY TERMS

factorial design   factorial notation   main effect   interaction effect

MODULE EXERCISES

(Answers to odd-numbered exercises appear in Appendix A.)

1. What is/are the advantage(s) of conducting a study with three or more levels of the independent variable?
2. What is the advantage of manipulating more than one independent variable in an experiment?
3. How many independent variables are in a 4 × 6 factorial design? How many conditions are in this design?
4. In a study a researcher manipulated the number of hours that participants studied (either 4, 6, or 8), the type of study technique they used (shallow processing versus deep processing), and whether participants studied individually or in groups. What is the factorial notation for this design?

5. What is the difference between a condition mean and the means used to interpret a main effect?
6. How many main effects and interaction effects are possible in a 2 × 6 factorial design?
7. What is the difference between a complete factorial design and an incomplete factorial design?
8. The condition means for two experiments follow. Determine whether there are any effects of factor A, factor B, and A × B for each experiment. In addition, draw a graph representing the data from each experiment.

Experiment 1	A_1	A_2
B_1	3	5
B_2	5	8

Experiment 2	A_1	A_2
B_1	12	4
B_2	4	12

CRITICAL THINKING CHECK ANSWERS

14.1

1. This is a 3 × 5 design. There are three types of crust and five types of toppings, so there are 15 conditions in the study.

2. A 4 × 6 factorial design has two independent variables. Thus there is the possibility of two main effects (one for each independent variable) and one interaction effect (the interaction between the two independent variables).

3. There appears to be a main effect of word type, with concrete words recalled better than abstract words. There also appears to be a main effect of rehearsal type, with those who used imagery rehearsal remembering more words than those who used rote rehearsal. In addition, there appears to be an interaction effect. When imagery rehearsal is used, word type makes no difference; recall is very high for both types of words. When rote rehearsal is used, word type makes a large difference; concrete words are recalled very well and abstract words very poorly.

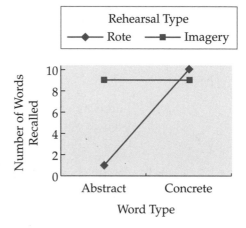

WEB RESOURCES

Check your knowledge of the content and key terms in this module with a practice quiz and interactive flashcards at **www.cengage.com/psychology/jackson,** or for step-by-step practice and information, check out the Statistics and Research Methods Workshops at **www.cengage.com/psychology/workshops**.

LAB RESOURCES

For hands-on experience using the research methods described in this module, see Chapters 5 ("One-Way Designs I"), 6 ("One-Way Designs II"), 7 ("Factorial Designs I"), and 8 ("Factorial Designs II") in *Research Methods Laboratory Manual for Psychology*, 2nd ed., by William Langston (Belmont, CA: Wadsworth, 2005).

CHAPTER SIX SUMMARY AND REVIEW: EXPLANATORY METHODS

Researchers need to consider several factors when designing and evaluating a true experiment. First, they need to address the issues of control and possible confounds. The study needs to be designed with strong control and no confounds to maximize internal validity. Second, researchers need to consider external validity in order to ensure that the study is as generalizable as possible while maintaining control. In addition, they should use the design most appropriate for the type of research they are conducting. Researchers should consider the strengths and weaknesses of each of the three types of designs (between-, within-, and matched-participants) when determining which is best for their study. Further, when conducting developmental studies, researchers can choose from three designs: a cross-sectional design, a longitudinal design, or a combination of the two, called a sequential design.

At times researchers need to determine whether a design using more than two levels of an independent variable might be appropriate. Advantages to such designs include being able to compare more than two kinds of treatment, to use fewer participants, to compare all treatments with a control group, and to use placebo groups. Researchers might also consider experimental designs that use more than one independent variable. We discussed several advantages of using such designs and introduced the concepts of factorial notation, main effects, and interaction effects. After reading the section on main and interaction effects, you should be able to create a graph with data from a factorial design and interpret it.

CHAPTER SIX REVIEW EXERCISES

(Answers to exercises appear in Appendix A.)

Fill-in Self-Test

Answer the following questions. If you have trouble answering any of the questions, restudy the relevant material before going on to the multiple-choice self-test.

1. An experiment in which different participants are assigned to each group is a _____.
2. When we use _____, we determine who serves in each group in an experiment randomly.
3. When the dependent variable is measured both before and after manipulation of the independent variable, we are using a _____ design.
4. _____ is the extent to which the results of an experiment can be attributed to the manipulation of the independent variable rather than to a confounding variable.
5. A(n) _____ is a threat to internal validity where the possibility of participants' naturally occurring changes is responsible for the observed results.
6. If there is a problem with the measuring device then there may be a(n) _____ effect.
7. If participants talk to each other about an experiment, there may be _____.
8. When neither the experimenter nor the participant know the condition to which each participant has been assigned, a _____ experiment is being used.

9. When the measuring device is limited in such a way that scores at the top of the scale cannot be differentiated, there is a _____ effect.

10. The extent to which the results of an experiment can be generalized is called _____.

11. When a study is based on another study but uses different methods, a different manipulation, or a different measure, we are conducting a _____ replication.

12. If the order of conditions affects the results in a within-participants design, then there are _____.

13. When participants from different age groups all serve together in the same experiment, a _____ developmental design is being used.

14. A _____ is an inert substance that participants believe is a treatment.

15. The notation that indicates how many independent variables were used in a study and how many levels there were for each variable is called _____.

16. An effect of a single independent variable is a _____.

17. In a 4 × 6 factorial design there are _____ independent variables, one with _____ levels and one with _____ levels.

Multiple-Choice Self-Test

Select the single best answer for each of the following questions. If you have trouble answering any of the questions, restudy the relevant material.

1. Manipulate is to measure as _____ is to _____.
   a. independent variable; dependent variable
   b. dependent variable; independent variable
   c. control group; experimental group
   d. experimental group; control group

2. In an experimental study of the effects of stress on appetite, stress is the _____.
   a. dependent variable
   b. independent variable
   c. control group
   d. experimental group

3. In an experimental study of the effects of stress on appetite, participants are randomly assigned to either the no-stress group or the stress group. These groups represent the _____ and the _____, respectively.
   a. independent variable; dependent variable
   b. dependent variable; independent variable
   c. control group; experimental group
   d. experimental group; control group

4. Within-participants design is to between participants design as _____ is to _____.
   a. using different participants in each group; using the same participants in each group
   b. using the same participants in each group; using different participants in each group
   c. matched-participants design; correlated-groups design
   d. experimental group; control group

5. The extent to which the results of an experiment can be attributed to the manipulation of the independent variable rather than to some confounding variable refers to _____.
   a. external validity
   b. generalization to populations
   c. internal validity
   d. both b and c

6. Joann conducted an experiment to test the effectiveness of an antianxiety program. The experiment took place over a 1-month time period. Participants in the control group and the experimental group (those who participated in the antianxiety program) recorded their anxiety levels several times each day. Joann was unaware that

midterm exams also happened to take place during the 1-month time period of her experiment. Joann's experiment is now confounded by _____.
a. a maturation effect
b. a history effect
c. regression to the mean
d. a mortality effect

7. Joe scored very low on the SAT the first time he took it. Based on the confound of _____, if Joe were to retake the SAT, his score should

_____.
a. instrumentation; increase
b. instrumentation; decrease
c. regression to the mean; increase
d. regression to the mean; decrease

8. What does the confound of mortality mean?
a. Participants are lost equally from both the experimental and control groups.
b. Participants die as a result of participating in the experiment.
c. Participants boycott the experiment.
d. Participants are lost differentially from the experimental and control groups.

9. Controlling participant effects is to controlling both participant and experimenter effects as _____ is to _____.
a. fatigue effects; practice effects
b. practice effects; fatigue effects
c. double-blind experiment; single-blind experiment
d. single-blind experiment; double-blind experiment

10. If you were to use a bathroom scale to weigh mice in an experimental setting, your experiment would most likely suffer from a _____ effect.
a. ceiling
b. floor
c. practice
d. fatigue

11. If we were to conduct a replication in which we increased the number of levels of the independent variable, we would be using a(n) _____ replication.

a. exact
b. conceptual
c. exact
d. systematic

12. Most psychology experiments suffer from the _____ problem because of the type of participants used.
a. diffusion of treatment
b. college sophomore
c. regression to the mean
d. mortality

13. What happens when we manipulate more than one independent variable in a study?
a. We have significant main effects.
b. We have at least one significant interaction effect.
c. We are using a factorial design.
d. All of the above.

14. In a study examining the effects of time of day (morning, afternoon, or evening) and teaching style (lecture only versus lecture with small group discussion) on student attentiveness, how many main effects are possible?
a. 3
b. 6
c. 5
d. 2

15. In a study examining the effects of time of day (morning, afternoon, or evening) and teaching style (lecture only versus lecture with small group discussion) on student attentiveness, how many interaction effects are possible?
a. 1
b. 2
c. 6
d. 5

16. In a study examining the effects of time of day (morning, afternoon, or evening) and teaching style (lecture only versus lecture with small group discussion) on student attentiveness, the factorial notation would be _____.
a. 2 × 2
b. 2 × 3
c. 2 × 5
d. 3 × 3

17. A 2 × 4 × 5 × 6 factorial design has _____ potential main effects.
    a. 2
    b. 3
    c. 4
    d. 24

18. An experiment with three independent variables, each with three levels, is a _____ design.
    a. 2 × 3
    b. 3 × 3
    c. 2 × 2 × 2
    d. 3 × 3 × 3

19. If the lines in a graph are not parallel, then there is most likely _____.
    a. a main effect of variable A
    b. a main effect of variable B
    c. an interaction effect
    d. all of the above

20. In terms of developmental designs, a _____ design is being used when the researcher tests the same participants at different ages over many years.
    a. matched-participants
    b. sequential
    c. cross-sectional
    d. longitudinal

KEY TERMS

Here are the terms from the glossary presented earlier. Go through the list and see if you can remember the definition of each.

Between-participants design	Double-blind experiment	Latin square	Pretest/posttest control group design
Ceiling effect	Exact replication	Longitudinal design	Sequential design
Cohort	Experimenter effect	Main effect	Single-blind experiment
Cohort effect	External validity	Matched-participants design	Subject (participant) effect
College sophomore problem	Factorial design	Maturation effect	Systematic replication
Conceptual replication	Factorial notation	Mortality (attrition)	Testing effect
Correlated-groups design	Floor effect	Order effects	Within-participants design
Counterbalancing	History effect	Placebo	
Cross-sectional design	Instrumentation effect	Placebo group	
Diffusion of treatment	Interaction effect	Posttest-only control group design	

CHAPTER 7

Descriptive Statistics

16 | TRANSFORMATION SCORES AND CORRELATION COEFFICIENTS

Types of Distributions
Normal Distributions
Kurtosis
Positively Skewed Distributions
Negatively Skewed Distributions

z-Scores
z-Scores, the Standard Normal Distribution, Probability, and Percentile
  Ranks

Correlation Coefficients
Advanced Correlational Techniques: Regression Analysis

SUMMARY
REVIEW OF KEY TERMS
MODULE EXERCISES
CRITICAL THINKING CHECK ANSWERS
WEB RESOURCES

CHAPTER SEVEN SUMMARY AND REVIEW: DESCRIPTIVE STATISTICS

In this chapter we begin to discuss what to do with the observations made in the course of a study, namely, how to describe the data set through the use of descriptive statistics. First, we consider ways of organizing the data. We need to take the large number of observations made during a study and present them in a manner that is easier to read and understand. Second, we discuss some simple descriptive statistics. These statistics allow us to do "number crunching," that is, to condense a large number of observations into a summary statistic or set of statistics. The concepts and statistics we describe in this chapter can be used to draw conclusions from data collected through descriptive, predictive, or explanatory methods. They do not come close to covering all that can be done with data gathered from a study. They do, however, provide a place to start.

MODULE **15**

Data Organization, Central Tendency, and Variance

LEARNING OBJECTIVES

- Organize data in either a frequency distribution or class interval frequency distribution.

- Graph data in either a bar graph, histogram, or frequency polygon.

- Differentiate measures of central tendency.

- Know how to calculate the mean, median, and mode

- Differentiate measures of variation.

- Know how to calculate the range, standard deviation, and variance.

ORGANIZING DATA

We discuss two methods of organizing data: frequency distributions and graphs.

Frequency Distributions

To illustrate the processes of organizing and describing data, let's use the data set presented in Table 15.1. These data represent the scores of 30 students on an introductory psychology exam. One reason for organizing data and using statistics is to draw meaningful conclusions. The list of exam scores in Table 15.1 is simply that—a list in no particular order. As shown, the data are not especially meaningful. One of the first steps in organizing these data might be to rearrange them from highest to lowest or from lowest to highest.

frequency distribution: A table in which all of the scores are listed along with the frequency with which each occurs.

Once the scores are ordered (see Table 15.2), we can condense the data into a **frequency distribution**, a table in which all of the scores are listed along with the frequency with which each occurs. We can also show the relative frequency, which is the proportion of the total observations included in each score. When a relative frequency is multiplied by 100, it is read as a percentage. A frequency distribution and a relative frequency distribution of our exam data are presented in Table 15.3.

class interval frequency distribution: A table in which the scores are grouped into intervals and listed along with the frequency of scores in each interval.

The frequency distribution is a way of presenting data that makes their pattern easier to see. We can make the data set still easier to read (especially desirable with large data sets) if we group the scores and create a class interval frequency distribution. In a **class interval frequency distribution** we combine individual scores into categories, or intervals, and list them along with the frequency of scores in each interval. In our exam score example the scores range from 45 to 95, a 50-point range. A rule of thumb when creating class intervals is to have between 10 and 20 categories (Hinkle, Wiersma, & Jurs, 1988). A quick method of calculating what the width of the interval should be is to subtract the lowest score from the highest score and then divide the result by the number of intervals we would like (Schweigert, 1994). If we want 10 intervals in our example, we proceed as follows:

$$\frac{95-45}{10} = \frac{50}{10} = 5$$

Table 15.4 is the frequency distribution using class intervals with a width of 5. Notice how much more compact the data appear when presented in a class interval frequency distribution. Although such distributions have the advantage of reducing the number of categories, they have the disadvantage of not providing as much information as a regular frequency distribution. Consequently, although we can see from the class interval frequency distribution that five people scored between 75 and 79, we do not know their exact scores within the interval.

Graphs

Frequency distributions provide valuable information, but sometimes a picture is of greater value. Several types of pictorial representations can be used to represent data. The choice depends on the type of data collected and what the researcher hopes to emphasize or illustrate. The most common graphs used by

TABLE **15.1**
Exam scores
for 30 Students

56	74
69	70
78	90
80	74
47	59
85	86
82	92
74	60
95	63
65	45
54	94
60	93
87	82
76	77
75	78

TABLE **15.2**
Exam Scores Ordered
from Lowest to Highest

45	76
47	77
54	78
56	78
59	80
60	82
60	82
63	85
65	86
69	87
70	90
74	92
74	93
74	94
75	95

TABLE **15.3**
Frequency and Relative Frequency Distributions
of Exam Data

Score	f (frequency)	rf (relative frequency)
45	1	.033
47	1	.033
54	1	.033
56	1	.033
59	1	.033
60	2	.067
63	1	.033
65	1	.033
69	1	.033
70	1	.033
74	3	.100
75	1	.033
76	1	.033
77	1	.033
78	2	.067
80	1	.033
82	2	.067
85	1	.033
86	1	.033
87	1	.033
90	1	.033
92	1	.033
93	1	.033
94	1	.033
95	1	.033
	$N = 30$	1.00

psychologists are bar graphs, histograms, and frequency polygons (line graphs). Graphs typically have two coordinate axes: the x-axis (the horizontal axis) and the y-axis (the vertical axis). The y-axis is usually shorter than the x-axis, typically 60–75% of the length of the x-axis.

Bar Graphs and Histograms

qualitative variable:
A categorical variable
for which each value
represents a discrete
category.

Bar graphs and histograms are frequently confused. If the data collected are on a nominal scale or if the variable is a **qualitative variable** (a categorical

TABLE **15.4**

A Class Interval Distribution of the Exam Data

Class Interval	f	rf
45–49	2	.067
50–54	1	.033
55–59	2	.067
60–64	3	.100
65–69	2	.067
70–74	4	.133
75–79	5	.166
80–84	3	.100
85–89	3	.100
90–94	4	.133
95–99	1	.033
	N = 30	1.00

bar graph: A graphical representation of a frequency distribution in which vertical bars are centered above each category along the x-axis and are separated from each other by a space, which indicates that the levels of the variable represent distinct, unrelated categories.

quantitative variable: A variable for which the scores represent a change in quantity.

histogram: A graphical representation of a frequency distribution in which vertical bars centered above scores on the x-axis touch each other to indicate that the scores on the variable represent related, increasing values.

variable for which each value represents a discrete category), then a bar graph is most appropriate. A **bar graph** is a graphical representation of a frequency distribution in which vertical bars are centered above each category along the x-axis and are separated from each other by a space, which indicates that the levels of the variable represent distinct, unrelated categories.

If the variable is a **quantitative variable** (the scores represent a change in quantity) or if the data collected are ordinal, interval, or ratio in scale, then a histogram can be used. A **histogram** is also a graphical representation of a frequency distribution in which vertical bars are centered above scores on the x-axis, but in a histogram the bars touch each other to indicate that the scores on the variable represent related, increasing values.

In both a bar graph and a histogram the height of each bar indicates the frequency for that level of the variable on the x-axis. The spaces between the bars on the bar graph indicate not only the qualitative differences among the categories but also that the order of the values of the variable on the x-axis is arbitrary. In other words, the categories on the x-axis in a bar graph can be placed in any order. The contiguous bars in a histogram indicate not only the increasing quantity of the variable but also that the values of the variable have a definite order that cannot be changed.

A bar graph for a hypothetical distribution is illustrated in Figure 15.1, which indicates the frequencies of individuals who affiliate with various political parties. Notice that the different political parties are listed on the x-axis, and frequency is recorded on the y-axis. Although the political parties are presented in a certain order, this order could be rearranged because the variable is qualitative.

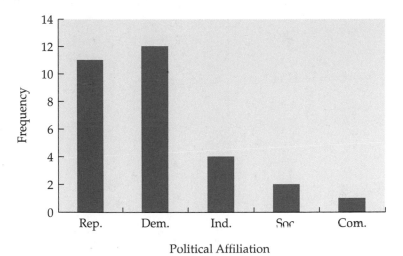

FIGURE **15.1** Bar graph representing political affiliation for a distribution of 30 individuals

Figure 15.2 illustrates a histogram. In this figure the frequencies of intelligence test scores from a hypothetical distribution are indicated. A histogram is appropriate because the IQ score variable is quantitative. The values of the variable have a specific order that cannot be rearranged.

frequency polygon:
A line graph of the frequencies of individual scores.

Frequency Polygons

We can also depict the data in a histogram as a **frequency polygon**, that is, a line graph of the frequencies of individual scores or intervals. Again, scores

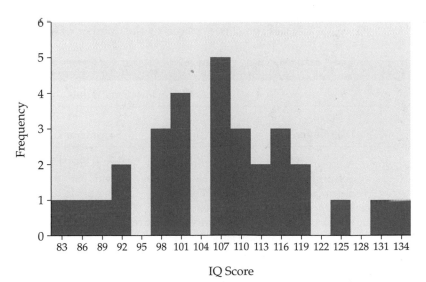

FIGURE **15.2** Histogram representing IQ score data for 30 individuals

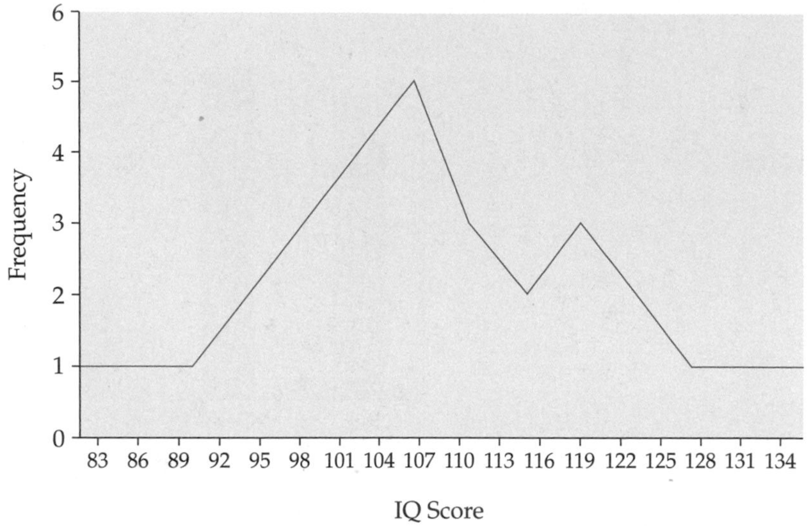

FIGURE **15.3** Frequency polygon of IQ score data for 30 individuals

(or intervals) are shown on the *x*-axis and frequencies on the *y*-axis. Once all the frequencies are plotted, the data points are connected. You can see the frequency polygon for the intelligence score data in Figure 15.3.

Frequency polygons are appropriate when the variable is quantitative or the data are ordinal, interval, or ratio. In this respect frequency polygons are similar to histograms. They are especially useful for continuous data (such as age, weight, or time) in which it is theoretically possible for values to fall anywhere along the continuum. For example, an individual may weigh 120.5 pounds or be 35.5 years old. Histograms are more appropriate when the data are discrete (measured in whole units), as for example the number of college classes taken or the number of siblings.

IN REVIEW	Data Organization			
Types of Organizational Tools				
	Frequency Distribution	Bar Graph	Histogram	Frequency Polygon
Description	A list of all scores occurring in the distribution along with the frequency of each	A pictorial graph with bars representing the frequency of occurrence of items for qualitative variables	A pictorial graph with bars representing the frequency of occurrence of items for quantitative variables	A line graph representing the frequency of occurrence of items for quantitative variables
Use with	Nominal, ordinal, interval, or ratio data	Nominal data	Typically ordinal, interval, or ratio data; most appropriate for discrete data	Typically ordinal, interval, or ratio data; most appropriate for continuous data

DESCRIPTIVE STATISTICS

descriptive statistics: Numerical measures that describe a distribution by providing information on the central tendency of the distribution, the width of the distribution, and the shape of the distribution.

Organizing data into tables and graphs can make a data set more meaningful. These methods, however, do not provide as much information as numerical measures. **Descriptive statistics** are numerical measures that describe a distribution by providing information on the central tendency of the distribution, the width of the distribution, and the distribution's shape.

Measures of Central Tendency

measure of central tendency: A number that characterizes the "middleness" of an entire distribution.

A **measure of central tendency** is a representative number that characterizes the "middleness" of an entire set of data. The three measures of central tendency are the mean, the median, and the mode.

Mean

mean: A measure of central tendency; the arithmetic average of a distribution.

The most commonly used measure of central tendency is the **mean**, that is, the arithmetic average of a group of scores. You are probably familiar with this idea. We can calculate the mean for our distribution of exam scores by adding all of the scores together and dividing the sum by the total number of scores. Mathematically, this is

$$\mu = \frac{\sum X}{N}$$

where

μ (pronounced "mu") represents the symbol for the population mean;

$\sum$ represents the symbol for "the sum of";

X represents the individual scores; and

N represents the number of scores in the distribution.

To calculate the mean, we sum all of the Xs, or scores, and divide by the total number of scores in the distribution (N). You may have also seen this formula represented as

$$\overline{X} = \frac{\sum X}{N}$$

In this formula $\overline{X}$ represents the sample mean and N the number of scores in the sample.

TABLE **15.5**

Frequency Distribution of Exam Scores, Including an fX Column

X	f	fX
45	1	45
47	1	47
54	1	54
56	1	56
59	1	59
60	2	120
63	1	63
65	1	65
69	1	69
70	1	70
74	3	222
75	1	75
76	1	76
77	1	77
78	2	156
80	1	80
82	2	164
85	1	85
86	1	86
87	1	87
90	1	90
92	1	92
93	1	93
94	1	94
95	1	95
N = 30		$\sum X = 2{,}220$

We can use either formula (they are the same) to calculate the mean for the distribution of exam scores. These scores are presented again in Table 15.5 along with a column showing the frequency (f) and another column showing the frequency of the score multiplied by the score (f times X or fX). The sum of all the values in the fX column is the sum of all the individual scores ($\sum X$). Using this sum in the formula for the mean, we have

$$\mu = \frac{\sum X}{N} = \frac{2{,}220}{30} = 74.00$$

You can also calculate the mean using statistical software packages such as SPSS or Excel or with the Stats function on most calculators. The procedures for calculating the mean using SPSS, Excel, and the TI84 calculator are presented in Appendix C. The use of the mean is constrained by the nature of the data: The mean is appropriate for interval and ratio data, but not for ordinal or nominal data.

Median

Another measure of central tendency, the median, is used when the mean might not be representative of a distribution. Let's use a different distribution of scores to demonstrate when it is appropriate to use the median rather than the mean. Imagine that you are considering taking a job with a small computer company. When you interview for the position, the owner of the company informs you that the mean salary for employees at the company is approximately $100,000 and that the company has 25 employees. Most people would view this as good news. Having learned in a statistics class that the mean might be influenced by extreme scores, however, you ask to see the distribution of 25 salaries. The distribution is shown in Table 15.6. The calculation of the mean for this distribution is

$$\frac{\sum X}{N} = \frac{2,498,000}{25} = 99,920$$

TABLE **15.6**
Yearly Salaries for 25 Employees

Salary	Frequency	fx
$ 15,000	1	15,000
20,000	2	40,000
22,000	1	22,000
23,000	2	46,000
25,000	5	125,000
27,000	2	54,000
30,000	3	90,000
32,000	1	32,000
35,000	2	70,000
38,000	1	38,000
39,000	1	39,000
40,000	1	40,000
42,000	1	42,000
45,000	1	45,000
1,800,000	1	1,800,000
	N = 25	$\sum X$ = 2,498,000

Notice that, as claimed, the mean salary of company employees is very close to $100,000. Notice also, however, that the mean in this case is not very representative of central tendency, or middleness. The mean is thrown off center or inflated by the one extreme score of $1,800,000 (the salary of the company's owner, needless to say). This extremely high salary pulls the mean toward it and thus increases or inflates the mean. Thus in distributions with one or a few extreme scores (either high or low), the mean is not a good indicator of central tendency. In such cases a better measure of central tendency is the median.

median: A measure of central tendency; the middle score in a distribution after the scores have been arranged from highest to lowest or lowest to highest.

The **median** is the middle score in a distribution after the scores have been arranged from highest to lowest or lowest to highest. The distribution of salaries in Table 15.6 is already ordered from lowest to highest. To determine the median, we simply have to find the middle score. In this case, with 25 scores, that is the 13th score. You can see that the median of the distribution is a salary of $27,000, which is far more representative of the central tendency for this distribution.

Why is the median not as influenced as the mean by extreme scores? Think about the calculation of each of these measures. When calculating the mean, we must add in the atypical income of $1,800,000, thus distorting the calculation. When determining the median, however, we do not consider the size of the $1,800,000 income; it is only a score at one end of the distribution whose numerical value does not have to be considered to locate the middle score in the distribution. The point to remember is that the median is not affected by extreme scores in a distribution because it is only a positional value. The mean is affected because its value is determined by a calculation that has to include the extreme values.

In the salary example the distribution has an odd number of scores ($N = 25$). Accordingly, the median is an actual score in the distribution (the 13th score). In distributions with an even number of observations, the median is calculated by averaging the two middle scores. That is, we determine the middle point between the two middle scores. Look back at the distribution of exam scores in Table 15.5. This distribution has 30 scores. The median is the average of the 15th and 16th scores (the two middle scores). Thus, the median is 75.5—not an actual score in the distribution, but the middle point nonetheless. Notice that in this distribution, the median (75.5) is very close to the mean (74.00). Why are they so similar? Because this distribution contains no extreme scores; both the mean and the median are representative of the central tendency of the distribution.

Like the mean, the median can be used with ratio and interval data and is inappropriate for use with nominal data, but unlike the mean, the median can be used with most ordinal data. In other words, it is appropriate to report the median for a distribution of ranked scores.

Mode

mode: A measure of central tendency; the score in a distribution that occurs with the greatest frequency.

The third measure of central tendency is the **mode**, the score in a distribution that occurs with the greatest frequency. In the distribution of exam scores the mode is 74 (similar to the mean and median). In the distribution of salaries the mode is $25,000 (similar to the median but not the mean). In some distributions all scores occur with equal frequency; such a distribution has no mode. In other distributions several scores occur with equal frequency. Thus a distribution may have two modes (bimodal), three modes (trimodal), or even more. The mode is the only indicator of central tendency that can be used with nominal data. Although it can also be used with ordinal, interval, or ratio data, the mean and median are more reliable indicators of the central tendency of a distribution, and the mode is seldom used.

IN REVIEW	Measures of Central Tendency		
	Types of Central Tendency Measures		
	Mean	**Median**	**Mode**
Definition	The arithmetic average	The middle score in a distribution of scores organized from highest to lowest or lowest to highest	The score occurring with greatest frequency
Use with	Interval and ratio data	Ordinal, interval, and ratio data	Nominal, ordinal, interval, or ratio data
Cautions	Not for use with distributions with a few extreme scores		Not a reliable measure of central tendency

CRITICAL THINKING CHECK 15.2

1. In the example described in Critical Thinking Check 15.1, a researcher collected data on drivers' gender, type of vehicle, and speed of travel. What is an appropriate measure of central tendency to calculate for each type of data?
2. If one driver was traveling at 100 mph (25 mph faster than anyone else), which measure of central tendency would you recommend against using?

MEASURES OF VARIATION

measure of variation: A number that indicates the degree to which scores are either clustered or spread out in a distribution.

A measure of central tendency provides information about the middleness of a distribution of scores but not about the width or spread of the distribution. To assess the width of a distribution, we need a measure of variation or dispersion. A **measure of variation** indicates the degree to which scores are either clustered or spread out in a distribution. As an illustration, consider the two very small distributions of exam scores shown in Table 15.7. Notice that the mean is the same for both distributions. If these data represented two very small classes of students, reporting that the two classes had the same mean on the exam might lead one to conclude that the classes performed essentially the same. Notice, however, how different the distributions are. Providing a measure of variation along with a measure of central tendency conveys the information that even though the distributions have the same mean, their spreads are very different.

The three measures of variation to be discussed are the range, the standard deviation, and variance. The range can be used with ordinal, interval, or ratio data, whereas the standard deviation and variance are appropriate for only interval and ratio data.

TABLE **15.7**

Two Distributions of
Exam Scores

Class 1	Class 2
0	45
50	50
100	55
$\sum = 150$	$\sum = 150$
$\mu = 50$	$\mu = 50$

range: A measure of
variation; the difference
between the lowest and
the highest scores in a
distribution.

standard deviation: A
measure of variation,
the average difference
between the scores in the
distribution and the mean
or central point of the
distribution or more
precisely the square root
of the average squared
deviation from the mean.

Range

The simplest measure of variation is the **range,** the difference between the lowest and the highest scores in a distribution. The range is usually reported with the mean of the distribution. To find the range, we simply subtract the lowest score from the highest score. In our hypothetical distributions of exam scores in Table 15.7, the range for Class 1 is 100 points, whereas the range for Class 2 is 10 points. The range therefore provides information concerning the difference in the spreads of the distributions. In this simple measure of variation, however, only the highest and lowest scores enter the calculation, and all other scores are ignored. For example, in the distribution of 30 exam scores presented in Table 15.1, only 2 of the 30 scores are used in calculating the range ($95 - 45 = 50$). Consequently the range is easily distorted by one unusually high or low score in a distribution.

Standard Deviation

More sophisticated measures of variation use all of the scores in the distribution in their calculation. The most commonly used measure of variation is the *standard deviation.* Most people have heard of this term before and may even have calculated a standard deviation if they have taken a statistics class. However, many people who know how to calculate a standard deviation do not really appreciate the information it provides.

To begin, let's think about what the phrase *standard deviation* means. Other words that might be substituted for the word *standard* include *average, normal,* and *usual.* The word *deviation* means to *diverge, move away from,* or *digress.* Putting these terms together, we see that the standard deviation means the average movement away from something—but what? It is the average movement away from the center of the distribution, that is, the mean.

The **standard deviation** then is the average distance of all the scores in the distribution from the mean or central point of the distribution or, as we will see shortly, the square root of the average squared deviation from the mean. To calculate the average distance of all the scores from the mean of the distribution, we first have to determine how far each score is from the mean; this is the deviation, or difference, score. Then we have to average these scores. This concept is the basic idea behind calculating the standard deviation.

Let's use the exam score data from Table 15.5 to calculate the average distance from the mean. Referring to Table 15.8, you can see that we begin by determining how much each score deviates from the mean, or

$$X - \mu$$

Then we need to sum the deviation scores. Notice, however, that if we were to sum these scores, they would add to zero. Therefore we square the deviation scores to "get rid of" the negative deviation scores, as shown in the third column of Table 15.8. To calculate the standard deviation, we sum the squared deviation scores:

$$\sum (X - \mu)^2$$

Next we divide the sum by the total number of scores to find the standard deviation and then take the square root of that number. Why? Squaring the deviation scores has inflated them. We now need to bring the squared

TABLE **15.8**

Calculations for the Sum of the Squared Deviation Scores

X	X − μ	(X − μ)²
45	−29.00	841.00
47	−27.00	729.00
54	−20.00	400.00
56	−18.00	324.00
59	−15.00	225.00
60	−14.00	196.00
60	−14.00	196.00
63	−11.00	121.00
65	−9.00	81.00
69	−5.00	25.00
70	−4.00	16.00
74	0.00	0.00
74	0.00	0.00
74	0.00	0.00
75	1.00	1.00
76	2.00	4.00
77	3.00	9.00
78	4.00	16.00
78	4.00	16.00
80	6.00	36.00
82	8.00	64.00
82	8.00	64.00
85	11.00	121.00
86	12.00	144.00
87	13.00	169.00
90	16.00	256.00
92	18.00	324.00
93	19.00	361.00
94	20.00	400.00
95	21.00	441.00
		$\sum(X - \mu)^2 - 5{,}580.00$

deviation scores back to the same level of measurement as the mean so that the standard deviation is measured on the same scale as the mean.

$$\sigma = \sqrt{\frac{\sum (X - \mu)^2}{N}}$$

This formula represents the standard deviation for a population. The symbol for the population standard deviation is σ (pronounced "sigma"). To derive the standard deviation for a sample, the calculation is the same, but the symbols differ; we simply use S rather than σ.

Now using the sum of the squared deviation scores (5,580.00) from Table 15.8, we can calculate the standard deviation:

$$\sigma = \sqrt{\frac{\sum (X - \mu)^2}{N}} = \sqrt{\frac{5580.00}{30}} = \sqrt{186.00} = 13.64$$

The standard deviation tells us that the exam scores fall an average of 13.64 points from the mean of 74.00.

If you have taken a statistics class, you may have used the raw-score (or computational) formula to calculate the standard deviation. The raw-score formula is shown in Table 15.9 in which it is used to calculate the standard deviation for the same distribution of exam scores. The numerator represents an algebraic transformation from the original formula that is somewhat shorter to use. Although the raw-score formula is slightly easier to use, it is more difficult to equate this formula with what the standard deviation actually is—the average deviation (or distance) from the mean for all the scores in the distribution. Thus the definitional formula allows you not only to calculate the statistic but also to understand it better.

If we are using sample data to *estimate* the population standard deviation, then the standard deviation formula must be slightly modified. The modification provides what is called an "unbiased estimator" of the population standard deviation based on sample data. The modified formula is

$$s = \sqrt{\frac{\sum (X - \overline{X})^2}{N - 1}}$$

TABLE **15.9**
Standard Deviation Raw-Score Formula

$$\sigma = \sqrt{\frac{\sum X^2 - \frac{(\sum X)^2}{N}}{N}} = \sqrt{\frac{169,860 - \frac{(2,220)^2}{30}}{30}} = \sqrt{\frac{169,860 - \frac{4,928,400}{30}}{30}}$$

$$= \sqrt{\frac{169,860 - 164,280}{30}} = \sqrt{\frac{5,580}{30}} = \sqrt{186} = 13.64$$

Notice that the symbol for the unbiased estimator of the population standard deviation is s (lowercase), whereas the symbol for the sample standard deviation is S (uppercase). The main difference, however, is the denominator $N - 1$ rather than N. The reason for this difference in the denominators between the two formulas is that the standard deviation within a small sample may not be representative of the population; that is, there may not be as much variability in the sample as there actually is in the population. We therefore divide by $N - 1$ when estimating the population standard deviation from sample data because dividing by a smaller number increases the standard deviation and therefore provides a better estimate of the population standard deviation.

We can use the formula for s to calculate the standard deviation on the same set of exam score data. Before we even begin the calculation, we know that because we are dividing by a smaller number $(N - 1)$, s should be larger than either σ or S (which were both 13.64). Normally we would not compute σ, S, and s on the same distribution of scores because σ is the standard deviation for the population, S is the standard deviation for a sample, and s is the unbiased estimator of the population standard deviation based on sample data. We do so here to illustrate the differences between the formulas.

$$s = \sqrt{\frac{\sum (X - \overline{X})^2}{N - 1}} = \sqrt{\frac{5580.00}{30 - 1}} = \sqrt{\frac{5580.00}{29}} = \sqrt{192.41379} = 13.87$$

Note that s (13.87) is slightly larger than σ and S (13.64). The procedures for calculating the standard deviation using SPSS, Excel, and the TI84 calculator are shown in Appendix C.

variance: The standard deviation squared.

One final measure of variability is called the **variance**, which is equal to the standard deviation squared. The variance for a population is σ^2, for a sample S^2, and for the unbiased estimator of the population s^2. Because the variance is not measured in the same level of measurement as the mean (it is the standard deviation squared), it is not as useful a descriptive statistic as the standard deviation. As a consequence we do not discuss it in great detail here. We will see, however, that it is used in more advanced statistical procedures presented later in the text.

The formulas for the standard deviation and variance all use the mean. Thus it is appropriate to use these measures with interval or ratio data but not with ordinal or nominal data.

IN REVIEW Measures of Variation

Types of Variation Measures

	Range	Standard Deviation
Definition	The difference between the lowest and highest scores in the distribution	The square root of the average squared deviation from the mean of a distribution
Use with	Primarily interval and ratio data	Interval and ratio data
Cautions	A simple measure that does not use all scores in the distribution in its calculation	The most sophisticated and most frequently used measure of variation

<table>
<tr>
<td>

CRITICAL
THINKING
CHECK 15.3

</td>
<td>

1. For a distribution of scores what information does a measure of variation convey that a measure of central tendency does not?
2. Today's weather report included information on the normal rainfall for this time of year. The amount of rain that fell today was 1.5 inches above normal. To decide whether this amount is abnormally high, you need to know that the standard deviation for rainfall is 0.75 inch. What would you conclude about how normal the amount of rainfall was today? Would your conclusion be different if the standard deviation were 2 inches rather than 0.75 inch?

</td>
</tr>
</table>

SUMMARY

In this module we discussed data organization and descriptive statistics. We presented several methods of data organization, including a frequency distribution, a bar graph, a histogram, and a frequency polygon. We also discussed the types of data appropriate for each of these methods.

Descriptive statistics that summarize a large data set include measures of central tendency (mean, median, and mode) and measures of variation (range and standard deviation). These statistics provide information about the central tendency, or "middleness," of a distribution of scores and about the spread of a distribution of scores.

REVIEW OF KEY TERMS

frequency distribution	quantitative variable	measure of central tendency	measure of variation
class interval frequency distribution	histogram	mean	range
	frequency polygon	median	standard deviation
qualitative variable	descriptive statistics	mode	variance
bar graph			

MODULE EXERCISES

(Answers to odd-numbered exercises appear in Appendix A.)

1. The following data represent a distribution of speeds (in miles per hour) at which individuals were traveling on a highway.

64	80	64	70
76	79	67	72
65	73	68	65
67	65	70	62
67	68	65	64

Organize these data into a frequency distribution with frequency (f) and relative frequency (rf) columns.

2. Organize the data in Exercise 1 into a class interval frequency distribution using 10 intervals with frequency (f) and relative frequency (rf) columns.
3. Which type of figure should be used to represent the data in Exercise 1: a bar graph, histogram, or frequency polygon? Why? Draw the appropriate figure for these data.

4. Calculate the mean, median, and mode for the data set in Exercise 1. Is the distribution normal or skewed? Which measure of central tendency is most appropriate for this distribution? Why?

5. Calculate the mean, median, and mode for the following four distributions (a–d):

a	b	c	d
2	1	1	2
2	2	3	3
4	3	3	4
5	4	3	5
8	4	5	6
9	5	5	6
10	5	8	6

a	b	c	d
11	5	8	7
11	6	8	8
11	6	9	8
	8	10	
	9	11	

6. Calculate the range and standard deviation for the following five distributions:
   a. 1, 2, 3, 4, 5, 6, 7, 8, 9
   b. −4, −3, −2, −1, 0, 1, 2, 3, 4
   c. 10, 20, 30, 40, 50, 60, 70, 80, 90
   d. 0.1, 0.2, 0.3, 0.4, 0.5, 0.6, 0.7, 0.8, 0.9
   e. 100, 200, 300, 400, 500, 600, 700, 800, 900

CRITICAL THINKING CHECK ANSWERS

15.1

1. One advantage is that it is easier to "see" the data set in a graphical representation. A picture makes it easier to determine where the majority of the scores are in the distribution. A frequency distribution requires more reading before a judgment can be made about the shape of the distribution.

2. Gender and the type of vehicle driven are qualitative variables, measured on a nominal scale; thus a bar graph should be used. The speed at which the drivers are traveling is a quantitative variable, measured on a ratio scale. Either a histogram or a frequency polygon could be used. A frequency polygon might be better because of the continuous nature of the variable.

15.2

1. Because gender and the type of vehicle driven are nominal data, only the mode can be determined; it is inappropriate to use the median or the mean with these data. Speed of travel is ratio in scale, so the mean, median, or mode could be used. Both the mean and median are better indicators of central tendency than the mode. If the distribution is skewed, however, the mean should not be used.

2. In this case the mean should not be used because of the single outlier (extreme score) in the distribution.

15.3

1. A measure of variation tells us about the spread of the distribution. In other words, are the scores clustered closely about the mean, or are they spread over a wide range?

2. The amount of rainfall for the indicated day is 2 standard deviations above the mean. The amount of rainfall was well above average. If the standard deviation were 2 rather than 0.75, then the amount of rainfall for the indicated day would be less than 1 standard deviation above the mean—above average but not greatly so.

WEB RESOURCES

Check your knowledge of the content and key terms in this module with a practice quiz and interactive flashcards at **www.cengage.com/ psychology/jackson,** or for step-by-step practice and information, check out the Statistics and Research Methods Workshops at **www.cengage. com/psychology/workshops.**

MODULE **16**

Transformation Scores and Correlation Coefficients

LEARNING OBJECTIVES

- Explain the difference between a normal distribution and a skewed distribution.

- Explain the difference between a positively skewed distribution and a negatively skewed distribution.

- Differentiate the types of kurtosis.

- Describe what a z-score is and know how to calculate it.

- Use the area under the normal curve to determine proportions and percentile ranks.

- Describe when it would be appropriate to use the Pearson product-moment correlation coefficient, the Spearman rank-order correlation coefficient, the point-biserial correlation coefficient, and the phi coefficient.

- Determine and explain r^2 for a correlation coefficient.

- Explain regression analysis.

- Determine the regression line for two variables.

TYPES OF DISTRIBUTIONS

In addition to knowing the central tendency and the width or spread of a distribution, it is important to know about the shape of the distribution.

Normal Distributions

normal curve: A symmetrical bell-shaped frequency polygon representing a normal distribution.

When a distribution of scores is very large, it often tends to approximate a pattern called a *normal distribution*. When plotted as a frequency polygon, a normal distribution forms a symmetrical, bell-shaped pattern often called a **normal curve** (see Figure 16.1). We say that the pattern *approximates* a normal distribution because a true normal distribution is a theoretical construct not actually observed in the real world.

normal distribution: A theoretical frequency distribution that has certain special characteristics.

The **normal distribution** is a theoretical frequency distribution that has certain special characteristics. First, it is bell-shaped and symmetrical: the right half is a mirror image of the left half. Second, the mean, median, and mode are equal and are located at the center of the distribution. Third, the normal distribution is unimodal, that is, it has only one mode. Fourth, most of the observations are clustered around the center of the distribution with far fewer observations at the ends, or "tails," of the distribution. Finally, when standard deviations are plotted on the *x*-axis, the percentage of scores falling between the mean and any point on the *x*-axis is the same for all normal curves. This important property of the normal distribution is discussed more fully later in the module.

Although we typically think of the normal distribution as being similar to the curve depicted in Figure 16.1, there are variations in the shape of normal distributions.

Kurtosis

kurtosis: How flat or peaked a normal distribution is.

mesokurtic: Normal curves that have peaks of medium height and distributions that are moderate in breadth.

Kurtosis refers to how flat or peaked a normal distribution is. In other words, kurtosis refers to the degree of dispersion among the scores, that is, whether the distribution is tall and skinny or short and fat. The normal distribution depicted in Figure 16.1 is called mesokurtic—the term "meso" means middle. **Mesokurtic** curves have peaks of medium height, and the distributions

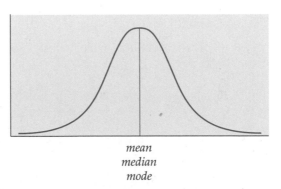

mean
median
mode

FIGURE **16.1** A normal distribution

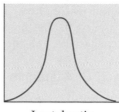 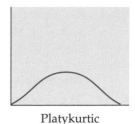

Leptokurtic   Platykurtic

FIGURE **16.2** Types of normal distributions: leptokurtic and platykurtic

leptokurtic: Normal curves that are tall and thin with only a few scores in the middle of the distribution having a high frequency.

platykurtic: Normal curves that are short and relatively more dispersed (broader).

positively skewed distribution: A distribution in which the peak is to the left of the center point and the tail extends toward the right or in the positive direction.

are moderate in breadth. Now look at the two distributions depicted in Figure 16.2. The normal distribution on the left is leptokurtic, the term "lepto" meaning thin. **Leptokurtic** curves are tall and thin with only a few scores in the middle of the distribution having a high frequency. Lastly, see the curve on the right side of Figure 16.2. This is a platykurtic curve, with "platy" meaning broad or flat. **Platykurtic** curves are short and more dispersed (broader). In a platykurtic curve there are many scores around the middle score that all have relatively high frequency.

Positively Skewed Distributions

Most distributions do not approximate a normal or bell-shaped curve. Instead, they are skewed or lopsided. In a skewed distribution scores tend to cluster at one end or the other of the x-axis with the tail of the distribution extending in the opposite direction. In a **positively skewed distribution** the peak is to the left of the center point and the tail extends toward the right or in the positive direction (see Figure 16.3).

Notice that it is the scores toward the right or positive direction that skew the distribution or throws it off center. A few individuals have extremely high scores that pull the distribution in that direction. Notice also what this skewing does to the mean, median, and mode. These three measures do not have the same value, nor are they all located at the center of the distribution as they are in a normal distribution. The mode—the score with the highest frequency—is

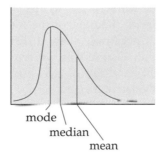 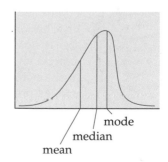

positively skewed distribution   negatively skewed distribution

FIGURE **16.3** Positively and negatively skewed distributions

the high point on the distribution. The median divides the distribution in half. The mean is pulled in the direction of the tail of the distribution because the few extreme scores pull the mean toward them and inflate it.

Negatively Skewed Distributions

negatively skewed distribution: A distribution in which the peak is to the right of the center point and the tail extends toward the left or in the negative direction.

The opposite of a positively skewed distribution is a **negatively skewed distribution,** a distribution in which the peak is to the right of the center point and the tail extends toward the left or in the negative direction. The term "negative" refers to the direction of the skew. In Figure 16.3, in a negatively skewed distribution, the mean is pulled toward the left by the few extremely low scores in the distribution. As in all distributions the median divides the distribution in half, and the mode is the most frequently occurring score in the distribution.

Knowing the shape of a distribution provides valuable information about the distribution. For example, would you prefer to have a negatively or positively skewed distribution of exam scores for an exam that you have taken? Students frequently answer that they would prefer a positively skewed distribution because they think the term "positive" means good. Keep in mind, though, that "positive" and "negative" describe the skew of the distribution not whether the distribution is "good" or "bad." Assuming that the exam scores span the entire possible range (say, 0–100), you should prefer a negatively skewed distribution, which means that most people have high scores and only a few have low scores.

Another example of the value of knowing the shape of a distribution is provided by Harvard paleontologist Stephen Jay Gould (1985). Gould was diagnosed in 1982 with a rare form of cancer. He immediately began researching the disease and learned that it was incurable and had a median mortality rate of only 8 months after discovery. Rather than immediately assuming that he would be dead in 8 months, Gould realized this meant that half of the patients lived longer than 8 months. Because he was diagnosed with the disease in its early stages and was receiving high-quality medical treatment, he reasoned that he could expect to be in the half of the distribution who lived beyond 8 months.

The other piece of information that Gould found encouraging was the shape of the distribution. Look again at the two distributions in Figure 16.3 and decide which you would prefer in this situation. With a positively skewed distribution, the cases to the right of the median could stretch out for years; this is not true for a negatively skewed distribution. The distribution of life expectancy for Gould's disease was positively skewed, and Gould was obviously in the far right-hand tail of the distribution because he lived and remained professionally active for another 20 years.

z-SCORES

The descriptive statistics and types of distributions discussed so far are valuable for describing a sample or group of scores. Sometimes, however, we want information about a single score. In our exam score distribution, we may want to know how one person's exam score compares with those of others in the class. Or we may want to know how an individual's exam score in one class, say psychology, compares with the same person's exam score in another class, say English. Because the two distributions of exam scores are different (different means and standard deviations), simply comparing the raw scores on the two exams does not provide this information. Let's say an individual who was in the psychology exam distribution example scored 86 on the exam. The exam had a mean of 74.00 with a standard deviation (S) of 13.64. The same person took an English exam and made a score of 91, and the English exam had a mean of 85 with a standard deviation of 9.58. On which exam did the student do better? Most people would immediately say the English exam because the score was higher. However, we are interested in how well the student did in comparison to everyone else who took the exams. That is, how well did the individual do in comparison to those taking the psychology exam versus in comparison to those taking the English exam?

To answer this question, we need to convert the exam scores to a form we can use to make comparisons. A **z-score**, or **standard score**, is a measure of how many standard deviation units an individual raw score falls from the mean of the distribution. We can convert each exam score to a z-score and then compare the z-scores because they are then in the same unit of measurement. We can think of z-scores as a translation of raw scores into scores of the same language for comparative purposes. The formulas for a z-score transformation are

z-score (standard score): A number that indicates how many standard deviation units a raw score is from the mean of a distribution.

$$z = \frac{X - \overline{X}}{S}$$

and

$$z = \frac{X - \mu}{\sigma}$$

where z is the symbol for the standard score. The difference between the two formulas is that the first is used when calculating a z-score for an individual in comparison to a sample and that the second is used when calculating a z-score for an individual in comparison to a population. Notice that the two formulas do exactly the same thing: they indicate the number of standard deviations an individual score is from the mean of the distribution.

Conversion to a z-score is a statistical technique that is appropriate for use with data on an interval or ratio scale of measurement (scales for which means are calculated). Let's use the formula to calculate the z-scores for the student's psychology and English exam scores. The necessary information is summarized in Table 16.1.

To calculate the z-score for the English test, we first calculate the difference between the score and the mean, and then divide by the standard deviation.

TABLE **16.1**

Raw Scores (X), Sample Means ($\overline{X}$), and Standard Deviations (S) for the English and Psychology Exams

	X	$\overline{X}$	S
English	91	85	9.58
Psychology	86	74	13.64

We use the same process to calculate the z-score for the psychology exam. These calculations are as follows:

$$z_{English} = \frac{X - \overline{X}}{S} = \frac{91 - 85}{9.58} = \frac{6}{9.58} = +0.626$$

$$z_{Psychology} = \frac{X - \overline{X}}{S} = \frac{86 - 74}{13.64} = \frac{12}{13.64} = +0.880$$

The individual's z-score for the English test is 0.626 standard deviation above the mean, and the z-score for the psychology test is 0.880 standard deviation above the mean. Consequently even though the student answered more questions correctly on the English exam (had a higher raw score) than on the psychology exam, the student performed better on the psychology exam relative to other students in that class than on the English exam in comparison to other English students.

The z-scores calculated in the previous example were both positive, indicating that the individual's scores were above the mean in both distributions. When a score is below the mean, the z-score is negative, indicating that the individual's score is lower than the mean of the distribution.

Another example enables you to practice calculating both positive and negative z-scores. Suppose you administered a test to a large sample of people and computed the mean and standard deviation of the raw scores with the following results:

$$\overline{X} = 45$$
$$S = 4$$

Suppose also that four of the individuals who took the test had the following scores:

Person	Score (X)
Rich	49
Debbie	45
Pam	41
Henry	39

Calculate the *z*-score equivalents for the raw scores of these individuals, beginning with Rich:

$$z_{Rich} = \frac{X_{Rich} - \overline{X}}{S} = \frac{49 - 45}{4} = \frac{4}{4} = +1$$

Notice that we substitute Rich's score (X_{Rich}) and then use the group mean ($\overline{X}$) and the group standard deviation (S). The positive sign (+) indicates that the *z*-score is positive or above the mean. We find that Rich's score of 49 is 1 standard deviation above the group mean of 45.

Now calculate Debbie's *z*-score:

$$z_{Debbie} = \frac{X_{Debbie} - \overline{X}}{S} = \frac{45 - 45}{4} = \frac{0}{4} = 0$$

Debbie's score is the same as the mean of the distribution. Therefore her *z*-score is 0, indicating that she scored neither above nor below the mean. Keep in mind that a *z*-score of 0 does not indicate a low score; rather it indicates a score right at the mean or average. Calculate the *z*-scores for Pam and Henry on your own. Do you get $z_{Pam} = -1$ and $z_{Henry} = -1.5$? Good work!

In summary the *z*-score tells whether an individual raw score is above the mean (a positive *z*-score) or below the mean (a negative *z*-score) as well as how many standard deviations the raw score is above or below the mean. Thus *z*-scores are a means of transforming raw scores to standard scores for purposes of comparison in both normal and skewed distributions. The procedure for calculating z scores using Excel and the TI84 calculator are shown in Appendix C.

z-Scores, the Standard Normal Distribution, Probability, and Percentile Ranks

standard normal distribution: A normal distribution with a mean of 0 and a standard deviation of 1.

If the distribution of scores for which you are calculating transformations (*z*-scores) is normal (symmetrical and unimodal), then it is referred to as the **standard normal distribution,** a normal distribution with a mean of 0 and a standard deviation of 1. The standard normal distribution is actually a theoretical distribution defined by a specific mathematical formula. All other normal curves approximate the Standard Normal Curve to a greater or lesser extent. The value of the Standard Normal Curve is that it provides information about the proportion of scores that are higher or lower than any other score in the distribution. A researcher can also determine the probability of occurrence of a score that is higher or lower than any other score in the distribution. The proportions under the Standard Normal Curve only hold for normal distributions, not for skewed distributions. Even though *z*-scores may be calculated on skewed distributions, the proportions under the Standard Normal Curve do not hold for skewed distributions.

Figure 16.4 represents the area under the Standard Normal Curve in terms of standard deviations. The figure shows that approximately 68% of the observations in the distribution fall between −1.0 and +1.0 standard deviations from the mean. This approximate percentage holds for all data that

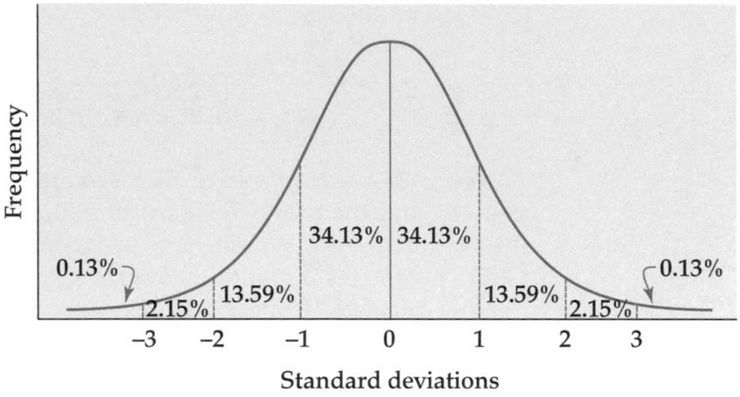

FIGURE **16.4** Area under the Standard Normal Curve

are normally distributed. Notice also that approximately 13.5% of the observations fall between −1.0 and −2.0 and another 13.5% between +1.0 and +2.0 and that approximately 2% of the observations fall between −2.0 and −3.0 and another 2% between +2.0 and +3.0. Only 0.13% of the scores are beyond a z-score of ±3.0. If we sum the percentages in Figure 16.4, we have 100%—all of the area under the curve, representing everybody in the distribution. If we sum half of the curve, we have 50%—half of the distribution.

probability: The expected relative frequency of a particular outcome.

With a curve that is normal (or symmetrical), the mean, median, and mode are all at the center point; thus 50% of the scores are above this number and 50% below it. This property helps us determine probabilities. A **probability** is defined as the expected relative frequency of a particular outcome, which could be the result of an experiment or any situation in which the result is not known in advance. For example, from the normal curve what is the probability of randomly choosing a score that falls above the mean? The probability is equal to the proportion of scores in that area, or .50. Figure 16.4 gives a rough estimate of the proportions under the normal curve. Luckily for us statisticians have determined the exact proportion of scores that fall between any two z-scores, say, between z-scores of +1.30 and +1.39. This information is provided in Table B.1 in Appendix B. A small portion of this table is shown in Table 16.2.

The columns across the top of the table are labeled z, Area between Mean and z, and Area beyond z. There are also pictorial representations. The z column contains the z-score with which you are working. The Area between Mean and z refers to the area under the curve between the mean of the distribution (where $z = 0$) and the z-score with which you are working, that is, the proportion of scores between the mean and the z-score in column 1. The Area beyond z refers to the area under the curve from the z-score out to the tail end of the distribution. Notice that the entire Table B.1 goes out to a z-score of only 4.00 because it is very unusual for a normally distributed population or sample of scores to include larger scores. Notice also that the table

TABLE **16.2**
A Portion of the Standard Normal Curve Table

	AREAS UNDER THE STANDARD NORMAL CURVE FOR VALUES OF z				
z	Area Between Mean and z	Area Beyond z	z	Area Between Mean and z	Area Beyond z
0.00	.0000	.5000	0.29	.1141	.3859
0.01	.0040	.4960	0.30	.1179	.3821
0.02	.0080	.4920	0.31	.1217	.3783
0.03	.0120	.4880	0.32	.1255	.3745
0.04	.0160	.4840	0.33	.1293	.3707
0.05	.0199	.4801	0.34	.1331	.3669
0.06	.0239	.4761	0.35	.1368	.3632
0.07	.0279	.4721	0.36	.1406	.3594
0.08	.0319	.4681	0.37	.1443	.3557
0.09	.0359	.4641	0.38	.1480	.3520
0.10	.0398	.4602	0.39	.1517	.3483
0.11	.0438	.4562	0.40	.1554	.3446
0.12	.0478	.4522	0.41	.1591	.3409
0.13	.0517	.4483	0.42	.1628	.3372
0.14	.0557	.4443	0.43	.1664	.3336
0.15	.0596	.4404	0.44	.1770	.3300
0.16	.0636	.4364	0.45	.1736	.3264
0.17	.0675	.4325	0.46	.1772	.3228
0.18	.0714	.4286	0.47	.1808	.3192
0.19	.0753	.4247	0.48	.1844	.3156
0.20	.0793	.4207	0.49	.1879	.3121
0.21	.0832	.4268	0.50	.1915	.3085
0.22	.0871	.4129	0.51	.1950	.3050
0.23	.0910	.4090	0.52	.1985	.3015
0.24	.0948	.4052	0.53	.2019	.2981
0.25	.0987	.4013	0.54	.2054	.2946
0.26	.1026	.3974	0.55	.2088	.2912
0.27	.1064	.3936	0.56	.2123	.2877
0.28	.1103	.3897	0.57	.2157	.2843

TABLE **16.2**

A Portion of the Standard Normal Curve Table (Continued)

AREAS UNDER THE STANDARD NORMAL CURVE FOR VALUES OF z					
z	Area Between Mean and z	Area Beyond z	z	Area Between Mean and z	Area Beyond z
0.58	.2190	.2810	0.71	.2611	.2389
0.59	.2224	.2776	0.72	.2642	.2358
0.60	.2257	.2743	0.73	.2673	.2327
0.61	.2291	.2709	0.74	.2704	.2296
0.62	.2324	.2676	0.75	.2734	.2266
0.63	.2357	.2643	0.76	.2764	.2236
0.64	.2389	.2611	0.77	.2794	.2206
0.65	.2422	.2578	0.78	.2823	.2177
0.66	.2454	.2546	0.79	.2852	.2148
0.67	.2486	.2514	0.80	9.2881	.2119
0.68	.2517	.2483	0.81	.2910	.2090
0.69	.2549	.2451	0.82	.2939	.2061
0.70	.2580	.2420	0.83	.2967	.2033

provides information only about positive z-scores even though the distribution of scores actually ranges from approximately -4.00 to $+4.00$. Because the distribution is symmetrical, the areas between the mean and z and beyond the z-scores are the same whether the z-score is positive or negative.

Some of the examples from earlier in the module illustrate how to use these proportions under the normal curve. Assume that the test data described earlier (with $\overline{X} = 45$ and $S = 4$) are normally distributed so that the proportions under the normal curve apply. We calculated z-scores for four individuals who took the test: Rich, Debbie, Pam, and Henry. Let's use Rich's z-score to illustrate the use of the normal curve table. Rich had a z-score equal to $+1.00$, 1 standard deviation above the mean. I like to begin by drawing a picture representing the normal curve and then sketch in the z-score with which I am working. Figure 16.5 shows a representation of the normal curve with a line drawn at a z-score of $+1.00$.

Before we look at the proportions under the normal curve, we can begin to gather information from this graphic. Rich's score is above the mean. Using the information from Figure 16.4, we see that roughly 34% of the area under the curve falls between his z-score and the mean of the distribution, whereas approximately 16% of the area falls beyond his z-score. Using

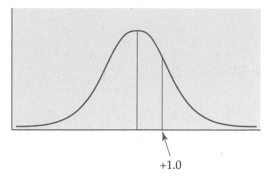

+1.0

FIGURE **16.5** Standard Normal Curve with z-score of +1.00 indicated

Table B.1 to get the exact proportions, we find (from the Area beyond z column) that the proportion of scores falling above the z-score of +1.0 is .1587. This number can be interpreted to mean that 15.87% of the scores are higher than Rich's score, or that the probability of randomly choosing a score with a z-score greater than +1.00 is .1587. To determine the proportion of scores falling below Rich's z-score, we need to use the Area between Mean and z column and add .50 to this proportion. According to the table the area between the mean and the z-score is .3413. Why add .50 to this number? The table provides information about only one side of the standard normal distribution. We must add in the proportion of scores represented by the other half of the distribution, a number that is always .50. In Figure 16.5 Rich's score is +1.00 above the mean, indicating that he did better than those between the mean and his z-score (.3413) and also better than everybody below the mean (.50). Hence, 84.13% of the scores are below Rich's score.

Debbie's z-score further illustrates the use of the z table. Debbie's z-score was 0.00, right at the mean. If she is at the mean (z = 0), then half of the distribution is below her score and half is above her score. Does this match what Table B.1 tells us? According to the table .5000 (50%) of scores are beyond this z-score, so the information in the table agrees with this reasoning.

Using the z table with Pam and Henry's z-scores is slightly more difficult because both Pam and Henry have negative z-scores. Remember, Pam has a z-score of −1.00, and Henry has a z-score of −1.50. Let's begin by drawing a normal distribution and then marking where both Pam and Henry fall on that distribution. This information is represented in Figure 16.6.

Before even looking at the z table, what do we know from Figure 16.6? We know that both Pam and Henry scored below the mean, that they are in the lower 50% of the class, that the proportion of people scoring higher than them is greater than .50, and that the proportion of people scoring lower than them is less than .50. Keep these observations in mind as we use Table B.1. Using Pam's z-score of −1.0, see if you can determine the proportion of scores lying above and below her score. If you determine that the proportion of scores above hers is .8413 and that the proportion below is .1587, you are correct! Why is the proportion above her score .8413? Look in the table at a z-score

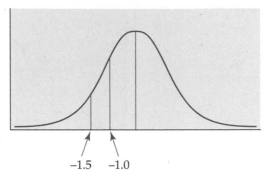

−1.5   −1.0

FIGURE **16.6** Standard Normal Curve with z-scores of −1.0 and −1.5 indicated

of 1.0 (there are no negatives in the table): The Area between Mean and z is .3413. Add the proportion of .50 in the top half of the curve. Adding these two proportions, we get .8413. The proportion below her score is represented by the area in the tail, the Area beyond z of .1587. Note that the proportions above and below should sum to 1.0 (.8413 + .1587 = 1.0). Now see if you can compute the proportions above and below Henry's z-score of −1.5.

Stop reading at this point and do the calculations. Then continue reading to check your answers.

Do you get .9332 above his score and .0668 below his score? Good work!

Now let's try something slightly more difficult by determining the proportion of scores that fall between Henry's z-score of −1.5 and Pam's z-score of −1.0. In Figure 16.6 we see that we are targeting the area between the two z-scores represented on the curve. Again, we use Table B.1 to provide the proportions. The area between the mean and Henry's z-score of −1.5 is .4332, and the area between the mean and Pam's z-score of −1.0 is .3413. To determine the proportion of scores that fall between the two, subtract .3413 from .4332, obtaining a difference of .0919. This result is illustrated in Figure 16.7.

The standard normal curve can also be used to determine an individual's **percentile rank**, the percentage of scores equal to or below the given raw score or the percentage of scores the individual's score is higher than. To determine a percentile rank, we must first know the individual's z-score.

percentile rank: A score that indicates the percentage of people who scored at or below a given raw score.

Let's say we want to calculate an individual's percentile rank based on the person's score on an intelligence test. The scores on the intelligence test are normally distributed, with $\mu = 100$ and $\sigma = 15$. Let's suppose the individual scored 119. Using the z-score formula, we have

$$z = \frac{X - \mu}{\sigma} = \frac{119 - 100}{15} = \frac{19}{15} = +1.27$$

Looking at the Area between Mean and z column for a score of +1.27, we find the proportion .3980. To determine all of the area below the score,

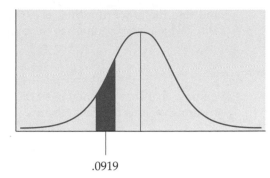

.0919

FIGURE **16.7** Proportion of scores between z-scores of −1.0 and −1.5

we must add .50 to .3980; the entire area below a z-score of +1.27 then is .8980. If we multiply this proportion by 100, we can describe the intelligence test score of 119 as being in the 89.80th percentile.

To practice calculating percentile ranks, see if you can calculate the percentile ranks for Rich, Debbie, Pam, and Henry from the previous examples. Stop reading at this point and do the calculations. Then check your answers with the following percentile ranks.

Person	Score (X)	z-Score	Percentile Rank
Rich	49	+1.0	84.13th
Debbie	45	0.0	50.00th
Pam	41	−1.0	15.87th
Henry	39	−1.50	6.68th

Students most often have trouble determining percentile ranks from negative z-scores. Always draw a figure representing the normal curve with the z-scores indicated; this figure helps you determine which column to use from the z table. When the z-score is negative, the proportion of the curve representing those who scored lower than the individual (the percentile rank) is found in the Area beyond z. When the z-score is positive, the proportion of the curve representing those who scored lower than the individual (the percentile rank) is found by using the Area between Mean and z and adding .50 (the bottom half of the distribution) to this proportion.

What if we know an individual's percentile rank and want to determine the person's raw score? Let's say we know that an individual scored at the 75th percentile on the intelligence test. We want to know what score has 75% of the scores below it. We begin by using Table B.1 to determine the z-score for this percentile rank. If the individual is at the 75th percentile, we know that the Area between Mean and z is .25 because the person scored higher than the 50% of people in the bottom half of the curve, and .75 − .50 = .25. Therefore we look in the column labeled Area between Mean and z and find the proportion that is closest to .25. The closest we come to .25 is .2486, which corresponds to a z-score of 0.67. The z-score formula is

$$z = \frac{X - \mu}{\sigma}$$

We know that $\mu = 100$ and $\sigma = 15$, and now we know that $z = 0.67$. What we want to find is the person's raw score, X. Solve for X:

$$z = \frac{X - \mu}{\sigma}$$

$$z\sigma = X - \mu$$

$$z\sigma + \mu = X$$

Substituting the values we have for μ, σ, and z, we find

$$X = z\sigma + \mu$$
$$X = .67(15) + 100$$
$$= 10.05 + 100$$
$$= 110.05$$

As you can see, the standard normal distribution is useful for determining how a single score compares with a population or sample of scores and also for determining probabilities and percentile ranks. Knowing how to use the proportions under the Standard Normal Curve increases the information we can derive from a single score.

IN REVIEW Distributions

	Types of Distributions		
	Normal	Positively Skewed	Negatively Skewed
Description	A symmetrical, bell-shaped, unimodal curve	A lopsided curve with a tail extending toward the positive or right side	A lopsided curve with a tail extending toward the negative or left side
z-score transformations applicable?	Yes	Yes	Yes
Percentile ranks and proportions under Standard Normal Curve applicable?	Yes	No	No

CRITICAL THINKING CHECK 16.1

1. On one graph draw two distributions with the same mean but different standard deviations. Draw a second set of distributions on another graph with different means but the same standard deviation.
2. Why is it not possible to use the proportions under the Standard Normal Curve with skewed distributions?
3. Students in the psychology department at General State University consume an average of 7 sodas per day with a standard deviation of 2.5. The distribution is normal.
   a. What proportion of students consume an amount equal to or greater than 6 sodas per day?
   b. What proportion of students consume an amount equal to or greater than 8.5 sodas per day?
   c. What proportion of students consume an amount between 6 and 8.5 sodas per day?
   d. What is the percentile rank for an individual who consumes 5.5 sodas per day?
   e. How many sodas would an individual at the 75th percentile drink per day?
4. Based on what you have learned about z-scores, percentile ranks, and the area under the Standard Normal Curve, fill in the missing information in the following table representing performance on an exam that is normally distributed with $\overline{X} = 55$ and $S = 6$.

	X	z-Score	Percentile Rank
John	63		
Ray		−1.66	
Betty			72

CORRELATION COEFFICIENTS

Let's turn to another descriptive statistic, correlation coefficients (first introduced in Modules 6 and 9). We will discuss several types of correlation coefficients. However, the formulas for these correlation coefficients are not presented because our coverage of statistics is necessarily selective. The type of correlation coefficient used depends on the type of data (nominal, ordinal, interval, or ratio) collected.

The most commonly used correlation coefficient is the **Pearson product-moment correlation coefficient**, usually referred to as **Pearson's r** (r is the statistical notation used to report this correlation coefficient). Pearson's r is used for data measured on an interval or ratio scale of measurement. Refer to Figure 9.1, which presents a scatterplot of height and weight data for 20 individuals. The data represented in Figure 9.1 are presented in Table 16.3. Because height and weight are both measured on a ratio scale, Pearson's r is applicable to these data.

Pearson product-moment correlation coefficient (Pearson's r): The most commonly used correlation coefficient when both variables are measured on an interval or ratio scale.

TABLE **16.3**

Height and Weight Data for 20 Individuals

WEIGHT (IN POUNDS)	HEIGHT (IN INCHES)
100	60
120	61
105	63
115	63
119	65
134	65
129	66
143	67
151	65
163	67
160	68
176	69
165	70
181	72
192	76
208	75
200	77
152	68
134	66
138	65

The development of this correlation coefficient is typically credited to Karl Pearson (hence the name for the coefficient), who published his formula for calculating r in 1895. Actually Francis Edgeworth published a similar formula for calculating r in 1892. Not realizing the significance of his work, however, Edgeworth embedded the formula in a statistical paper that was very difficult to follow, and it was not noted until years later. Consequently, although Edgeworth had published the formula 3 years earlier, Pearson received the recognition (Cowles, 1989).

The obtained correlation between height and weight for the 20 individuals represented in Table 16.3 is +.94. Can you interpret this correlation coefficient? The positive sign tells us that the variables increase and decrease together. The large magnitude (close to 1.00) tells us that there is a strong positive relationship between height and weight: Those who are taller tend to weigh more, whereas those who are shorter tend to weigh less. You can see how to use either SPSS, Excel, or the TI84 calculator to calculate Pearson's r in Appendix C.

In addition to interpreting the correlation coefficient, it is important to calculate the coefficient of determination. Calculated by squaring the correlation coefficient, the **coefficient of determination** (r^2) is a measure of the proportion of the variance in one variable that is accounted for by another variable. In our group of 20 individuals there is variation in both the height and weight variables, and some of the variation in one variable can be accounted for by the other. We could say that some of the variation in the weights of the 20 individuals can be explained by the variation in their heights. Some of the variation in their weights, however, cannot be explained by the variation in height. It might be explained by other factors such as genetic predisposition, age, fitness level, or eating habits. The coefficient of determination tells us how much of the variation in weight is accounted for by the variation in height. Squaring the obtained coefficient of $+.94$, we have $r^2 = .8836$. We typically report r^2 as a percentage. Hence, 88.36% of the variance in weight can be accounted for by the variance in height—a very high coefficient of determination. Depending on the research area, the coefficient of determination may be much lower and still be important. It is up to the researcher to interpret the coefficient of determination.

As noted previously, the type of correlation coefficient used depends on the type of data collected in the research study. Pearson's correlation coefficient is used when both variables are measured on an interval or ratio scale. Alternative correlation coefficients can be used with ordinal and nominal scales of measurement.

When one or more of the variables is measured on an ordinal (ranking) scale, the appropriate correlation coefficient is **Spearman's rank-order correlation coefficient**. If one of the variables is interval or ratio in nature, it must be ranked (converted to an ordinal scale) before the calculations are done. If one of the variables is measured on a dichotomous (having only two possible values such as gender) nominal scale and the other is measured on an interval or ratio scale, the appropriate correlation coefficient is the **point-biserial correlation coefficient**. Finally, if both variables are dichotomous and nominal, the **phi coefficient** is used.

All of the preceding correlation coefficients are based on Pearson's formula and can be found in a more comprehensive statistics text. Each of these coefficients is reported on a scale of -1.00 to $+1.00$. Accordingly, each is interpreted in a fashion similar to Pearson's r. Further, like Pearson's r, the coefficient of determination (r^2) can be calculated for each of these correlation coefficients in order to determine the proportion of variance in one variable accounted for by the other.

Although both the point-biserial and phi coefficients are used to calculate correlations with dichotomous nominal variables, keep in mind one of the cautions mentioned in Module 9 concerning potential problems when interpreting correlation coefficients, specifically the one regarding restricted ranges. Clearly, a variable with only two levels has a restricted range. What would the scatterplot for such a correlation look like? The points would have to be clustered in columns or groups depending on whether one or both of the variables were dichotomous.

---

coefficient of determination (r^2): A measure of the proportion of the variance in one variable that is accounted for by another variable; calculated by squaring the correlation coefficient.

Spearman's rank-order correlation coefficient: The correlation coefficient used when one or more of the variables are measured on an ordinal (ranking) scale.

point-biserial correlation coefficient: The correlation coefficient used when one of the variables is measured on a dichotomous nominal scale and the other is measured on an interval or ratio scale.

phi coefficient: The correlation coefficient used when both measured variables are dichotomous and nominal.

| IN REVIEW | Correlation Coefficients | | | |

Types of Coefficients

	Pearson	Spearman	Point-Biserial	Phi
Type of data	Both variables must be interval or ratio	Both variables are ordinal (ranked)	One variable is interval or ratio, and one is nominal and dichotomous	Both variables are nominal and dichotomous
Correlation reported	$\pm 0.0 - 1.0$	$\pm 0.0 - 1.0$	$\pm 0.0 - 1.0$	$\pm 0.0 - 1.0$
r^2 Applicable?	Yes	Yes	Yes	Yes

> **CRITICAL THINKING CHECK 16.2**
>
> 1. In a recent study researchers were interested in determining for a group of college students the relationship between gender and the amount of time spent studying. Which correlation coefficient should be used to assess this relationship?

ADVANCED CORRELATIONAL TECHNIQUES: REGRESSION ANALYSIS

regression analysis: A procedure that allows us to predict an individual's score on one variable based on knowing one or more other variables.

As we have seen, the correlational procedure allows us to predict from one variable to another, and the degree of accuracy with which we can predict depends on the strength of the correlation. A tool that enables us to predict an individual's score on one variable based on knowing one or more other variables is **regression analysis**. Imagine that you are an admissions counselor at a university and you want to predict how well a prospective student might do at your school based on both SAT scores and high school GPA. Or imagine that you work in a human resources office and you want to predict how well future employees might perform based on test scores and performance measures. Regression analysis allows you to make such predictions by developing a regression equation.

Regression analysis involves determining the equation for the best fitting line for a data set. This equation is based on the equation for representing a line that you may remember from algebra class: $y = mx + b$, where m is the slope of the line and b is the y-intercept (the point where the line crosses the y-axis). For a linear regression analysis the formula is essentially the same, although the symbols differ:

$$Y' = bX + a$$

where Y' is the predicted value on the Y variable, b is the slope of the line, X represents an individual's score on the X variable, and a is the y-intercept.

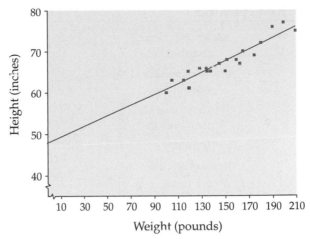

FIGURE **16.8** The relationship between height and weight with the regression line indicated

Using this formula then we can predict an individual's approximate score on variable Y based on that person's score on variable X. With the height and weight data, for example, we can predict an individual's approximate height based on knowing that person's weight. You can picture what we are talking about by looking at Figure 16.8 which shows the **regression line**, that is, the best-fitting straight line drawn through the center of a scatterplot, for these variables. In this figure we can see that if we know an individual's weight (read from the x-axis), we can predict the person's height (by finding the corresponding value on the y-axis).

regression line: The best-fitting straight line drawn through the center of a scatterplot that indicates the relationship between the variables.

SUMMARY

In this module we continued our discussion of descriptive statistics. A distribution may be normal, positively skewed, or negatively skewed. The shape of the distribution affects the relationships among the mean, median, and mode.

We also discussed the calculation of z-score transformations as a means of standardizing raw scores for comparative purposes. Although z-scores may be used with either normal or skewed distributions, the proportions under the Standard Normal Curve can be applied only to data that approximate a normal distribution.

Finally, we introduced four different correlation coefficients (Pearson's, Spearman's, point-biserial, and phi) along with when each should be used. Also we discussed the coefficient of determination and regression analysis, which provides a tool for predicting from one variable to another.

REVIEW OF KEY TERMS

normal curve	negatively skewed distribution	Pearson product-moment correlation coefficient (Pearson's *r*)	point-biserial correlation coefficient
normal distribution			
kurtosis	z-score (standard score)		phi coefficient
mesokurtic		coefficient of determination (r^2)	regression analysis
leptokurtic	standard normal distribution		regression line
platykurtic	probability	Spearman's rank-order correlation coefficient	
positively skewed distribution	percentile rank		

MODULE EXERCISES

(Answers to odd-numbered exercises appear in Appendix A.)

1. The results of a recent survey indicate that the average new car costs $23,000 with a standard deviation of $3,500. The prices of cars are normally distributed.
   a. If someone buys a car for $32,000, what proportion of cars cost an equal amount or more than this?
   b. If someone buys a car for $16,000, what proportion of cars cost an equal amount or more than this?
   c. At what percentile rank is a car that sells for $30,000?
   d. At what percentile rank is a car that sells for $12,000?
   e. What proportion of cars are sold for an amount between $12,000 and $30,000?
   f. For what price would a car at the 16th percentile have sold?

2. A survey of college students was conducted during final exam week to assess the number of cups of coffee consumed each day. The mean number of cups was 5 with a standard deviation of 1.5 cups. The distribution was normal.
   a. What proportion of students drank 7 or more cups of coffee per day?
   b. What proportion of students drank 2 or more cups of coffee per day?
   c. What proportion of students drank between 2 and 7 cups of coffee per day?

   d. How many cups of coffee would an individual at the 60th percentile rank drink?
   e. What is the percentile rank for an individual who drinks 4 cups of coffee a day?
   f. What is the percentile rank for an individual who drinks 7.5 cups of coffee a day?

3. Fill in the missing information in the following table representing performance on an exam that is normally distributed with $\overline{X} = 75$ and $S = 9$.

	X	z-Score	Percentile Rank
Ken	73		
Drew		1.55	
Cecil			82

4. Assuming that the regression equation for the relationship between IQ score and psychology exam score is $Y' = 9 + .274X$, what would you expect the psychology exam scores to be for the following individuals given their IQ exam scores?

Individual	IQ Score (x)	Psychology Exam Score (y)
Tim	118	
Tom	98	
Tina	107	
Tory	103	

CRITICAL THINKING CHECK ANSWERS

16.1

1.

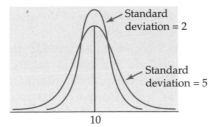

Same Mean, Different Standard Deviations

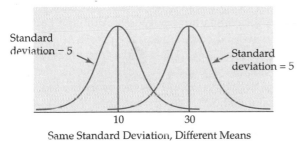

Same Standard Deviation, Different Means

2. The proportions hold for only normal (symmetrical) distributions in which one half of the distribution is equal to the other. If the distribution were skewed, this condition would be violated.

3. a. .6554
   b. .2743
   c. .3811
   d. 27.43rd
   e. 8.68

4.

	X	z-Score	Percentile Rank
John	63	+1.33	90.82
Ray	45.05	−1.66	4.85
Betty	58.48	+0.58	72

16.2

1. In this study gender is nominal in scale, and the amount of time spent studying is ratio in scale. Thus a point-biserial correlation coefficient is appropriate.

WEB RESOURCES

Check your knowledge of the content and key terms in this module with a practice quiz and interactive flashcards at **www.cengage.com/psychology/jackson**, or for step-by-step practice and information, check out the Statistics and Research Methods Workshops at **www.cengage.com/psychology/workshops**.

CHAPTER SEVEN SUMMARY AND REVIEW: DESCRIPTIVE STATISTICS

In this chapter we discussed data organization and descriptive statistics. We presented several methods of data organization, including a frequency distribution, a bar graph, a histogram, and a frequency polygon. We also discussed the types of data appropriate for each of these methods.

Descriptive statistics that summarize a large data set include measures of central tendency (mean, median, and mode) and measures of variation (range, standard deviation, and variance). These statistics provide information about the central tendency, or "middleness," of a distribution of scores and about the spread or width of the distribution, respectively. A distribution may be normal, positively skewed, or negatively skewed. The shape of the distribution affects the relationships among the mean, median, and mode.

In addition, we discussed the calculation of z-score transformations as a means of standardizing raw scores for comparative purposes. Although z-scores may be used with either normal or skewed distributions, the proportions under the Standard Normal Curve can be applied only to data that approximate a normal distribution. Based on our discussion of these descriptive methods, you can begin to organize and summarize a large data set and also compare the scores of individuals to the entire sample or population.

We also introduced four different correlation coefficients (Pearson's, Spearman's, point-biserial, and phi), explaining when each should be used. Also we discussed the coefficient of determination and regression analysis, which provide a tool for predicting from one variable to another.

CHAPTER SEVEN REVIEW EXERCISES

(Answers to exercises appear in Appendix A.)

Fill-in Self-Test

Answer the following questions. If you have trouble answering any of the questions, restudy the relevant material before going on to the multiple choice self-test.

1. A _____ is a table in which all of the scores are listed along with the frequency at which each occurs.
2. A categorical variable for which each value represents a discrete category is a _____ variable.
3. A graphical representation of a frequency distribution in which vertical bars centered above scores on the x-axis touch each other to indicate that the scores on the variable represent related, increasing values is a _____.
4. Measures of _____ are numbers intended to characterize an entire distribution.
5. The _____ is the middle score in a distribution after the scores have been arranged from highest to lowest or lowest to highest.
6. Measures of _____ are numbers that indicate how dispersed scores are around the mean of the distribution.
7. When we divide the squared deviation scores by $N - 1$ rather than by N, we are using the _____ of the population standard deviation.

8. Sigma (σ) represents the _____ standard deviation and S represents the _____ standard deviation.

9. A number that indicates how many standard deviation units a raw score is from the mean of a distribution is a _____.

10. The normal distribution with a mean of 0 and a standard deviation of 1 is the _____.

11. The _____ correlation coefficient is used when both variables are measured on an interval-ratio scale.

12. The _____ correlation coefficient is used when one variable is measured on an interval-ratio scale and the other on a nominal scale.

13. To measure the proportion of variance in one of the variables accounted for by the other variable, we use the _____.

14. _____ is a procedure that allows us to predict an individual's score on one variable based on knowing the person's score on a second variable.

Multiple-Choice Self-Test

Select the single best answer for each of the following questions. If you have trouble answering any of the questions, restudy the relevant material.

1. A _____ is a graphical representation of a frequency distribution in which vertical bars are centered above each category along the x-axis and are separated from each other by spaces, indicating that the levels of the variable represent distinct, unrelated categories.
   a. histogram
   b. frequency polygon
   c. bar graph
   d. class interval histogram

2. Qualitative variable is to quantitative variable as _____ is to _____.
   a. categorical variable; numerical variable
   b. numerical variable; categorical variable

c. bar graph; histogram
d. both a and c

3. Seven Girl Scouts reported the following individual earnings from their sale of cookies: $17, $23, $13, $15, $12, $19, and $13. In this distribution of individual earnings, the mean is _____ the mode and _____ the median.
   a. equal to; equal to
   b. greater than; equal to
   c. equal to; less than
   d. greater than; greater than

4. When Dr. Thomas calculated her students' history test scores, she noticed that one student had an extremely high score. Which measure of central tendency should be used in this situation?
   a. mean
   b. standard deviation
   c. median
   d. either a or c

5. Imagine that 4,999 people who are penniless live in Medianville. An individual whose net worth is $500,000,000 moves to Medianville. Now the mean net worth in this town is _____ and the median net worth is _____.
   a. 0; 0
   b. $100,000; 0
   c. 0; $100,000
   d. $100,000; $100,000

6. The middle score in the distribution is to _____ as the score occurring with the greatest frequency is to _____.
   a. mean; median
   b. median; mode
   c. mean; mode
   d. mode; median

7. Mean is to _____ as mode is to _____.
   a. ordinal, interval, and ratio data only; nominal data only
   b. nominal data only; ordinal data only
   c. interval and ratio data only; all types of data
   d. none of the above

8. Imagine that distribution A contains the following scores: 11, 13, 15, 18, 20. Imagine that distribution B contains the following scores: 13, 14, 15, 16, 17. Distribution A has a _____ standard deviation and a _____ range in comparison to distribution B.
    a. larger; larger
    b. smaller; smaller
    c. larger; smaller
    d. smaller; larger

9. Which of the following is not true?
    a. All scores in the distribution are used in the calculation of the range.
    b. The variance is calculated by squaring the standard deviation.
    c. The standard deviation is calculated by taking the square root of the variance.
    d. None of the above.

10. If the shape of a frequency distribution is lopsided with a long tail projecting longer to the left than to the right, how would the distribution be skewed?
    a. normally
    b. negatively
    c. positively
    d. average

11. If Jack scored 15 on a test with a mean of 20 and a standard deviation of 5, what is his z-score?
    a. +1.5
    b. −1.0
    c. 0.0
    d. cannot be determined

12. Faculty in the physical education department at State University consume an average of 2,000 calories per day with a standard deviation of 250 calories. The distribution is normal. What proportion of faculty consume an amount between 1,600 and 2,400 calories?
    a. .4452
    b. .8904
    c. .50
    d. none of the above

13. If the average weight for women is normally distributed with a mean of 135 pounds and a standard deviation of 15 pounds, then approximately 68% of all women should weigh between _____ and _____ pounds.
    a. 120, 150
    b. 120, 135
    c. 105, 165
    d. Cannot say from the information given.

14. Sue's first philosophy exam score is −1 standard deviation from the mean in a normal distribution. The test has a mean of 82 and a standard deviation of 4. Sue's percentile rank would be approximately _____%.
    a. 78
    b. 84
    c. 16
    d. Cannot say from the information given.

15. The _____ is the correlation coefficient that should be used when both variables are measured on an ordinal scale.
    a. Spearman rank-order correlation coefficient
    b. coefficient of determination
    c. point-biserial correlation coefficient
    d. Pearson product-moment correlation coefficient

16. Suppose that the correlation between age and hearing ability for adults is −.65. What proportion (or percentage) of the variability in hearing ability is accounted for by the relationship with age?
    a. 65%
    b. 35%
    c. 42%
    d. unable to determine

17. Drew is interested is assessing the degree of relationship between belonging to a Greek organization and number of alcoholic drinks consumed per week. Drew should use the _____ correlation coefficient to assess this.
    a. partial
    b. point-biserial
    c. phi
    d. Pearson product-moment

18. Regression analysis allows us to
    a. predict an individual's score on one variable based on knowing the person's score on another variable.
    b. determine the degree of relationship between two interval-ratio variables.
    c. determine the degree of relationship between two nominal variables.
    d. predict an individual's score on one variable based on knowing that the variable is interval-ratio in scale.

KEY TERMS

Here are the terms from the glossary presented earlier. Go through the list and see if you can remember the definition of each.

Bar graph

Class interval frequency distribution

Coefficient of determination (r^2)

Descriptive statistics

Frequency distribution

Frequency polygon

Histogram

Kurtosis

Leptokurtic

Mean

Measure of central tendency

Measure of variation

Median

Mesokurtic

Mode

Negatively skewed distribution

Normal curve

Normal distribution

Pearson product-moment correlation coefficient (Pearson's r)

Percentile rank

Phi coefficient

Platykurtic

Point-biserial correlation coefficient

Positively skewed distribution

Probability

Qualitative variable

Quantitative variable

Range

Regression analysis

Regression line

Spearman's rank-order correlation coefficient

Standard deviation

Standard normal distribution

Variance

z-score (standard score)

CHAPTER 8

Inferential Statistics I

CHAPTER EIGHT SUMMARY AND REVIEW: INFERENTIAL STATISTICS I

hypothesis testing: The process of determining whether a hypothesis is supported by the results of a research study.

In this chapter you are introduced to the concept of **hypothesis testing**, the process of determining whether a hypothesis is supported by the results of a research project. Our introduction to hypothesis testing includes a discussion of the null and alternative hypotheses, Type I and Type II errors, and one- and two-tailed tests of hypotheses as well as an introduction to statistical significance and probability as they relate to inferential statistics.

inferential statistics: Procedures for drawing conclusions about a population based on data collected from a sample.

In the remainder of this chapter we begin our discussion of **inferential statistics**, procedures for drawing conclusions about a population based on data collected from a sample. We address one statistical test: the t test for independent groups. After reading this chapter, engaging in the critical thinking checks, and working through the module exercises and chapter review and summary, you should understand when and how to use this statistical test.

Hypothesis Testing

LEARNING OBJECTIVES

- Differentiate null and alternative hypotheses.
- Differentiate one- and two-tailed hypothesis tests.
- Explain how Type I and Type II errors are related to hypothesis testing.
- Explain what statistical significance means.

Research is usually designed to answer a specific question such as do science majors score higher on tests of intelligence than students in the general population? The process of determining whether this statement is supported by the results of the research project is referred to as *hypothesis testing.*

Suppose a researcher wants to examine the relationship between the type of after-school program attended by a child and the child's intelligence level. The researcher is interested in whether students who attend after-school programs that are academically oriented (math, writing, and computer use) score higher on an intelligence test than students who do not attend such programs. The researcher forms a hypothesis. The hypothesis might be that children in academic after-school programs have higher IQ scores than children in the general population. Because most intelligence tests are standardized with a mean score (μ) of 100 and a standard deviation (σ) of 15, the students in academic after-school programs must score higher than 100 for the hypothesis to be supported.

NULL AND ALTERNATIVE HYPOTHESES

Most of the time researchers are interested in demonstrating the truth of a statement, that is, they are interested in supporting their hypothesis. It is impossible statistically, however, to demonstrate that something is true. In fact, statistical techniques are much better at demonstrating that something is not true. This presents a dilemma for researchers. They want to support their hypotheses, but the techniques available to them are better for showing that something is false. But there is another way to apply the techniques. The logical route is to propose exactly the opposite of what they want to demonstrate to be true and then disprove or falsify that hypothesis. What is left (the initial hypothesis) must then be true (Kranzler & Moursund, 1995).

In the sample hypothesis above we want to show that children who attend academic after-school programs have different (higher) IQ scores than those who do not. We understand that statistics cannot demonstrate the truth of this statement. We therefore construct what is known as a *null hypothesis.* Whatever the research topic, the **null hypothesis** (H_0) always predicts that there is no difference between the groups being compared. This lack of difference is typically what the researcher does not expect to find. Think about the meaning of *null*—nothing or zero. The null hypothesis means we have found nothing, no difference between the groups.

For the sample study the null hypothesis is that children who attend after-school programs have the same intelligence level as other children.

null hypothesis: The hypothesis predicting that no difference exists between the groups being compared.

Statistics allow us only to disprove or falsify a hypothesis. Therefore if the null hypothesis is not supported, then our original hypothesis that children who attend academic after-school programs have different IQs than other children is all that is left. In statistical notation the null hypothesis for this study is

$$H_0: \mu_0 = \mu_1, \quad \text{or} \quad \mu_{\text{academic program}} = \mu_{\text{general population}}$$

The purpose of the study then is to decide whether H_0 is probably true or probably false.

The hypothesis that the researcher wants to support is known as the **alternative hypothesis** (H_a), or the **research hypothesis** (H_1). The statistical notation for H_a is

$$H_a: \mu_0 > \mu_1, \quad \text{or} \quad \mu_{\text{academic program}} > \mu_{\text{general population}}$$

When we use inferential statistics, we are trying to reject H_0; this rejection means that H_a is supported.

alternative hypothesis (research hypothesis): The hypothesis that the researcher wants to support and that predicts a significant difference exists between the groups being compared.

ONE- AND TWO-TAILED HYPOTHESIS TESTS

one-tailed hypothesis (directional hypothesis): An alternative hypothesis in which the researcher predicts the direction of the expected difference between the groups.

The manner in which the previous research hypothesis (H_a) was stated reflects what is known statistically as a **one-tailed hypothesis**, or a **directional hypothesis**, that is, an alternative hypothesis in which the researcher predicts the direction of the expected difference between the groups. In this case the researcher predicts the direction of the difference, namely, that children in academic after-school programs are more intelligent than children in the general population. When we use a directional alternative hypothesis, the null hypothesis is also in some sense directional. If the alternative hypothesis is that children in academic after-school programs have higher intelligence test scores, then the null hypothesis is that being in academic after-school programs either has no effect on intelligence test scores or decreases intelligence test scores. Thus the null hypothesis for the one-tailed directional test might more appropriately be written as

$$H_0: \mu_0 \leq \mu_1, \quad \text{or} \quad \mu_{\text{academic program}} \leq \mu_{\text{general population}}$$

In other words, if the alternative hypothesis for a one-tailed test is $\mu_0 > \mu_1$ then the null hypothesis is $\mu_0 \leq \mu_1$, and to reject H_0, the children in academic after-school programs have to have intelligence test scores higher than those in the general population.

two-tailed hypothesis (nondirectional hypothesis): An alternative hypothesis in which the researcher predicts that the groups being compared differ but does not predict the direction of the difference.

The alternative to a one-tailed or directional test is a **two-tailed hypothesis**, or a **nondirectional hypothesis**, that is, an alternative hypothesis in which the researcher expects to find differences between the groups but is unsure what the differences are. In our example the researcher would predict a difference in IQ scores between children in academic after-school programs and those in the general population, but the direction of the difference would not be predicted. Those in academic programs would be expected to have either higher or lower IQs but not the same IQs as the general population of children. The statistical notation for a two-tailed test is

$$H_0: \mu_0 = \mu_1, \quad \text{or} \quad \mu_{\text{academic program}} = \mu_{\text{general population}}$$
$$H_a: \mu_0 \neq \mu_1, \quad \text{or} \quad \mu_{\text{academic program}} \neq \mu_{\text{general population}}$$

In our example a two-tailed hypothesis does not really make sense.

Assume that the researcher has selected a random sample of children from academic after-school programs to compare their IQs with the IQs of children in the general population (we know that the mean IQ for the population is 100). If we collected data and found that the mean intelligence level of the children in academic after-school programs is "significantly" (a term to be discussed shortly) higher than the mean intelligence level for the population, we could reject the null hypothesis (that there is no difference between the sample and the population). Consequently the researcher concludes that the null hypothesis is not supported. When the null hypothesis is rejected, the alternative hypothesis that those in academic programs have higher IQ scores than those in the general population is supported. We can say that the evidence suggests that the sample of children in academic after-school programs represents a specific population that scores higher on the IQ test than the general population.

On the other hand, if the mean IQ score of the children in academic after-school programs is not significantly different from the population's mean score, then the researcher has failed to reject the null hypothesis and by default has failed to support the alternative hypothesis. In this case the alternative hypothesis that the children in academic programs have higher IQs than the general population is not supported.

TYPE I AND TYPE II ERRORS IN HYPOTHESIS TESTING

Anytime we make a decision using statistics, there are four possible outcomes (see Table 17.1). Two of the outcomes represent correct decisions, whereas two represent errors. Let's use our example to illustrate these possibilities.

If we reject the null hypothesis (that there is no IQ difference between groups), we may be correct or incorrect. If our decision to reject H_0 is correct, then there truly is a difference in IQ between children in academic after-school programs and those in the general population. However, our decision could be incorrect. The result may have been due to chance. Even though we

TABLE **17.1**
The Four Possible Outcomes in Statistical Decision Making

	The Truth (Unknown to the Researcher)	
The Researcher's Decision	H_0 is True	H_0 is False
Reject H_0 (say it is false)	Type I error	Correct decision
Fail to reject H_0 (say it is true)	Correct decision	Type II error

Type I error: An error in hypothesis testing in which the null hypothesis is rejected when it is true.

Type II error: An error in hypothesis testing in which there is a failure to reject the null hypothesis when it is false.

statistical significance: An observed difference between two descriptive statistics such as means that is unlikely to have occurred by chance.

observed a significant difference in IQs between the children in our study and the general population, the result might have been a fluke—perhaps the children in our sample just happened to guess correctly on a lot of the questions. In this case we have made what is known as a **Type I error**—we rejected H_0 when in reality we should have failed to reject it (it is true that there really is no IQ difference between the sample and the population). Type I errors can be thought of as false alarms: we said there was a difference, but in reality there is none.

What if our decision is not to reject H_0, thus concluding that there is no difference in IQs between the children in academic after-school programs and children in the general population? This decision could be correct, which would mean that there is no IQ difference between the sample and the population. However, it could also be incorrect. In this case we would be making a **Type II error**, saying there is no difference between groups when in reality there is. Somehow we have missed the difference that really exists and have failed to reject the null hypothesis when it is false. These possibilities are summarized in Table 17.1.

STATISTICAL SIGNIFICANCE AND ERRORS

Suppose we actually do the study on IQ levels and academic after-school programs. Further, suppose we find that there is a difference between the IQ levels of children in academic after-school programs and children in the general population, that is, those in academic programs score higher. And finally, suppose this difference is statistically significant at the .05 (or the 5%) level (also known as the .05 alpha level). To say that a result has **statistical significance** at the .05 level means that a difference as large as or larger than what we observed between the sample and the population could have occurred by chance only 5 times or less out of 100. In other words, the likelihood that this result is due to chance is small. If the result is not due to chance, then it is most likely due to a true or real difference between the groups. If our result is statistically significant, we can reject the null hypothesis and conclude that we have observed a significant difference in IQ scores between the sample and the population.

However, when we reject the null hypothesis, we could be correct in our decision or we could be making a Type I error. Maybe the null hypothesis is true, and the result is one of those 5 or fewer times out of 100 when the observed differences between the sample and the population did occur by chance. This means that when we adopt the .05 level of significance (the .05 alpha level), as often as 5 times out of 100, we could make a Type I error. The .05 level then is the probability of making a Type I error. In the social and behavioral sciences alpha is typically set at .05 (as opposed to .01 or .08 or anything else). This practice means that researchers in these areas are willing to accept up to a 5% risk of making a Type I error.

What if you want to reduce the risk of making a Type I error and decide to use the .01 alpha level, that is, reducing the risk of a Type I error to 1 out of 100 times? Implementing this decision seems simple enough: Simply reduce alpha to .01, and you reduce the chance of making a Type I error. By making this reduction, however, you increase the chance of making a Type II error. By reducing the risk of making a false alarm, saying a difference is there when it really is not, you increase the risk of missing a difference that really is there. In reducing the alpha level, you are insisting on more stringent conditions for accepting the research, making it more likely that you could miss a significant difference when it is present.

Which type of error, Type I or Type II, do you think is considered more serious by researchers? Most researchers consider a Type I error the more serious. They would rather miss a result (Type II error) than conclude that there is a meaningful difference when there really is not (Type I error). This preference holds true in other arenas, for example in the courtroom. A jury could make a correct decision in a case (find guilty when the defendant is truly guilty or find innocent when truly innocent). They could also make either a Type I error (find guilty when innocent) or a Type II error (find innocent when guilty). Which is more serious? Most people believe that a Type I error is worse in this situation. On the other hand, in the medical profession a doctor who is attempting to determine whether a patient has cancer could make one of the two correct decisions or one of the two types of errors. The Type I error is saying that cancer is present when in fact it is not. The Type II error is saying that there is no cancer when in fact there is. In this situation most people would consider a Type II error to be more serious.

IN REVIEW	Hypothesis Testing	
Concept	**Description**	**Example or Explanation**
Null hypothesis	The hypothesis stating that the independent variable has no effect and that there is no difference between the two groups	$H_0: \mu_0 = \mu_1$ (two-tailed) $H_0: \mu_0 \geq \mu_1$ (one-tailed) $H_0: \mu_0 \leq \mu_1$ (one-tailed)
Alternative hypothesis, or research hypothesis	The hypothesis stating that the independent variable has an effect and that there is a difference between the two groups	$H_a: \mu_0 \neq \mu_1$ (two-tailed) $H_a: \mu_0 < \mu_1$ (one-tailed) $H_a: \mu_0 > \mu_1$ (one-tailed)
Two-tailed, or nondirectional test	An alternative hypothesis stating that a difference is expected between the groups, but there is no prediction as to which group will perform better or worse	The mean of the sample is different from or unequal to the mean of the general population
One-tailed, or directional test	An alternative hypothesis stating that a difference is expected between the groups, and it is expected to occur in a specific direction	The mean of the sample is greater than the mean of the population, or the mean of the sample is less than the mean of the population
Type I error	The error of rejecting H_0 when we should fail to reject it	Equivalent to a "false alarm," saying that there is a difference between the groups when in reality there is none

Type II error	The error of failing to reject H_0 when we should reject it	Equivalent to a "miss," saying that there is not a difference between the groups when in reality there is
Statistical significance	When the probability of a Type I error is low (.05 or less)	The difference between the groups is so large that we conclude it is due to something other than chance

---

CRITICAL THINKING CHECK 17.1

1. A researcher hypothesizes that children in the South weigh less (because they spend more time outside) than the national average. Identify H_0 and H_a. Is this a one- or two-tailed test?
2. A researcher collects data on children's weights from a random sample of children in the South and concludes that children living there weigh less than the national average. The researcher, however, does not realize that the sample includes many children who are small for their age and that in reality there is no difference in weight between children in the South and the national average. What type of error is the researcher making?
3. If a researcher decides to use the .10 level rather than the conventional .05 level of significance, what type of error is more likely to be made? Why? If the .01 level is used, what type of error is more likely? Why?

PARAMETRIC STATISTICS FOR TWO-GROUP DESIGNS

parametric test: A statistical test that involves making assumptions about estimates of population characteristics, or parameters.

nonparametric test: A statistical test that does not involve the use of any population parameters; μ and σ are not needed, and the underlying distribution does not have to be normal.

Parametric tests are tests that require us to make certain assumptions about estimates of population characteristics, or parameters. These assumptions typically involve knowing the mean (μ) and standard deviation (σ) of the population and knowing that the population distribution is normal. Parametric statistics are generally used with interval or ratio data. There are also statistical tests that are nonparametric inferential tests. **Nonparametric tests** are tests that do not involve the use of any population parameters. In other words, μ and σ are not needed, and the underlying distribution does not have to be normal. Nonparametric tests are most often used with ordinal or nominal data. Although nonparametric tests are not covered in this text, you can find an explanation of them in a basic statistics text.

In the two-group design two samples (representing two populations) are compared by having one group receive nothing (the control group) and the second group receive some level of the independent variable (the experimental group). It is also possible to have two experimental groups and no control group (see Module 12). In this case members of each group receive a different level of the independent variable. The null hypothesis tested in a two-group design using a two-tailed test is that the populations represented by the two groups do not differ:

$$H_0: \mu_1 = \mu_2$$

The alternative hypothesis is that we expect differences in performance between the two populations but we are unsure which group will perform better or worse:

$$H_a: \mu_1 \neq \mu_2$$

As discussed in this module, for a one-tailed test the null hypothesis is either

$$H_0: \mu_1 \leq \mu_2, \quad \text{or} \quad H_0: \mu_1 \geq \mu_2$$

depending on which alternative hypothesis is being tested:

$$H_a: \mu_1 > \mu_2, \quad \text{or} \quad H_a: \mu_1 < \mu_2$$

respectively.

A significant difference between the two groups (samples representing populations) depends on the critical value for the statistical test being conducted. The norm with most statistical tests alpha is typically set at .05 ($\alpha = .05$).

SUMMARY

In this module we introduced hypothesis testing and inferential statistics. The discussion of hypothesis testing included the null and alternative hypotheses, one- and two-tailed hypothesis tests, and Type I and Type II errors in hypothesis testing. In addition, we defined the concept of statistical significance and parametric and nonparametric statistical tests.

REVIEW OF KEY TERMS

hypothesis testing	alternative hypothesis (research hypothesis)	two-tailed hypothesis (nondirectional hypothesis)	statistical significance
inferential statistics	one-tailed hypothesis (directional hypothesis)	Type I error	parametric test
null hypothesis		Type II error	nonparametric test

MODULE EXERCISES

(Answers to odd-numbered questions appear in Appendix A.)

1. The admissions counselors at Brainy University believe that the freshman class they have just recruited is the brightest yet. If they wanted to test this belief (that the freshmen are brighter than the other classes), what would the null and alternative hypotheses be? Is this a one- or two-tailed hypothesis test?

2. To test the hypothesis in Exercise 1, the admissions counselors select a random sample of freshmen and compare their scores on the SAT to those of the

population of upperclassmen. They find that the freshmen do in fact have a higher mean SAT score. However, what they are unaware of is that the sample of freshmen was not representative of all freshmen at Brainy University. In fact, the sample over-represented those with high scores and un-derrepresented those with low scores. What type of error (Type I or Type II) did the counselors make?

3. A researcher believes that family size has increased in the last decade in comparison to the previous decade, that is, people are now having more children than they were before. What would the null and alternative hypotheses be in a study designed to assess this contention? Is this a one- or two-tailed hypothesis test?

4. What are the appropriate H_0 and H_a for each of the following research studies? In addition, note whether the hypothesis test is one- or two-tailed.
   a. A study in which researchers want to test whether there is a difference in spatial ability between left- and right-handed people

b. A study in which researchers want to test whether nurses who work 8-hour shifts deliver higher-quality work than those who work 12-hour shifts

c. A study in which researchers want to determine whether crate-training puppies is superior to training without a crate

5. Assume that each of the following conclusions represents an error in hypothesis testing. Indicate whether each of the statements is a Type I or II error.
   a. Based on the data, the null hypothesis was rejected.
   b. There was no significant difference in the quality of work between nurses who work 8- and 12-hour shifts.
   c. There was a significant difference between right- and left-handers in their ability to perform a spatial task.
   d. The researcher failed to reject the null hypothesis based on these data.

CRITICAL THINKING CHECK ANSWERS

17.1

1. H_0: $\mu_{\text{Southern children}} \geq \mu_{\text{children in general}}$
   H_a: $\mu_{\text{Southern children}} < \mu_{\text{children in general}}$

   This is a one-tailed test.

2. The researcher concluded that there is a difference between the sample and the population when in reality there is none. This is a Type I error.

3. With the .10 level of significance the researcher is willing to accept a higher

probability that the result may be due to chance. Therefore a Type I error is more likely to be made than if the researcher used the more traditional .05 level of significance. With a .01 level of significance the researcher is willing to accept only a .01 probability that the result may be due to chance. In this case a true result is more likely to be missed, and a Type II error is more likely.

WEB RESOURCES

Check your knowledge of the content and key terms in this module with a practice quiz and interactive flashcards at **www.cengage.com/psychology/jackson**, or for step-by-step practice and information, check out the Statistics and Research Methods Workshops at **www.cengage.com/psychology/workshops**.

The *t* Test for Independent Groups

LEARNING OBJECTIVES

- Explain when the *t* test for independent-groups should be used.
- Calculate an independent-groups *t* test.
- Interpret an independent-groups *t* test.
- Calculate and interpret Cohen's *d*.
- Explain the assumptions of the independent-groups *t* test.

n the two-group design two samples (representing two populations) are compared by having one group receive nothing (the control group) and the second group receive some level of the manipulated variable (the experimental group). It is also possible to have two experimental groups and no control group. In this case members of each group receive a different level of the manipulated variable. The null hypothesis tested in a two-group design is that the populations represented by the two groups do not differ:

$$H_0: \mu_1 = \mu_2$$

The alternative hypothesis is either that we expect differences in performance between the two populations but are unsure which group will perform better or worse (a two-tailed test):

$$H_0: \mu_1 \neq \mu_2$$

As discussed in Module 17, for a one-tailed test, the null hypothesis is either

$$H_0: \mu_1 \leq \mu_2 \quad \text{or} \quad H_0: \mu_1 \geq \mu_2$$

depending on which alternative hypothesis is being tested:

$$H_a: \mu_1 > \mu_2 \quad \text{or} \quad H_a: \mu_1 < \mu_2, \text{ respectively.}$$

A significant difference between the two groups (samples representing populations) depends on the critical value for the statistical test being conducted. As described in Module 17, alpha is typically set at .05 ($\alpha = .05$).

Remember from Module 17 that parametric tests such as the *t* test are inferential statistical tests designed for sets of data that meet certain requirements. The most basic requirement is that the data fit a bell-shaped distribution. In addition, parametric tests involve data for which certain parameters are known such as the mean (μ) and the standard deviation (σ). Finally, parametric tests use interval-ratio data.

---

t TEST FOR INDEPENDENT GROUPS: WHAT IT IS AND WHAT IT DOES

independent-groups *t* test: A parametric inferential test for comparing sample means of two independent groups of scores.

The **independent-groups *t* test** is a parametric statistical test that compares the performance of two different samples of participants. It indicates whether the two samples perform so similarly that we conclude that they are likely from the same population or whether they perform so differently that we conclude that they represent two different populations. Imagine that a researcher wants to study the effects on exam performance of massed versus spaced study. All participants in the experiment study the same material for the same amount of time. The difference between the groups is that one group studies for 6 hours all at once (massed study), whereas the other group studies for 6 hours broken into three 2-hour blocks (spaced study). Because the researcher believes that the spaced study method will lead to better performance, the null and alternative hypotheses are

$$H_0: \text{Spaced Study} \leq \text{Massed Study} \quad \text{or} \quad \mu_1 \leq \mu_2$$
$$H_a: \text{Spaced Study} > \text{Massed Study} \quad \text{or} \quad \mu_1 > \mu_2$$

The 20 participants are chosen by random sampling and assigned to the groups randomly. Because of the random assignment of participants, we are confident that there are no major differences between the groups prior to the study. The dependent variable is the participants' scores on a 30-item test of the material; these scores are listed in Table 18.1.

Notice that the mean performance of the spaced-study group ($\overline{X}_1 = 22$) is better than that of the massed-study group($\overline{X}_2 = 16.9$). However, we want to be able to say more than this. In other words, we need to statistically analyze the data in order to determine whether the observed difference is statistically significant. As you may recall, statistical significance indicates that an observed difference between two descriptive statistics (such as means) is unlikely to have occurred by chance. For this analysis we will use an independent-groups *t* test. If your instructor prefers you calculate the *t* test using a

TABLE **18.1**

Number of Items Answered Correctly by Each Participant under Spaced Versus Massed Study Conditions Using a Between-Participants Design (*N* = 20)

Spaced Study	Massed Study
23	17
18	18
23	21
22	15
20	15
24	16
21	17
24	19
21	14
24	17
$\overline{X}_1 = 22$	$\overline{X}_2 = 16.9$

data analysis tool, rather than by hand, instructions on using SPSS, Excel, or the TI84 calculator to conduct this independent-groups *t* test appear in Appendix C.

Calculations for the Independent-Groups *t* Test

The formula for an independent-groups *t* test is

$$t_{\text{obt}} = \frac{\overline{X}_1 - \overline{X}_2}{s_{\overline{X}_1 - \overline{X}_2}}$$

standard error of the difference between means: The standard deviation of the sampling distribution of differences between the means of independent samples in a two-sample experiment.

This formula allows us to compare two sample means. The denominator in the equation represents the **standard error of the difference between means,** the estimated standard deviation of the sampling distribution of differences between the means of independent samples in a two-sample experiment. When conducting an independent-groups *t* test, we are determining how far from the difference between the population means the difference between the sample means falls. If the difference between the sample means is large, it will fall in one of the tails of the distribution (far from the difference between the population means). Remember, our null hypothesis says that the difference between the population means is zero.

To determine how far the difference between sample means is from the difference between the population means, we need to convert our mean differences to standard errors. The formula for this conversion is

$$s_{\overline{X}_1 - \overline{X}_2} = \sqrt{\frac{s_1^2}{n_1} + \frac{s_2^2}{n_2}}$$

The standard error of the difference between the means does have a logical meaning. If you took thousands of pairs of samples from these two populations and found $\overline{X}_1 - \overline{X}_2$ for each pair, those differences between means would not all be the same. They would form a distribution. The mean of that distribution would be the difference between the means of the populations ($\mu_1 - \mu_2$), and its standard deviation would be $s_{\overline{X}_1 - \overline{X}_2}$.

Putting all of this together, we see that the formula for determining *t* is

$$t_{\text{obt}} = \frac{\overline{X}_1 - \overline{X}_2}{\sqrt{\frac{s_1^2}{n_1} + \frac{s_2^2}{n_2}}}$$

where

    t_{obt} = the value of *t* obtained
    $\overline{X}_1$ and $\overline{X}_2$ = the means for the two groups
    s_1^2 and s_2^2 = the variances of the two groups
    n_1 and n_2 = the number of participants in each of the two groups (we use *n* to refer to the subgroups and *N* to refer to the total number of people in the study)

Let's use this formula to determine whether there are any significant differences between our spaced and massed study groups.

$$\overline{X}_1 = \frac{\sum X_1}{n_1} = \frac{220}{10} = 22 \qquad \overline{X}_2 = \frac{\sum X_2}{n_2} = \frac{169}{10} = 16.9$$

$$s_1^2 = \frac{\sum (X_1 - \overline{X}_1)^2}{n_1 - 1} = \frac{36}{9} = 4.00 \qquad s_2^2 = \frac{\sum (X_2 - \overline{X}_2)^2}{n_2 - 1} = \frac{38.9}{9} = 4.32$$

$$t = \frac{\overline{X}_1 - \overline{X}_2}{\sqrt{\dfrac{S_1^2}{n_1} + \dfrac{S_2^2}{n_2}}} = \frac{22 - 16.9}{\sqrt{\dfrac{4.00}{10} + \dfrac{4.32}{10}}} = \frac{5.1}{\sqrt{.832}} = \frac{5.1}{.912} = 5.59$$

"THIS IS THE PART I ALWAYS HATE."

© 2005 Sidney Harris. Reprinted with permission.

Interpreting the Independent-Groups *t* Test

degrees of freedom (df): The number of scores in a sample that are free to vary.

The $t_{obt} = 5.59$. We must now consult Table B.2 in Appendix B to determine the critical value for t (t_{cv}). First we need to determine the **degrees of freedom (df)**, the number of scores in a sample that are free to vary, that for an independent-groups t test are $(n_1 - 1) + (n_1 - 2)$ or $n_1 + n_2 - 2$. In the present study, with 10 participants in each group, there are 18 degrees of freedom ($10 + 10 - 2 = 18$). The alternative hypothesis was one-tailed, and $\alpha = .05$.

Consulting Table B.2, we find that for a one-tailed test with 18 degrees of freedom, the critical value of t at the .05 level is 1.734. Our t_{obt} falls beyond the critical value (is larger than the critical value). Thus the null hypothesis is rejected, and the alternative hypothesis that participants in the spaced study condition performed better on a test of the material than did participants in the massed study condition is supported. Because the *t*-score was significant at the .05 level, we should check for significance at the .025, .01, .005, and .0005 levels provided in Table B.2. Our t_{obt} of 5.59 is larger than the critical values at all of the levels of significance provided in Table B.2. This result is pictured in Figure 18.1. In APA style it would be reported as follows: $t\,(18) =$ 5.59, $p < .0005$ (one-tailed), which conveys in a concise manner the *t*-score, the degrees of freedom, and that the result was significant at the .0005 level. Keep in mind that when a result is significant, the *p* value is reported as less than ($<$) .05 (or some smaller probability) not greater than ($>$), an error commonly made by students. Remember, the *p* value, or alpha level, indicates the probability of a Type I error. We want this probability to be small, meaning we are confident that there is only a small probability that our results were due to chance. This small probability means it is highly probable that the observed difference between the groups is truly a meaningful difference, that it is actually due to the independent variable.

Look back at the formula for *t*, and think about what will affect the size of the *t*-score. We would like the *t*-score to be large in order to increase the chance that it will be significant. What will increase the size of the *t*-score? Anything that increases the numerator or decreases the denominator in the equation will increase the *t*-score. What will increase the numerator? A larger difference between the means for the two groups (a greater difference produced by the independent variable) will increase the numerator. This difference is somewhat difficult to influence. However, if we minimize chance in our study and the independent variable truly does have an effect, then the means should be different. What will decrease the size of the denominator? Because the denominator is the standard error of the difference between the means ($s_{\overline{X}_1 - \overline{X}_2}$) and is derived by using *s* (the unbiased estimator of the population standard deviation), we can decrease $s_{\overline{X}_1 - \overline{X}_2}$ by decreasing the variability within each condition or group or by increasing sample size. Look at the

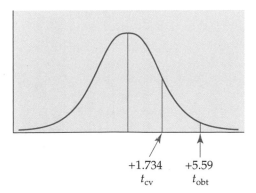

$$+1.734 \qquad +5.59$$
$$t_{cv} \qquad\quad t_{obt}$$

FIGURE **18.1** The obtained *t*-score in relation to the *t* critical value formula and think about why this would be so. In summary then, three aspects of a study can increase power:

- Greater differences produced by the independent variable
- Smaller variability of raw scores in each condition
- Increased sample size

Graphing the Means

Typically when a significant difference is found between two means, the means are graphed to provide a pictorial representation of the difference. In creating a graph, we place the independent variable on the *x*-axis and the dependent variable on the *y*-axis. As noted in Module 15, the *y*-axis should be 60–75% of the length of the *x*-axis. For a line graph we plot each mean and connect them with a line. For a bar graph we draw separate bars whose heights represent the means. Figure 18.2 shows a bar graph representing the data from the spaced versus massed study experiment. Recall that the mean number of items answered correctly by those in the spaced study condition was 22 compared with a mean of 16.9 for those in the massed study condition.

Effect Size: Cohen's *d*

effect size: The proportion of variance in the dependent variable that is accounted for by the manipulation of the independent variable.

In addition to the reported statistic, alpha level, and graph, the American Psychological Association (2009) recommends that we also look at **effect size,** the proportion of variance in the dependent variable that is accounted for by the manipulation of the independent variable. Effect size indicates how big a role the conditions of the independent variable play in determining scores on the dependent variable. It is therefore an estimate of the effect of the independent variable, regardless of sample size. The larger the effect size, the more consistent is the influence of the independent variable. In other words, the greater the effect size, the better knowledge of the conditions of

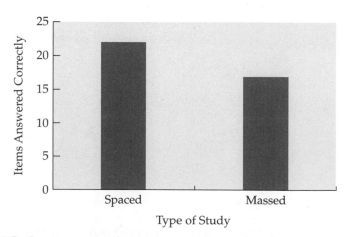

FIGURE **18.2** Mean number of items answered correctly under spaced and massed study conditions

the independent variable improves our accuracy in predicting participants' scores on the dependent variable. For the *t* test one formula for effect size, known as Cohen's *d*, is

$$d = \frac{\overline{X}_1 - \overline{X}_2}{\sqrt{\frac{s_1^2}{2} + \frac{s_2^2}{2}}}$$

Cohen's *d*: An inferential statistic for measuring effect size.

Cohen's *d* is an inferential statistic for measuring effect size.

Let's begin by working on the denominator, using the data from the spaced versus massed study experiment:

$$\sqrt{\frac{s_1^2}{2} + \frac{s_2^2}{2}} = \sqrt{\frac{4.00}{2} + \frac{4.32}{2}} = \sqrt{2.00 + 2.16} = \sqrt{4.16} = 2.04$$

We can now put this denominator into the formula for Cohen's *d*:

$$d = \frac{22 - 16.9}{2.04} = \frac{5.1}{2.04} = 2.50$$

According to Cohen (1988, 1992), a small effect size is one of at least 0.20, a medium effect size is at least 0.50, and a large effect size is at least 0.80. Obviously our effect size of 2.50 is far greater than 0.80, indicating a very large effect size (most likely a result of using fabricated data). Using APA style, we report that the effect size estimated with Cohen's *d* is 2.50. You can also report Cohen's *d* with the *t*-score in the following manner

$$t(18) = 5.59, p < .0005 \text{ (one-tailed)}, d = 2.50$$

The preceding example illustrates a *t* test for independent groups with equal *n* values (sample sizes). In situations in which the *n* values are unequal, a modified version of the previous formula is used. If you need this formula, you can find it in an undergraduate statistics texts.

Assumptions of the Independent-Groups *t* Test

The assumptions of the independent-groups *t* test are

- The data are interval-ratio scale.
- The underlying distributions are bell-shaped.
- The observations are independent.
- There is homogeneity of variance: if we could compute the true variance of the population represented by each sample, the variance in each population would be the same.

If any of these assumptions were violated, it would be appropriate to use another statistic. For example, if the scale of measurement is not interval-ratio or if the underlying distribution is not bell-shaped, it may be more appropriate to use a nonparametric statistic. If the observations are not independent, then it is appropriate to use a statistic for a correlated-groups design (described in the next chapter).

IN REVIEW	Independent-Groups *t* Test
What it is	A parametric test for a two-group between-participants design
What it does	Compares performance of the two groups to determine whether they represent the same population or different populations
Assumptions	Interval-ratio data Bell-shaped distribution Independent observations Homogeneity of variance

CRITICAL THINKING CHECK 18.1

1. How is effect size different from significance level? In other words, how is it possible to have a significant result and yet a small effect size?
2. How does increasing sample size affect a *t* test? Why does it affect it in this manner?
3. How does decreasing variability affect a *t* test? Why does it affect it in this manner?

SUMMARY

In this module we began our discussion of inferential statistics, procedures for drawing conclusions about a population based on data collected from a sample. The *t* test for independent groups was introduced along with Cohen's *d*, the measure of effect size used with this test. The *t* test for independent groups is used to compare the performance of two groups, using a between-participants design, to determine whether the performance of the two groups differs significantly.

REVIEW OF KEY TERMS

independent-groups *t* test

standard error of the difference between means

degrees of freedom
effect size

Cohen's *d*

MODULE EXERCISES

(Answers to odd-numbered questions appear in Appendix A.)

1. Explain when it would be appropriate to use the independent-groups *t* test.

2. What is the standard error of the difference between means?

3. Why does APA recommend that we calculate a measure of effect size in addition to calculating the test statistic?

4. A college student is interested in whether there is a difference between male and female students in the amount of time spent studying each week. The student gathers information from a random sample of male and female students on campus. Amount of time spent studying is normally distributed. The data follow.

Males	Females
27	25
25	29
19	18
10	23
16	20
22	15
14	19

a. What statistical test should be used to analyze these data?
b. Identify H_0 and H_a for this study.
c. Conduct the appropriate analysis.
d. Should H_0 be rejected? What should the researcher conclude?
e. If significant, compute the effect size and interpret.
f. If significant, draw a graph representing the data.

5. A student is interested in whether students who study with music playing devote as much attention to their studies as do students who study under quiet conditions.

He randomly assigns the 18 participants to either music or no music conditions and has them read and study the same passage of information for the same amount of time. Participants are then all given the same 10-item test on the material. Their scores appear below. Scores on the test represent interval-ratio data and are normally distributed.

Music	No Music
6	10
5	9
6	7
5	7
6	6
6	6
7	8
8	6
5	9

a. What statistical test should be used to analyze these data?
b. Identify H_0 and H_a for this study.
c. Conduct the appropriate analysis.
d. Should H_0 be rejected? What should the researcher conclude?
e. If significant, compute the effect size and interpret.
f. If significant, draw a graph representing the data.

CRITICAL THINKING CHECK ANSWERS

Critical Thinking Check 18.1

1. The effect size indicates the magnitude of the experimental treatment regardless of sample size. A result can be statistically significant because sample size was very large, but the effect of the independent variable was not so large. Effect size would indicate whether this situation was the case because in this type of situation the effect size should be small.

2. In the long run it means that the obtained t is more likely to be significant. This outcome is so because in terms of the formula used to calculate t, increasing sample size will decrease the standard error of the difference between means ($s_{\overline{X}_1-\overline{X}_2}$). This consequence in turn will increase the size of the obtained t, which is more likely to exceed the critical value and be significant.

3. Decreasing variability also makes a *t* test more powerful (likely to be significant). It does so because decreasing variability also means that $s_{\overline{X}_1-\overline{X}_2}$ (the standard error of the difference between means) will be smaller. This outcome in turn will increase the size of the obtained *t*, which is more likely to exceed the critical value and be significant.

WEB RESOURCES

Check your knowledge of the content and key terms in this module with a practice quiz and interactive flashcards at **www.cengage.com/ psychology/jackson,** or for step-by-step practice and information, check out the Statistics and Research Methods Workshops at **www.cengage .com/psychology/workshops**.

STATISTICAL SOFTWARE RESOURCES

For hands-on experience using statistical software to complete the analyses described in this module, see Chapter 7 ("The *t* Statistic: Two Samples") in *The Excel Statistics Companion, Version 2.0* by Kenneth M. Rosenberg (Belmont, CA: Thomson Wadsworth, 2007).

CHAPTER EIGHT SUMMARY AND REVIEW: INFERENTIAL STATISTICS I

In this chapter we discussed hypothesis testing and introduced inferential statistics. This survey included a discussion of the null and alternative hypotheses, one- and two-tailed hypothesis tests, and Type I and Type II errors. One parametric inferential statistic used with a two-group design was presented in this chapter, the independent-groups t test. After reading this chapter, you should be able to conduct an independent-groups t test, interpret it, determine Cohen's d, and graph the means.

CHAPTER EIGHT REVIEW EXERCISES

(Answers to exercises appear in Appendix A.)

Fill-in Self-Test

Answer the following questions. If you have trouble answering any of the questions, restudy the relevant material before going on to the multiple choice self-test.

1. A(n) _____ is a parametric inferential test for comparing sample means of two independent groups of scores.
2. The hypothesis predicting that no difference exists between the groups being compared is the _____.
3. An alternative hypothesis in which the researcher predicts the direction of the expected difference between the groups is a _____.
4. An error in hypothesis testing in which the null hypothesis is rejected when it is true is a _____.
5. When an observed difference, say between two means, is unlikely to have occurred by chance we say that the result has _____.
6. _____ tests are statistical tests that do not involve the use of any population parameters.
7. _____ is an inferential statistic for measuring effect size with t tests.

Multiple-Choice Self-Test

Select the single best answer for each of the following questions. If you have trouble answering any of the questions, restudy the relevant material.

1. Inferential statistics allow us to infer something about the _____ based on the _____.
   a. sample; population
   b. population; sample
   c. sample; sample
   d. population; population
2. The hypothesis predicting that differences exist between the groups being compared is the _____ hypothesis.
   a. null
   b. alternative
   c. one-tailed
   d. two-tailed
3. Null hypothesis is to alternative hypothesis as _____ is to _____.
   a. effect; no effect
   b. Type I error; Type II error
   c. no effect; effect
   d. both b and c
4. One-tailed hypothesis is to directional hypothesis as _____ hypothesis is to _____ hypothesis.
   a. null; alternative
   b. alternative; null
   c. two-tailed; nondirectional
   d. two-tailed; one-tailed
5. When using a one-tailed hypothesis, the researcher predicts which of the following?
   a. the direction of the expected difference between the groups
   b. only that the groups being compared will differ in some way

c. nothing
d. only one thing

6. In a study of the effects of caffeine on driving performance, researchers predict that those in the group given more caffeine will exhibit the worse driving performance. The researchers are using a _____ hypothesis.
   a. two-tailed
   b. directional
   c. one-tailed
   d. both b and c

7. What is the effect of a conservative statistical test?
   a. It minimizes the chances of both Type I and Type II errors.
   b. It minimizes the chance of Type I errors but increases the chance of Type II errors.
   c. It minimizes the chance of Type II errors but increases the chance of Type I errors.
   d. It decreases the chance of Type II errors.

8. In a recent study researchers concluded that caffeine significantly increased stress levels. What the researchers were unaware of, however, was that several of the participants in the no-caffeine group were also taking antianxiety medications. The researchers' conclusion is a(n) _____ error.
   a. Type II
   b. Type I
   c. null hypothesis
   d. alternative hypothesis

9. What does it mean when alpha is .05?
   a. The probability of a Type II error is .95.
   b. The probability of a Type II error is .05.
   c. The probability of a Type I error is .95.
   d. The probability of a Type I error is .05.

10. Which test should be used when we are comparing the sample means for two unrelated groups?
    a. correlated-groups t test
    b. independent-groups t test
    c. ANOVA
    d. z-score

11. The value of the t test _____ as sample variance decreases.

a. increases
b. decreases
c. stays the same
d. is not affected

12. Which of the following t test results has the greatest chance of statistical significance?
    a. $t(28) = 3.12$
    b. $t(14) = 3.12$
    c. $t(18) = 3.12$
    d. $t(10) = 3.12$

13. If the null hypothesis is false, then the t test should be _____.
    a. equal to 0.00
    b. greater than 1
    c. greater than 0.05
    d. greater than 0.95

14. Imagine that you conducted an independent-groups t test with 10 participants in each group. For a one-tailed test the t_{cv} at $\alpha = .05$ would be _____.
    a. ±1.729
    b. ±2.101
    c. ±1.734
    d. ±2.093

15. If a researcher reported for an independent-groups t test that $t(26) = 2.90$, $p < .005$, how many participants were there in the study?
    a. 13
    b. 26
    c. 27
    d. 28

16. Ha: $\mu_1 \neq \mu_2$ is the _____ hypothesis for a _____ tailed test.
    a. null; two-
    b. alternative; two-
    c. null; one-
    d. alternative; one-

17. Cohen's d is a measure of _____ for a _____.
    a. significance; t test
    b. significance; x^2 test
    c. effect size; t test
    d. effect size; x^2 test

18. $t_{cv} = 2.15$ and $t_{obt} = -2.20$. Based on these
    results, we _____.
    a. reject H_0
    b. fail to reject H_0

    c. accept H_0
    d. reject H_a

KEY TERMS

Here are the terms from the glossary presented earlier. Go through the list and see if you can remember the definition of each.

Alternative hypothesis (research hypothesis)	Independent-groups t-test	One-tailed hypothesis (directional hypothesis)	Statistical significance
Cohen's d	Inferential statistics	Parametric test	Two-tailed hypothesis (nondirectional Hypothesis)
Degrees of freedom	Nonparametric test	Standard error of the difference between means	Type I error
Effect size	Null hypothesis		Type II error
Hypothesis testing			

CHAPTER 9

Inferential Statistics II

Assumptions of the One-Way Randomized ANOVA
Tukey's Post Hoc Test

One-Way Repeated Measures and Two-Way ANOVAs

SUMMARY
REVIEW OF KEY TERMS
MODULE EXERCISES
CRITICAL THINKING CHECK ANSWERS
WEB RESOURCES
LAB RESOURCES
STATISTICAL SOFTWARE RESOURCES

CHAPTER NINE SUMMARY AND REVIEW: INFERENTIAL STATISTICS II

In this chapter we continue our discussion of inferential statistics. We begin by discussing the analog to the *t* test for independent groups discussed in Module 18—the *t* test for correlated groups. This inferential test compares the performance of participants across two conditions, but in this case, the design is correlated groups, that is, either a within-participants design or a matched-participants design. In addition, we discuss another extension of the independent-groups *t* test, the analysis of variance (ANOVA), which is used when we have three or more groups to compare.

t Test for Correlated Groups (Samples)

LEARNING OBJECTIVES

- Explain when the *t* test for correlated-groups should be used.
- Calculate a correlated-groups *t* test.
- Interpret a correlated-groups *t* test.
- Calculate and interpret Cohen's *d*.
- Explain the assumptions of the correlated-groups *t* test.

t TEST FOR CORRELATED GROUPS: WHAT IT IS AND WHAT IT DOES

correlated-groups *t* test: A parametric inferential test used to compare the means of two related (within- or matched-participants) samples.

Like the previously discussed *t* test, the **correlated-groups *t* test** compares the performance of participants in two groups. In this case, however, the same people are used in each group (a within-participants design) or different participants are matched between groups (a matched-participants design). The test indicates whether there is a difference in sample means and whether this difference is greater than would be expected based on chance. In a correlated-groups design the sample includes two scores for each person (or matched pair in a matched-participants design), instead of just one. To conduct the *t* test for correlated groups (also called the *t* test for dependent groups or samples), we must convert the two scores for each person into one score. That is, we compute a difference score for each person by subtracting one score from the other for that person (or for the two individuals in a matched pair). Although this process may sound confusing, the dependent-groups *t* test is actually easier to compute than the independent-groups *t* test. Because the two samples are related, the analysis becomes easier because we work with pairs of scores. The null hypothesis is that there is no difference between the two scores; that is, a person's score in one condition is the same as that (or a matched) person's score in the second condition. The alternative hypothesis is that there is a difference between the paired scores, that the individuals (or matched pairs) performed differently in each condition.

To illustrate the use of the correlated-groups *t* test, imagine that we conduct a study in which participants are asked to learn two lists of words. One list is composed of 20 concrete words (for example, *desk, lamp,* and *bus*); the other is composed of 20 abstract words (for example, *love, hate,* and *deity*). Each participant is tested twice, once in each condition.

Because each participant provides one pair of scores, a correlated-groups *t* test is the appropriate way to compare the means of the two conditions. We expect to find that recall performance is better for the concrete words. Thus the null hypothesis is

$$H_0: \mu_1 - \mu_2 = 0$$

and the alternative hypothesis is

$$H_a: \mu_1 - \mu_2 > 0$$

representing a one-tailed test of the null hypothesis.

To better understand the correlated-groups *t* test, consider the sampling distribution for the test. This is a sampling distribution of the differences between pairs of sample means. In other words, imagine the population of people who must recall abstract words versus the population of people who must recall concrete words. Further, imagine that samples of eight participants are chosen (the eight participants in each individual sample come from one population) and that each sample's mean score in the abstract condition is subtracted from the mean score in the concrete condition. We use this procedure repeatedly until the entire population has been sampled. If the null hypothesis

TABLE **19.1**

Number of Abstract and Concrete Words Recalled by Each Participant Using a Correlated-Groups (Within-Participants) Design

Participant	Concrete	Abstract
1	13	10
2	11	9
3	19	13
4	13	12
5	15	11
6	10	8
7	12	10
8	13	13

is true, the differences between the sample means should be zero or very close to zero. If, as the researcher suspects, participants remember more concrete words than abstract words, the difference between the sample means should be significantly larger than zero.

The data representing each participant's performance are presented in Table 19.1.

Notice that we have two sets of scores, one for the concrete word list and one for the abstract list. Our calculations for the correlated-groups *t* test involve transforming the two sets of scores into one set by determining **difference scores,** which represent the difference between participants' performance in one condition and their performance in the other condition. The difference scores for our study are shown in Table 19.2. If your instructor

difference scores: Scores representing the difference between participants' performance in one condition and their performance in a second condition.

TABLE **19.2**

Number of Concrete and Abstract Words Recalled by Each Participant with Difference Scores Provided

Participant	Concrete	Abstract	*d* (Difference Score)
1	13	10	3
2	11	9	2
3	19	13	6
4	13	12	1
5	15	11	4
6	10	8	2
7	12	10	2
8	13	13	0
			$\sum = 20$

would prefer you calculate the correlated-groups *t* test using SPSS, Excel, or the TI84 calculator rather than by hand, you can find the instructions for this in Appendix C.

Calculations for the Correlated-Groups *t* Test

After calculating the difference scores, we have one set of scores representing the performance of participants in both conditions. We can now compare the mean of the difference scores with zero (based on the null hypothesis stated previously).

$$t = \frac{\overline{D} - 0}{s_{\overline{D}}}$$

where

$\overline{D}$ = the mean of the difference scores

$s_{\overline{D}}$ = the standard error of the difference scores

standard error of the difference scores: The standard deviation of the sampling distribution of mean differences between dependent samples in a two-group experiment.

The **standard error of the difference scores** ($s_{\overline{D}}$) represents the standard deviation of the sampling distribution of mean differences between dependent samples in a two-group experiment. It is calculated as follows:

$$s_{\overline{D}} = \frac{s_D}{\sqrt{N}}$$

where s_D = the estimated standard deviation of the difference scores. The estimated standard deviation of the difference scores is calculated in the same manner as the standard deviation for any set of scores:

$$s_D = \sqrt{\frac{\sum(D - \overline{D})^2}{N - 1}}$$

Or, if you prefer, you may use the raw score formula for the standard deviation:

$$s_D = \sqrt{\frac{\sum D^2 - \frac{(\sum D)^2}{N}}{N - 1}}$$

Let's use the first formula to determine s_D, $s_{\overline{D}}$, and the final *t*-score.

We begin by determining the mean of the difference scores ($\overline{D}$), which is $20/8 = 2.5$, and then use this calculation to determine the difference scores, the squared difference scores, and the sum of the squared difference scores. These scores are shown in Table 19.3. We then use this sum (24) to determine s_D.

$$s_D = \sqrt{\frac{24}{7}} = \sqrt{3.429} = 1.85$$

TABLE **19.3**

Difference Scores and Squared Difference Scores
for Concrete and Abstract Words

D (Difference Score)	$D - \overline{D}$	$(D - \overline{D})^2$
3	0.5	0.25
2	−0.5	0.25
6	3.5	12.25
1	−1.5	2.25
4	1.5	2.25
2	−0.5	0.25
2	−0.5	0.25
0	−2.5	6.25
		$\sum = 24$

Next we use the estimated standard deviation ($s_D = 1.85$) to calculate the standard error of the difference scores ($s_{\overline{D}}$):

$$s_{\overline{D}} = \frac{s_D}{\sqrt{N}} = \frac{1.85}{\sqrt{8}} = \frac{1.85}{2.83} = 0.65$$

Finally, we use the standard error of the difference scores ($s_{\overline{D}} = 0.65$) and the mean of the difference scores (2.5) in the *t* test formula:

$$t = \frac{\overline{D} - 0}{s_{\overline{D}}} = \frac{2.5 - 0}{0.65} = \frac{2.5}{0.65} = 3.85$$

Interpreting the Correlated-Groups *t* Test and Graphing the Means

The degrees of freedom for a correlated-groups *t* test are equal to $N - 1$; in this case, $8 - 1 = 7$. We can use Table B.2 in Appendix B to determine t_{cv} for a one-tailed test with $\alpha = .05$ and $df = 7$. Consulting this table, we find that $t_{cv} = 1.895$. Our $t_{obt} = 3.85$ and therefore falls in the region of rejection. Because the *t*-score was significant at the .05 level, we should check for significance at the .025, .01, .005, and .0005 levels provided in Table B.2. Our t_{obt} of 3.85 is larger than the critical values of the .025, .01, and .005 levels. Figure 19.1 shows this t_{obt} in relation to the t_{cv}. In APA style this result would be reported as $t(7) = 3.85$, $p < .005$, (one-tailed), indicating that there is a significant difference in the number of words recalled in the two conditions.

This difference is illustrated in Figure 19.2 in which the mean number of concrete and abstract words recalled by the participants have been graphed. We can therefore conclude that participants performed significantly better in the concrete word condition, supporting the alternative (research) hypothesis.

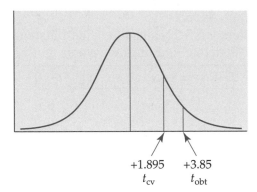

FIGURE **19.1** The obtained *t*-score in relation to the *t* critical value

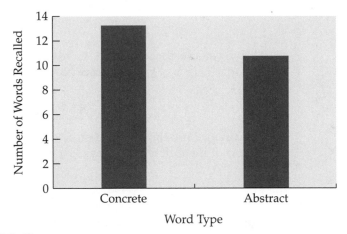

FIGURE **19.2** Mean number of items recalled correctly under concrete and abstract word conditions

Effect Size: Cohen's *d*

As with the independent-groups *t* test we should also compute Cohen's *d* (the proportion of variance in the dependent variable that is accounted for by the manipulation of the independent variable) for the correlated-groups *t* test. Remember, effect size indicates how big a role the conditions of the independent variable play in determining scores on the dependent variable. For the correlated-groups *t* test the formula for Cohen's *d* is

$$d = \frac{\overline{D}}{s_D}$$

where $\overline{D}$ is the mean of the difference scores and s_D is the standard deviation of the difference scores. We have already calculated each of these as part of the t test. Thus

$$d = \frac{2.5}{1.85} = 1.35$$

Cohen's d for a correlated-groups design is interpreted in the same manner as d for an independent-groups design. That is, a small effect size is one of at least 0.20, a medium effect size is at least 0.50, and a large effect size is at least 0.80. Obviously, our effect size of 1.35 is far greater than 0.80, indicating a very large effect size.

Assumptions of the Correlated-Groups t Test

The assumptions for the correlated-groups t test are the same as those for the independent-groups t test, except for the assumption that the observations are independent. In this case the observations are not independent; rather, they are correlated (dependent).

IN REVIEW	Correlated-Groups t Tests
	Correlated Groups t Tests
What it is	A parametric test for a two-group within-participants or matched-participants design
What it does	Analyzes whether each individual performed in a similar or different manner across conditions
Assumptions	Interval-ratio data
	Bell-shaped distribution
	Correlated (dependent) observations
	Homogeneity of variance

CRITICAL THINKING CHECK 19.1

1. Explain what difference scores are and how they are calculated for a correlated-groups t test.
2. Why is H_0 for a correlated-groups t test H_0: $\mu_1 - \mu_2 = 0$? In other words, why should the difference scores be equal to 0 if H_0 is true?

SUMMARY

In this module we continued our discussion of inferential statistics. The t test for correlated groups was introduced along with Cohen's d for this test. The t test for correlated groups is used to compare the performance of two conditions, using a within- or matched-participants design, to determine whether the performance between the two conditions differs significantly.

REVIEW OF KEY TERMS

correlated-groups *t* test   difference scores   standard error of the difference scores

MODULE EXERCISES

(Answers to odd-numbered questions appear in Appendix A.)

1. What is the difference between an independent-groups *t* test and a correlated-groups *t* test in terms of when each should be used.
2. What are the assumptions of a correlated-groups *t* test?
3. When using a correlated-groups *t* test, how do we take the two scores recorded for each participant and "turn them into" one score for each participant?
4. What measure of effect size is used for a correlated-groups *t* test?
5. A researcher is interested in whether participating in sports positively influences self-esteem in young girls. She identifies a group of girls who have not played sports before but are now planning to begin participating in organized sports. She gives them a 50-item self-esteem inventory before they begin playing sports and administers it again after six months of playing sports. The self-esteem inventory is measured on an interval scale, with higher numbers indicating higher self-esteem. In addition, scores on the inventory are normally distributed. The scores appear below.

Before	After
44	46
40	41
39	41
46	47
42	43
43	45

a. What statistical test should be used to analyze these data?

b. Identify H_0 and H_a for this study.
c. Conduct the appropriate analysis.
d. Should H_0 be rejected? What should the researcher conclude?
e. If significant, compute the effect size and interpret.
f. If significant, draw a graph representing the data.

6. The student in Question 5 from Module 18 decides to conduct the same study using a within-participants design in order to control for differences in cognitive ability. He selects a random sample of participants and has them study different material of equal difficulty in both the music and no music conditions. The data appear below. As before, they are measured on an interval-ratio scale and are normally distributed.

Music	No Music
6	10
7	7
6	8
5	7
6	7
8	9
8	8

a. What statistical test should be used to analyze these data?
b. Identify H_0 and H_a for this study.
c. Conduct the appropriate analysis.
d. Should H_0 be rejected? What should the researcher conclude?
e. If significant, compute the effect size and interpret.
f. If significant, draw a graph representing the data.

CRITICAL THINKING CHECK ANSWERS

19.1

1. Difference scores represent the difference in performance for each participant between his or her score in one condition versus the other condition in the experiment. Consequently we simply take the participant's score from one condition and subtract it from her or his score in the other condition, always subtracting in the same order (e.g., condition one from condition two or vice versa).

2. If H_0 is true, then the independent variable in the study should not have had any effect. If there is no effect, then the difference score for each participant should be zero because his or her performance in each condition should be the same.

WEB RESOURCES

Check your knowledge of the content and key terms in this module with a practice quiz and interactive flashcards at **www.cengage.com/psychology/jackson,** or for step-by-step practice and information, check out the Statistics and Research Methods Workshops at **www.cengage.com/psychology/workshops.**

Analysis of Variance (ANOVA)

LEARNING OBJECTIVES

- Identify what a one-way randomized ANOVA is and what it does.
- Describe what between-groups variance is.
- Describe what within-groups variance is.
- Understand conceptually how an F-ratio is derived.

n this module we continue to discuss the types of parametric statistical analyses used by psychologists, but now we look at tests designed for between-participants designs in which there are more than two levels of the independent variable. This design means that the *t* tests described in the last two modules are not suitable in these circumstances because they allow us to compare only the means of two groups. We begin our discussion by outlining some of the advantages of having more than two levels of an independent variable in a study and then turn to the appropriate statistical analysis for such studies.

COMPARING MORE THAN TWO KINDS OF TREATMENT IN ONE STUDY

To illustrate the advantage of more complex experimental designs, let's assume we want to compare the effects of various types of rehearsal on memory. We have participants study a list of 10 words using either rote rehearsal (repetition) or some form of elaborative rehearsal. In addition, we specify the type of elaborative rehearsal to be used in the different experimental groups. Group 1 (the control group) uses rote rehearsal, group 2 uses an imagery mnemonic technique, and group 3 uses a story mnemonic device. Why don't we simply conduct three studies or comparisons, comparing group 1 to group 2, group 2 to group 3, and group 1 to group 3 in three different experiments? This practice is not recommended for several reasons.

A *t* test is used to compare performance between two groups or conditions (Modules 18 and 19). If we do three experiments, we need to use three *t* tests to determine the differences. The problem is that using multiple tests inflates the Type I error rate (we reject the null hypothesis when we should fail to reject it, that is, we claim that the independent variable has an effect when it does not). For most statistical tests we use the .05 alpha level, that is, we are willing to accept a 5% risk of making a Type I error. Although the chance of making a Type I error on one *t* test is .05, the overall chance of making such an error increases as more tests are conducted.

Suppose we conducted three *t* tests or comparisons among the three groups in the memory experiment. The probability of a Type I error on any single comparison is .05. The probability of a Type I error on at least one of the three tests, however, is considerably higher. To determine the chance of a Type I error when making multiple comparisons, we use the formula $1 - (1 - \alpha)^c$ where c equals the number of comparisons performed. Using this formula for the present example, we get

$$1 - (1 - .05)^3 = 1 - (.95)^3 = 1 - .86 = .14$$

Thus the probability of a Type I error on at least one of the three tests is .14, or 14%.

One way of counteracting the increased chance of a Type I error is to use a more stringent alpha level. The **Bonferroni adjustment** in which the desired alpha level is divided by the number of tests or comparisons is typically used for this purpose. For example, if we are using the *t* test to make the three comparisons, we divide .05 by 3 and get .017. By not accepting the result as significant unless the alpha level is .017 or less, we minimize the chance of a Type I error when making multiple comparisons. We know from discussions in previous modules, however, that although using a more stringent alpha level decreases the chance of a Type I error, it increases the chance of a Type II error (failing to reject the null hypothesis when it should have been rejected, namely, missing an effect of an independent variable). Consequently the Bonferroni adjustment is not the best method of handling the problem. A better method is to use a single statistical test that compares all groups rather than using multiple comparisons and statistical tests. Luckily there is a statistical technique that does this: the analysis of variance (ANOVA), which is discussed in the next section.

Bonferroni adjustment: Setting a more stringent alpha level for multiple tests to minimize Type I errors.

ANALYZING THE MULTIPLE-GROUP EXPERIMENT

ANOVA (analysis of variance): An inferential statistical test for comparing the means of three or more groups.

Because *t* tests are not recommended for comparing performance across groups in a multiple-group design due to the increased probability of a Type I error, for multiple-group designs in which interval-ratio data are collected, the recommended statistical analysis is the **ANOVA (analysis of variance)**, an inferential parametric statistical test for comparing the means of three or more groups. As its name indicates, this procedure allows us to analyze the variance in a study. (See the discussion of variance in Module 15.) Nonparametric analyses are also available for designs in which ordinal data are collected (the Kruskal-Wallis analysis of variance) and for designs in which nominal data are collected (the chi-square test). You can find coverage of these statistics in a statistics text.

BETWEEN-PARTICIPANTS DESIGNS: ONE-WAY RANDOMIZED ANOVA

We begin our coverage of statistics appropriate for multiple-group designs by discussing those used with data collected from a between-participants design. Recall that in a between-participants design different participants serve in each condition. In the previously described rehearsal experiment, let's say we ask participants to study a list of 10 words using rote rehearsal or one of two forms of elaborative rehearsal. A total of 24 participants are randomly assigned, 8 to each condition. Table 20.1 lists the number of words correctly recalled by each participant.

Because these data represent an interval-ratio scale of measurement and because there are more than two groups, an ANOVA is the appropriate test to analyze the data. In addition, because this is a between-participants design,

TABLE **20.1**

Numbers of Words Recalled Correctly in Rote Rehearsal, Imagery, and Story Conditions

Rote Rehearsal	Imagery	Story
2	4	6
4	5	5
3	7	9
5	6	10
2	5	8
7	4	7
6	8	10
$\underline{3}$	$\underline{5}$	$\underline{9}$
$\overline{X}=4$	$\overline{X}=5.5$	$\overline{X}=8$

Grand Mean = 5.833

we use a one-way randomized ANOVA. The term "randomized" indicates that participants are randomly assigned to conditions in a between-participants design. The term "one-way" indicates that the design uses only one independent variable, in this case type of rehearsal. Please note that although all of the studies used to illustrate the ANOVA procedure in this module have an equal number of participants in each condition, this is not a requirement when using the ANOVA procedure.

One-Way Randomized ANOVA: What It Is and What It Does

The analysis of variance, or ANOVA, is a parametric inferential statistical test for comparing the means of three or more groups. In addition to helping maintain an acceptable Type I error rate, the ANOVA has the advantage over using multiple t tests of being more powerful and therefore less susceptible to a Type II error. In this section we discuss the simplest use of ANOVA: a design with one independent variable with three levels.

The null hypothesis (H_0) for an ANOVA is that the sample means represent the same population (H_0: $\mu_1 = \mu_2 = \mu_3$). The alternative hypothesis (H_a) is that they represent different populations (H_a: at least one $\mu \neq$ another μ). A rejection of H_0 using an ANOVA signifies that the independent variable affected the dependent variable to the extent that at least one group mean differs from the others by more than would be expected based on chance. Failing to reject H_0 indicates that the means do not differ from each other more than would be expected based on chance. In other words, there is not enough evidence to suggest that the sample means represent at least two different populations.

In the current experiment and given the data in Table 20.1, remember that we are interested in the effects of rehearsal type on memory. The mean number of words recalled in the rote rehearsal condition is 4, in the imagery condition 5.5, and in the story condition 8. The data indicate that most

grand mean: The mean performance across all participants in a study.

participants in each condition did not score exactly at the mean for that condition. That is, there is variability within each condition. The **grand mean**, the mean performance across all participants in all conditions, is 5.833. Because none of the participants in any condition recalled 5.833 words, there is also variability between conditions. The question is whether this variability is primarily due to the independent variable (differences in rehearsal type) or to **error variance**, the amount of variability among the scores caused by chance or uncontrolled variables such as individual differences between participants.

error variance: The amount of variability among the scores caused by chance or uncontrolled variables.

The error variance can be estimated by looking at the amount of variability *within* each condition. Each participant in each condition was treated similarly; each was instructed to rehearse the words in the same manner. Because the participants in each condition were treated in the same manner, any differences observed in the number of words recalled are attributable only to error variance. In other words, some participants may have been better motivated, or more distracted, or better at memory tasks, all factors that would contribute to error variance in this case. Accordingly, the **within-groups variance** (the variance within each condition or group) is an estimate of the population error variance.

within-groups variance: The variance within each condition, an estimate of the population error variance.

Now we can compare the means between the groups. If the independent variable (rehearsal type) had an effect, we would expect some of the group means to differ from the grand mean. If the independent variable had no effect on the number of words recalled, we would still expect the group means to vary from the grand mean slightly as a result of error variance attributable to individual differences. That is, all participants in a study do not score exactly the same. Therefore even when the independent variable has no effect, we do not expect the group means to exactly equal the grand mean. If there is no effect of the independent variable, then the variance between groups should be small and is due to error.

Between-groups variance may be attributed to several sources. There could be systematic differences between the groups, referred to as *systematic variance*. This kind of variance between the groups could be due to the effects of the independent variable (variance due to the experimental manipulation). However, it could also be due to the influence of uncontrolled confounding variables (variance due to extraneous variables). In addition, there is always some error variance in any between-groups variance estimate. In sum **between-groups variance** is an estimate of systematic variance (the effect of the independent variable and any confounds) *and* error variance.

between-groups variance: An estimate of the effect of the independent variable *and* error variance.

F-ratio: The ratio of between-groups variance to within-groups variance.

By looking at the ratio of between-groups variance to within-groups variance, known as the **F-ratio**, we can determine whether most of the variability is attributable to systematic variance (hopefully due to the independent variable and not to confounds) or to chance and random factors (error variance):

$$F = \frac{\text{Between-group variance}}{\text{Within-group variance}} = \frac{\text{Systematic variane} + \text{Error variance}}{\text{Error variance}}$$

Looking at the F-ratio, we can see that, if the systematic variance (which we assume is due to the effect of the independent variable) is substantially greater than the error variance, the ratio will be substantially greater than 1. If there is no systematic variance, then the ratio will be approximately 1.00 (error variance divided by error variance).

There are two points to remember regarding F-ratios. First, for an F-ratio to be significant (show a statistically meaningful effect of an independent variable), it must be substantially greater than 1 (we discuss exactly how much greater later in the module). Second, if an F-ratio is approximately 1, then the between-groups variance equals the within-groups variance and there is no effect of the independent variable.

Refer to Table 20.1, and think about the within-groups versus between-groups variance in this study. Notice that the amount of variance within the groups is small; the scores within each group vary from each individual group mean but not by very much. The between-groups variance, on the other hand, is large: the scores across the three conditions vary to a greater extent. With these data then it appears that we have a relatively large between-groups variance and a smaller within-groups variance. Our F-ratio is therefore greater than 1.00. To assess how large it is, we need to conduct the appropriate calculations (described in the next section). At this point, however, you should have a general understanding of how an ANOVA analyzes variance in order to determine whether the independent variable has an effect.

CRITICAL THINKING CHECK 20.1	
	1. Imagine that a researcher wants to compare four different types of treatment. The researcher decides to conduct six individual studies to make these comparisons. What is the probability of a Type I error, with alpha = .05, across the six comparisons? Use the Bonferroni adjustment to determine the suggested alpha level for the six tests.
	2. Imagine that the following data are from the study of the effects of type of rehearsal on the number of words recalled. Do you think that the between-groups and within-groups variances are large, moderate, or small? Will the corresponding F-ratio be greater than, equal to, or less than 1.00?

Rote Rehearsal	Imagery	Story
2	4	5
4	2	2
3	5	4
5	3	2
2	2	3
7	7	6
6	6	3
3	2	7
$\overline{X} = 4$	$\overline{X} = 3.88$	$\overline{X} = 4$ Grand Mean $= 3.96$

Calculations for the One-Way Randomized ANOVA

To see exactly how ANOVA works, we begin by calculating the sums of squares (*SS*). We used sums of squares as part of the calculation for standard deviation in Module 15. The sum of squares in that formula represented the sum of the squared deviations of each score from the overall mean. If your instructor prefers that you use SPSS, Excel, or the TI84 calculator to conduct this one-way ANOVA, you can find instructions on using these tools in Appendix C.

Several types of sums of squares are used in the calculation of an ANOVA. This section contains *definitional formulas*, which follow the definitions for the various types and give you the basic idea of how they are calculated. When we are dealing with very large data sets, however, definitional formulas can become cumbersome. Consequently statisticians have transformed the definitional formulas into *computational formulas*, which are easier to use in terms of the number of steps required. However, each computational formula does not follow the definition of the particular *SS* and therefore does not necessarily make sense in terms of its definition. If your instructor prefers that you use the computational formulas, they are provided in Appendix D.

total sum of squares:
The sum of the squared deviations of each score from the grand mean.

The first sum of squares that we need to describe is the **total sum of squares** (SS_{Total}), the sum of the squared deviations of each score from the grand mean. In a definitional formula this sum is represented as $\sum (X - \overline{X}_G)^2$ where X represents each individual score and $\overline{X}_G$ is the grand mean. In other words, we determine how much each individual participant varies from the grand mean, square that deviation score, and sum all of the squared deviation scores. For our study of the effects of rehearsal type on memory, the total sum of squares (SS_{Total}) = 127.32. Table 20.2 illustrates the application of this formula.

TABLE **20.2**

Calculation of SS_{Total} Using the Definitional Formula

Rote Rehearsal		Imagery		Story	
X	$(X - \overline{X}_G)^2$	X	$(X - \overline{X}_G)^2$	X	$(X - \overline{X}_G)^2$
2	14.69	4	3.36	6	.03
4	3.36	5	.69	5	.69
3	8.03	7	1.36	9	10.03
5	.69	6	.03	10	17.36
2	14.69	5	.69	8	4.70
7	1.36	4	3.36	7	1.36
6	.03	8	4.70	10	17.36
3	8.03	5	.69	9	10.03
	$\sum = \overline{50.88}$		$\sum = \overline{14.88}$		$\sum = \overline{61.56}$

$SS_{Total} = 50.88 + 14.88 + 61.56 = 127.32$

Note: All numbers have been rounded to two decimal places.

(For the computational formula, see Appendix D.) Once we calculate the sum of squares within and between groups (as we do in the following paragraphs) and add them together, they should equal the total sum of squares. In this way we can check our calculations for accuracy. If the sums of squares within and between do not equal the sum of squares total, then you know there is an error in at least one of the calculations.

Because an ANOVA analyzes the variances between groups and within groups, we need to use different formulas to determine the variance attributable to these two factors. The **within-groups sum of squares** is the sum of the squared deviations of each score from its group mean, or condition mean, and is a reflection of the amount of error variance. In the definitional formula it would be $\sum(X - \overline{X}_g)^2$ where X refers to each individual score and $\overline{X}_g$ is the mean for each group or condition. To determine SS_{Within}, we find the difference between each score and its group mean, square these deviation scores, and then sum all of the squared deviation scores. The use of the definitional formula to calculate SS_{Within} is illustrated in Table 20.3. The computational formula appears in Appendix D. So rather than comparing every score in the entire study to the grand mean of the study (as is done for SS_{Total}), we compare each score in each condition to the mean of that condition. Thus SS_{Within} is a reflection of the amount of variability within each condition. Because the participants in each condition were treated in a similar manner, we would expect little variation among the scores within each group. This lack of variation means that the within-groups sum of squares (SS_{Within}) should be small, indicating a small amount of error variance in the study. For our memory study the within-groups sum of squares (SS_{Within}) is 62.

within-groups sum of squares: The sum of the squared deviations of each score from its group mean.

TABLE **20.3**

Calculation of SS_{Within} Using the Definitional Formula

Rote Rehearsal		Imagery		Story	
X	$(X - \overline{X}_g)^2$	X	$(X - \overline{X}_g)^2$	X	$(X - \overline{X}_g)^2$
2	4	4	2.25	6	4
4	0	5	.25	5	9
3	1	7	2.25	9	1
5	1	6	.25	10	4
2	4	5	.25	8	0
7	9	4	2.25	7	1
6	4	8	6.25	10	4
3	1	5	.25	9	1
	$\sum = 24$		$\sum = 14$		$\sum = 24$

$SS_{\text{Within}} = 24 + 14 + 24 = 62$

Note: All numbers have been rounded to two decimal places.

TABLE **20.4**

Calculation of SS_{Between} Using the Definitional Formula

Rote Rehearsal

$(\overline{X}_g - \overline{X}_G)^2 n = (4 - 5.833)^2 8 = (-1.833)^2 8 = (3.36)8 = 26.88$

Imagery

$(\overline{X}_g - \overline{X}_G)^2 n = (5.5 - 5.833)^2 8 = (-.333)^2 8 = (.11)8 = .88$

Story

$(\overline{X}_g - \overline{X}_G)^2 n = (8 - 5.833)^2 8 = (2.167)^2 8 = (4.696)8 = 37.57$

$SS_{\text{Between}} = 26.88 + .88 + 37.57 = 65.33$

---

between-groups sum of squares: The sum of the squared deviations of each group's mean from the grand mean, multiplied by the number of participants in each group.

The **between-groups sum of squares** is the sum of the squared deviations of each group's mean from the grand mean, multiplied by the number of participants in each group. In the definitional formula this would be $\sum[(\overline{X}_g - \overline{X}_G)^2 n]$ where $\overline{X}_g$ refers to the mean for each group, $\overline{X}_G$ refers to the grand mean, and n refers to the number of participants in each group. The use of the definitional formula to calculate SS_{Between} is illustrated in Table 20.4. The computational formula appears in Appendix D. The between-groups variance is an indication of the systematic variance across the groups (the variance due to the independent variable and any confounds) and error. The basic idea behind the between-groups sum of squares is that if the independent variable had no effect (if there were no differences between the groups), then we would expect all the group means to be about the same. If all the group means are similar, they are also approximately equal to the grand mean, and there is little variance across conditions. However, if the independent variable caused changes in the means of some conditions (caused them to be larger or smaller than other conditions), then the condition means would not only differ from each other but would also differ from the grand mean, indicating variance across conditions. In our memory study $SS_{\text{Between}} = 65.33$.

We can check the accuracy of our calculations by adding SS_{Within} and SS_{Between}. When added, these numbers should equal SS_{Total}. Thus, SS_{Within} (62) + SS_{Between} (65.33) = 127.33. The SS_{Total} that we calculated earlier was 127.32 and is essentially equal to $SS_{\text{Within}} + SS_{\text{Between}}$ when taking into account rounding errors.

Calculating the sums of squares is an important step in the ANOVA. It is not, however, the end step. We must transform SS_{Total}, SS_{Within}, and SS_{Between} into the mean squares. The term **mean square (MS)** is an abbreviation of mean squared deviation scores. The MS scores are estimates of variance between and within the groups. To calculate the MS for each group (MS_{Within} and MS_{Between}), we divide each SS by the appropriate df (degrees of freedom) because the MS scores are variance estimates. Recall that when calculating standard deviation and variance, we divide the sum

mean square: An estimate of either variance between groups or variance within groups.

of squares by N (or $N - 1$ for the unbiased estimator) to get the average deviation from the mean (Module 15). In this same manner we divide the SS scores by their degrees of freedom (the number of scores that contributed to each SS minus 1).

In our example we first determine the degrees of freedom for each type of variance. Let's begin with df_{Total}, which we use to check our accuracy when calculating df_{Within} and $df_{Between}$ (these should sum to df_{Total}). We determined SS_{Total} by calculating the deviations around the grand mean. We therefore have one restriction on our data—the grand mean. This restriction leaves us with $N - 1$ total degrees of freedom (the total number of participants in the study minus the one restriction). For our study on the effects of rehearsal type on memory,

$$df_{Total} = 24 - 1 = 23$$

If we use a similar logic, the degrees of freedom within each group would then be $n - 1$ (the number of participants in each condition minus 1). However, we have more than one group: We have k groups in which k refers to the number of groups or conditions in the study. The degrees of freedom within groups is therefore $k(n - 1)$ or $(N - k)$. For our example

$$df_{Within} = 24 - 3 = 21$$

Finally, the degrees of freedom between groups is the variability of k means around the grand mean. Consequently $df_{Between}$ equals the number of groups (k) minus $1(k - 1)$. For our study this is

$$df_{Between} = 3 - 1 = 2$$

Notice that the sum of df_{Within} and $df_{Between}$ is df_{Total}: $21 + 2 = 23$. This sum allows us to check our calculations for accuracy. If the degrees of freedom between and within do not sum to the degrees of freedom total, we know there is a mistake somewhere.

We can now use the sums of squares and their degrees of freedom to calculate estimates of the variances between and within groups. As stated previously, the variance estimates are called mean squares and are determined by dividing each SS by its corresponding df. In our example

$$MS_{Between} = SS_{Between}/df_{Between} = 65.33/2 = 32.67$$

$$MS_{Within} = SS_{Within}/df_{Within} = 62/21 = 2.95$$

We can now use the estimates of between-groups and within-groups variances to determine the F-ratio:

$$F = MS_{Between}/MS_{Within} = 32.67/2.95 = 11.07$$

The definitional formulas for the sums of squares, along with the formulas for the degrees of freedom, mean squares, and the final F-ratio, are summarized in Table 20.5. The ANOVA summary table for the F-ratio just calculated is presented in Table 20.6. This latter table presents a common format for summarizing ANOVA findings. You will often see ANOVA summary

TABLE **20.5**

ANOVA Summary Table: Definitional Formulas

Source	df	SS	MS	F
Between groups	$k-1$	$\sum[(\overline{X}_g - \overline{X}_G)^2 n]$	SS_b/df_b	MS_b/MS_w
Within groups	$N-k$	$\sum(X - \overline{X}_g)^2$	SS_w/df_w	
Total	$N-1$	$\sum(X - \overline{X}_G)^2$		

TABLE **20.6**

ANOVA Summary Table for the Memory Study

Source	df	SS	MS	F
Between groups	2	65.33	32.67	11.07
Within groups	21	62	2.95	
Total	23	127.33		

tables in journal articles because they are a concise way of presenting the results from an analysis of variance.

Interpreting the One-Way Randomized ANOVA

The obtained F-ratio of 11.07 is obviously greater than 1.00. However, we do not know whether it is large enough to let us reject the null hypothesis. To make this decision, we need to compare the obtained $F(F_{obt})$ of 11.07 with the F_{cv}, the critical value that determines the cutoff for statistical significance. The underlying F distribution is actually a family of distributions, each based on the degrees of freedom between and within each group. Remember that the alternative hypothesis is that the population means represented by the sample means are not from the same population. Table B.3 in Appendix B provides the critical values for the family of F distributions when $\alpha = .05$ and when $\alpha = .01$. To use the table, look at the df_{Within} running down the left-hand side of the table and the $df_{Between}$ running across the top of the table. F_{cv} is found where the row and column of these two numbers intersect. For our example $df_{Within} = 21$ and $df_{Between} = 2$. Because there is no 21 in the df_{Within} column, we use the next lower number, 20. According to Table B.3, F_{cv} for the .05 level is 3.49. Because our F_{obt} exceeds this figure, it is statistically significant at the .05 level. Let's check the .01 level also. The critical value for the .01 level is 5.85. Our F_{obt} is greater than this critical value also. We can therefore conclude that F_{obt} is significant at the .01 level. In APA publication format this information is written as $F(2, 21) = 11.07, p < .01$. Accordingly, we reject H_0 and support H_a. In other words, at least one group mean differs significantly from the others.

Let's consider what factors might affect the size of the final F_{obt}. Because F_{obt} is derived using the between-groups variance as the numerator and the within-groups variance as the denominator, anything that increases the numerator or decreases the denominator increases F_{obt}. Using stronger controls in the experiment could increase the numerator because it makes any differences between the groups more noticeable or larger. This means that $MS_{Between}$ (the numerator in the F-ratio) becomes larger and therefore leads to a larger final F-ratio.

To decrease the denominator, once again use better control to reduce the overall error variance, or increase the sample size, an action that increases df_{Within} and ultimately decreases MS_{Within}. Either measure decreases the size of MS_{Within}, which is the denominator in the F-ratio. Dividing by a smaller number leads to a larger final F-ratio and therefore a greater chance that it is significant.

Graphing the Means and Effect Size

We usually graph the means when we find a significant difference between them, with the independent variable on the x-axis and the dependent variable on the y-axis. A bar graph representing the mean performance of each group is shown in Figure 20.1. In our experiment those in the rote rehearsal condition remembered an average of 4 words, those in the imagery condition an average of 5.5 words, and those in the story condition an average of 8 words.

In addition to graphing the data, we should assess effect size. Based on F_{obt}, we know that there was more variability between groups than within groups, namely, the between-groups variance (the numerator in the F-ratio) was larger than the within-groups variance (the denominator in the F-ratio). However, it is useful to know how much of the variability in the dependent variable can be attributed to the independent variable, that is, to have

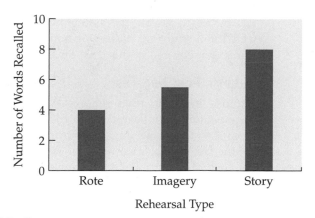

FIGURE **20.1** Mean number of words recalled as a function rehearsal type

eta-squared (η^2): An inferential statistic for measuring effect size with an ANOVA.

a measure of effect size. For an ANOVA, effect size can be estimated using **eta-squared** (η^2), which is calculated as follows:

$$\eta^2 = SS_{Between}/SS_{Total}$$

Because $SS_{Between}$ reflects the differences between the means from the various levels of an independent variable and SS_{Total} reflects the total differences among all scores in the experiment, η^2 reflects the proportion of the total differences in the scores associated with differences between sample means, or how much of the variability in the dependent variable (memory) is attributable to the manipulation of the independent variable (rehearsal type).

Using the $SS_{Between}$ and SS_{Total} from Table 20.6, η^2 is calculated as follows:

$$\eta^2 = 65.33/127.33 = .51$$

So approximately 51% of the variance among the scores can be attributed to the rehearsal condition to which the participant was assigned. In our example the independent variable of rehearsal type is fairly important in determining the number of words recalled by participants because the η^2 of 51% represents a considerable effect.

Assumptions of the One-Way Randomized ANOVA

As with most statistical tests certain conditions must be met to ensure that the statistic is being used properly. The assumptions for the randomized one-way ANOVA are similar to those for the t test for independent groups:

- The data are on an interval-ratio scale.
- The underlying distribution is normally distributed.
- The variances among the populations being compared are homogeneous.

Because the ANOVA is a robust statistical test, violations of some of these assumptions do not necessarily affect the results. Specifically, if the distributions are slightly skewed rather than normally distributed, they do not affect the results of the ANOVA. In addition, if the sample sizes are equal, the assumption of homogeneity of variances can be violated. However, it is not acceptable to violate the assumption of interval-ratio data. If the data collected in a study are ordinal or nominal in scale, other nonparametric procedures (not covered in this text) must be used.

Tukey's Post Hoc Test

post hoc test: When used with an ANOVA, a means of comparing all possible pairs of groups to determine which ones differ significantly from each other.

Because the results from our ANOVA indicate that at least one of the sample means differs significantly from the others (represents a different population from the others), we must now compute a post hoc test (a test conducted after the fact—in this case after the ANOVA). A **post hoc test** involves comparing each of the groups in the study with each of the other groups in order to determine which ones differ significantly from each other. This process may sound a lot like what a t test does, and in this sense the two tests are alike. However, remember that a series of multiple t tests inflates the probability of a Type I error. A post hoc test is designed to permit multiple comparisons and maintain alpha (the probability of a Type I error) at .05.

Tukey's honestly significant difference (HSD): A post hoc test used with ANOVAs for making all pairwise comparisons when conditions have equal n.

The post hoc test presented here is **Tukey's honestly significant difference (HSD)**, which allows a researcher to make all pairwise comparisons among the sample means in a study while maintaining an acceptable alpha (usually .05 but possibly .01) when the conditions have equal n. If there is not an equal number of participants in each condition, then another post hoc test such as Fisher's protected t test, which can be used with equal or unequal n, is appropriate. Because the coverage of statistics in this text is necessarily selective, you'll need to consult a more comprehensive statistics text regarding alternative post hoc tests if you need them.

Tukey's test identifies the smallest difference between any two means that is significant with alpha $=.05$ or .01. The formula for Tukey's HSD is

$$HSD_{.05} = Q(k, df_{\text{Within}}) \sqrt{\frac{MS_{\text{Within}}}{n}}$$

Using this formula, we can determine the HSD for the .05 alpha level. This involves looking up the value for Q in Table B.4 in Appendix B. To look up Q, we need k (the number of means being compared—in our study on memory k is 3) and df_{Within} which can be found in Table 20.6. Referring to Table B.4 for $k = 3$ and $df_{\text{Within}} = 21$ (because there is no 21 in the table, we use 20), we find that at the .05 level $Q = 3.58$. In addition, we need MS_{Within} from Table 20.6 and n (the number of participants in each group). Using these numbers, we calculate HSD:

$$HSD_{.05} = (3.58) \sqrt{\frac{2.95}{8}} = (3.58) \ \sqrt{.369} = (3.58)(.607) = 2.17$$

This result tells us that a difference of 2.17 or greater for any pair of means is significant at the .05 level. In other words, the difference between the means is greater than what would be expected based on chance.

Table 20.7 summarizes the differences between the means for each pairwise comparison. Can you identify which comparisons are significant using Tukey's HSD?

If you identify the differences between the story condition and the rote rehearsal condition and between the story condition and the imagery condition as the two honestly significant differences, you are correct because the difference between the means is greater than 2.17. Because these differences are significant at alpha $=.05$, we should also check $HSD_{.01}$. To do so, we use the

TABLE **20.7**

Differences between Each Pair of Means in the Memory Study

	Rote Rehearsal	Imagery	Story
Rote Rehearsal	—	1.5	4.0
Imagery		—	2.5
Story			—

same formula, but we use Q for the .01 alpha level from Table B.4. The calculations are as follows:

$$HSD_{.01} = (4.64)\sqrt{\frac{2.95}{8}} = (4.64)(.607) = 2.82$$

The only difference significant at this level is between the rote rehearsal and the story conditions. Based on these data, those in the story condition recalled significantly more words than those in the imagery condition ($p < .05$) and those in the rote rehearsal condition ($p < .01$).

IN REVIEW One-Way Randomized ANOVA

Concept	Description
Null hypothesis (H_0)	The independent variable had no effect; the samples all represent the same population
Alternative hypothesis (H_a)	The independent variable had an effect; at least one of the samples represents a different population than the others
F-ratio	The ratio formed when the between-groups variance is divided by the within-groups variance
Between-groups variance	An estimate of the variance of the group means about the grand mean; it includes both systematic variance and error variance
Within-groups variance	An estimate of the variance within each condition in the experiment; it is also known as error variance, or variance due to chance factors
Eta-squared	A measure of effect size; the variability in the dependent variable that is attributable to the independent variable
Tukey's post hoc test	A test conducted in order to determine which conditions in a study with more than two groups differ significantly from each other

---

CRITICAL THINKING CHECK 20.2

1. Of the following four F-ratios, which appears to indicate that the independent variable had an effect on the dependent variable?

   1.25/1.11   0.91/1.25   1.95/0.26   0.52/1.01

2. The following ANOVA summary table represents the results from a study of the effects of exercise on stress. There were three conditions in the study: a control group, a moderate exercise group, and a high exercise group. Each group had 10 participants, and the mean stress levels for each group were control = 75.0, moderate exercise = 44.7, and high exercise = 63.7. Stress was measured using a 100-item stress scale, with 100 representing the highest level of stress. Complete the ANOVA summary table, and determine whether the F-ratio is significant. In addition, calculate eta-squared and Tukey's HSD, if necessary.

ANOVA summary table				
Source	df	SS	MS	F
Between		4,689.27		
Within		82,604.20		
Total				

ONE-WAY REPEATED MEASURES AND TWO-WAY ANOVAs

If the design of the experiment is correlated-groups, the data are interval-ratio, and there are more than two levels of the independent variable, an ANOVA is once again the appropriate statistic. However, in this case because the design is correlated-groups, the appropriate ANOVA is a one-way repeated-measures ANOVA. The term "repeated measures" refers to the fact that we are repeatedly taking measures on the same people. In other words, we are using a correlated-groups design in which the same people serve in every condition. Although detailed coverage of this statistic is beyond the scope of this text, the resulting F-ratio is interpreted in a similar fashion to that from a one-way randomized ANOVA. Moreover, the ANOVA model can be extended to two-way ANOVAs, three-way ANOVAs and so on. This extension simply means that we are increasing the number of independent variables in the study. For example, a two-way ANOVA has two independent variables, and a three-way ANOVA has three. Once again the resulting F-ratios from these ANOVAs are interpreted in a similar fashion to that from a one-way ANOVA.

SUMMARY

In this module we discussed designs that use more than two levels of an independent variable. These designs allow researchers to compare more than two kinds of treatment in a single study. In addition, we discussed the statistical analyses most appropriate for use with these designs, most commonly with interval-ratio data an ANOVA. A randomized one-way ANOVA is used for between-participants designs, a repeated measures one-way ANOVA for correlated-groups designs, and a two-way ANOVA for designs with two independent variables. Also discussed were appropriate post hoc tests (Tukey's HSD) and measures of effect size (eta-squared).

REVIEW OF KEY TERMS

Bonferroni adjustment
ANOVA (analysis of variance)

one-way randomized ANOVA
grand mean

error variance
within-groups variance

between-groups variance
F-ratio

total sum of squares	between-groups sum of squares	eta-squared (η^2)	Tukey's honestly
within-groups sum of squares	mean square	post hoc test	significant difference (HSD)

MODULE EXERCISES

(Answers to odd-numbered exercises appear in Appendix A.)

1. What is the difference between a randomized ANOVA and a repeated measures ANOVA? What does the term "one-way" mean with respect to an ANOVA?
2. Explain between-groups variance and within-groups variance.
3. If a researcher decides to use multiple comparisons in a study with three conditions, what is the probability of a Type I error across these comparisons? Use the Bonferroni adjustment to determine the suggested alpha level.
4. If H_0 is true, what should the F-ratio equal or be close to? If H_a is supported, should the F-ratio be greater than, less than, or equal to 1?
5. What information does eta-squared (η^2) provide?
6. A researcher conducts a study on the effects of the amount of sleep on creativity. The creativity scores for four levels of sleep (2 hours, 4 hours, 6 hours, and 8 hours) for $n = 5$ participants follow.

Amount of Sleep (in Hours)

2	4	6	8
3	4	10	10
5	7	11	13
6	8	13	10
4	3	9	9
2	2	10	10

a. Complete the following ANOVA summary table. (If your instructor wants you to calculate the sums of squares, use the preceding data to do so.)

Source	df	SS	MS	F
Between groups		187.75		
Within groups		55.20		
Total		242.95		

b. Is F_{obt} significant at $\alpha = .05$?
c. Perform post hoc comparisons if necessary.
d. What conclusions can be drawn from the F-ratio and the post hoc comparisons?
e. What is the effect size, and what does it mean?
f. Graph the means.

7. In a study of the effects of stress on illness, a researcher tallied the number of colds people contracted during a 6-month period as a function of the amount of stress they reported during that same time period. There were three stress levels: minimal, moderate, and high. The sums of squares appear in the following ANOVA summary table. The mean for each condition and the number of participants per condition are also noted.

Source	df	SS	MS	F
Between groups		22.167		
Within groups		14.750		
Total		36.917		

Stress Level	Mean	n
Minimal	3	4
Moderate	4	4
High	6	4

a. Complete the ANOVA summary table.
b. Is F_{obt} significant at $\alpha = .05$?
c. Perform post hoc comparisons, if necessary.
d. What conclusions can be drawn from the F-ratio and the post hoc comparisons?
e. What is the effect size, and what does it mean?
f. Graph the means.

8. A researcher interested in the effects of exercise on stress had participants exercise for 30, 60, or 90 minutes per day. The mean

stress level on a 100-point stress scale (with 100 indicating high stress) for each condition follows along with the ANOVA summary table with the sums of squares indicated.

Source	df	SS	MS	F
Between groups		4,689.27		
Within groups		82,604.20		
Total		87,293.47		

Exercise Level	Mean	n
30 minutes	75.0	10
60 minutes	44.7	10
90 minutes	63.7	10

a. Complete the ANOVA summary table.
b. Is F_{obt} significant at $\alpha = .05$?
c. Perform post hoc comparisons if necessary.
d. What conclusions can be drawn from the F-ratio and the post hoc comparisons?
e. What is the effect size, and what does it mean?
f. Graph the means.

9. A researcher conducted an experiment on the effects of a new drug on depression. The researcher had a control group who received nothing, a placebo group,

and an experimental group who received the drug. A depression inventory that provided a measure of depression on a 50-point scale was used (with 50 indicating that an individual is very high on the depression variable). The ANOVA summary table follows along with the mean depression score for each condition.

Source	df	SS	MS	F
Between groups		1,202.313		
Within groups		2,118.00		
Total		3,320.313		

Drug Condition	Mean	n
Control	36.26	15
Placebo	33.33	15
"Drug"	24.13	15

a. Complete the ANOVA summary table.
b. Is F_{obt} significant at $\alpha = .05$?
c. Perform post hoc comparisons if necessary.
d. What conclusions can be drawn from the F-ratio and the post hoc comparisons?
e. What is the effect size, and what does it mean?
f. Graph the means.

CRITICAL THINKING CHECK ANSWERS

20.1

1. The probability of a Type I error is 26.5%: $[1 - (1 - .05)^6] = [1 - (.95)^6] = [1 - .735] = 26.5\%$. With the Bonferroni adjustment the alpha level is .008 for each comparison.
2. Both the within-groups and between-groups variances are moderate to small. This ratio should lead to an F-score of approximately 1.

20.2

1. The F-ratio $1.95/0.26 = 7.5$ suggests that the independent variable had an effect on the dependent variable.

2. ANOVA summary table

Source	df	SS	MS	F
Between	2	4,689.27	2,344.64	0.766
Within	27	82,604.20	3,059.41	
Total	29	87,293.47		

The resulting F-ratio is less than 1 and thus not significant. Although stress levels differ across some of the groups, the difference is not large enough to be significant.

WEB RESOURCES

Check your knowledge of the content and key terms in this module with a practice quiz and interactive flashcards at **www.cengage.com/psychology/jackson,** or for step-by-step practice and information, check out the Statistics and Research Methods Workshops at **www.cengage.com/psychology/workshops.**

LAB RESOURCES

For hands-on experience using the research methods described in this module, see Chapters 5 ("One-Way Designs I") and 6 ("One-Way Designs II") in *Research Methods Laboratory Manual for Psychology*, 2nd ed., by William Langston (Belmont, CA: Wadsworth, 2005).

STATISTICAL SOFTWARE RESOURCES

For hands-on experience using statistical software to complete the analyses described in this module, see Chapters 8 ("Single-Factor ANOVA") and 9 ("Two-Factor ANOVA") in *The Excel Statistics Companion, Version 2.0,* by Kenneth M. Rosenberg (Belmont, CA: Thomson Wadsworth, 2007).

CHAPTER NINE SUMMARY AND REVIEW: INFERENTIAL STATISTICS II

In this chapter we discussed one parametric inferential statistic used with a correlated two-group design: the correlated-groups t test. In addition, we discussed designs that use more than two levels of an independent variable. One advantage to such designs is being able to compare more than two kinds of treatment. Further, we discussed the statistical analyses most appropriate for use with these designs, the most common with interval-ratio data being an ANOVA. A randomized one-way ANOVA is used for between-participants designs. We also discussed appropriate post hoc tests (Tukey's HSD) and measures of effect size (eta-squared). After completing this chapter, you should appreciate the advantages of using more complicated designs, and you should understand the basic statistics used to analyze such designs.

CHAPTER NINE REVIEW EXERCISES

(Answers to exercises appear in Appendix A.)

Fill-in Self-Test

Answer the following questions. If you have trouble answering any of the questions, restudy the relevant material before going on to the multiple-choice self-test.

1. When using a correlated-groups t test we calculate _____, scores representing the difference between participants' performance in one condition and their performance in a second condition.
2. The standard deviation of the sampling distribution of mean differences between dependent samples in a two-group experiment is the _____.
3. The _____ provides a means of setting a more stringent alpha level for multiple tests in order to minimize Type I errors.
4. A(n) _____ is an inferential statistical test for comparing the means of three or more groups.
5. The mean performance across all participants is represented by the _____.
6. The _____ variance is an estimate of the effect of the independent variable, confounds, and error variance.

7. The sum of squared deviations of each score from the grand mean is the _____.
8. When we divide an SS score by its degrees of freedom, we have calculated a _____.
9. _____ is an inferential statistic for measuring effect size with an ANOVA.
10. For an ANOVA we use _____ to compare all possible pairs of groups in order to determine which ones differ significantly from each other.

Multiple-Choice Self-Test

Select the single best answer for each of the following questions. If you have trouble answering any of the questions, restudy the relevant material.

1. If a correlated-groups t test and an independent-groups t test both have $df = 10$, which experiment used fewer participants?
   a. they both used the same number of participants ($n = 10$)
   b. they both used the same number of participants ($n = 11$)
   c. the correlated-groups t test
   d. the independent-groups t test

2. If researchers reported that for a correlated-groups design $t(15) = 2.57$, $p < .05$, you can conclude that_____.
   a. a total of 16 people participated in the study
   b. a total of 17 people participated in the study
   c. a total of 30 people participated in the study
   d. there is no way to determine how many people participated in the study

3. The F-ratio is determined by dividing _____ by _____.
   a. error variance; systematic variance
   b. between-groups variance; within-groups variance
   c. within-groups variance; between-groups variance
   d. systematic variance; error variance

4. If between-groups variance is large, then we have observed _____.
   a. experimenter effects
   b. large systematic variance
   c. large error variance
   d. possibly both b and c

5. The larger the F-ratio is, the greater the chance that _____.
   a. a mistake has been made in the computation
   b. large systematic effects are present
   c. the experimental manipulation probably did not have the predicted effects
   d. the between-groups variation is no larger than would be expected by chance alone and no larger than the within-groups variance

6. One reason to use an ANOVA rather than a t test is to reduce the risk of _____.

   a. a Type II error
   b. a Type I error
   c. confounds
   d. error variance

7. If the null hypothesis for an ANOVA is false, then the F-ratio should be _____.
   a. greater than 1.00
   b. a negative number
   c. 0.00
   d. 1.00

8. If in a randomized ANOVA there are four groups with 15 participants in each group, then the df for the F-ratio is equal to _____.
   a. 60
   b. 59
   c. 3, 56
   d. 3, 57

9. For an F-ratio with $df = 3, 20$ the F_{cv} for $\alpha = .05$ is _____.
   a. 3.10
   b. 4.94
   c. 8.66
   d. 5.53

10. If a researcher reported an F-ratio with $df = 2, 21$ for a randomized one-way ANOVA, then there were _____ conditions in the experiment and _____ total participants.
   a. 2; 21
   b. 3; 23
   c. 2; 24
   d. 3; 24

11. Systematic variance and error variance comprise the _____ variance.
   a. within-groups
   b. total
   c. between-groups
   d. participant

12. If a randomized one-way ANOVA produced $MS_{Between} = 25$ and $MS_{Within} = 5$, then the F-ratio would be _____.
   a. $25/5 = 5$
   b. $5/25 = 0.20$
   c. $25/30 = 0.83$
   d. $30/5 = 6$

KEY TERMS

Here are the terms from the glossary presented earlier. Go through the list and see if you can remember the definition of each.

ANOVA (analysis of variance)

Between-groups sum of squares

Between-groups variance

Bonferroni adjustment

Correlated-groups t test

Difference scores

Error variance

Eta-squared (η^2)

F-ratio

Grand mean

Mean square

One-way randomized ANOVA

Post hoc test

Standard error of the difference scores

Total sum of squares

Tukey's honestly significant difference (HSD)

Within-groups sum of squares

Within-groups variance

CHAPTER **10**

APA Communication Guidelines

22 | APA SAMPLE MANUSCRIPT

CHAPTER TEN SUMMARY AND REVIEW: APA COMMUNICATION GUIDELINES

In this final chapter we cover the guidelines set forth by the APA for writing style. APA has very specific writing style guidelines, which can be found in the sixth edition of the *Publication Manual of the American Psychological Association* (APA, 2009). We discuss general writing style, including clarity and grammar, how to cite others' work properly and avoid plagiarism, and basic typing or word processing configurations for your document. In addition, we describe the basic organization of an APA-style paper and look at a sample paper. Finally, we examine briefly guidelines for presenting your research at a conference.

Communicating Research Findings

LEARNING OBJECTIVES

- Identify and briefly describe the basic components of an APA-format paper.

- Be familiar with the basic word processing skills necessary to create an APA-style paper.

WRITING CLEARLY

The APA style guidelines are intended to facilitate clear paper writing. First, the APA recommends an orderly and organized presentation of ideas. Toward this end you should prepare an outline of the paper before you begin writing. Second, the APA guidelines stress smoothness of expression, or clear and logical communication. To meet this goal, provide transitions from paragraph to paragraph and from section to section, do not change topics suddenly, and make sure you have not omitted something that is necessary to understand the material being presented. Third, the APA recommends striving for economy of expression, avoiding wordiness and redundancy. Following are some examples of wordiness:

Wordy	*Better*
at the present time	now
based on the fact that	because
the present study	this study

In the following examples from the APA manual, the italicized words are redundant and can be omitted:

Six *different* groups saw

a total of 45 participants

in *close* proximity

just exactly

has been *previously* found

The APA manual provides several strategies to improve writing style and avoid potential problems, including: writing from an outline; putting aside the first draft, rereading the initial draft after a delay; and asking a colleague or peer to critique the draft for you.

AVOIDING GRAMMATICAL PROBLEMS

Among other things, clarity and smoothness depend on grammatical correctness. Be sure to check for subject and verb agreement. If the subject is singular, then the verb in the sentence must be singular; if the subject is plural, then the verb should be plural.

Incorrect: Participant apathy as well as performance on the task decrease with practice.
Correct: Participant apathy as well as performance on the task decreases with practice.

A pronoun must agree with its antecedent. Pronouns replace nouns (antecedents). If the antecedent is singular, then the pronoun must be singular; if the antecedent is plural, then the pronoun should be plural.

Incorrect: The participant first entered their four-digit code.
Correct: The participants first entered their four-digit code.
Or: The participant first entered his or her four-digit code.

In addition, pronouns must agree in gender (i.e., masculine, feminine, or neuter) with the nouns they replace. This rule also applies to relative pronouns, a pronoun that links subordinate clauses to nouns. The relative pronoun *who* should be used for human beings, whereas *that* or *which* should be used for nonhuman animals and for things.

> *Incorrect:* The subjects that volunteered were asked to complete a survey.
> *Correct:* The subjects who volunteered were asked to complete a survey.

Another common problem in student papers is the misuse of homophones. Homophones are words that sound the same or are pronounced the same but are spelled differently and have different meanings. For example, *to, too,* and *two* are homophones as are *rite, write,* and *right* and *their, there,* and *they're.* Make sure you understand the proper use of each of these homophones.

Two other errors frequently made by students that resemble homophone errors are confusing *then* and *than* and *effect* and *affect.* The word *then* is an adverb meaning "at that time"; the word *than* is a conjunction meaning "in comparison with." The following examples illustrate correct usage:

> *Then:* I was at work then.
> I want to go to the gym first and then go to the store.
> *Than:* She is a better dancer than I.
> I would rather go to the game than study for my exam.

The word *effect* can be a noun or a verb. As a noun it means "what is produced by a cause"; as a verb it means "to bring about or accomplish."

> *Effect* (noun): The amount of practice had a significant effect on reaction time.
> *Effect* (verb): I effected a change in the grading policy.

The word *affect* can also be a noun or a verb. As a noun it refers to emotion; as a verb it means "to act on or to move."

> *Affect* (noun): The participants in the placebo group maintained a flat affect.
> *Affect* (verb): The amount of practice affected reaction time.

Other common problems include distinguishing between *that* and *which* and between *while* and *since.* *That* and *which* are relative pronouns used to introduce an element that is subordinate to the main clause of the sentence. *That* clauses are restrictive; that is, they are essential to the meaning of the sentence.

> *Example:* The animals that performed well in the first experiment were used in the second experiment.

In other words, only those animals that performed well were used in the second experiment. *Which* clauses are nonrestrictive and merely add further information.

> *Example:* The animals, which performed well in the first experiment, were not proficient in the second experiment.

In other words, the second experiment was more difficult for all of the animals.

While and *since* are subordinate conjunctions that also introduce an element that is subordinate to the main clause of the sentence. Although some style authorities accept the use of *while* and *since* when they do not refer strictly to time, the APA manual calls for the use of *while* and *since* primarily when referring to time. *While* should be used to refer to simultaneous events; *since* should be used to refer to a subsequent event.

While: The participants performed well while listening to music.
Since: Since this original study, many others have been published.

When the writer is not referring to temporal events, the APA manual suggests using *although, whereas, and*, or *but* rather than *while* and *because* rather than *since*.

Beware of misusing nouns of foreign origin such as *data*, which is a Latin plural noun (the singular is *datum*).

Incorrect: The data is presented in Table 1.
Correct: The data are presented in Table 1.

Other nouns of foreign origin with plural forms that are frequently misused include the following:

Singular	*Plural*
phenomenon	phenomena
stimulus	stimuli
analysis	analyses
hypothesis	hypotheses

Finally, the APA prefers the use of active voice rather than passive voice because verbs are vigorous, direct communicators. Although the passive voice is acceptable in other forms of writing, in APA-style writing we are focusing on the actor. The following examples illustrate the use of active versus passive voice.

Nonpreferred: The data were analyzed using a two-way randomized ANOVA.
Preferred: We analyzed the data using a two-way randomized ANOVA.

REPORTING NUMBERS

You will most likely be reporting many numbers in your research paper, from the number of participants used to the statistics that you calculated. How should they be reported—as numbers or in words? The general rule for APA papers is to use words when expressing numbers below 10 that do not represent precise measurements and to use numerals for all numbers 10 and higher. This general rule, however, has some exceptions.

- When starting a sentence with a number, use words.
  Example: Sixty students participated in the study.

- When reporting a percentage, use numerals followed by a percent sign.
  Example: The participants in the imagery practice condition improved by 40%, whereas those in the nonimagery practice condition improved by only 8%.

- When describing ages, use numerals.
  Example: The 10-year-olds performed better than the 8-year-olds.
- When describing sample size, use numerals.
  Example: There were 9 females and 9 males in each condition.
- When reporting statistics, mathematical formulas, functions, or decimal quantities use numerals.
  Example: The mean score for the females was 6.
- When referring to times or dates use numerals.
  Example: Subjects had 2 hours to work on the task.
- When numbers above or at 10 and below 10 are being compared in the same sentence, use numerals.
  Example: Participants worked on either 5 or 10 logic problems.

One final consideration with respect to reporting numbers is how to report statistics. As noted, they are reported as numbers. However, each statistical term is represented by an italicized abbreviation. The abbreviations for some of the more commonly used descriptive statistics are given here:

M	Mean
SD	Standard deviation
df	Degrees of freedom
N	Total number of participants

When we report the results of a statistical significance test, APA style is to report the abbreviation for the test with the degrees of freedom in parentheses, the calculated value of the test statistic, and the probability level.

> *Example:* The participants in the imagery rehearsal condition remembered more words ($M = 7.9$) than the participants in the rote rehearsal condition ($M = 4.5$), $t(18) = 4.86$, $p < .01$ (one-tailed).

Table 21.1 provides examples of the correct APA format for reporting the results from several statistical significance tests.

TABLE **21.1**

Statistical Abbreviations and Examples of Correct APA Format
for Reporting Test Results

Statistical Abbreviation	Statistical Test	Example of Correct APA Reporting Format
r	Pearson's product-moment correlation coefficient	$r(20) = .89, p < .01$
t	t test	$t(18) = 3.95, p < .001$
χ^2	χ^2 test	$\chi^2(1) = 4.13, p < .05$
F	ANOVA	$F(2, 24) = 5.92, p < .01$

CITING AND REFERENCING

Another important element of an APA-style paper is citing and referencing properly. The most important general rule to keep in mind is that any information obtained from another source, whether quoted or simply reported, must be cited and referenced. The author's name and the publication date of the work are cited in the body of the paper. All sources cited in the paper must then appear in the references list, which in turn should contain entries only for those works cited in the text of the paper. This practice enables readers to identify the source of ideas and then to locate the published sources.

Citation Style: One Author

APA journals use the author-date method of citation. Accordingly, the surname of the author and the date of publication are inserted in the text at the appropriate point.

> Jones (1999) found that ...
> A recent study of rehearsal type (Jones, 1999) suggests ...
> According to a recent study (Jones, 1999), imagery rehearsal ...
> Participants who used rote rehearsal remembered fewer words than those who used imagery rehearsal (Jones, 1999).

When the name of the author appears as part of the text, cite the year of publication in parentheses. When the name of the author is not part of the narrative, both the author and the date appear in parentheses and are separated by a comma. This parenthetical citation may fall either within a sentence or at its end. Within a paragraph there is no need to include the year of publication in subsequent citations of the same study as long as the study cannot be confused with others cited.

Citation Style: Multiple Authors

When a work has two authors, cite both authors every time the reference occurs. When a work has three to five authors, cite all authors the first time the reference occurs. After that, cite only the first author's surname followed by the abbreviation "et al." (and others).

> *First citation:* Burns, Menendez, Block, and Follows (2001) found ...
> *Subsequent citation within the same paragraph:* Burns et al. found ...
> *Subsequent first citation per paragraph thereafter:* Burns et al. (2001) found ...

When a paper has six or more authors, cite only the surname of the first author followed by "et al." and the year of publication for the first and subsequent citations. When the paper appears in the references, however, include the names of all authors. Note that when two or more authors are cited in parentheses, the word "and" is replaced by an ampersand (&).

Reference Style

APA reference style differs for journal articles, books, edited books, dissertations, magazines, newspaper articles, and information from the Web. When in doubt about referencing format, it is best to consult the APA *Publication Manual* (2009). References are typed in alphabetical order by the first author's last name. Each reference has several sections that are separated by periods, for example, author name(s), publication date, article title, and journal. The title of a journal (or book) and the volume number of the journal are italicized. The first line of each reference begins at the left margin, and all subsequent lines are indented—known as a hanging indent. Like the rest of the manuscript, the references are double-spaced. The following are the correct formats for some of the more commonly used types of references. If you are referencing a source that is not covered here, consult the *Publication Manual*.

Journal Article

Karau, S. J., & Williams, K. D. (1993). Social loafing: A meta-analytic review and theoretical integration. *Journal of Personality and Social Psychology, 65,* 681–706.

Book: One Author, First Edition

Hunt, M. (1993). *The story of psychology.* New York: Doubleday.

Book: Multiple Authors, Second or Later Edition

Bordens, K. S., & Abbott, B. B. (1999). *Research design and methods: A process approach* (4th ed.). Mountain View, CA: Mayfield.

Edited Book

Sternberg, R. J., & Barnes, M. L. (Eds.). (1988). *The psychology of love.* New Haven, CT: Yale University Press.

Chapter or Article in an Edited Book

Massaro, D. (1992). Broadening the domain of the fuzzy logical model of perception. In H. L. Pick, Jr., P. van den Broek, & D. C. Knill (Eds.), *Cognition: Conceptual and methodological issues* (pp. 51–84). Washington, DC: American Psychological Association.

Magazine

King, P. (1991, March 18). Bawl players. *Sports Illustrated,* 14–17.

Diagnostic and Statistical Manual of Mental Disorders

American Psychiatric Association. (1994). *Diagnostic and statistical manual of mental disorders* (4th ed.). Washington, DC: Author.

Paper Presented at a Meeting

Roediger, H. L., III. (1991, August). *Remembering, knowing, and reconstructing the past.* Paper presented at the annual meeting of the American Psychological Association, San Francisco.

Poster Presented at a Meeting

Griggs, R. A., Jackson, S. L., Christopher, A. N., & Marek, P. (1999, January). *Introductory psychology textbooks: An objective analysis and update.* Poster session presented at the annual meeting of the National Institute on the Teaching of Psychology, St. Pete Beach, FL.

Internet Article Based on a Print Source

Jacobson, J. W., Mulick, J. A., & Schwartz, A. A. (1995). A history of facilitated communication: Science, pseudoscience, and antiscience. *American Psychologist, 50,* 750–765. doi: 10.1037/0003-066X.50.9.750

Article in an Internet-Only Journal

Fredrickson, B. L. (2000, March 7). Cultivating positive emotions to optimize health and well-being. *Prevention & Treatment, 3,* Article 0001a. Retrieved from http://journals.apa.org/prevention/volume3/pre0030001a.html

TYPING AND WORD PROCESSING

In APA style the entire manuscript is double-spaced. This double-spacing includes the title page, headings, footnotes, quotations, and references. Single or one-and-a-half spacing may be used in tables and figures. Use a 12-point font size in a serif style such as Times New Roman. Margins should be at least 1 inch at the top, bottom, left, and right of every page. Justify the left margin, but you should leave the right margin uneven, or ragged. Do not divide words at the end of a line, and do not use a hyphen to break words at the ends of lines. Use one space after commas, colons, semicolons, periods in citations, and all periods in the reference section. The APA prefers two spaces after periods at the end of sentences. Begin numbering the manuscript on the title page and number all pages thereafter. The running head (the information at the top of each page) and page numbers should be about ½ inch from the top of the page. Paragraphs should be indented five to seven spaces.

ORGANIZING THE PAPER

An APA-style manuscript has a specific organization. The proper order is title page, abstract, introduction, method, results, discussion, and references, and any footnotes. Finally, tables, figures, and appendices appear at the very end of the manuscript. In the following sections we discuss the basic content for each of these parts of the manuscript. Refer to the sample paper in Module 22 as you read through each of the following sections.

Title Page

The title page in an APA-style manuscript contains more information than simply the title of the paper. Refer to the title page in Module 22. At the top of the page is the running head—an abbreviated title—that is preceded by the phrase "Running head"; however, this phrase only appears on the title page. The running head itself is typed in all capital letters. In the sample paper the running head is "WILLINGNESS TO DATE." The running head is left-justified and appears about ½ inch from the top of the page. Thus it is actually printed in the top margin of the page. It should be a maximum of 50 characters, counting letters, punctuation, and spaces between words. Right-justified on the same line as the running head, is the page number, beginning with the title page as page 1. The running head and page number appear on every page of the manuscript (remember, although the running head appears on every page of the paper, it is preceded by the phrase "Running head" only on the title page). If you are using a word processing program, use the header/footer function to insert the running head and page number. Do not try to manually type the running head on each page. APA style requires the running head so that those reviewing the manuscript have an easier time keeping the paper together and the pages in the correct order. In addition, if the paper is published in a journal, the running head will appear at the top of either odd- or even-numbered pages of the article. Thus the running head should convey in brief what the paper is about.

The title is centered below the running head and page number in the top half of the page. A title should be no more than 12 words and should clearly and simply summarize the main idea of the paper. Notice that the title of the sample paper, "The Effects of Salary on Willingness to Date," states the effects of an independent variable on a dependent variable. Below the title of the paper is the author's name, and below that is his or her institutional affiliation. Lastly, author notes appear on the title page. Author notes include the heading "Author Note" followed by the departmental affiliation of each author and the sources of financial support. It can also provide such background information about the study as that it was based on the author's master's thesis or dissertation. The author note also provides acknowledgments to colleagues who may have helped with the study. Further, the author note tells the reader whom to contact for further information concerning the article.

Abstract

Page 2 of the manuscript is the abstract. See the abstract in Module 22. The word "Abstract" is centered at the top of the page, the abstract itself is written as a block-style paragraph (no paragraph indent), and the running head and page number are in top margin of the page. The abstract is a brief comprehensive summary of the contents of the manuscript. It should be between 150 and 250 words. Although the abstract appears at the beginning of the manuscript, it is usually easier to write it after you have written the entire paper because it is a very brief description of the entire paper. When writing the abstract, try to describe each section of the paper (introduction, Method, Results, and Discussion) in one or two concise sentences. Describe the problem under investigation and the purpose of the study; the participants and general methodology; the findings with statistical significance levels, and/or effects sizes, and confidence intervals; and the conclusions and implications or applications of the study. If your manuscript is published, the abstract will appear in collections of abstracts such as those in the *Psychological Abstracts* described in Module 3.

Introduction

The introduction begins on page 3. It is not labeled "Introduction"; instead, the title of the manuscript, exactly as it appears on the title page, is centered at the top of the page. The introduction has three basic components. The first part introduces the problem under study. The second part contains relevant previous research to provide an appropriate history and cites works that are pertinent to the issue but not works of marginal or peripheral significance. When summarizing earlier works, emphasize pertinent findings, relevant methodological issues, and major conclusions. Do not include nonessential details. The third part of the introduction states the purpose and rationale for the study. You should explain your approach to solving the problem, define the variables, and state your hypotheses along with the rationale for each hypothesis.

Method

The Method section begins wherever the introduction ends; it does not begin on a new page. The heading "**Method**" in boldfaced font is centered wherever the Method section begins. This section describes exactly how the study was conducted, in sufficient detail that it can be replicated by anyone who has read the Method section. This section is generally divided into subsections. Although the subsections vary across papers, the most common are "participants" (or "subjects") and "procedure," although it is also possible to have a separate materials or apparatus section as in the sample paper in Module 22. The participants subsection should include a description of the participants and how they were obtained. Major demographic characteristics such as gender, age, and ethnicity should be described when appropriate, and the total number of participants should be indicated. A materials subsection if used usually describes the testing materials used, such as a particular test or inventory or a type of problem that participants were asked to solve. An apparatus subsection if used describes specific equipment employed. The procedure subsection summarizes each step in the execution of the research, including the groups used in the study, instructions given to the participants, the experimental manipulation employed, any counterbalancing or randomization used, and specific control features utilized in the design. If the design is particularly complex, you may want to consider having a separate design subsection preceding the procedure.

Results

The Results section begins right after the Method section, with the heading "**Results**" in boldfaced print centered before the section begins. This section summarizes the data collected and the type of statistic(s) used to analyze the data. It should include a description of the results only, not an explanation of the results. In addition to using the APA format (as explained earlier in the module), it is also common to use tables and figures when presenting the results. Tables usually provide exact values and can be used to display complex data and analyses in an easy-to-read format. Figures provide a visual impression and can be used to illustrate complex relationships, but they are generally not as precise as tables. Remember that tables and figures are used to supplement the text. When using them, you must refer to them in the text, telling the reader what to look for. Although tables and figures are referred to in the Results section of the paper (and will be included here if the manuscript is published), the actual tables and figures appear at the end of the manuscript, following the references and footnotes.

Discussion

The Discussion section begins immediately after the Results section with the heading "**Discussion**" centered at the beginning of the section. The Discussion section allows you to evaluate and interpret the results. Typically this section begins with a restatement of the predictions of the study. You then discuss whether the predictions were supported. Next comes a discussion of the relationship between the results and past research and theories. Lastly, include any criticisms of the study (such as possible confounds) and implications for future research. If the Discussion is relatively brief, it can be combined with the Results section as a Results and Discussion section or Results and Conclusions section.

References

Use the correct format for references (as described earlier in the module). The references begin on a new page after the end of the discussion. Center the word "References" (no boldfaced print here) at the top of the page. Remember to double-space the references, use a hanging indent, and include the running head and page number in the top margin of each page. Also remember that any works cited in the text must appear in the references but that only works cited in the text should be included.

Appendices

Appendices are used to provide information that might be distracting if presented in the text. Some examples of material that might be included in an appendix are a computer program specifically designed for the research study, an unpublished test, a mathematical proof, and a survey instrument.

Tables and Figures

Although tables and figures are typically used and referred to in the Results section to supplement the text, they appear at the end of the manuscript. Tables always precede figures at the end of the manuscript, no matter what order they were referred to in the text. Each table appears on a separate page.

TABLE **21.2**
Sample Table

Table 1				
Means of Personality Variables by Major and Gender				
	Science		Humanities	
	Helping first	Mood first	Helping first	Mood first
Males	22.22	23.00	45.40	61.11
Females	14.67	9.50	50.22	52.09

There are no specific rules for formatting tables, other than that they should not appear cramped, that horizontal lines should be used to define areas of the table, and that vertical lines may not be used. The columns and rows of the table should be labeled clearly. The running head and page number continue to be used on the pages with tables. In addition, each table should be numbered and have a brief explanatory title. Because the sample paper in Module 22 has no tables, the example in Table 21.2 illustrates the basic table format.

Figures are always placed after the tables at the end of the manuscript. The running head and page number appear on the figure pages also. If there is more than one figure in the manuscript, each figure appears on a separate page. The figure caption appears at the bottom of the page and can be single-, one-and-a-half-, or double-spaced. It is preceded by the identifier in italics "*Figure 1.*" or "*Figure 2.*" etc. A figure can consist of a graph, chart, photograph, map, or drawing. Several figures appear in Modules 15, 18, 19, and 20. You can use these or the figure that appears in the sample paper as guides. In graphs the levels of the independent variable are plotted on the *x*-axis, and the values of the dependent variable are plotted on the *y*-axis. If a study has more than one independent variable, the levels of the second and successive independent variables are labeled within the figure.

The Use of Headings

APA-style papers use one to five levels of headings. Examples of the types of headings follow:

Level 1   **Centered, Boldface, Uppercase and Lowercase Heading**
The heading is centered and boldface. The first letter of each word is capitalized. The text begins indented on a new line.

Level 2   **Flush Left, Boldface, Uppercase and Lowercase Heading**
The heading is typed in boldface, flush on the left margin. The first letter of each word is capitalized, and the text begins indented on a new line.

Level 3   **Indented, boldface, lowercase paragraph heading ending with a period.** The heading is indented, typed in boldface, and has a period at the end. The first letter of the first word is capitalized, and the text begins on the same line.

Level 4   *Indented, boldface, italicized, lowercase paragraph heading ending with a period.* The heading is indented, typed in boldface and italics, and has a period at the end. The first letter of the first word is capitalized, and the text begins on the same line.

Level 5   *Indented, italicized, lowercase paragraph heading ending with a period.* The heading is indented, typed in italics, and has a period at the end. The first letter of the first word is capitalized, and the text begins on the same line.

Most papers will use Level 1-3 headings. It might be necessary to use Level 4 and 5 headings in more complex papers.

Level 1 headings are used for major sections such as the Method, Results, and Discussion. The heading is centered, and the first letter of each word is capitalized. (Please note that the APA does not consider the abstract, title of the paper in the introduction, or the references headings. So although they are centered at the top of their respective sections, they are not boldface.) Level 2 headings are used to divide the major sections into subsections. In the sample paper Level 2 headings divide the Method section into subsections. These headings are typed in boldface, flush on the left margin, and the first letter of each word is capitalized. Level 3 headings may be used to organize material within a subsection. Consequently the procedure subsection might be further subdivided into categories of instructions to participants, or the materials subsection might be further divided into categories of tests. A Level 3 heading begins on a new line, indented, and typed in boldface. Only the first letter in the first word is capitalized. The heading ends with a period, and the text begins on the same line.

APA-FORMATTING CHECKLIST

The checklist in Table 21.3 itemizes some of the most common errors found in student papers. Before finalizing a research paper, reread the manuscript and review this checklist for potential errors.

CONFERENCE PRESENTATIONS

Psychologists conducting research frequently attend research conferences at which they present their findings. Their presentations typically take one of two forms: an oral presentation or a poster presentation. Brief descriptions of each of these presenting methods follow.

Oral Presentations

Most oral presentations have one thing in common: you are limited in the amount of time you have to present. Typically you have 10 to 15 minutes to present your research and answer questions. Thus the first dilemma is how to condense your entire paper to a 10- to 15-minute presentation. According to the *Publication Manual*, the material you deliver verbally should differ in the level of detail from your written work. It is appropriate to omit many of the details of the scientific procedures because someone listening to your

TABLE **21.3**
APA-Formatting Checklist

General Formatting and Typing
- There are at least 1-inch margins on all four sides of each page of the manuscript.
- The font is the correct size (12 point on a word processor) and the correct style (a serif font such as Times New Roman).
- The manuscript is double-spaced throughout, including title page, references, and appendices. Tables and figures can be single, one-and-a-half-, or double-spaced.
- The page number appears on the same line with the running head with the running head left-justified and the page number right-justified.
- The running head and page number are typed at the top of each page 1/2 inch from the top of the page (in the top margin).
- There is only one space after commas, colons, semicolons, periods in citations, and all periods in the reference section. Two spaces are preferred after periods at the ends of sentences.
- Arabic numerals are used correctly to express numbers that are 10 or greater; numbers that immediately precede a unit of measurement; numbers that represent fractions and percentages; numbers that represent times, dates, ages, participants, samples, populations, scores, or points on a scale; and numbers less than 10 when those numbers are compared to a number greater than 10.
- Words are used correctly to express numbers less than 10 and numbers at the beginning of a title, sentence, or heading.

Title Page
- The entire title page is double-spaced.
- The running head is aligned with the left margin and is less than 50 characters and spaces long and appears in the top margin 1/2 inch from the top of the page. It is preceded by the phrase "Running head:" on the title page only. The running head itself is in all capital letters but not the phrase "Running head:".
- The page number appears on the same line as the running head and is right-justified.
- The title of the paper is centered in the top 1/3 of the page with the author's names and affiliations centered below it.
- The author note appears on the title page at the bottom of the page with the header "Author Note" centered above it.

Abstract
- "Abstract" is centered at the top of the page—not in boldface.
- The first line of the abstract is even with the left margin (block style, not indented).
- The abstract is between 150 and 250 words.

Body of the Manuscript
- The title of the paper appears centered at the top of page 3 and is not in boldface.
- There are no one-sentence paragraphs.
- The word "while" is used primarily to indicate events that take place simultaneously (alternatives: "although," "whereas," and "but").
- Abbreviated terms are written out completely the first time they are used and then always abbreviated thereafter.
- The word "and" is used in citations outside of parentheses.
- The ampersand (&) is used in citations within parentheses.
- Each and every citation used in the manuscript has a corresponding entry in the references section.
- The phrase "et al." is used only when there are three or more authors.
- In the Results section all test statistics (F, t, χ^2, p) are italicized.
- The section headings Method, Results, and Discussion are in boldface.

References Section
- "References" is centered at the top of the first page—not in boldface.
- The first line of each reference is flush left, and subsequent lines are indented (a hanging indent).
- All entries are typed in alphabetical order.
- Authors' names are separated by commas.
- Authors' last names appear with first and (if provided) middle initials (do not type out first or middle names).
- The name of the journal and the volume number are italicized.
- Each and every entry is cited in the body of the manuscript.

presentation cannot process at the same level of detail as someone reading a written paper. Decide on a limited number of significant ideas you want the audience to process. In addition, use clear, simple language free of jargon to state what you studied, how you went about the research, what you discovered, and the implications of your results. It is appropriate to be redundant in order to emphasize important ideas. Also consider using transparencies, slides, or PowerPoint slides as part of your presentation. It is also recommended that you write your presentation out and practice delivering it out loud to learn it and to determine its length. You should also consider presenting your paper to a critical audience before delivering it at a conference. When you actually deliver the paper, do not read it. Instead, try to speak directly to the audience and refer when necessary to an outline of key points. In addition, make sure to leave time for questions. Finally, have copies of your paper ready for distribution (APA, 2001a).

Poster Presentations

Poster presentations differ from oral paper presentations in that they provide the opportunity for the presenter and the audience to talk with one another. Typically posters are presented in an exhibit area with other posters, which are often on a similar topic and are being presented at the same time. In this manner those interested in the topic can visit the exhibit area, wander about, view the posters, and speak with the authors. Each presenter has a bulletin board, usually about 3.5 feet high by 3 feet wide, on which to display a poster. Bring your own thumbtacks. In constructing the poster, use a few simple guidelines. As with paper presentations minimize jargon and try to use clear and simple language to describe what you studied, how you went about the research, what you discovered, and what the implications of your results are. Pictures, tables, and figures work very well in poster presentations. Make sure you use an appropriate font size when preparing the poster; viewers should be able to read it easily from a distance of 3 feet. As with oral paper presentations have copies of your paper ready for distribution.

CRITICAL THINKING CHECK 21.1	1. Explain what the running head is and where it appears in the manuscript. 2. Identify and briefly explain what the subsections in a Method section should be. 3. Explain what information should and should not appear in a Results section.

SUMMARY

After reading this module, you should have an understanding of APA's writing standards. We presented basic APA formatting and writing guidelines. We discussed how to write clearly, avoid grammatical problems, report numbers, and properly cite and reference the works of others. In addition, we described the organization of an APA-style manuscript, with frequent references to the sample paper in Module 22. Finally, we discussed presenting your research at conferences using either an oral paper presentation format or a poster presentation format.

MODULE EXERCISES

(Answers to odd-numbered exercises appear in Appendix A.)

1. What information is contained on the title page of a manuscript?
2. Briefly describe the type of information that should be in an introduction.
3. Identify the grammatical or formatting errors in each of the following statements:

   a. 50 students participated in the study.
   b. The F-score was 6.54 with a p-value of .05 and 1 and 12 degrees of freedom.
   c. The data is presented in Table 1.
   d. One group of participants took the medication while the other group did not.

CRITICAL THINKING CHECK ANSWERS

21.1

1. The running head that appears on the title page of the manuscript is preceded by the phrase "Running head:" whereas the running head that appears on the remainder of the manuscript pages is not preceded by this phrase. The running head briefly (in 50 characters or less) conveys the nature of the paper. If the paper is ultimately published, the running head will appear at the top of either odd- or even-numbered pages of the journal article.
2. The participants (subjects) subsection should be first. It provides a description of the participants and may include gender, age, and ethnicity. Next may appear a materials or apparatus subsection, describing testing materials or equipment used. The final subsection is usually a procedure (or a design and procedure) subsection. It should describe the variables in the study and the procedure used to collect the data in sufficient detail that another researcher can replicate the study after reading the section.
3. The Results section should identify the statistics used to analyze the data and the results of the analyses. It should not include any explanation or qualification of the results, nor should it relate the results to the hypothesis being tested. These matters are covered in the Discussion section.

WEB RESOURCES

Check your knowledge of the content and key terms in this module with a practice quiz and interactive flashcards at **www.cengage.com/psychology/jackson**, or for step-by-step practice and information, check out the Statistics and Research Methods Workshops at **www.cengage.com/psychology/workshops**.

MODULE 22

APA Sample Manuscript

T his sample paper by Kim J. Driggers and Tasha Helms was originally published in the *Psi Chi Journal of Undergraduate Research* (2000, Vol. 5, pp. 76–80). This paper is reprinted with permission.

Running head: WILLINGNESS TO DATE

1

Running head is left justified and provides a short (50 characters or less) description of the topic of the paper. It is typed in all capital letters and preceded by the phrase "Running head:" on the title page only. The page number is right-justified on the same line.

The Effects of Salary on Willingness to Date

Kim J. Driggers and Tasha Helms

Oklahoma State University

Title, author's name(s), and affiliation(s) are centered and double-spaced.

Author Note

Kim J. Driggers and Tasha Helms, Department of Psychology, Oklahoma State University.

Correspondence concerning this article should be addressed to Kim J. Driggers, Department of Psychology, Oklahoma State University, Stillwater, OK 74078.

The abstract is typed in block paragraph format and is between 150 and 250 words.

Abstract

Abstract is centered at the top of page 2.

The present experiment tested the role of salary in date selection by men and women. Male and female college students ($N = 150$) viewed pictures of the opposite sex and rated the target's attractiveness and their own willingness to date the target was varied among 3 conditions. The level of salary (i.e., \$20,000, \$60,000, and \$100,000) listed. Statistical analyses yielded support for the hypothesis that as the target's salary increased, a participant's willingness to date the target would also increase. That is, as salary increased, both men's and women's willingness to date a target increased. We also found a significant main effect for the sex of participants; as salary increased, women's willingness to date a person increased significantly more than men's willingness.

WILLINGNESS TO DATE   3

The Effects of Salary on Willingness to Date

To properly review current research in the area of date selection, it is first necessary to highlight theories that form the foundations upon which this research was built. Scientists have studied human mate selection for over a century. Darwin (1871) proposed that physical attractiveness and survival attributes were the essence of mate selection (a.k.a. *natural selection*). Many anthropologists and biologists have, explained the factors of physical attractiveness and socioeconomic status (SES) on the basis of evolutionary principles. Often when selecting a mate, one's instinct is a driving factor. Men, according to sociobiologists, search for the most attractive woman to mate with in order to ensure reproductive success (Buss, 1987). Men thus must use physical appearance or related factors (e.g., age and health) to predict the fertility and genes of a woman. To men, mating with a highly attractive woman ensures that their offspring will have a "good" (i.e., viable) genetic makeup. Yet the suggested pattern for women is somewhat different. In terms of evolution, women are more selective than men in their mate selection. Women have more potential risks when choosing a mate (e.g., pregnancy, childbirth, child rearing) and thus concentrate more on a man's ability to pro-vide for her and her offspring (Townsend & Levy, 1990b); hence commitment and the man's ability to offer resources are important factors when it comes to a woman's selection of a man.

WILLINGNESS TO DATE   4

Social psychologists explain these differences in mate selection as a social exchange between the sexes. Scientists have found the exchange of a man's security for an attractive woman is the basis of mate selection (Rusbult, 1980). Elder (1969) found that men's personal prestige ratings increased when they were paired with an attractive woman. However, ratings of women in Elder's study were based on physical attractiveness only. Therefore, women are exchanging attractiveness for the resources men can provide.

These diverse theories highlight the importance of physical attractiveness and SES. Research (Buss, 1987; Darwin, 1871; Elder, 1969; Rusbult, 1980; Townsend & Levy, 1990b) suggests that physical attractiveness is a better predictor of mate selection in men, and SES is a better predictor of mate selection in women. Current studies have also found that both of these attributes play an integral part in female and male mate selection (e.g., Buss, 189; Davis, 1985; Goode, 1996; Hill, Nocks, & Gardner, 1987; Hudson & Henze, 1969; Joshi & Rai, 1989; Sprecher, 1989; Townsend & Levy, 1990a, 1990b).

Townsend and Levy (1990a) questioned participants regarding different types of relationships ranging from casual conversation to dating, sex, and other types of serious relationships. Participants rated their willingness to engage in these types of relationships based on a slide photograph of a person (face and torso were depicted in the picture). Results indicated that men and women were more likely

In parentheses multiple citations are separated by semicolons.

When there are three to five authors give all authors' names in the first citation, and use the first author's name followed by "et al." for subsequent citations. If there are six or more authors, use the "et al." form for the first and subsequent citations.

Use "and" when authors' names are part of the text.

WILLINGNESS TO DATE   5

to engage in all types of relationships when a person was physically attractive. Sprecher (1989), on the other hand, presented only a description of a person (e.g., occupation, salary, favorite color) as the stimulus. Sprecher also found that physical attractiveness played an important factor, even in the absence of visual stimuli.

Other current studies have noted SES as an important predictor of interpersonal attraction. SES includes factors such as career, salary, and the attitudes and behaviors attributed to the concerned person (Joshi & Rai, 1989). Research indicates SES is an important element among both sexes in terms of date selection (Bell 1976; Goode, 1996; Hill et al., 1987; Townsend & Levy, 1990b). For example Hill et al. found that attractiveness ratings by both men and women of an unattractive target of the opposite sex increased as their SES increases. Although important to both sexes, SES is even more important to women than to men in terms of date selection (Bell; Buss, 1987; Goode; Hill et al.; Nevid, 1984; Townsend & Levy, 1990a). Nevid (1984) asked participants to rate personal qualities (e.g., appearance, career, etc.) in terms of their degree of importance in determining their choice of a romantic partner. No visual stimuli were used when the participant determined the order of importance of qualities. Results indicated that women rated SES higher (i.e., as more important) than men in their ranking of importance qualities. Townsend and Levy (990a, 199b) asked men and women

> When there are three to five authors, use the first author's name followed by "et al." for subsequent citations.

how willing they were to enter into relationships after presenting them with a picture and description of a person. They found that SES was a better predictor for women than men when deciding whether or not to enter a serious relationship.

The previously mentioned studies have evaluated the importance of SES in combination with other attributes. Moreover, SES typically has been studied as a global construct, it has never been broken down into its counterparts (i.e., career, salary, attitudes, and behaviors) for evaluation. What are the effects of salary alone on mate selection? How important is salary alone in the overall effect of SES? The present study examined the significance of salary on willingness to date. In order to eliminate the influence of physical attractiveness on ratings, the pictures used in the present study were considered low in physical attractiveness. The independent variable was the salary associated with the photo (three levels: $20,000, $60,000, and $100,000). The dependent variable was the participant's willingness to date a person. The primary hypothesis was that the participant's willingness to date a person would increase as the target's salary increases. Based on previous research, we hypothesized that this relation would be stronger for women.

WILLINGNESS TO DATE   7

The Method section begins right after the introduction ends, not on a new page. The word "Method" is centered in boldface.

Method

Participants

Subsection headings are typed, in boldface, flush on the left margin. Subsection headings stand alone on a line.

The participants in this study consisted of 150 college students (75 men, 75 women) attending a large Midwestern university. The average age of participants was 21 years. The ethnic background of participants varied, with 71% of the sampling being Caucasian, 14% Asian American, 8% African American, and 7% Native American. Researchers accessed participants from the college library, dormitories, the student union, and laundry facilities. In these facilities, researchers accessed 55 participants at student organizational meetings, 75 participants at the university library, and the remaining 20 participants in the mezzanines of the dormitories. Only three participants approached refused to participate. Participants were assigned to conditions (n = 50 each condition) based on the order in which they were approached by the experimenters.

Materials

The materials for the present study consisted of two pictures (one man, one woman) with a short description posted below each picture, and a questionnaire packet (i.e., informed consent sheet, short description of study, and questionnaire). A pre-testing group of 20 students selected the pictures used in this experiment. The pretest group selected the most unattractive male and female picture out of 30 different photographs. The male and female pictures the pretest group selected most often as unattractive were used in this study to control for attractiveness. The pictures focused on the faces and upper torso of a Caucasian man and a Caucasian woman separately, both dressed in casual clothes. Included in the short description paired with the picture was the person's age (i.e., 24), occupation (i.e., business field), pets (i.e., none), and marital status (i.e., single), with the only manipulated variable being salary. The salary values were $20,000, $60,000, and $100,000. The short descriptions were the same for both the female and male conditions.

The seven questions in the survey measured the participant's perception of the target's attractiveness and popularity and the participant's willingness to date the target individual. These questions were based on a 7-point Likert scale with the anchors being 1 (*not willing*) and 7 (*extremely willing*). The focus question in this study was "How willing would you be to go on a date with this person?" The other questions were fillers to distract the participant from determining the true purpose of the research.

Procedure

The three salary levels defined the three conditions for both the male and female groups. Each participant experienced only one of the three conditions, receiving a picture of the opposite sex. Each condition utilized the same female and male picture.

WILLINGNESS TO DATE   9

One of us was present for each individual participant and each of us tested 75 participants. We told the participants that the purpose of the study was to assess individuals' perceptions. Once the participant finished reading the brief description of the study and signed the informed consent, we presented the participant with a picture that included one of the short descriptions below it. Participants were allotted 1 min to look at the picture, but they generally looked at it for 30 s or less. After reading the description of the person and observing the picture, the participant responded to the questionnaire. Once completed, the questionnaire and picture were gathered, and the participant was debriefed.

As with the Method section the Results section does not begin on a new page. The heading is centered in boldface.

Results

We analyzed the scores of the focus question (willingness to date), in each condition, to determine any significant differences that might exist between conditions and sex. There was a significant increase in willingness to date across salary levels for both men and women (see Figure 1). Effects of sex and salary level were analyzed using a two-way analysis of variance (ANOVA). A main effect for sex was found to be significant, $F(1, 150) = 4.58$, $p < .05$, with women $(M = 3.27, SD = 2.07)$ receiving higher ratings than men $(M = 2.97, SD = 1.68)$. A main effect for salary level was significant, $F(1, 150) = 294.96$, $p < .01$, with scores increasing as salary increased. An interaction between sex and condition was also

Tables and figures must be referred to in the text.

When statistical significance tests are presented, the name of the symbol for the test (e.g., F, t, r) is italicized. It is followed by the degrees of freedom in parentheses, the test score, and the p-value (with "p" italicized).

WILLINGNESS TO DATE   10

significant, $F(2, 150) = 5.40$, $p < .01$. Subsequent analyses, indicated that men and women did not differ at the two lower salary levels; however, the willingness scores of the women were significantly higher than those of the men for the highest ($100,000) salary level $t(48) = 3.213$, $p < .05$.

The Discussion section follows immediately after the Results section, not on a new page.

Discussion

The purpose of this study was to examine the significance of salary on date selection preferences, while holding status and attractiveness constant. The first hypothesis was that participants' willingness to date a person would increase as the target's salary increased. We also hypothesized that this relationship would be stronger for women. The data supported both hypotheses. Participants' willingness to date ratings increased as salary increased, and women were more willing than men to engage in a dating relationship, at least at the highest salary level.

Although evolutionary principles were not tested in this experiment, the results do overlap with findings based on these principles. Evolutionists have found that in terms of mate selection, women hold SES as a more important element than men. Thus, a woman may seek out a mate that has high SES in order to ensure support for her family (Townsend & Levy, 1990b). These results support these evolutionary principles in that women's willingness-to-date ratings did increase significantly more than men's ratings as salary increased.

One contradictory result of the present study to these principles is that men's ratings also increased as salary increased, although not as much as women's. A possible explanation may be that this finding is due to an environmental influence because in today's society SES is an important attribute to both men and women (Bell, 1976; Goode, 1996; Hill et al., 1987; Townsend & Levy). Thus evolutionary principles may explain the significant difference in men and women's willingness ratings, whereas environmental influences might account for the significant importance overall of SES to both men and women.

The findings presented in this study were not consistent with social psychology theories of mate selection. A common view is that mate selection is a social exchange between the man and the woman (i.e., man's security in exchange for an attractive woman; Rusbult, 1980). If this social exchange theory played a significant part in mate selection, men's ratings of the women would have been consistent across conditions because there was no change in attractiveness.

Although past studies (Goode, 1996; Hill et al., 1987; Joshi & Rai, 1989; Sprecher, 1989; Townsend & Levy, 1990b) have tested the role of physical attractiveness and other attributes combined, this study isolated the influence of salary. SES was found to be a significant factor in these past studies when combined with other attributes. After isolating salary as a single variable to be tested in date selection, the present findings were similar to past studies that combined

WILLINGNESS TO DATE   12

salary with other attributes (Goode; Hill et al.; Joshi & Rai; Sprecher; Townsend & Levy).

This study was a partial replication of Townsend and Levy's study (1990b). The present study used the same format of questions (i.e., willingness to engage in specific relationships based on a Likert scale response), similar stimuli (i.e., pictures), and also similar methods of analysis. Their results indicated that SES in combination with other attributes (e.g., appearance, personality characteristics, etc.) was an important predictor of date selection in both men and women, but more so for women. This study supported past evidence when identifying the differences between men and women in the role of salary in date selection (Bell, 1976; Buss, 1987; Goode, 1996; Hill et al., 1987; Nevid, 1984; Townsend & Levy, 1990a).

Although the present findings support past research, the design involved a sample of college students whose responses were to hypothetical relationships with hypothetical partners, in only one region of the United States. A replication of this study with a sample encompassing a larger region or multiple regions would help to further support this hypothesis for the purpose of generalization to a more diverse population. Also, personal SES factors of the participants might influence ratings of the target. Controlling for this variable in future studies would broaden the knowledge of this attribute in date selection.

WILLINGNESS TO DATE   13

Other methods need to be developed to continue to test the role of SES in date selection. Showing a video of a person or having a person-to-person interaction are suggestions for future stimuli to further test this hypothesis. Future studies could also evaluate the impact of the participants' personal SES in their selections of romantic partners. If a participant has a high income, how important is that attribute to that person when selecting a date? Another future study might also investigate the importance of salary among lesbian and gay male relationships.

WILLINGNESS TO DATE   14

References

Bell, Q. (1976). *On human finery*. New York: Schocken Books.

Buss, D. M. (1987). Sex differences in human mate selection
criteria: An evolutionary perspective. In C. B. Crawford, M. Smith,
& D. Krebs (Eds.), *Sociobiology and psychology: Ideas, issues
and applications* (pp. 335–352). Hillsdale, NJ: Erlbaum.

Buss, D. M. (1989). Sex differences in human mate preferences:
Evolutionary hypotheses tested in 37 cultures. *The Behavioral
and Brain Sciences, 12,* 1–49.

Darwin, C. (1871). *The descent of man, and selection in relation to
sex*. London: John Murray.

Davis, K (1985). The meaning and significance of marriage in con-
temporary society. In K Davis (Ed.), *Contemporary marriage:
Comparative perspectives on a changing institution* (pp. 1–21).
New York: Russell Sage.

Elder, G. H., Jr. (1969). Appearance and education in marriage mobil-
ity. *American Sociological Review, 34,* 519–533. doi:10.2307/2091

Goode, E. (1996). Gender and courtship entitlement: Responses to
personal ads. *Sex Roles, 34,* 141–169. doi:10.1007/BF01544

Hill, E. M., Nocks, E. S., & Gardner, L. (1987). Physical attractiveness: Manipulation by physique and status displays. *Ethology and
Sociobiology, 8,* 143–154. doi:10.1016/0162-3095(87)90037-9

Hudson, J. W., & Henze, L. F. (1969). Campus values in mate selection: A replication. *Journal of Marriage and the Family, 31,*
772–775.

Joshi, K., & Rai, S. N. (1989). Effect of physical attractiveness and
social status upon interpersonal attraction. *Psychological Studies,*
34, 193–197.

Nevid, J. S. (1984). Sex differences in factors of romantic attraction.
Sex Roles, 11, 401–411. doi:10.1007/BF00287468

Rusbult, C. E. (1980). Commitment and satisfaction in romantic
associations: A test of the investment model. *Journal of Experi-*
mental Social Psychology, 16, 172–186. doi:10.1016/0022-1031
(80)90007-4

Sprecher, S. (1989). The importance to males and females of physical
attractiveness, earning potential, and expressiveness in initial
attraction. *Sex Roles, 21,* 591–607. doi:10.1007/BF00289173

Townsend, J. M., & Levy, G. D. (1990a). Effects of potential partners' costume and physical attractiveness on sexuality and partner
selection. *Journal of Psychology, 124,* 371–389.

Townsend, J. M., & Levy, G. D. (1990b). Effects of potential partners' physical attractiveness and socioeconomic status on sexuality and partner selection. *Archives of Sexual Behavior, 19,*
149–164. doi:10.1007/BF01542229

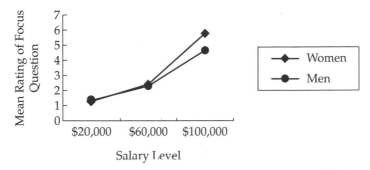

Figure 1. Mean rating of male and female participants for each conditions ($20,000, $60,000, $100,000) on focus question ("How willing would you be to go on a date with this person?").

CHAPTER TEN SUMMARY AND REVIEW: APA COMMUNICATION GUIDELINES

Basic APA formatting and writing guidelines were presented in this chapter. This presentation included how to write clearly, avoid grammatical problems, report numbers, and properly cite and reference the works of others. Additionally, the organization of an APA-style manuscript was described, with frequent references to the sample paper in Module 22.

CHAPTER TEN REVIEW EXERCISES

(Answers to exercises appear in Appendix A.)

Fill-in Self-Test

Answer the following questions. If you have trouble answering any of the questions, restudy the relevant material before going on to the multiple choice self-test.

1. The subsections in a Method section of an APA-format paper include the _____.
2. Statistical findings are reported in the _____ section of an APA-format paper.
3. The page after the title page in an APA-format paper is always the _____.

Multiple-Choice Self-Test

Select the single best answer for each of the following questions. If you have trouble answering any of the questions, restudy the relevant material.

1. A description of prior findings in the area of study is to the _____ as a report of statistical findings is to _____.
   a. introduction; method section
   b. method section; introduction
   c. introduction; results section
   d. results section; method section

2. A summary of the entire research project is to _____ as an interpretation of the findings is to _____.
   a. abstract; results section
   b. method section; results section
   c. abstract; discussion section
   d. results; discussion section

3. Which list below represents the correct ordering of the sections of an APA paper?
   a. abstract, method, introduction, results
   b. introduction, abstract, method, results
   c. discussion, abstract, introduction, method
   d. title page, abstract, introduction, method

4. Based on APA style, what is wrong with the following reference?
   Karau, Steven. J., & Williams, Kenneth. D. (1993). Social loafing: A meta-analytic review and theoretical integration. *Journal of Personality and Social Psychology, 65*, 681–706.
   a. The name of the journal should be underlined.
   b. Only the initials for the authors' first and middle names should be used.
   c. The first letters of the words in the title of the paper should be capitalized.
   d. Nothing is wrong with the reference.

Answers to Odd-Numbered Exercises

Module 1

1. The answers provided to this question will obviously vary. The following are examples of information gained through each of the sources of knowledge discussed in the chapter.

   Superstition-Intuition:
   Breaking a mirror leads to 7 years of bad luck.

   A black cat crossing your path signifies bad luck.

   I have a feeling that something bad is going to happen on my trip next week.

   Authority:
   You read in the newspaper that more Americans are overweight now than 10 years ago.

   You recently saw a TV commercial for a new diet product that was endorsed by a very slim soap opera star.

   Tenacity:
   You have heard the SlimFast slogan so many times that you believe it must be true.

   Rationalism:
   SUVs use more gas and spew more emissions than many other vehicles. Because emissions contribute significantly to air pollution, those who drive SUVs must be less concerned about polluting the environment.

Empiricism:

I have observed that using note cards can be an effective means of studying for an examination.

I have observed that using note cards can be an ineffective means of studying for an examination.

Science:

Studies have shown that smoking has been linked to lung disease.

Studies have shown that elaborative rehearsal leads to better retention than rote rehearsal.

3. Many scientists view being called a skeptic as a compliment because in their opinion being skeptical means that they do not blindly accept findings or information. In other words, being a skeptic means that they require data to support an idea and that they insist on proper testing procedures when the data are collected. In addition, being a skeptic means applying the three criteria that help to define science: systematic empiricism, public verification, and empirically solvable problems.

5. Applied research has the obvious advantage of being able to apply the findings immediately. This research helps to solve problems and apply the answers to help improve lives. Basic research, on the other hand, might not be applied so readily. It is designed to answer questions in the search of knowledge. However, much basic research has led to applications that improve lives.

Module 2

1. Research methods are equally important to all areas of psychology because all that we know about a discipline is gained through research. Thus for those planning on pursuing careers in clinical or counseling psychology, a knowledge of research methods is important in order to determine whether a particular counseling method or drug is an effective treatment.

3. a. The independent variable is the amount of caffeine.
   b. The dependent variable is level of anxiety.
   c. The control group is made up of those who receive no caffeine, whereas the experimental group consists of those who receive caffeine.
   d. The independent variable is manipulated.

CHAPTER ONE REVIEW

Fill-In Self-Test

1. intuition
2. tenacity
3. hypothesis
4. skeptic
5. solvable problems
6. pseudoscience
7. description, prediction, explanation

8. applied
9. case study
10. population
11. correlational
12. participant (subject)
13. independent
14. control

Multiple-Choice Self-Test

1. d	4. d	7. b	10. b
2. a	5. a	8. b	11. d
3. b	6. c	9. c	12. d

CHAPTER TWO

Module 3

1. There is no correct answer to this question. It requires library work.

Module 4

1. Debriefing entails providing information about the true purpose of the study as soon as possible after the completion of data collection. Through the debriefing process participants should learn more about the benefits of research to them and to society in general. The researcher also has the opportunity to alleviate any discomfort the participants may be experiencing. During debriefing the researcher should try to bring the participants back to the same state of mind that they were in before they participated in the study.

3. In addition to treating the animals humanely throughout all experimental procedures, the APA guidelines on the use of animals mandate that there must be justification for the research, that the personnel interacting with the animals must be properly trained, that there must be adequate care and housing for the animals, and that the animals are acquired in the appropriate manner.

CHAPTER TWO REVIEW

Fill-In Self-Test

1. PsycINFO, PsycLIT
2. Social Science Citation Index (SSCI)
3. informed consent
4. deception
5. Institutional Review Board (IRB)

Multiple-Choice Self-Test

1. c	2. a	3. a	4. c

CHAPTER THREE

Module 5

1. Answer c represents an operational definition of depression.

Module 6

1. c. + .83. Although this correlation coefficient is not the strongest, it is the strongest positive correlation. It is therefore the best measure of reliability.
3. If the observers disagreed 32 times out of 75, then they agreed 43 times out of 75. Thus the interrater reliability is 43/75 = .57. Because the interrater reliability is moderate, the librarians should use these data with caution. In other words, there may be a problem either with the measuring instrument or with the individuals using the instrument, and therefore the data are not very reliable.

CHAPTER THREE REVIEW

Fill-In Self-Test Answers

1. operational definition
2. magnitude (ordinality)
3. nominal
4. interval
5. self-report measures
6. reactivity
7. test-retest reliability
8. interrater reliability
9. content validity
10. construct validity

Multiple-Choice Self-Test

1. d	4. b	7. a	10. b
2. b	5. a	8. d	11. d
3. a	6. b	9. c	12. b

CHAPTER FOUR

Module 7

1. This research might best be conducted by means of some form of naturalistic observation. It would probably be best to use a disguised type of observation, either nonparticipant or participant. Thus the researcher could have data collectors stationed at all of the locations of interest. These individuals could either be hidden or appear to be part of the normal environment. In either case it would not be noticeable that they were collecting data. With respect to data collection, if the data recorders were hidden, a checklist could be used. However, if the data recorders were disguised participants, then a narrative record might be best so

that drivers would not notice that they were being observed; the person collecting the data could either use a hidden audio recorder or communicate with another individual via a cell phone. The concerns would be those already indicated. Should you use a disguised nonparticipant observation or a disguised participant observation? Also the type of data collection used depends on which of the two previous methods was used.

3. Narrative records involve recording what is taking place while observing participants. This narrative record can be done via audio- or videotape recorder or simply by taking very detailed notes. After the observations have been recorded, the researcher must convert the narrative record into data for analytical purposes. This conversion usually entails using more than one coder or rater so that interrater reliability can be established. Thus narrative records begin as a subjective record that must be converted into something more objective.

   Checklists, on the other hand, begin as an objective list of behaviors or characteristics, and the researcher simply checks off whether or not the behavior or characteristic is present or absent. This procedure sounds far easier than using a narrative record, but the creation of the checklist can be very time-consuming. Consequently with checklists more work takes place before the data are collected, whereas with narrative records more work takes place after they are collected and the coding begins.

5. The archival method involves describing data that existed before the time of the study. In other words, the data were not generated as part of the study. One of the biggest advantages of archival research is that the problem of reactivity is somewhat minimized because the data have already been collected and the researcher does not have to interact with the participants in any way. Another advantage of archival research is that it is usually less time-consuming than most other research methods because the data already exist. Therefore, researchers are not confronted with the problems of getting participants for their study and taking the time to observe them—these tasks have already been done for them.

7. Action research is research conducted by a group of people to identify a problem, attempt to resolve it, and then assess how successful the efforts were. This research is highly applied in that it is typically conducted by those who have a problem in order to solve the problem. In other words, action research follows the old adage "If you want something done right, do it yourself." So rather than hire someone to analyze a social program in order to assess its effectiveness, those who work in the program would identify a problem to be evaluated, explore the problem, and then define an agenda for action.

Module 8

1. The researcher is using the personal interview method. She could use either open-ended, close-ended, partially open-ended, or Likert scale questions. However, close-ended and Likert scale questions would make it easier to record answers. The researcher is randomly sampling students who visit the student center. However, this group of students is not a random sample of

the entire university. A better way to sample would be to obtain a list of all students at the university and randomly select a sample of those students. She could then contact them regarding participating in the survey, or if she changed the type of survey (e.g., to a mail or phone survey), she could mail the survey to them or phone the random sample of students.

CHAPTER FOUR REVIEW

Fill-In Self-Test

1. nonparticipant
2. ecological validity
3. disguised
4. narrative records
5. static
6. sampling bias
7. socially desirable response
8. random selection (or sampling)
9. stratified random sampling
10. closed-ended questions
11. Likert scale
12. leading question

Multiple-Choice Self-Test

1. c	4. c	7. b	10. a
2. a	5. b	8. d	11. b
3. a	6. a	9. c	12. a

CHAPTER FIVE

Module 9

1. The first problem is with the correlation coefficient that was calculated. Correlation coefficients can vary between -1.0 and $+1.0$. They cannot be greater than ± 1.0. Thus the calculated correlation coefficient is incorrect. Second, correlation does not mean causation, and observing a correlation between exercise and health does not mean that we can conclude that exercise causes better health; they are simply related.
3. We would expect the correlation between GRE scores and graduate school GPAs to be much lower than that between SAT scores and undergraduate GPAs because both GRE scores and graduate school GPAs are restricted in range.

Module 10

1. In a true experimental design there is a manipulated independent variable. However, when using a quasi-experimental design, there may be no independent variable, that is, only one group is used and given the treatment. Or there may be a nonmanipulated independent variable, that is,

although two groups are used, they come to the study already differing, or they choose on their own to participate or not participate in some treatment. Consequently although we can assume a causal relationship based on data from a true experimental design, we cannot do so based on data collected from a quasi-experimental design.

3. In this situation the researcher would use a single-group posttest-only design in which each exam given across the semester serves as a posttest measure. Because she has no comparison group, this type of study has limitations.

Module 11

1. A researcher may want information only on the single participant being studied and thus choose to use single-case research. Second, single-case designs allow for easier replication because only one additional participant is needed rather than another group. Third, group designs may contribute to error variance due to the increase in individual differences. Single-case research therefore would minimize error variance.

3. In a multiple-baseline design rather than reversing the treatment and baseline conditions numerous times, the introduction of the treatment is assessed over multiple participants, behaviors, or situations. This procedure allows us to control for confounds not by reverting to baseline after treatment as in a reversal design but by introducing the treatment at different times across different people, behaviors, or situations.

CHAPTER FIVE REVIEW

Fill-In Self-Test

1. scatterplot
2. negative
3. causality; directionality
4. restricted range
5. regression analysis
6. participant (subject)
7. single-group posttest only
8. single-group time series
9. nonequivalent control group pretest/posttest design
10. single-case design
11. small-n design
12. ABA reversal design
13. multiple baseline design across participants

Multiple-Choice Self-Test

1. c	5. d	9. d	13. d
2. b	6. b	10. d	14. b
3. c	7. d	11. d	15. a
4. c	8. a	12. a	16. b

CHAPTER SIX

Module 12

1. This is a between-participants design. If participants are randomly assigned to one of the two conditions, then different participants are used in each condition.
3. A ceiling effect is possible. In other words, the test was so easy that everyone in the class did well (performed at the top). In this case the test would not be sensitive enough to detect differences in knowledge of biology.

Module 13

1. A Latin square design allows a researcher to utilize a form of incomplete counterbalancing. Thus with designs that have several conditions, the researcher uses as many orders as there are conditions. For example, in a design with 4 conditions, the researcher uses 4 orders rather than the 24 orders that would be necessary if complete counterbalancing were used. This use of four orders means that the researcher can still counterbalance the study without the counterbalancing procedure becoming too difficult.
3. These are all examples of developmental designs, designs in which age is the manipulated variable. With cross-sectional designs individuals of different ages are studied at the same time, whereas with longitudinal designs the same people are studied over many years or decades. A sequential design is a combined cross-sectional and longitudinal design. A researcher begins with participants of different ages (a cross-sectional design) and tests or measures them. Then, either months or years later, the research retests or measures the same individuals (a longitudinal design).

Module 14

1. Conducting a study with three or more levels of the independent variable allows a researcher to compare more than two kinds of treatment in one study, to compare two or more kinds of treatment with a control group, and to compare a placebo group to both the control and experimental groups.
3. There are two independent variables in a 4 × 6 design. One variable has four levels and the other has six levels. There would be 24 conditions in a 4 × 6 design.
5. A condition mean represents the performance in a single condition of an experiment. The row and column means (used to interpret main effects) represent the performance collapsed across all levels of each independent variable. Thus there would be two or more condition means contributing to each row or column mean.
7. In a complete factorial design all levels of each independent variable are paired with all levels of every other independent variable. In an incomplete factorial design there is more than one independent variable, but there is not a complete pairing of all levels of each independent variable with all levels of every other independent variable.

CHAPTER SIX REVIEW

Fill-In Self-Test Answers

1. between-participants design
2. random assignment
3. pretest/posttest
4. internal validity
5. maturation effect
6. instrumentation
7. diffusion of treatment
8. double-blind
9. ceiling
10. external validity
11. conceptual
12. order effects
13. cross-sectional
14. placebo
15. factorial notation
16. main effect
17. two; four; six

Multiple-Choice Self-Test

1. a	6. b	11. d	16. b
2. b	7. c	12. b	17. c
3. c	8. d	13. c	18. d
4. b	9. d	14. d	19. c
5. c	10. b	15. a	20. d

CHAPTER SEVEN

Module 15

1.

Speed	f	rf
62	1	.05
64	3	.15
65	4	.20
67	3	.15
68	2	.10
70	2	.10
72	1	.05
73	1	.05
76	1	.05
79	1	.05
80	1	.05
	20	1.00

3. Either a histogram or a frequency polygon could be used to graph these data. However, due to the continuous nature of the speed data, a frequency polygon might be most appropriate. Both a histogram and a frequency polygon of the data are presented.

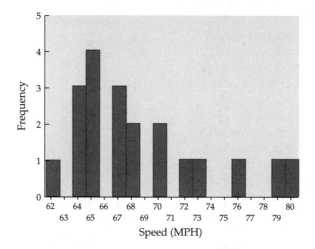

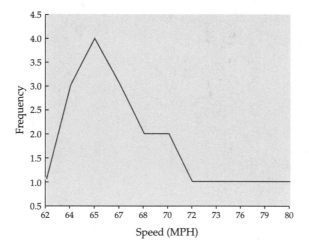

5. a. $\overline{X} = 7.3$
    Median = 8.5
    Mode = 11
  b. $\overline{X} = 4.83$
    Median = 5
    Mode = 5
  c. $\overline{X} = 6.17$
    Median = 6.5
    Mode = 3, 8
  d. $\overline{X} = 5.5$
    Median = 6
    Mode = 6

Module 16

1. a. $z = +2.57$; proportion of cars that cost an equal amount or more $= .0051$
    b. $z = -2.0$; proportion of cars that cost an equal amount or more $= .9772$
    c. $z = +2.0$; percentile rank $= 97.72$
    d. $z = -3.14$; percentile rank $= 0.08$
    e. $z = -3.14$, $z = +2.0$; proportion between $= .4992 + .4772 = .9764$
    f. 16th percentile converts to a z-score of -0.99; $-0.99(3,500) + 23,000 = \$19,535$

3.

	X	z-Score	Percentile Rank
Ken	73.00	−0.22	41.29
Drew	88.95	+1.55	93.94
Cecil	83.28	+0.92	82.00

CHAPTER SEVEN REVIEW

Fill-In Self-Test Answers

1. frequency distribution
2. qualitative
3. histogram
4. central tendency
5. median
6. variation
7. unbiased estimator
8. population; sample
9. z-score
10. standard normal distribution
11. Pearson product-moment
12. point biserial
13. coefficient of determination
14. Regression analysis

Multiple-Choice Self-Test Answers

1. c	6. b	11. b	16. c
2. d	7. c	12. b	17. b
3. d	8. a	13. a	18. a
4. c	9. a	14. c	
5. b	10. b	15. a	

CHAPTER EIGHT

Module 17

1. H_0: $\mu_{\text{Freshman}} = \mu_{\text{All other classes}}$, or,
    $\mu_{\text{Freshman}} \leq \mu_{\text{All other classes}}$
    H_a: $\mu_{\text{Freshman}} > \mu_{\text{All other classes}}$

This is a one-tailed test.

3. H_0: $\mu_{\text{Family size now}} = \mu_{\text{Family size in previous decade}}$, or
$\mu_{\text{Family size now}} \leq \mu_{\text{Family size in previous decade}}$
H_a: $\mu_{\text{Family size now}} > \mu_{\text{Family size in previous decade}}$
This is a one-tailed test.

5. a. Type I error
   b. Type II error
   c. Type I error
   d. Type II error

Module 18

1. An independent-groups t test is used when we have interval-ratio data, a between-participants design, and one independent variable with two levels.

3. The APA recommends that we calculate a measure of effect size in addition to the test statistic because a measure of effect size tells us the true effect of the independent variable controlling for sample size. In other words, a measure of effect size tells us how much of the difference in dependent variable can be attributed to the independent variable.

5. a. An independent samples t test should be used.
   b. H_0: $\mu_{\text{Music}} = \mu_{\text{No music}}$, or $\mu_{\text{Music}} \geq \mu_{\text{No music}}$
      H_a: $\mu_{\text{Music}} < \mu_{\text{No music}}$
   c. $t(16) = 2.60$, $p < 0.01$.
   d. Reject H_0. Studying with no music leads to significantly higher test scores.
   e. $d = 1.22$—there is a large effect size.
   f.

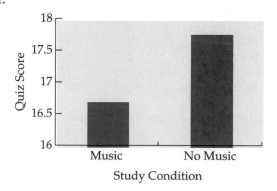

CHAPTER EIGHT REVIEW

Fill-In Self-Test

1. independent-groups t test
2. null hypothesis
3. one-tailed (directional) hypothesis

4. Type I error
5. statistical significance
6. nonparametric
7. Cohen's *d*

Multiple-Choice Self-Test

1. b	6. d	11. a	16. b
2. b	7. b	12. a	17. c
3. c	8. b	13. b	18. a
4. c	9. d	14. c	
5. a	10. b	15. d	

CHAPTER NINE

Module 19

1. Both *t* tests are used to compare two groups when interval-ratio data are collected. The difference is that an independent-groups *t* test is used with a between-participants design, whereas a correlated-groups *t* test is used with a correlated-groups design.

3. We turn them into one score by calculating difference scores: the difference between each participant's score in one condition versus the second condition. If the independent variable had no effect, we would expect the difference scores to be zero, whereas if the independent variable had an effect, we would expect the difference scores to be greater than zero.

5. a. A correlated-groups *t* test should be used.
   b. H_0: $\mu_{before} = \mu_{after}$, or H_0: $\mu_{before} \geq \mu_{after}$
      H_a: $\mu_{before} < \mu_{after}$
   c. $t(5) = 6.82$, $p < .005$
   d. Reject H_0. Participating in sports leads to significantly higher self-esteem scores.
   e. $d = 2.78$—a large effect size.
   f.

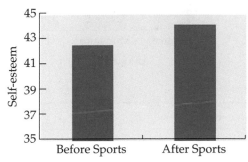

Module 20

1. A randomized ANOVA is used with a between-participants design, whereas a repeated measures ANOVA is used with a correlated-groups design. The term one-way means that there is one independent variable in the study.

3. The probability of a Type I error with three comparison is .14. Using the Bonferroni adjustment, the suggested alpha level is .017.

5. Eta-squared tells us how much of the variability in the dependent variable can be attributed to the independent variable.

7. a.

Source	df	SS	MS	F
Between-groups	2	22.167	11.08	6.76
Within-groups	9	14.750	1.64	
Total	11	36.917		

b. Yes, $F(2, 9) = 6.76$, $p < .05$.

c. $HSD_{.05} = 2.53$
   $HSD_{.01} = 3.47$

d. Stress had a significant effect on the number of colds that people had. Specifically, those reporting the highest level of stress had significantly more colds than those reporting the lowest level of stress.

e. The effect size $(\eta^2) = 60\%$. In other words, knowing the stress condition from which a person came can account for 60% of the variance in colds.

f.

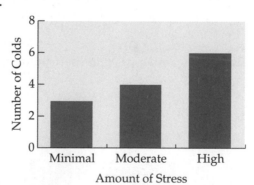

9. a.

Source	df	SS	MS	F
Between-groups	2	1,202.313	601.16	11.92
Within-groups	42	2,118.00	50.43	
Total	44	3,320.313		

b. Yes, $F(2, 42) = 11.92, p < .01$

c. $HSD_{.05} = 6.30$
   $HSD_{.01} = 8.00$

d. The new drug had a significant effect on depression. Specifically, those receiving the new "drug" had significantly lower depression levels than those in both the placebo and control groups.

e. The effect size (η^2) is 36%. Knowing the drug condition to which a participant was assigned accounts for 36% of the variance in depression scores.

f.

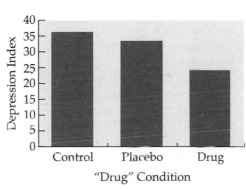

CHAPTER NINE REVIEW

Fill-In Self-Test Answers

1. difference scores
2. standard error of the difference scores
3. Bonferroni adjustment
4. ANOVA
5. grand mean
6. between-groups
7. total sum of squares
8. mean square
9. Eta-squared
10. post hoc tests or Tukey's HSD

Multiple-Choice Self-Test Answers

1. c	4. d	7. a	10. d
2. a	5. b	8. c	11. c
3. b	6. b	9. a	12. a

CHAPTER TEN

Module 21

1. The title page contains the running head in the top margin, aligned on the left margin, along with the page number, aligned on the right margin. The title of the paper is centered in the top third of the page followed by the author's name(s) (centered) and then the author's affiliation(s) (centered). The Author Note is centered at the bottom of the page. The entire title page is double-spaced.

3. a. The number *50* should be written out because it begins a sentence. Alternatively the sentence could be rewritten so that it does not begin with a number.

b. The proper way to report an *F*-ratio is as follows: $F(1, 12) = 6.54$, $p < .05$.

c. The word *data* is plural. Thus the sentence should read: "The data are presented in Table 1."

d. The word "while" typically refers to time. The sentence would be better as follows: "One group of participants took the medication whereas the other group did not."

CHAPTER TEN REVIEW

Fill-In Self-Test Answers

1. participants, apparatus/materials, and procedure
2. Results
3. abstract

Multiple-Choice Self Test Answers

1. c
2. c
3. d
4. b

APPENDIX B

Statistical Tables

TABLE **B.1**
Area under the Normal Curve (z Table)

z	Area between Mean and z	Area beyond z	z	Area between Mean and z	Area beyond z
0.00	0.00000	0.50000	0.32	0.12552	0.37448
0.01	0.00400	0.49600	0.33	0.12931	0.37069
0.02	0.00798	0.49202	0.34	0.13307	0.36693
0.03	0.01198	0.48802	0.35	0.13684	0.36316
0.04	0.01595	0.48405	0.36	0.14058	0.35942
0.05	0.01995	0.48005	0.37	0.14432	0.35568
0.06	0.02392	0.47608	0.38	0.14803	0.35197
0.07	0.02791	0.47209	0.39	0.15174	0.34826
0.08	0.03188	0.46812	0.40	0.15542	0.34458
0.09	0.03587	0.46413	0.41	0.15911	0.34089
0.10	0.03983	0.46017	0.42	0.16276	0.33724
0.11	0.04381	0.45619	0.43	0.16641	0.33359
0.12	0.04776	0.45224	0.44	0.17003	0.32997
0.13	0.05173	0.44827	0.45	0.17366	0.32634
0.14	0.05567	0.44433	0.46	0.17724	0.32276
0.15	0.05963	0.44037	0.47	0.18083	0.31917
0.16	0.06356	0.43644	0.48	0.18439	0.31561
0.17	0.06751	0.43249	0.49	0.18794	0.31206
0.18	0.07142	0.42858	0.50	0.19146	0.30854
0.19	0.07536	0.42464	0.51	0.19498	0.30502
0.20	0.07926	0.42074	0.52	0.19847	0.30153
0.21	0.08318	0.41682	0.53	0.20195	0.29805
0.22	0.08706	0.41294	0.54	0.20540	0.29460
0.23	0.09096	0.40904	0.55	0.20885	0.29115
0.24	0.09483	0.40517	0.56	0.21226	0.28774
0.25	0.09872	0.40128	0.57	0.21567	0.28433
0.26	0.10257	0.39743	0.58	0.21904	0.28096
0.27	0.10643	0.39357	0.59	0.22242	0.27758
0.28	0.11026	0.38974	0.60	0.22575	0.27425
0.29	0.11410	0.38590	0.61	0.22908	0.27092
0.30	0.11791	0.38209	0.62	0.23237	0.26763
0.31	0.12173	0.37827	0.63	0.23566	0.26434

(continued)

TABLE **B.1**
Area under the Normal Curve (z Table) (*continued*)

z	Area between Mean and z	Area beyond z	z	Area between Mean and z	Area beyond z
0.64	0.23891	0.26109	0.96	0.33147	0.16853
0.65	0.24216	0.25784	0.97	0.33399	0.16601
0.66	0.24537	0.25463	0.98	0.33646	0.16354
0.67	0.24858	0.25142	0.99	0.33892	0.16108
0.68	0.25175	0.24825	1.00	0.34134	0.15866
0.69	0.25491	0.24509	1.01	0.34376	0.15624
0.70	0.25804	0.24196	1.02	0.34614	0.15386
0.71	0.26116	0.23884	1.03	0.34851	0.15149
0.72	0.26424	0.23576	1.04	0.35083	0.14917
0.73	0.26732	0.23268	1.05	0.35315	0.14685
0.74	0.27035	0.22965	1.06	0.35543	0.14457
0.75	0.27338	0.22662	1.07	0.35770	0.14230
0.76	0.27637	0.22363	1.08	0.35993	0.14007
0.77	0.27936	0.22064	1.09	0.36215	0.13785
0.78	0.28230	0.21770	1.10	0.36433	0.13567
0.79	0.28525	0.21475	1.11	0.36651	0.13349
0.80	0.28814	0.21186	1.12	0.36864	0.13136
0.81	0.29104	0.20896	1.13	0.37077	0.12923
0.82	0.29389	0.20611	1.14	0.37286	0.12714
0.83	0.29674	0.20326	1.15	0.37494	0.12506
0.84	0.29955	0.20045	1.16	0.37698	0.12302
0.85	0.30235	0.19765	1.17	0.37901	0.12099
0.86	0.30511	0.19489	1.18	0.38100	0.11900
0.87	0.30786	0.19214	1.19	0.38299	0.11701
0.88	0.31057	0.18943	1.20	0.38493	0.11507
0.89	0.31328	0.18672	1.21	0.38687	0.11313
0.90	0.31594	0.18406	1.22	0.38877	0.11123
0.91	0.31860	0.18140	1.23	0.39066	0.10934
0.92	0.32121	0.17879	1.24	0.39251	0.10749
0.93	0.32383	0.17617	1.25	0.39436	0.10564
0.94	0.32639	0.17361	1.26	0.39617	0.10383
0.95	0.32895	0.17105	1.27	0.39797	0.10203

(*continued*)

TABLE **B.1**
Area under the Normal Curve (z Table) (*continued*)

z	Area between Mean and z	Area beyond z	z	Area between Mean and z	Area beyond z
1.28	0.39973	0.10027	1.60	0.44520	0.05480
1.29	0.40149	0.09851	1.61	0.44631	0.05369
1.30	0.40320	0.09680	1.62	0.44738	0.05262
1.31	0.40491	0.09509	1.63	0.44846	0.05154
1.32	0.40658	0.09342	1.64	0.44950	0.05050
1.33	0.40825	0.09175	1.65	0.45054	0.04946
1.34	0.40988	0.09012	1.66	0.45154	0.04846
1.35	0.41150	0.08850	1.67	0.45255	0.04745
1.36	0.41309	0.08691	1.68	0.45352	0.04648
1.37	0.41467	0.08533	1.69	0.45450	0.04550
1.38	0.41621	0.08379	1.70	0.45543	0.04457
1.39	0.41775	0.08225	1.71	0.45638	0.04362
1.40	0.41924	0.08076	1.72	0.45728	0.04272
1.41	0.42074	0.07926	1.73	0.45820	0.04180
1.42	0.42220	0.07780	1.74	0.45907	0.04093
1.43	0.42365	0.07635	1.75	0.45995	0.04005
1.44	0.42507	0.07493	1.76	0.46080	0.03920
1.45	0.42648	0.07352	1.77	0.46165	0.03835
1.46	0.42785	0.07215	1.78	0.46246	0.03754
1.47	0.42923	0.07077	1.79	0.46328	0.03672
1.48	0.43056	0.06944	1.80	0.46407	0.03593
1.49	0.43190	0.06810	1.81	0.46486	0.03514
1.50	0.43319	0.06681	1.82	0.46562	0.03438
1.51	0.43449	0.06551	1.83	0.46639	0.03361
1.52	0.43574	0.06426	1.84	0.46712	0.03288
1.53	0.43700	0.06300	1.85	0.46785	0.03215
1.54	0.43822	0.06178	1.86	0.46856	0.03144
1.55	0.43944	0.06056	1.87	0.46927	0.03073
1.56	0.44062	0.05938	1.88	0.46995	0.03005
1.57	0.44180	0.05820	1.89	0.47063	0.02937
1.58	0.44295	0.05705	1.90	0.47128	0.02872
1.59	0.44409	0.05591	1.91	0.47194	0.02806

(*continued*)

TABLE **B.1**
Area under the Normal Curve (z Table) (*continued*)

z	Area between Mean and z	Area beyond z	z	Area between Mean and z	Area beyond z
1.92	0.47257	0.02743	2.25	0.48779	0.01221
1.93	0.47321	0.02679	2.26	0.48809	0.01191
1.94	0.47381	0.02619	2.27	0.48841	0.01159
1.95	0.47442	0.02558	2.28	0.48870	0.01130
1.96	0.47500	0.02500	2.29	0.48900	0.01100
1.97	0.47559	0.02441	2.30	0.48928	0.01072
1.98	0.47615	0.02385	2.31	0.48957	0.01043
1.99	0.47672	0.02328	2.32	0.48983	0.01017
2.00	0.47725	0.02275	2.33	0.49011	0.00989
2.01	0.47780	0.02220	2.34	0.49036	0.00964
2.02	0.47831	0.02169	2.35	0.49062	0.00938
2.03	0.47883	0.02117	2.36	0.49086	0.00914
2.04	0.47932	0.02068	2.37	0.49112	0.00888
2.05	0.47983	0.02017	2.38	0.49134	0.00866
2.06	0.48030	0.01970	2.39	0.49159	0.00841
2.07	0.48078	0.01922	2.40	0.49180	0.00820
2.08	0.48124	0.01876	2.41	0.49203	0.00797
2.09	0.48170	0.01830	2.42	0.49224	0.00776
2.10	0.48214	0.01786	2.43	0.49246	0.00754
2.11	0.48258	0.01742	2.44	0.49266	0.00734
2.12	0.48300	0.01700	2.45	0.49287	0.00713
2.13	0.48342	0.01658	2.46	0.49305	0.00695
2.14	0.48382	0.01618	2.47	0.49325	0.00675
2.15	0.48423	0.01577	2.48	0.49343	0.00657
2.16	0.48461	0.01539	2.49	0.49362	0.00638
2.17	0.48501	0.01499	2.50	0.49379	0.00621
2.18	0.48537	0.01463	2.51	0.49397	0.00603
2.19	0.48575	0.01425	2.52	0.49413	0.00587
2.20	0.48610	0.01390	2.53	0.49431	0.00569
2.21	0.48646	0.01354	2.54	0.49446	0.00554
2.22	0.48679	0.01321	2.55	0.49462	0.00538
2.23	0.48714	0.01286	2.56	0.49477	0.00523
2.24	0.48745	0.01255	2.57	0.49493	0.00507

(*continued*)

TABLE **B.1**
Area under the Normal Curve (z Table) (*continued*)

z	Area between Mean and z	Area beyond z	z	Area between Mean and z	Area beyond z
2.58	0.49506	0.00494	2.90	0.49813	0.00187
2.59	0.49521	0.00479	2.91	0.49820	0.00180
2.60	0.49534	0.00466	2.92	0.49825	0.00175
2.61	0.49548	0.00452	2.93	0.49832	0.00168
2.62	0.49560	0.00440	2.94	0.49836	0.00164
2.63	0.49574	0.00426	2.95	0.49842	0.00158
2.64	0.49585	0.00415	2.96	0.49846	0.00154
2.65	0.49599	0.00401	2.97	0.49852	0.00148
2.66	0.49609	0.00391	2.98	0.49856	0.00144
2.67	0.49622	0.00378	2.99	0.49862	0.00138
2.68	0.49632	0.00368	3.00	0.49865	0.00135
2.69	0.49644	0.00356	3.02	0.49874	0.00126
2.70	0.49653	0.00347	3.04	0.49882	0.00118
2.71	0.49665	0.00335	3.06	0.49889	0.00111
2.72	0.49674	0.00326	3.08	0.49896	0.00104
2.73	0.49684	0.00316	3.10	0.49903	0.00097
2.74	0.49693	0.00307	3.12	0.49910	0.00090
2.75	0.49703	0.00297	3.14	0.49916	0.00084
2.76	0.49711	0.00289	3.16	0.49921	0.00079
2.77	0.49721	0.00279	3.18	0.49926	0.00074
2.78	0.49728	0.00272	3.20	0.49931	0.00069
2.79	0.49738	0.00262	3.25	0.49943	0.00057
2.80	0.49744	0.00256	3.30	0.49952	0.00048
2.81	0.49753	0.00247	3.35	0.49961	0.00039
2.82	0.49760	0.00240	3.40	0.49966	0.00034
2.83	0.49768	0.00232	3.45	0.49973	0.00027
2.84	0.49774	0.00226	3.50	0.49977	0.00023
2.85	0.49782	0.00218	3.60	0.49984	0.00016
2.86	0.49788	0.00212	3.70	0.49989	0.00011
2.87	0.49796	0.00204	3.80	0.49993	0.00007
2.88	0.49801	0.00199	3.90	0.49995	0.00005
2.89	0.49808	0.00192	4.00	0.49997	0.00003

Source: Lehman, R. S. (1995). *Statistics in the Behavioral Sciences: A Conceptual Introduction.* Pacific Grove, CA: Brooks/Cole Publishing.

TABLE **B.2**

Critical Values for the Student's *t* Distribution

	Level of Significance for One-Tailed Test					
	.10	.05	.025	.01	.005	.0005
	Level of Significance for Two-Tailed Test					
df	.20	.10	.05	.02	.01	.001
1	3.078	6.314	12.706	31.821	63.657	636.619
2	1.886	2.920	4.303	6.965	9.925	31.598
3	1.638	2.353	3.182	4.541	5.841	12.941
4	1.533	2.132	2.776	3.747	4.604	8.610
5	1.476	2.015	2.571	3.365	4.032	6.859
6	1.440	1.943	2.447	3.143	3.707	5.959
7	1.415	1.895	2.365	2.998	3.499	5.405
8	1.397	1.860	2.306	2.896	3.355	5.041
9	1.383	1.833	2.262	2.821	3.250	4.781
10	1.372	1.812	2.228	2.764	3.169	4.587
11	1.363	1.796	2.201	2.718	3.106	4.437
12	1.356	1.782	2.179	2.681	3.055	4.318
13	1.350	1.771	2.160	2.650	3.012	4.221
14	1.345	1.761	2.145	2.624	2.977	4.140
15	1.341	1.753	2.131	2.602	2.947	4.073
16	1.337	1.746	2.120	2.583	2.921	4.015
17	1.333	1.740	2.110	2.567	2.898	3.965
18	1.330	1.734	2.101	2.552	2.878	3.922
19	1.328	1.729	2.093	2.539	2.861	3.883
20	1.325	1.725	2.086	2.528	2.845	3.850
21	1.323	1.721	2.080	2.518	2.831	3.819
22	1.321	1.717	2.074	2.508	2.819	3.792
23	1.319	1.714	2.069	2.500	2.807	3.767
24	1.318	1.711	2.064	2.492	2.797	3.745
25	1.316	1.708	2.060	2.485	2.787	3.725
26	1.315	1.706	2.056	2.479	2.779	3.707
27	1.314	1.703	2.052	2.473	2.771	3.690
28	1.313	1.701	2.048	2.467	2.763	3.674
29	1.311	1.699	2.045	2.462	2.756	3.659
30	1.310	1.697	2.042	2.457	2.750	3.646
40	1.303	1.684	2.021	2.423	2.704	3.551
60	1.296	1.671	2.000	2.390	2.660	3.460
120	1.289	1.658	1.980	2.358	2.617	3.373
∞	1.282	1.645	1.960	2.326	2.576	3.291

Source: Lehman, R. S. (1995). *Statistics in the Behavioral Sciences: A Conceptual Introduction.* Pacific Grove, CA: Brooks/Cole Publishing.

TABLE **B.3**
Critical Values for the *F* Distribution

df for Denominator (df within or error)	α	\multicolumn{12}{c}{*df* for Numerator (*df* between)}
		1	2	3	4	5	6	7	8	9	10	11	12
1	.05	161	200	216	225	230	234	237	239	241	242	243	244
2	.05	18.5	19.0	19.2	19.2	19.3	19.3	19.4	19.4	19.4	19.4	19.4	19.4
	.01	98.5	99.0	99.2	99.2	99.3	99.3	99.4	99.4	99.4	99.4	99.4	99.4
3	.05	10.1	9.55	9.28	9.12	9.01	8.94	8.89	8.85	8.81	8.79	8.76	8.74
	.01	34.1	30.8	29.5	28.7	28.2	27.9	27.7	27.5	27.3	27.2	27.1	27.1
4	.05	7.71	6.94	6.59	6.39	6.26	6.16	6.09	6.04	6.00	5.96	5.94	5.91
	.01	21.2	18.0	16.7	16.0	15.5	15.2	15.0	14.8	14.7	14.5	14.4	14.4
5	.05	6.61	5.79	5.41	5.19	5.05	4.95	4.88	4.82	4.77	4.74	4.71	4.68
	.01	16.3	13.3	12.1	11.4	11.0	10.7	10.5	10.3	10.2	10.1	9.96	9.89
6	.05	5.99	5.14	4.76	4.53	4.39	4.28	4.21	4.15	4.10	4.06	4.03	4.00
	.01	13.7	10.9	9.78	9.15	8.75	8.47	8.26	8.10	7.98	7.87	7.79	7.72
7	.05	5.59	4.74	4.35	4.12	3.97	3.87	3.79	3.73	3.68	3.64	3.60	3.57
	.01	12.2	9.55	8.45	7.85	7.46	7.19	6.99	6.84	6.72	6.62	6.54	6.47
8	.05	5.32	4.46	4.07	3.84	3.69	3.58	3.50	3.44	3.39	3.35	3.31	3.28
	.01	11.3	8.65	7.59	7.01	6.63	6.37	6.18	6.03	5.91	5.81	5.73	5.67
9	.05	5.12	4.26	3.86	3.63	3.48	3.37	3.29	3.23	3.18	3.14	3.10	3.07
	.01	10.6	8.02	6.99	6.42	6.06	5.80	5.61	5.47	5.35	5.26	5.18	5.11
10	.05	4.96	4.10	3.71	3.48	3.33	3.22	3.14	3.07	3.02	2.98	2.94	2.91
	.01	10.0	7.56	6.55	5.99	5.64	5.39	5.20	5.06	4.94	4.85	4.77	4.71
11	.05	4.84	3.98	3.59	3.36	3.20	3.09	3.01	2.95	2.90	2.85	2.82	2.79
	.01	9.65	7.21	6.22	5.67	5.32	5.07	4.89	4.74	4.63	4.54	4.46	4.40
12	.05	4.75	3.89	3.49	3.26	3.11	3.00	2.91	2.85	2.80	2.75	2.72	2.69
	.01	9.33	6.93	5.95	5.41	5.06	4.82	4.64	4.50	439	4.30	4.22	4.16
13	.05	4.67	3.81	3.41	3.18	3.03	2.92	2.83	2.77	2.71	2.67	2.63	2.60
	.01	9.07	6.70	5.74	5.21	4.86	4.62	4.44	4.30	4.19	4.10	4.02	3.96
14	.05	4.60	3.74	3.34	3.11	2.96	2.85	2.76	2.70	2.65	2.60	2.57	2.53
	.01	8.86	6.51	5.56	5.04	4.69	4.46	4.28	4.14	4.03	3.94	3.86	3.80
15	.05	4.54	3.68	3.29	3.06	2.90	2.79	2.71	2.64	2.59	2.54	2.51	2.48
	.01	8.68	6.36	5.42	4.89	4.56	4.32	4.14	4.00	3.89	3.80	3.73	3.67
16	.05	4.49	3.63	3.24	3.01	2.85	2.74	2.66	2.59	2.54	2.49	2.46	2.42
	.01	8.53	6.23	5.29	4.77	4.44	4.20	4.03	3.89	3.78	3.69	3.62	3.55

(continued)

TABLE **B.3**
Critical Values for the *F* Distribution (*continued*)

df for Numerator (df between)													df for Denominator (df within or error)
15	20	24	30	40	50	60	100	120	200	500	∞	α	
246	248	249	250	251	252	252	253	253	254	254	254	.05	1
19.4	19.4	19.5	19.5	19.5	19.5	19.5	19.5	19.5	19.5	19.5	19.5	.05	2
99.4	99.4	99.5	99.5	99.5	99.5	99.5	99.5	99.5	99.5	99.5	99.5	.01	
8.70	8.66	8.64	8.62	8.59	8.58	8.57	8.55	8.55	8.54	8.53	8.53	.05	3
26.9	26.7	26.6	26.5	26.4	26.4	26.3	26.2	26.2	26.2	26.1	26.1	.01	
5.86	5.80	5.77	5.75	5.72	5.70	5.69	5.66	5.66	5.65	5.64	5.63	.05	4
14.2	14.0	13.9	13.8	13.7	13.7	13.7	13.6	13.6	13.5	13.5	13.5	.01	
4.62	4.56	4.53	4.50	4.46	4.44	4.43	4.41	4.40	4.39	4.37	4.36	.05	5
9.72	9.55	9.47	9.38	9.29	9.24	9.20	9.13	9.11	9.08	9.04	9.02	.01	
3.94	3.87	3.84	3.81	3.77	3.75	3.74	3.71	3.70	3.69	3.68	3.67	.05	6
7.56	7.40	7.31	7.23	7.14	7.09	7.06	6.99	6.97	6.93	6.90	6.88	.01	
3.51	3.44	3.41	3.38	3.34	3.32	3.30	3.27	3.27	3.25	3.24	3.23	.05	7
6.31	6.16	6.07	5.99	5.91	5.86	5.82	5.75	5.74	5.70	5.67	5.65	.01	
3.22	3.15	3.12	3.08	3.04	3.02	3.01	2.97	2.97	2.95	2.94	2.93	.05	8
5.52	5.36	5.28	5.20	5.12	5.07	5.03	4.96	4.95	4.91	4.88	4.86	.01	
3.01	2.94	2.90	2.86	2.83	2.80	2.79	2.76	2.75	2.73	2.72	2.71	.05	9
4.96	4.81	4.73	4.65	4.57	4.52	4.48	4.42	4.40	4.36	4.33	4.31	.01	
2.85	2.77	2.74	2.70	2.66	2.64	2.62	2.59	2.58	2.56	2.55	2.54	.05	10
4.56	4.41	4.33	4.25	4.17	4.12	4.08	4.01	4.00	3.96	3.93	3.91	.01	
2.72	2.65	2.61	2.57	2.53	2.51	2.49	2.46	2.45	2.43	2.42	2.40	.05	11
4.25	4.10	4.02	3.94	3.86	3.81	3.78	3.71	3.69	3.66	3.62	3.60	.01	
2.62	2.54	2.51	2.47	2.43	2.40	2.38	2.35	2.34	2.32	2.31	2.30	.05	12
4.01	3.86	3.78	3.70	3.62	3.57	3.54	3.47	3.45	3.41	3.38	3.36	.01	
2.53	2.46	2.42	2.38	2.34	2.31	2.30	2.26	2.25	2.23	2.22	2.21	.05	13
3.82	3.66	3.59	3.51	3.43	3.38	3.34	3.27	3.25	3.22	3.19	3.17	.01	
2.46	2.39	2.35	2.31	2.27	2.24	2.22	2.19	2.18	2.16	2.14	2.13	.05	14
3.66	3.51	3.43	3.35	3.27	3.22	3.18	3.11	3.09	3.06	3.03	3.00	.01	
2.40	2.33	2.29	2.25	2.20	2.18	2.16	2.12	2.11	2.10	2.08	2.07	.05	15
3.52	3.37	3.29	3.21	3.13	3.08	3.05	2.98	2.96	2.92	2.89	2.87	.01	
2.35	2.28	2.24	2.19	2.15	2.12	2.11	2.07	2.06	2.04	2.02	2.01	.05	16
3.41	3.26	3.18	3.10	3.02	2.97	2.93	2.86	2.84	2.81	2.78	2.75	.01	

(*continued*)

TABLE **B.3**
Critical Values for the *F* Distribution (*continued*)

df for Denominator (df within or error)	α	1	2	3	4	5	6	7	8	9	10	11	12
17	.05	4.45	3.59	3.20	2.96	2.81	2.70	2.61	2.55	2.49	2.45	2.41	2.38
	.01	8.40	6.11	5.18	4.67	4.34	4.10	3.93	3.79	3.68	3.59	3.52	3.46
18	.05	4.41	3.55	3.16	2.93	2.77	2.66	2.58	2.51	2.46	2.41	2.37	2.34
	.01	8.29	6.01	5.09	4.58	4.25	4.01	3.84	3.71	3.60	3.51	3.43	3.37
19	.05	4.38	3.52	3.13	2.90	2.74	2.63	2.54	2.48	2.42	2.38	2.34	2.31
	.01	8.18	5.93	5.01	4.50	4.17	3.94	3.77	3.63	3.52	3.43	3.36	3.30
20	.05	4.35	3.49	3.10	2.87	2.71	2.60	2.51	2.45	2.39	2.35	2.31	2.28
	.01	8.10	5.85	4.94	4.43	4.10	3.87	3.70	3.56	3.46	3.37	3.29	3.23
22	.05	4.30	3.44	3.05	2.82	2.66	2.55	2.46	2.40	2.34	2.30	2.26	2.23
	.01	7.95	5.72	4.82	4.31	3.99	3.76	3.59	3.45	3.35	3.26	3.18	3.12
24	.05	4.26	3.40	3.01	2.78	2.62	2.51	2.42	2.36	2.30	2.25	2.21	2.18
	.01	7.82	5.61	4.72	4.22	3.90	3.67	3.50	3.36	3.26	3.17	3.09	3.03
26	.05	4.23	3.37	2.98	2.74	2.59	2.47	2.39	2.32	2.27	2.22	2.18	2.15
	.01	7.72	5.53	4.64	4.14	3.82	3.59	3.42	3.29	3.18	3.09	3.02	2.96
28	.05	4.20	3.34	2.95	2.71	2.56	2.45	2.36	2.29	2.24	2.19	2.15	2.12
	.01	7.64	5.45	4.57	4.07	3.75	3.53	3.36	3.23	3.12	3.03	2.96	2.90
30	.05	4.17	3.32	2.92	2.69	2.53	2.42	2.33	2.27	2.21	2.16	2.13	2.09
	.01	7.56	5.39	4.51	4.02	3.70	3.47	3.30	3.17	3.07	2.98	2.91	2.84
40	.05	4.08	3.23	2.84	2.61	2.45	2.34	2.25	2.18	2.12	2.08	2.04	2.00
	.01	7.31	5.18	4.31	3.83	3.51	3.29	3.12	2.99	2.89	2.80	2.73	2.66
60	.05	4.00	3.15	2.76	2.53	2.37	2.25	2.17	2.10	2.04	1.99	1.95	1.92
	.01	7.08	4.98	4.13	3.65	3.34	3.12	2.95	2.82	2.72	2.63	2.56	2.50
120	.05	3.92	3.07	2.68	2.45	2.29	2.17	2.09	2.02	1.96	1.91	1.87	1.83
	.01	6.85	4.79	3.95	3.48	3.17	2.96	2.79	2.66	2.56	2.47	2.40	2.34
200	.05	3.89	3.04	2.65	2.42	2.26	2.14	2.06	1.98	1.93	1.88	1.84	1.80
	.01	6.76	4.71	3.88	3.41	3.11	2.89	2.73	2.60	2.50	2.41	2.34	2.27
∞	.05	3.84	3.00	2.60	2.37	2.21	2.10	2.01	1.94	1.88	1.83	1.79	1.75
	.01	6.63	4.61	3.78	3.32	3.02	2.80	2.64	2.51	2.41	2.32	2.25	2.18

df for Numerator (*df* between)

(*continued*)

TABLE **B.3**
Critical Values for the *F* Distribution (*continued*)

15	20	24	30	40	50	60	100	120	200	500	∞	α	df for Denominator (df within or error)
						df for Numerator (*df* between)							
2.31	2.23	2.19	2.15	2.10	2.08	2.06	2.02	2.01	1.99	1.97	1.96	.05	17
3.31	3.16	3.08	3.00	2.92	2.87	2.83	2.76	2.75	2.71	2.68	2.65	.01	
2.27	2.19	2.15	2.11	2.06	2.04	2.02	1.98	1.97	1.95	1.93	1.92	.05	18
3.23	3.08	3.00	2.92	2.84	2.78	2.75	2.68	2.66	2.62	2.59	2.57	.01	
2.23	2.16	2.11	2.07	2.03	2.00	1.98	1.94	1.93	1.91	1.89	1.88	.05	19
3.15	3.00	2.92	2.84	2.76	2.71	2.67	2.60	2.58	2.55	2.51	2.49	.01	
2.20	2.12	2.08	2.04	1.99	1.97	1.95	1.91	1.90	1.88	1.86	1.84	.05	20
3.09	2.94	2.86	2.78	2.69	2.64	2.61	2.54	2.52	2.48	2.44	2.42	.01	
2.15	2.07	2.03	1.98	1.94	1.91	1.89	1.85	1.84	1.82	1.80	1.78	.05	22
2.98	2.83	2.75	2.67	2.58	2.53	2.50	2.42	2.40	2.36	2.33	2.31	.01	
2.11	2.03	1.98	1.94	1.89	1.86	1.84	1.80	1.79	1.77	1.75	1.73	.05	24
2.89	2.74	2.66	2.58	2.49	2.44	2.40	2.33	2.31	2.27	2.24	2.21	.01	
2.07	1.99	1.95	1.90	1.85	1.82	1.80	1.76	1.75	1.73	1.71	1.69	.05	26
2.81	2.66	2.58	2.50	2.42	2.36	2.33	2.25	2.23	2.19	2.16	2.13	.01	
2.04	1.96	1.91	1.87	1.82	1.79	1.77	1.73	1.71	1.69	1.67	1.65	.05	28
2.75	2.60	2.52	2.44	2.35	2.30	2.26	2.19	2.17	2.13	2.09	2.06	.01	
2.01	1.93	1.89	1.84	1.79	1.76	1.74	1.70	1.68	1.66	1.64	1.62	.05	30
2.70	2.55	2.47	2.39	2.30	2.25	2.21	2.13	2.11	2.07	2.03	2.01	.01	
1.92	1.84	1.79	1.74	1.69	1.66	1.64	1.59	1.58	1.55	1.53	1.51	.05	40
2.52	2.37	2.29	2.20	2.11	2.06	2.02	1.94	1.92	1.87	1.83	1.80	.01	
1.84	1.75	1.70	1.65	1.59	1.56	1.53	1.48	1.47	1.44	1.41	1.39	.05	60
2.35	2.20	2.12	2.03	1.94	1.88	1.84	1.75	1.73	1.68	1.63	1.60	.01	
1.75	1.66	1.61	1.55	1.50	1.46	1.43	1.37	1.35	1.32	1.28	1.25	.05	120
2.19	2.03	1.95	1.86	1.76	1.70	1.66	1.56	1.53	1.48	1.42	1.38	.01	
1.72	1.62	1.57	1.52	1.46	1.41	1.39	1.32	1.29	1.26	1.22	1.19	.05	200
2.13	1.97	1.89	1.79	1.69	1.63	1.58	1.48	1.44	1.39	1.33	1.28	.01	
1.67	1.57	1.52	1.46	1.39	1.35	1.32	1.24	1.22	1.17	1.11	1.00	.05	∞
2.04	1.88	1.79	1.70	1.59	1.52	1.47	1.36	1.32	1.25	1.15	1.00	.01	

Source: Lehman, R. S. (1995). *Statistics in the Behavioral Sciences: A Conceptual Introduction.* Pacific Grove, CA: Brooks/Cole Publishing.

TABLE **B.4**
Studentized Range Statistic

| Error *df* (*df* within) | α | \multicolumn{10}{c}{k = Number of Means or Number of Steps between Ordered Means} |
		2	3	4	5	6	7	8	9	10	11
5	.05	3.64	4.60	5.22	5.67	6.03	6.33	6.58	6.80	6.99	7.17
	.01	5.70	6.98	7.80	8.42	8.91	9.32	9.67	9.97	10.24	10.48
6	.05	3.46	4.34	4.90	5.30	5.63	5.90	6.12	6.32	6.49	6.65
	.01	5.24	6.33	7.03	7.56	7.97	8.32	8.61	8.87	9.10	9.30
7	.05	3.34	4.16	4.68	5.06	5.36	5.61	5.82	6.00	6.16	6.30
	.01	4.95	5.92	6.54	7.01	7.37	7.68	7.94	8.17	8.37	8.55
8	.05	3.26	4.04	4.53	4.89	5.17	5.40	5.60	5.77	5.92	6.05
	.01	4.75	5.64	6.20	6.62	6.96	7.24	7.47	7.68	7.86	8.03
9	.05	3.20	3.95	4.41	4.76	5.02	5.24	5.43	5.59	5.74	5.87
	.01	4.60	5.43	5.96	6.35	6.66	6.91	7.13	7.33	7.49	7.65
10	.05	3.15	3.88	4.33	4.65	4.91	5.12	5.30	5.46	5.60	5.72
	.01	4.48	5.27	5.77	6.14	6.43	6.67	6.87	7.05	7.21	7.36
11	.05	3.11	3.82	4.26	4.57	4.82	5.03	5.20	5.35	5.49	5.61
	.01	4.39	5.15	5.62	5.97	6.25	6.48	6.67	6.84	6.99	7.13
12	.05	3.08	3.77	4.20	4.51	4.75	4.95	5.12	5.27	5.39	5.51
	.01	4.32	5.05	5.50	5.84	6.10	6.32	6.51	6.67	6.81	6.94
13	.05	3.06	3.73	4.15	4.45	4.69	4.88	5.05	5.19	5.32	5.43
	.01	4.26	4.96	5.40	5.73	5.98	6.19	6.37	6.53	6.67	6.79
14	.05	3.03	3.70	4.11	4.41	4.64	4.83	4.99	5.13	5.25	5.36
	.01	4.21	4.89	5.32	5.63	5.88	6.08	6.26	6.41	6.54	6.66
15	.05	3.01	3.67	4.08	4.37	4.59	4.78	4.94	5.08	5.20	5.31
	.01	4.17	4.84	5.25	5.56	5.80	5.99	6.16	6.31	6.44	6.55
16	.05	3.00	3.65	4.05	4.33	4.56	4.74	4.90	5.03	5.15	5.26
	.01	4.13	4.79	5.19	5.49	5.72	5.92	6.08	6.22	6.35	6.46
17	.05	2.98	3.63	4.02	4.30	4.52	4.70	4.86	4.99	5.11	5.21
	.01	4.10	4.74	5.14	5.43	5.66	5.85	6.01	6.15	6.27	6.38
18	.05	2.97	3.61	4.00	4.28	4.49	4.67	4.82	4.96	5.07	5.17
	.01	4.07	4.70	5.09	5.38	5.60	5.79	5.94	6.08	6.20	6.31
19	.05	2.96	3.59	3.98	4.25	4.47	4.65	4.79	4.92	5.04	5.14
	.01	4.05	4.67	5.05	5.33	5.55	5.73	5.89	6.02	6.14	6.25
20	.05	2.95	3.58	3.96	4.23	4.45	4.62	4.77	4.90	5.01	5.11
	.01	4.02	4.64	5.02	5.29	5.51	5.69	5.84	5.97	6.09	6.19

(*continued*)

TABLE **B.4**
Studentized Range Statistic (*continued*)

12	13	14	15	16	17	18	19	20	α	Error *df* (*df* within)
\multicolumn{11}{c}{*k* = Number of Means or Number of Steps between Ordered Means}										
7.32	7.47	7.60	7.72	7.83	7.93	8.03	8.12	8.21	.05	5
10.70	10.89	11.08	11.24	11.40	11.55	11.68	11.81	11.93	.01	
6.79	6.92	7.03	7.14	7.24	7.34	7.43	7.51	7.59	.05	6
9.48	9.65	9.81	9.95	10.08	10.21	10.32	10.43	10.54	.01	
6.43	6.55	6.66	6.76	6.85	6.94	7.02	7.10	7.17	.05	7
8.71	8.86	9.00	9.12	9.24	9.35	9.46	9.55	9.65	.01	
6.18	6.29	6.39	6.48	6.57	6.65	6.73	6.80	6.87	.05	8
8.18	8.31	8.44	8.55	8.66	8.76	8.85	8.94	9.03	.01	
5.98	6.09	6.19	6.28	6.36	6.44	6.51	6.58	6.64	.05	9
7.78	7.91	8.03	8.13	8.23	8.33	8.41	8.49	8.57	.01	
5.83	5.93	6.03	6.11	6.19	6.27	6.34	6.40	6.47	.05	10
7.49	7.60	7.71	7.81	7.91	7.99	8.08	8.15	8.23	.01	
5.71	5.81	5.90	5.98	6.06	6.13	6.20	6.27	6.33	.05	11
7.25	7.36	7.46	7.56	7.65	7.73	7.81	7.88	7.95	.01	
5.61	5.71	5.80	5.88	5.95	6.02	6.09	6.15	6.21	.05	12
7.06	7.17	7.26	7.36	7.44	7.52	7.59	7.66	7.73	.01	
5.53	5.63	5.71	5.79	5.86	5.93	5.99	6.05	6.11	.05	13
6.90	7.01	7.10	7.19	7.27	7.35	7.42	7.48	7.55	.01	
5.46	5.55	5.64	5.71	5.79	5.85	5.91	5.97	6.03	.05	14
6.77	6.87	6.96	7.05	7.13	7.20	7.27	7.33	7.39	.01	
5.40	5.49	5.57	5.65	5.72	5.78	5.85	5.90	5.96	.05	15
6.66	6.76	6.84	6.93	7.00	7.07	7.14	7.20	7.26	.01	
5.35	5.44	5.52	5.59	5.66	5.73	5.79	5.84	5.90	.05	16
6.56	6.66	6.74	6.82	6.90	6.97	7.03	7.09	7.15	.01	
5.31	5.39	5.47	5.54	5.61	5.67	5.73	5.79	5.84	.05	17
6.48	6.57	6.66	6.73	6.81	6.87	6.94	7.00	7.05	.01	
5.27	5.35	5.43	5.50	5.57	5.63	5.69	5.74	5.79	.05	18
6.41	6.50	6.58	6.65	6.73	6.79	6.85	6.91	6.97	.01	
5.23	5.31	5.39	5.46	5.53	5.59	5.65	5.70	5.75	.05	19
6.34	6.43	6.51	6.58	6.65	6.72	6.78	6.84	6.89	.01	
5.20	5.28	5.36	5.43	5.49	5.55	5.61	5.66	5.71	.05	20
6.28	6.37	6.45	6.52	6.59	6.65	6.71	6.77	6.82	.01	

(*continued*)

TABLE **B.4**
Studentized Range Statistic (*continued*)

Error *df* (*df* within)	α	2	3	4	5	6	7	8	9	10	11
		\multicolumn{10}{c}{*k* = Number of Means or Number of Steps between Ordered Means}									
24	.05	2.92	3.53	3.90	4.17	4.37	4.54	4.68	4.81	4.92	5.01
	.01	3.96	4.55	4.91	5.17	5.37	5.54	5.69	5.81	5.92	6.02
30	.05	2.89	3.49	3.85	4.10	4.30	4.46	4.60	4.72	4.82	4.92
	.01	3.89	4.45	4.80	5.05	5.24	5.40	5.54	5.65	5.76	5.85
40	.05	2.86	3.44	3.79	4.04	4.23	4.39	4.52	4.63	4.73	4.82
	.01	3.82	4.37	4.70	4.93	5.11	5.26	5.39	5.50	5.60	5.69
60	.05	2.83	3.40	3.74	3.98	4.16	4.31	4.44	4.55	4.65	4.73
	.01	3.76	4.28	4.59	4.82	4.99	5.13	5.25	5.36	5.45	5.53
120	.05	2.80	3.36	3.68	3.92	4.10	4.24	4.36	4.47	4.56	4.64
	.01	3.70	4.20	4.50	4.71	4.87	5.01	5.12	5.21	5.30	5.37
∞	.05	2.77	3.31	3.63	3.86	4.03	4.17	4.29	4.39	4.47	4.55
	.01	3.64	4.12	4.40	4.60	4.76	4.88	4.99	5.08	5.16	5.23

(*continued*)

TABLE **B.4**
Studentized Range Statistic (*continued*)

k = Number of Means or Number of Steps between Ordered Means										Error *df*
12	13	14	15	16	17	18	19	20	α	(*df* within)
5.10	5.18	5.25	5.32	5.38	5.44	5.49	5.55	5.59	.05	24
6.11	6.19	6.26	6.33	6.39	6.45	6.51	6.56	6.61	.01	
5.00	5.08	5.15	5.21	5.27	5.33	5.38	5.43	5.47	.05	30
5.93	6.01	6.08	6.14	6.20	6.26	6.31	6.36	6.41	.01	
4.90	4.98	5.04	5.11	5.16	5.22	5.27	5.31	5.36	.05	40
5.76	5.83	5.90	5.96	6.02	6.07	6.12	6.16	6.21	.01	
4.81	4.88	4.94	5.00	5.06	5.11	5.15	5.20	5.24	.05	60
5.60	5.67	5.73	5.78	5.84	5.89	5.93	5.97	6.01	.01	
4.71	4.78	4.84	4.90	4.95	5.00	5.04	5.09	5.13	.05	120
5.44	5.50	5.56	5.61	5.66	5.71	5.75	5.79	5.83	.01	
4.62	4.68	4.74	4.80	4.85	4.89	4.93	4.97	5.01	.05	∞
5.29	5.35	5.40	5.45	5.49	5.54	5.57	5.61	5.65	.01	

Source: Abridged from Table 29 in E. S. Pearson and H. O. Hartley, eds. *Biometrika Tables for Statisticians*, 3rd ed., 1966, Vol. 1, pp. 176–177. Reprinted by permission of the Biometrika Trustees and the author.

Excel, SPSS, and TI84 Exercises

Many of the problems worked in the modules appear in the exercises below. SPSS, Excel, and the TI84 either do not compute, or do not easily compute all of the statistics covered in this text. Thus if a particular statistics is missing from the exercises, it is for one of these reasons.

EXCEL EXERCISES FOR EXCEL 2007

Before you begin to use Excel to analyze data, you may need to install the Data Analysis ToolPak. This installation can be accomplished by launching Excel and then clicking on the Microsoft icon at the top left of the page. At the bottom of the drop-down menu there is a tab labeled **Excel Options**. Click on this tab and a dialog box of options will appear. On the left-hand side of the dialog box is a list of options; double-click on **Add-Ins**. The very top option should be **Analysis ToolPak**. Click on this option and then **GO**. A dialog box in which the first two options are **Analysis Toolpak** and **Analysis Toolpak-VBA** will appear. Check both of these and then click **OK**. The toolpak should now be installed on your computer.

Module 15 (Measures of Central Tendency and Variation)

To begin using Excel to conduct data analyses, the data must be entered into an Excel spreadsheet. This procedure simply involves opening Excel and entering the data into the spreadsheet. You can see in the following spreadsheet that I have entered the exam grade data from Table 15.5 (in Module 15) into an Excel spreadsheet.

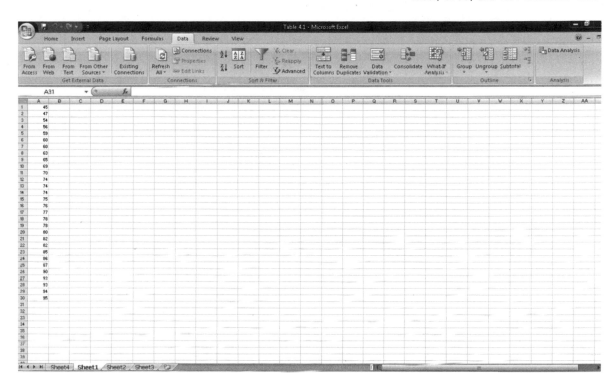

Once the data have been entered, we use the Data Analysis tool to calculate descriptive statistics. This calculation is accomplished by clicking on the **Data** tab or ribbon (as in the preceding window) and then clicking the **Data Analysis** icon on the far top right side of the window. Once the Data Analysis tab is active, a dialog box of options will appear (see below).

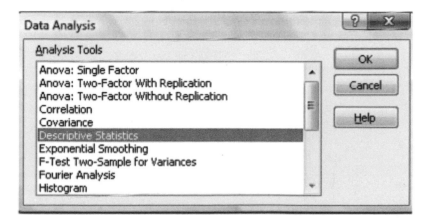

Select **Descriptive Statistics** as is indicated in the preceding box, and then click **OK**. This action will lead to the following dialog box.

Descriptive Statistics

Input
Input Range: `$A$1:$A$30`

Grouped By:
- ⦿ Columns
- ○ Rows

☐ Labels in First Row

Output options
- ○ Output Range:
- ⦿ New Worksheet Ply:
- ○ New Workbook

☑ Summary statistics
☐ Confidence Level for Mean: 95 %
☐ Kth Largest: 1
☐ Kth Smallest: 1

OK
Cancel
Help

With the cursor in the **Input Range** box, highlight the data that you want analyzed from Column A in the Excel spreadsheet so that they appear in the input range. In addition, check the **Summary statistics** box. Once you have done so, click **OK**. The summary statistics will appear in a new Worksheet as seen below.

	A	B
1	Column1	
2		
3	Mean	74
4	Standard Error	2.532546762
5	Median	75.5
6	Mode	74
7	Standard Deviation	13.8713299
8	Sample Variance	192.4137931
9	Kurtosis	-0.60744581
10	Skewness	-0.391850234
11	Range	50
12	Minimum	45
13	Maximum	95
14	Sum	2220
15	Count	30

As you can see, there are several descriptive statistics reported including measures of central tendency (mean, median, and mode) and measures of variation (range, standard deviation, and variance).

Module 16 (Standard Scores or *z*-Scores)

To calculate *z*-scores using Excel, we use a function other than the Data Analysis Toolpak. Open Excel and click on the **Formulas** tab. You can see in the following Excel worksheet that this tab is highlighted.

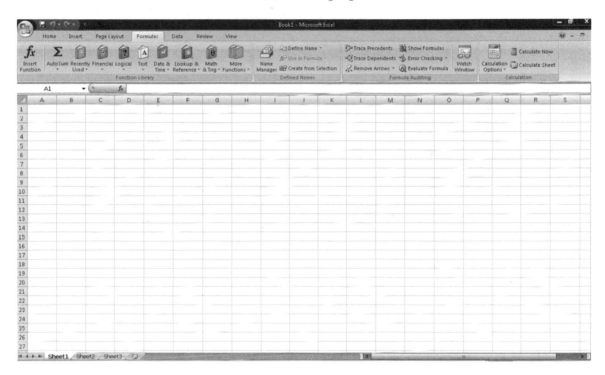

We'll use the English exam data from Table 16.1 (in Module 16) to calculate a *z*-score. You can see from that table that the individual in question scored 91 on the English exam and the exam had a mean of 85 and a standard deviation of 9.58. To calculate the *z*-score, click on the *fX* button on the far right side of the formulas ribbon to receive the following dialog box. Enter the students English exam score into the *X* box and the mean and standard deviation where indicated. Then click on **OK**.

Excel will give you the output above where you can see the *z*-score of +.626305 in the A1 column.

Module 16 (Correlation Coefficients)

To illustrate how Excel can be used to calculate a correlation coefficient, let's use the data from Table 16.3 with which we will calculate Pearson's product-moment correlation coefficient just as we did in Module 16 in the text. In order to make this calculation, we begin by entering the data from Table 16.3 into Excel, as illustrated in the following figure, with the weight data being entered in Column A and the height data in Column B.

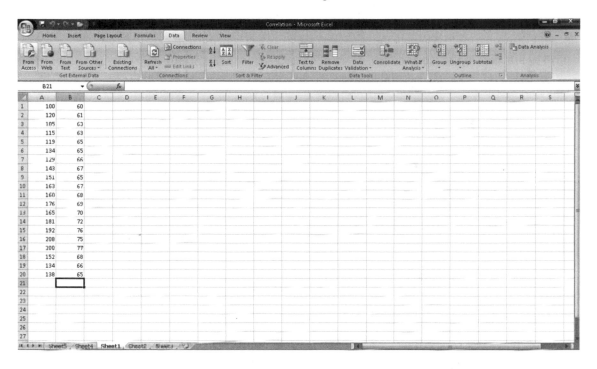

Next, with the **Data** ribbon active as in the preceding window, click on **Data Analysis** in the upper right corner. The following dialog box will appear.

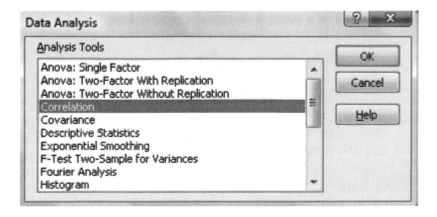

Highlight **Correlation,** and then click **OK.** The subsequent dialog box will appear.

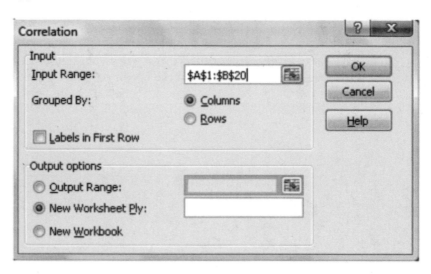

With the cursor in the **Input Range** box, highlight the data in Columns A and B, and click **OK.** The output worksheet generated from this operation is very small and simply reports the correlation coefficient of +.94 as seen below.

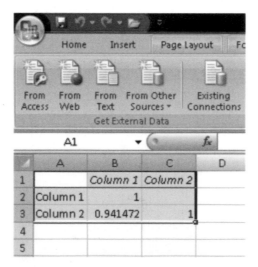

Module 16 (Regression Analysis)

To illustrate how Excel can be used to calculate a regression analyses, let's use the data from Table 16.3 on which we will calculate a regression line just as we did in Module 16 in the text. In order to make this calculation, we begin by entering the data from Table 16.3 into Excel, as illustrated in the following figure, with the weight data being entered in Column A and the height data in Column B.

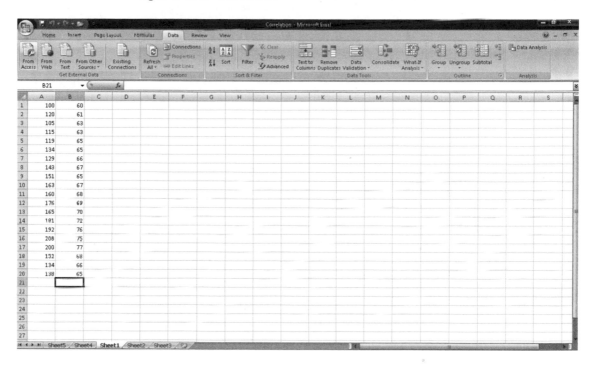

Next, with the **Data** ribbon active as in the preceding window, click on **Data Analysis** in the upper right corner. The following drop down box will appear.

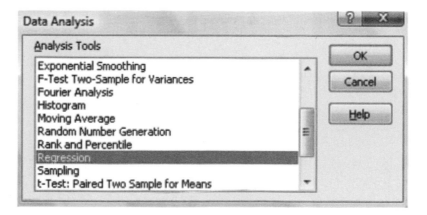

Highlight **Regression** and then click **OK**. The dialog box that follows will appear.

With the cursor in the **Input Y Range** box, highlight the height data in Column B so that it appears in the Input Y Range box. Do the same with the **Input X Range** box and the data from Column A (we place the height data in the Y box because height is what we are predicting based on knowing one's weight). Then click **OK**. The following output will be produced.

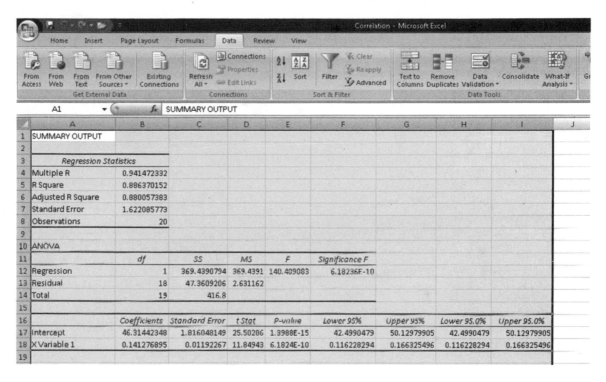

We are really only interested in the data necessary to create the regression line. These data can be found on lines 17 and 18 of the output worksheet in the first column labeled Coefficients. We see that the Y-intercept is 46.31 and the slope is .141. Thus the regression equation would be $Y' = .141(X) + 46.31$.

Module 18 (Independent-Groups *t* Test)

We'll use the data from Table 18.1 (in Module 18) to illustrate how to use Excel to calculate an independent-groups *t* test. The data represent the number of items answered correctly for two groups of participants when one group used a spaced study technique and the other used a massed study technique. The researcher predicted that those in the spaced study condition would perform better. The data from Table 18.1 have been entered into the following Excel worksheet with the data from the spaced condition in Column A and the data from the massed condition in Column B.

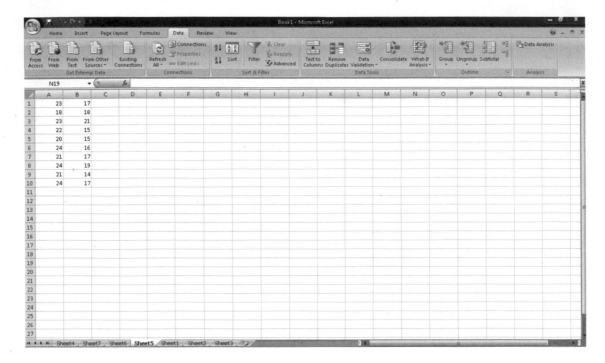

Next we click on **Data Analysis** in the top right corner of the screen; the following dialog box will appear.

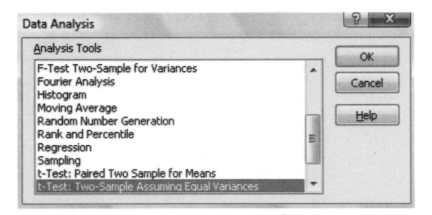

You can see that I have selected *t*-**Test: Two-Sample Assuming Equal Variances**. After you have done the same, click **OK**, and you will then see the following dialog box.

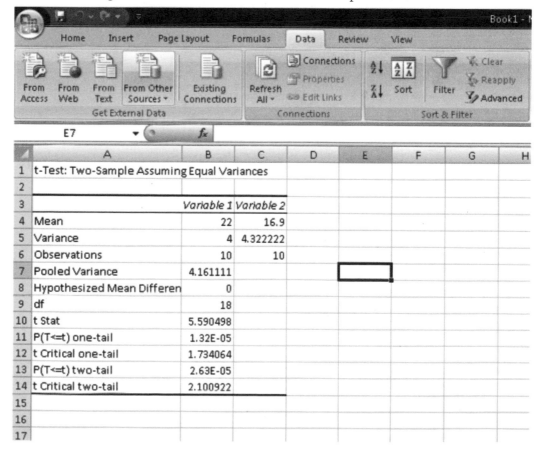

With the cursor in the **Variable 1 Range** box, highlight the data in the A Column in the Excel spreadsheet so that they are entered in to the **Variable 1 Range** box. Do the same for Column B, and enter these data into the **Variable 2 Range** box. Then click **OK**. You will see the output below.

	A	B	C
1	t-Test: Two-Sample Assuming Equal Variances		
2			
3		Variable 1	Variable 2
4	Mean	22	16.9
5	Variance	4	4.322222
6	Observations	10	10
7	Pooled Variance	4.161111	
8	Hypothesized Mean Differen	0	
9	df	18	
10	t Stat	5.590498	
11	P(T<=t) one-tail	1.32E-05	
12	t Critical one-tail	1.734064	
13	P(T<=t) two-tail	2.63E-05	
14	t Critical two-tail	2.100922	
15			
16			
17			

We are provided with the *t* test statistics of 5.59 along with the probability and critical values for both one- and two-tailed tests. We can see based on the one-tailed critical value of *t* that the test is significant at $p < .0000132$.

Module 19 (Correlated-Groups *t* Test)

Using Excel to calculate a correlated-groups *t* test is very similar to using it to calculate an independent-groups *t* test. We'll use the data from Table 19.1 (in Module 19) to illustrate its use. You might remember that for this *t* test we are comparing memory for concrete versus abstract words for a group of 8 participants. Each participant served in both conditions. First enter the data from Table 19.1 into an Excel spreadsheet (as illustrated below). The data for the concrete word condition are entered in Column A and the data for the abstract word condition in Column B.

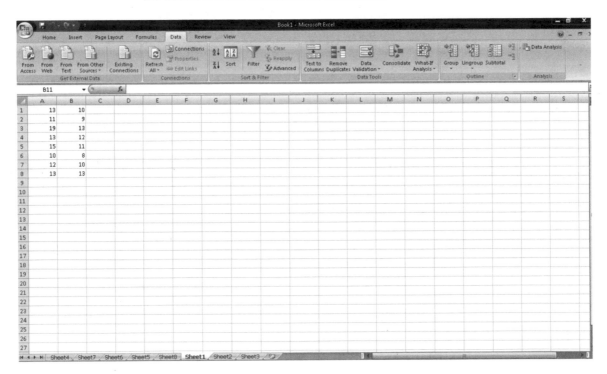

Then click on the **Data Analysis** tab, and select ***t*-Test: Paired Two Sample for Means** as indicated in the following dialog box. Click **OK** after doing this.

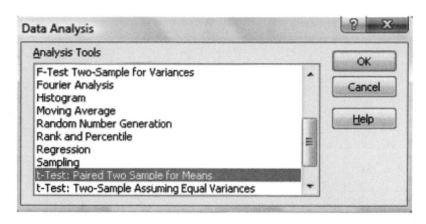

You will then get the following dialog box into which you will enter the data from Column A into the **Variable 1 Range** box by clicking in the Variable 1 Range box and then highlighting the data in Column A. Next do the same with the data in Column B and the **Variable 2 Range** box. After these operations the dialog box should appear as below.

Next click **OK,** and you will receive the output as it appears below.

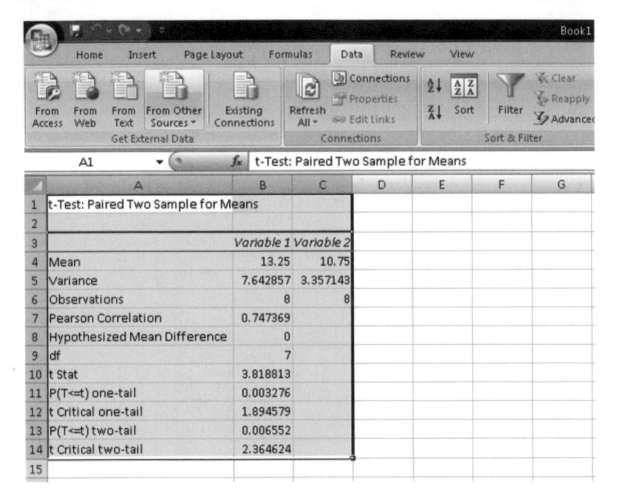

We can see that $t(7) = 3.82$, $p < .003$ (one-tailed).

Module 20 (One-Way Randomized ANOVA)

We'll use the data from Table 20.1 (in Module 20) to illustrate the use of Excel to compute a one-way randomized ANOVA. In this study we had participants use one of three different types of rehearsal (rote, imagery, or story) and then had them perform a recall task. Thus we manipulated rehearsal and measured memory for the 10 words participants studied. Because there were different participants in each condition, we use a randomized ANOVA. We begin by entering the data into Excel with the data from each condition appearing in a different column, as illustrated below.

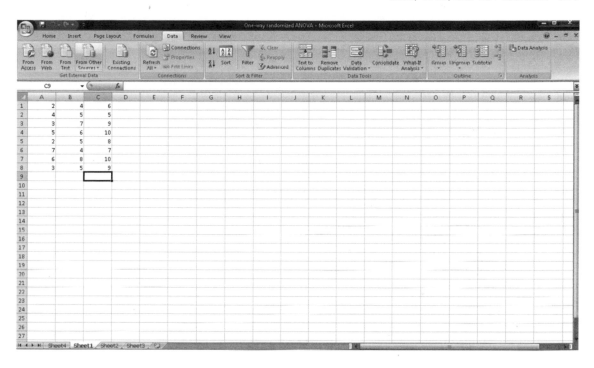

Next, with the **Data** ribbon highlighted, click on the **Data Analysis** tab in the top right corner. You should receive the following dialog box.

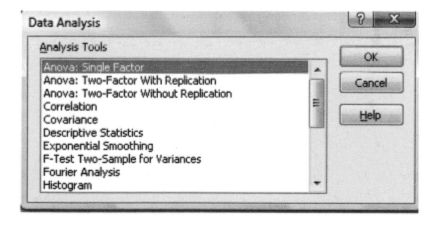

Select **Anova: Single Factor** as in the preceding box, and click **OK**. The following dialog box will appear.

With the cursor in **the Input Range** box, highlight the three columns of data so that they are entered into the Input Range box as they are in the preceding box. Then click **OK**.

The output from the ANOVA will appear on a new Worksheet as seen below.

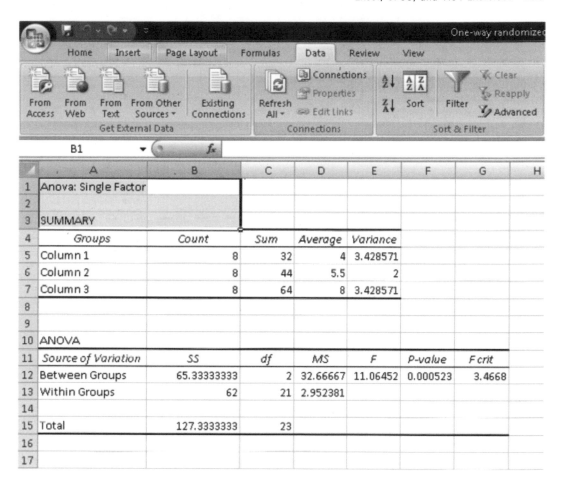

You can see from the ANOVA Summary Table provided by Excel that $F(2,21) = 11.06$, $p = 0.000523$. In addition to the full ANOVA Summary Table, Excel also provides the mean and variance for each condition.

SPSS EXERCISES

Module 15 (Measures of Central Tendency and Variation)

To begin using SPSS to conduct data analyses, the data must be entered into an SPSS spreadsheet. This operation simply involves opening SPSS and entering the data into the spreadsheet. You can see in the following spreadsheet that I have entered the exam grade data from Table 15.5 (in Module 15) into an SPSS spreadsheet. (Please note: When you enter the data into your spreadsheet, consult Table 15.5 from the text, not the figure below, and enter all of the data from Table 15.5. Due to space constraints all of the data do not appear in the figure below.)

Notice that the variable is simply named VAR0001. To rename the variable to something appropriate for your data set, click on the **Variable View** tab on the bottom left of the screen. You will see the following window.

File	Edit	View	Data	Transform	Analyze	Graphs	Utilities	Add-ons	Window	Help				
		Name	Type	Width	Decimals	Label		Values	Missing	Columns	Align		Measure	
1		VAR00001	Numeric	8	2			None	None	8	⬛ Right		✎ Scale	
2														
3														
4														
5														
6														
7														
8														
9														
10														
11														
12														
13														
14														
15														
16														
17														
18														
19														
20														
21														
22														
23														
24														
25														
26														
27														
28														
29														

Data View   **Variable View**

Type the name you wish to give the variable in the highlighted data box. The variable name cannot have any spaces in it. Because these data represent exam grade data, we'll type in **Examgrade** and then highlight the **Data View** tab on the bottom left of the screen in order to get back the data spreadsheet. Once you have navigated back to the data spreadsheet, click on the **Analyze** tab at the top of the screen and a dropdown menu with various statistical analyses will appear. Select **Descriptive Statistics** and then **Descriptives...** The following dialog box will appear.

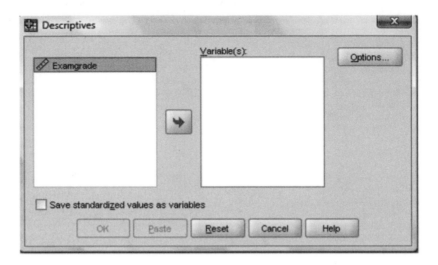

Examgrade will be highlighted, as above. Click on the arrow in the middle of the window, and the Examgrade variable will be moved over to the **Variables** box. Then click on **Options** to receive the following dialog box.

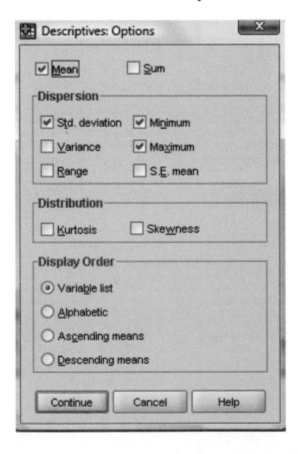

You can see that the Mean, Standard Deviation, Minimum, and Maximum are all checked. However, you could select any of the descriptive statistics you want calculated. After making your selections, click **Continue** and then **OK**. The output will appear on a separate page as an Output file like the one below.

Descriptives

Descriptive Statistics

	N	Minimum	Maximum	Mean	Std. Deviation
Exam Grade	30	45.00	95.00	74.0000	13.87133
Valid N (listwise)	30				

Module 16 (Correlation Coefficients)

To illustrate how SPSS can be used to calculate a correlation coefficient, let's use the data from Table 16.3 on which we will calculate Pearson's product-moment correlation coefficient just as we did in Module 16 in the text. In order to make this calculation, we begin by entering the data from Table 16.3 into SPSS, as illustrated in the following figure, with the weight data being entered in Column B and the height data in Column C. The data in Column A represent the participants (there were 20).

File	Edit	View	Data	Transform	Analyze	Graphs	Utilities

27 : Participant	

	Participant	Weight	Height	var
1	1.00	100.00	60.00	
2	2.00	120.00	61.00	
3	3.00	105.00	63.00	
4	4.00	115.00	63.00	
5	5.00	119.00	65.00	
6	6.00	134.00	65.00	
7	7.00	129.00	66.00	
8	8.00	143.00	67.00	
9	9.00	151.00	65.00	
10	10.00	163.00	67.00	
11	11.00	160.00	68.00	
12	12.00	176.00	69.00	
13	13.00	165.00	70.00	
14	14.00	181.00	72.00	
15	15.00	192.00	76.00	
16	16.00	208.00	75.00	
17	17.00	200.00	77.00	
18	18.00	152.00	68.00	
19	19.00	134.00	66.00	
20	20.00	138.00	65.00	

Next click on **Analyze,** followed by **Correlate** and then **Bivariate.** The dialog box that follows will be produced.

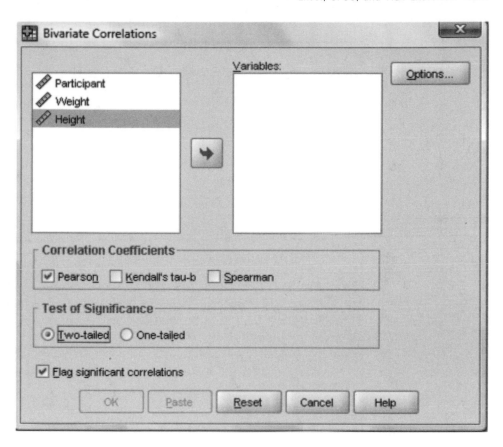

Move the two variables you want correlated (weight and height) into the **Variables** box. In addition, click **One-tailed** because this was a one-tailed test, and lastly, click on **Options** and select **Means and Standard Deviations**, thus letting SPSS know that you want descriptive statistics on the two variables. The output will appear as below.

Correlations
[DataSet0]

Descriptive Statistics

	Mean	Std. Deviation	N
Weight	149.2500	31.21213	20
Height	67.4000	4.68368	20

Correlations

		Weight	Height
Weight	Pearson Correlation	1	.941**
	Sig. (1-tailed)		.000
	N	20	20
Height	Pearson Correlation	.941**	1
	Sig. (1-tailed)	.000	
	N	20	20

**Correlation is significant at the 0.01 level (1-tailed).

The correlation coefficient of .941 is provided along with the one-tailed significance level and the mean and standard deviation for each of the variables.

Module 16 (Regression Analysis)

To illustrate how SPSS can be used to calculate a regression analysis, let's use the data from Table 16.3 on which we will calculate a regression line just as we did in Module 16. In order to make this calculation, we begin by entering the data from Table 16.3 into SPSS, as illustrated in the following figure, with the data being entered just as they were when we used SPSS to calculate a correlation on the same data.

File	Edit	View	Data	Transform	Analyze	Graphs	Utilities

27 : Participant

	Participant	Weight	Height	var
1	1.00	100.00	60.00	
2	2.00	120.00	61.00	
3	3.00	105.00	63.00	
4	4.00	115.00	63.00	
5	5.00	119.00	65.00	
6	6.00	134.00	65.00	
7	7.00	129.00	66.00	
8	8.00	143.00	67.00	
9	9.00	151.00	65.00	
10	10.00	163.00	67.00	
11	11.00	160.00	68.00	
12	12.00	176.00	69.00	
13	13.00	165.00	70.00	
14	14.00	181.00	72.00	
15	15.00	192.00	76.00	
16	16.00	208.00	75.00	
17	17.00	200.00	77.00	
18	18.00	152.00	68.00	
19	19.00	134.00	66.00	
20	20.00	138.00	65.00	

Next click on **Analyze,** followed by **Regression** and then **Linear.** The dialog box that follows will be produced.

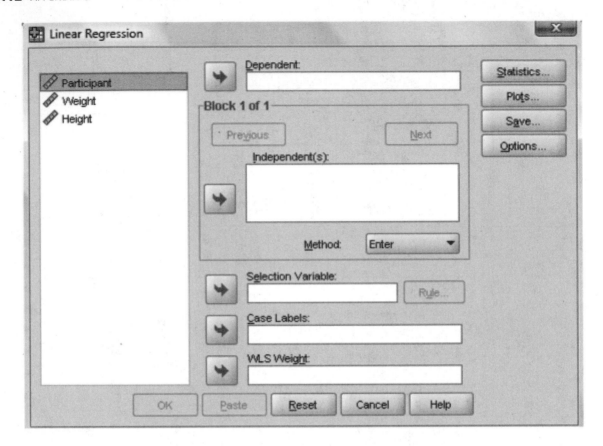

For this regression analysis we tried to predict height based on knowing an individual's weight. Thus we are using height as the dependent measure in our model and weight as the independent measure. Enter height into the **Dependent** box and weight into the **Independent** box by using the appropriate arrows. Then click **OK**. The output will be generated in the output window.

Regression

Variables Entered/Removed[b]

Model	Variables Entered	Variables Removed	Method
1	Weight[a]		Enter

[a]All requested variables entered.
[b]Dependent Variable: Height.

Model Summary

Model	R	R Square	Adjusted R Square	Std. Error of the Estimate
1	.941[a]	.886	.880	1.62209

[a]Predictors: (Constant), Weight.

Coefficients[a]

Model		Unstandardized Coefficients		Standardized Coefficients		
		B	Std. Error	Beta	t	Sig.
1	(Constant)	46.314	1.816		25.503	.000
	Weight	.141	.012	.941	11.849	.000

[a]Dependent Variable: Height.

We are most interested in the data necessary to create the regression line. This data can be found in the box labeled Coefficients. We see that the Y-intercept (Constant) is 46.314 and the slope is .141. Consequently the regression equation would be $Y' = .141(X) + 46.31$.

Module 18 (Independent-Groups *t* Test)

We'll use the text problem from Module 18 to illustrate the use of SPSS for an Independent-Groups *t* Test. In this study researchers have participants use one of two types of study, spaced or massed, and then measure exam performance. The data from Table 18.1 are entered into SPSS as in the following window.

File	Edit	View	Data	Transform	Analyze	Graphs	Utilities	Add-ons	Window	Help

1 : Typeofstudy		1.0				

	Typeofstudy	Examscore	var	var	var	var
1	1.00	23.00				
2	1.00	18.00				
3	1.00	23.00				
4	1.00	22.00				
5	1.00	20.00				
6	1.00	24.00				
7	1.00	21.00				
8	1.00	24.00				
9	1.00	21.00				
10	1.00	24.00				
11	2.00	17.00				
12	2.00	18.00				
13	2.00	21.00				
14	2.00	15.00				
15	2.00	15.00				
16	2.00	16.00				
17	2.00	17.00				
18	2.00	19.00				
19	2.00	14.00				
20	2.00	17.00				
21						

Notice that the independent variable of Typeofstudy has been converted to a numeric variable where the number 1 represents the spaced study condition and the number 2 represents the massed study condition. Thus the data in rows 1–10 represent spaced study data and that in rows 11–20 the massed study data. Click on the **Analyze** tab, and then **Compare Means** followed by **Independent-Samples T Test.** The following dialog box will appear.

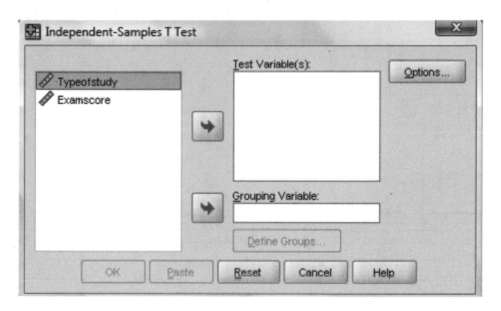

We'll place the Examscore data into the **Test Variable** (dependent variable) box and the Typeofstudy data into the **Grouping Variable** (independent variable) box. Once you have done these operations, click on the **Grouping Variable** box and the **Define Groups** box below that will become active. Click on the **Define Groups** box, and you will receive a dialog box as follows.

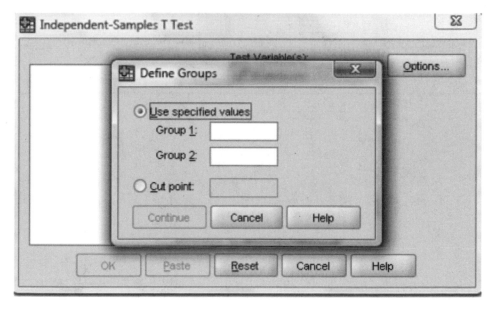

We have to let SPSS know what values we used to designate the spaced versus the massed study groups. So enter a 1 into the **Group 1** box and a 2

into the **Group 2** box, and click **Continue**. Then click **OK** in the Independent-Samples **T Test** window. You should receive output similar to the following.

T-Test

Group Statistics

	Type of study	N	Mean	Std. Deviation	Std. Error Mean
Exam score	1.00	10	22.0000	2.0000	.63246
	2.00	10	16.9000	2.07900	.65744

Independent Samples Test

		Levene's Test for Equality of Variances		t-test for Equality of Means							
										95% Confidence interval of the Difference	
		F	Sig.	t	df	Sig. (2-tailed)	Mean Difference	Std. Error Difference	Lower	Upper
Exam score	Equal variances assumed	.022	.884	5.590	18	.000	5.1000	.91226	3.18341	7.01659
	Equal variances not assumed			5.590	17.973	.000	5.10000	.91226	3.18320	7.01680

Descriptive statistics for the two conditions are reported in the first table, followed by the *t* test score of 5.590. Because we are assuming equal variances, we use the *df*, *t* score, and other data from that row in the table. Moreover, the two-tailed significance level is provided, but because this was a one-tailed test, the critical values table from Appendix B should be consulted for the one-tailed significance level. We are also provided with the 95% confidence interval for the *t* test.

Module 19 (Correlated-Groups *t* Test)

To illustrate the Correlated-Groups *t* Test, we'll use the problem from the text in Module 19 in which a researcher has a group of participants study a list of 20 concrete words and 20 abstract words and then measures recall for the words within each condition. The researcher predicts that the participants will have better recall for the concrete words. The data from Table 19.1 are entered into SPSS as follows. We have 8 participants, with each serving in both conditions. Thus the scores for each participant in both conditions appear in a single row.

File	Edit	View	Data	Transform	Analyze	Graphs	Utilities	Add-ons	Window	Help

1 : Participant | 1.0

	Participant	Concretewords	Abstractwords	var	var	var
1	1.00	13.00	10.00			
2	2.00	11.00	9.00			
3	3.00	19.00	13.00			
4	4.00	13.00	12.00			
5	5.00	15.00	11.00			
6	6.00	10.00	8.00			
7	7.00	12.00	10.00			
8	8.00	13.00	13.00			
9						
10						

Next we click on the **Analyze** tab, followed by the **Compare Means** tab and then **Paired-Samples T Test**. These operations will produce the following dialog box.

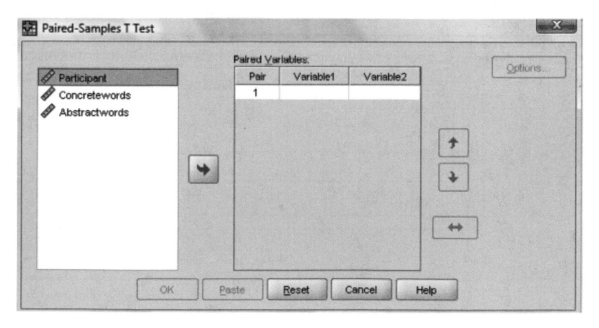

Highlight the **Concretewords** variable, and then click the arrow button in the middle of the screen. The concretewords variable should now appear under **Variable1** in the box on the right of the window. Do the same for the **Abstractwords** variable, and it should appear under **Variable2** in the box on the right. The dialog box should now appear as follows.

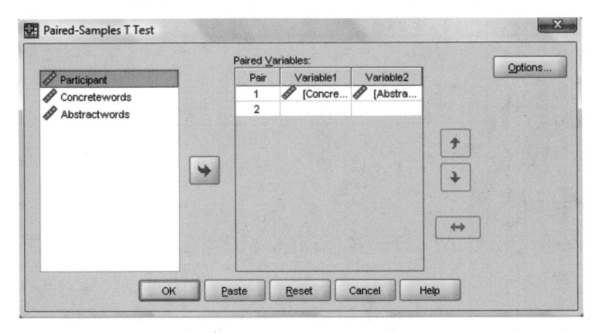

Click **OK**, and the output will appear in an output window as below.

T-Test

Paired Samples Statistics

		Mean	N	Std. Deviation	Std. Error Mean
Pair 1	Concretewords	13.2500	8	2.76457	.97742
	Abstractwords	10.7500	8	1.83225	.64780

Paired Samples Correlations

		N	Correlation	Sig.
Pair 1	Concretewords & Abstractwords	8	.747	.033

Paired Samples Test

		Paired Differences							
					95% Confidence Interval of the Difference				
		Mean	Std. Deviation	Std. Error Mean	Lower	Upper	t	df	Sig. (2-tailed)
Pair 1	Concrete-words-Abstract words	2.50000	1.85164	.65465	.95199	4.04801	3.819	7	.007

As in the independent-samples t test descriptive statistics appear in the first table, followed by the correlation between the variables. Additionally, the correlated-groups t test results appear in the third table with the t-score of 3.819, 7 degrees of freedom, and the two-tailed significance level, but as this was a one-tailed test, we can find the significance level for this in the critical values table in Appendix B. As in the previous t test the 95% confidence interval is also reported.

Module 20 (One-Way Randomized ANOVA)

We'll use the data from Table 20.1 (in Module 20) to illustrate the use of SPSS to compute a one-way randomized ANOVA. In this study we had participants use one of three different types of rehearsal (rote, imagery, or story) and then had them perform a recall task. Thus we manipulated rehearsal and measured memory for the 10 words participants studied. Because there were different participants in each condition, we use a randomized ANOVA. We begin by entering the data into SPSS. The first column is labeled Rehearsaltype and indicates which type of rehearsal the participants used (1 for rote, 2 for imagery, and 3 for story). The recall data for each of the three conditions appear in the second column labeled Recall.

	File Edit View Data Transform Analyze Graphs		
	27 : Rehearsaltype		
	Rehearsaltype	Recall	var
1	1.00	2.00	
2	1.00	4.00	
3	1.00	3.00	
4	1.00	5.00	
5	1.00	2.00	
6	1.00	7.00	
7	1.00	6.00	
8	1.00	3.00	
9	2.00	4.00	
10	2.00	5.00	
11	2.00	7.00	
12	2.00	6.00	
13	2.00	5.00	
14	2.00	4.00	
15	2.00	8.00	
16	2.00	5.00	
17	3.00	6.00	
18	3.00	5.00	
19	3.00	9.00	
20	3.00	10.00	
21	3.00	8.00	
22	3.00	7.00	
23	3.00	10.00	
24	3.00	9.00	
25			

Next, click on **Analyze**, followed by **Compare Means** and then **One-Way ANOVA**. You should receive the dialog box below.

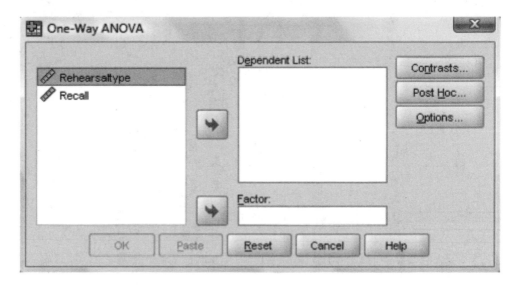

Enter Rehearsaltype into the **Factor** box by highlighting it and using the appropriate arrow. Do the same for Recall by entering it into the **Dependent List** box. After doing these operations, the dialog box should appear as follows.

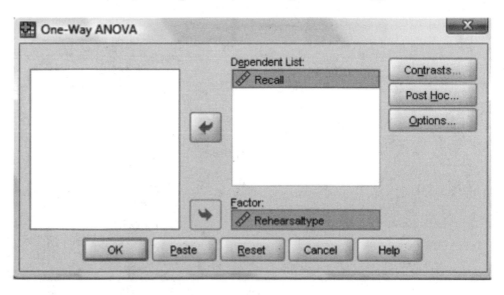

Next click on the **Options** button, and select **Descriptive** and **Continue**. Then click on the **Post Hoc** button, and select **Tukey** and then **Continue**. Then click on **OK**.

The output from the ANOVA will appear in a new output window as seen below.

One way

Descriptives

Recall

	N	Mean	Std. Deviation	Std. Error	95% Confidence Interval for Mean		Minimum	Maximum
					Lower Bound	Upper Bound		
1	8	4.0000	1.85164	.65465	2.4520	5.5480	2.00	7.00
2	8	5.5000	1.41421	.50000	4.3177	6.6823	4.00	8.00
3	8	8.0000	1.85164	.65465	6.4520	9.5480	5.00	10.00
Total	24	5.8333	2.35292	.48029	4.8398	6.8269	2.00	10.00

Anova

Recall

	Sum of Squares	df	Mean Square	F	Sig.
Between Groups	65.333	2	32.667	11.065	.001
Within Groups	62.000	21	2.952		
Total	127.333	23			

Post Hoc Tests

Multiple Comparisons

Recall
Tukey HSD

(I) Rehearsal type	(j) Rehearsal type	Mean Difference (I-J)	Std. Error	Sig.	95% Confidence Interval	
					Lower Bound	Upper Bound
1.00	2.00	−1.50000	.85912	.212	−3.6655	.6655
	3.00	−4.00000*	.85912	.000	−6.1655	−1.8345
2.00	1.00	1.50000	.85912	.212	−.6655	3.6655
	3.00	−2.50000*	.85912	.022	−4.6655	−.3345
3.00	1.00	4.00000*	.85912	.000	1.8345	6.1655
	2.00	2.50000*	.85912	.022	.3345	4.6655

* The mean difference is significant at the 0.05 level.

You can see that the descriptive statistics for each conditions are provided followed by the ANOVA Summary Table in which $F(2,21) = 11.065$, $p < .001$. In addition to the full ANOVA Summary Table, SPSS also calculated Tukey's HSD and provides all pair-wise comparisons between the three conditions along with whether or not the comparison was significant.

TI84 EXERCISES

(These exercises can also be performed on the TI83.)

Module 15 (Measures of Central Tendency)

TI84 Exercise: Calculation of the Mean

1. With the calculator on, press the STAT key.
2. EDIT will be highlighted. Press the ENTER key.
3. Under L1 enter the data from Table 15.5.
4. Press the STAT key again and highlight CALC.
5. Number 1: 1—VAR STATS will be highlighted. Press ENTER.
6. Press ENTER once again.

The statistics for the single variable on which you entered data will be presented on the calculator screen. The mean is presented first as $\overline{X}$.

Module 15 (Measures of Variability)

TI84 Exercise: Calculation of σ and s

1. With the calculator on, press the STAT key.
2. EDIT will be highlighted. Press the ENTER key.
3. Under L1 enter the data from Table 15.5.
4. Press the STAT key once again, and highlight CALC.
5. Number 1: 1—VAR STATS will be highlighted. Press ENTER.
6. Press ENTER once again.

Descriptive statistics for the single variable on which you entered data will be shown. The population standard deviation (σ) is indicated by the symbol σ_X. The unbiased estimator of the population standard deviation (s) is indicated by the symbol S_X.

Module 16 (Pearson Product-Moment Correlation Coefficient and Regression Analysis)

TI84 Exercise: Calculation of Pearson Product-Moment Correlation Coefficient, Coefficient of Determination, and Regression Analysis

Let's use the data from Table 16.3 to conduct the analyses in Module 16 using the TI84 calculator.

1. With the calculator on, press the STAT key.
2. EDIT will be highlighted. Press the ENTER key.
3. Under L1 enter the weight data from Table 16.3.
4. Under L2 enter the height data from Table 16.3.

5. Press the 2nd key and 0 [catalog], scroll down to DiagnosticOn, and press ENTER. Press ENTER once again. (The message DONE should appear on the screen.)
6. Press the STAT key, and highlight CALC. Scroll down to 8:LinReg(a + bx), and press ENTER.
7. Type L_1 (by pressing the 2nd key, followed by the 1 key), followed by a comma and L_2 (by pressing the 2nd key, followed by the 2 key) next to LinReg(a + bx). The screen should appear as follows: LinReg(a + bx) L_1,L_2.
8. Press ENTER.

The values of a (46.31), b (.141), r^2 (.89), and r (.94) should appear on the screen. (Please note: Any differences between the numbers calculated on the TI84 and those calculated previously by hand are due to rounding.)

Module 18 (Independent-Groups *t* Test)

TI84 Exercise: Calculation of the Independent-Groups *t* Test
Let's use the data from Table 18.1 to conduct the test using the TI84 calculator.

1. With the calculator on, press the STAT key.
2. EDIT will be highlighted. Press the ENTER key.
3. Under L1 enter the data from Table 18.1 for the Spaced Study Group.
4. Under L2 enter the data from Table 18.1 for the Massed Study Group.
5. Press the STAT key once again, and highlight TESTS.
6. Scroll down to 2-SampTTest. Press the ENTER key.
7. Highlight DATA. Enter L_1 next to List1 (by pressing the 2nd key, followed by the 1 key). Enter L_2 next to List2 (by pressing the 2nd key, followed by the 2 key).
8. Scroll down to µ1:, and select >µ2 (for a one-tailed test in which we predict that the spaced study group will do better than the massed study group). Press ENTER.
9. Scroll down to Pooled:, and highlight YES. Press ENTER.
10. Scroll down to and highlight CALCULATE. Press ENTER.

The *t*-score of 5.59 should be displayed, followed by the significance level of .000013 and the *df* of 18. In addition, descriptive statistics for both variables on which you entered data will be shown.

Module 19 (Correlated-Groups *t* Test)

TI84 Exercise: Calculation of the Correlated-Groups *t* Test
Let's use the data from Table 19.2 to conduct the test using the TI84 calculator.

1. With the calculator on, press the STAT key.
2. EDIT will be highlighted. Press the ENTER key.
3. Under L1 enter the difference scores from Table 19.2.
4. Press the STAT key once again, and highlight TESTS.
5. Scroll down to T-Test. Press the ENTER key.

6. Highlight DATA. Enter 0 next to μ_0:. Enter L_1 next to List (by pressing the 2nd key, followed by the 1 key).
7. Scroll down to μ:, and select $> \mu_0$ (for a one-tailed test in which we predict that the difference between the scores for each condition will be greater than 0). Press ENTER.
8. Scroll down to and highlight CALCULATE. Press ENTER.

The t-score of 3.82 should be displayed, followed by the significance level of .0033. (Please note: The slight difference between the t-score displayed on the calculator and that calculated in the text is due to rounding. The TI84 does not round, whereas I have rounded to two decimal places in the example in the text.) In addition, descriptive statistics will be shown.

Module 20 (One-Way Randomized ANOVA)

TI84 Exercise: Calculation of the Randomized One-Way ANOVA

Let's use the data from Table 20.1 to check our hand calculations by using the TI84 to conduct the analysis.

1. With the calculator on, press the STAT key.
2. EDIT will be highlighted. Press the ENTER key.
3. Under L1 enter the data from Table 20.1 for the Rote Group.
4. Under L2 enter the data from Table 20.1 for the Imagery Group.
5. Under L3 enter the data from Table 14.1 for the Story Group.
6. Press the STAT key once again, and highlight TESTS.
7. Scroll down to ANOVA. Press the ENTER key.
8. Next to ANOVA enter (L1,L2,L3) using the 2nd function key with the appropriate number keys. Make sure that you use commas. The finished line should read "ANOVA(L1,L2,L3)."
9. Press ENTER.

The F-score of 11.065 should be displayed, followed by the significance level of .0005, and the df, SS, and MS between-groups (listed as Factor) and within-groups (listed as Error).

Computational Formulas for ANOVAs

TABLE **D.1**

Alternative Table 20.5 ANOVA Summary Table Using Computational Formulas

SOURCE	DF	SS	MS	F
Between groups	$k-1$	$\sum\left[\dfrac{\left(\sum X_g\right)^2}{n_g}\right] - \dfrac{\left(\sum X\right)^2}{N}$	$\dfrac{SS_b}{df_b}$	$\dfrac{MS_b}{MS_W}$
Within groups	$N-k$	$\sum\left[\sum X_g^2 - \dfrac{\left(\sum X_g\right)^2}{n_g}\right]$	$\dfrac{SS_W}{df_W}$	
Total	$N-1$	$\sum X^2 - \dfrac{\left(\sum X\right)^2}{N}$		

REFERENCES

Ainsworth, M. D. S., & Bell, S. M. (1970). Attachment, exploration, and separation: Illustrated by the behavior of one-year-olds in a strange situation. *Child Development, 41*, 49–67.

American Psychological Association. (1996). *Guidelines for ethical conduct in the care and use of animals*. Washington, DC: Author.

American Psychological Association. (2001). *Publication manual of the American Psychological Association* (5th ed.). Washington, DC: Author.

American Psychological Association. (2002). Ethical principles of psychologists and code of conduct. *American Psychologist, 57*, 1060–1073.

American Psychological Association. (2007). *Thesaurus of psychological index terms* (11th ed.). Washington, DC: Author.

American Psychological Association. (2009). *Publication manual of the American Psychological Association* (6th ed.). Washington, DC: Author.

Anastasi, A., & Urbina, S. (1997). *Psychological testing* (7th ed.). Upper Saddle River, NJ: Prentice Hall.

Aronson, E., & Carlsmith, J. M. (1968). Experimentation in social psychology. In G. Lindzey & E. Aronson (Eds.), *Handbook of social psychology* (2nd ed., pp. 1–79). Reading, MA: Addison-Wesley.

Berg, B. L. (2009). *Qualitative research methods for the social sciences*. Boston: Allyn & Bacon.

Bolt, M. (1998). *Instructor's resources to accompany David G. Myers, Psychology* (5th ed.). New York: Worth.

Bourque, L. B., & Fielder, E. P. (2003). *How to conduct self-administered and mail surveys* (2nd ed.). Thousand Oaks, CA: Sage.

Bratton, R. L., Montero, D. P., Adams, K. S., Novas, M. A., McKay, R. C., Hall, L. J., et al. (2002). Effect of "ionized" wrist bracelets on musculoskeletal pain: A randomized, double-blind placebo-controlled trial. *Mayo Clinic Proceedings, 77*, 1164–1168.

Campbell, D. T. (1969). Reforms as experiments. *American Psychologist, 24*, 409–429.

Campbell, D. T., & Stanley, J. C. (1963). *Experimental and quasi-experimental designs for research*. Boston: Houghton Mifflin.

Cohen, J. (1988). *Statistical power analysis for the behavioral sciences*. Hillsdale, NJ: Erlbaum.

Cohen, J. (1992). A power primer. *Psychological Bulletin, 112*, 155–159.

Cook, T. D., & Campbell, D. T. (1979). *Quasi-experimentation: Design & analysis issues for field settings*. Boston: Houghton Mifflin.

Cowles, M. (1989). *Statistics in psychology: An historical perspective*. Hillsdale, NJ: Erlbaum.

Cozby, P. C. (2001). *Methods in behavioral research* (7th ed.). Mountain View, CA: Mayfield.

Dillman, D. A. (1978). *Mail and telephone surveys: The total design method*. New York: Wiley.

Dillman, D. A. (2007). *Mail and internet surveys: The tailored design method* (2nd ed.). Hoboken, NJ: Wiley.

Dillman, D. A., Smyth, J. D., & Christian, L. M. (2009). *Internet, mail and mixed-mode surveys: The tailored design method* (3rd ed.). Hoboken, NJ: Wiley.

Erdos, P. L. (1983). *Professional mail surveys*. Malabar, FL: Robert E. Krieger.

Esterberg, K. G. (2002). *Qualitative methods in social research*. Boston: McGraw Hill.

Gilovich, T. (1991). *How we know what isn't so: The fallibility of human reason in everyday life*. New York: Free Press.

Goldstein, W. M., & Goldstein, I. (1978). *How we know: An exploration of the scientific process*. New York: Plenum.

Gould, S. J. (1985, June). The median isn't the message. *Discover, 6*(6), 40–42.

Greene, J., Speizer, H., & Wiitala, W. (2008). Telephone and web: Mixed-mode challenge. *Health Research and Educational Trust, 43,* 230–248.

Griggs, R. A., & Cox, J. R. (1982). The elusive thematic-materials effect in Wason's selection task. *British Journal of Psychology, 73,* 407–420.

Groves, R. M., & Kahn, R. L. (1979). *Surveys by telephone: A national comparison with personal interviews.* New York: Academic Press.

Hall, R. H., Axelrod, S., Foundopoulos, M., Shellman, J., Campbell, R. A., & Cranston, S. S. (1971). The effective use of punishment to modify behavior in the classroom. *Educational Technology, 11*(4), 24–26. (Reprinted from *Classroom management: The successful use of behavior modification,* by K. D. O'Leary & S. O'Leary, Eds, 1972, New York: Pergamon)

Hinkle, D. E., Wiersma, W., & Jurs, S. G. (1988). *Applied statistics for the behavioral sciences* (2nd ed.). Boston: Houghton Mifflin.

Hite, S. (1987). *Women and love: A cultural revolution in progress.* New York: Knopf.

Jones, J. H. (1981). *Bad blood: The Tuskegee syphilis experiment.* New York: Free Press.

Jones, J. L. (1995). *Understanding psychological science.* New York: HarperCollins.

Keppel, G. (1991). *Design and analysis: A researcher's handbook* (3rd ed.). Englewood Cliffs, NJ: Prentice Hall.

Kerlinger, F. N. (1986). *Foundations of behavioral research* (4th ed.). New York: Holt, Rinehart & Winston.

Kranzler, G., & Moursund, J. (1995). *Statistics for the terrified.* Englewood Cliffs, NJ: Prentice Hall.

Leary, M. R. (2001). *Introduction to behavioral research methods* (3rd ed.). Needham Heights, MA: Allyn & Bacon.

Li, C. (1975). *Path analysis: A primer.* Pacific Grove, CA: Boxwood Press.

Likert, R. (1932). A technique for the measurement of attitudes. *Archives of Psychology, 19,* 44–53.

Messer, W., Griggs, R. A., & Jackson, S. L. (1999). A national survey of undergraduate psychology degree options and major requirements. *Teaching of Psychology, 26,* 164–171.

Milgram, S. (1963). Behavioral study of obedience. *Journal of Abnormal and Social Psychology, 67,* 371–378.

Milgram, S. (1974). *Obedience to authority.* New York: Harper & Row.

Milgram, S. (1977). Ethical issues in the study of obedience. In S. Milgram (Ed.), *The individual in a social world* (pp. 188–199). Reading, MA: Addison-Wesley.

Mitchell, M., & Jolley, J. (2004). *Research design explained* (5th ed.). Belmont, CA: Wadsworth/Thomson.

Olson, R. K., & Forsberg, H. (1993). Disabled and normal readers' eye movements in reading and nonreading tasks. In D. M. Willows, R. Kruk, & E. Corcos (Eds.), *Visual processes in reading and reading disabilities* (pp. 377–391). Hillsdale, NJ: Erlbaum.

Paul, G. L. (1966). *Insight vs. desensitization in psychotherapy.* Stanford, CA: Stanford University Press.

Paul, G. L. (1967). Insight vs. desensitization in psychotherapy two years after termination. *Journal of Consulting Psychology, 31,* 333–348.

Pfungst, O. (1911). *Clever Hans (the horse of Mr. von Osten): A contribution to experimental, animal, and human psychology* (C. L. Rahn, Trans.). New York: Holt, Rinehart & Winston. (Republished 1965)

Rewey, K. L., June, J. A., Weiser, A., & Davis, S. F. (2000). "Is this REALLY APA format?": A presubmission checklist for the PSI CHI Journal of Undergraduate Research. *PSI CHI Journal of Undergraduate Research, 5,* 87–89.

Rosenhan, D. C. (1973). On being sane in insane places. *Science, 179,* 250–258.

Salkind, N. J. (1997). *Exploring research* (3rd ed.). Upper Saddle River, NJ: Prentice Hall.

Schweigert, W. A. (1994). *Research methods & statistics for psychology.* Pacific Grove, CA: Brooks/Cole.

Shadish, W. R., Cook, T. D., & Campbell, D. T. (2002). *Experimental and quasi-experimental designs for generalized causal inference.* Boston: Houghton Mifflin.

Sidman, M. (1960). *Tactics of scientific research.* New York: Basic Books.

Stanovich, K. E. (2007). *How to think straight about psychology* (8th ed.). Boston: Allyn & Bacon.

U.S. Department of Health and Human Services. (1981, January 26). Final regulations amending basic HHS policy for the protection of human subjects. *Federal Register, 46,* 16.

Wallis, C. (1987, October 12). Back off, buddy. *Time,* pp. 68–73.

Williams, T. M. (Ed.). (1986). *The impact of television: A natural experiment in three communities.* Orlando, FL: Academic Press.

Zimbardo, P. G. (1972). Pathology of imprisonment. *Transaction/Society, 9,* 4–8.

ABA reversal design A single-case design in which baseline measures are taken, the independent variable is introduced and behavior is measured, and the independent variable is then removed (a return to baseline condition) and measures are taken again.

ABAB reversal design A design in which baseline and independent variable conditions are reversed twice.

absolute zero A property of measurement in which assigning a score of zero indicates an absence of the variable being measured.

action item A type of item used on a checklist to note the presence or absence of behaviors.

action research A method in which research is conducted by a group of people to identify a problem, attempt to resolve it, and then assess how successful their efforts were.

alternate-forms reliability A reliability coefficient determined by assessing the degree of relationship between scores on two equivalent tests.

alternative explanation The idea that another uncontrolled, extraneous variable may be responsible for an observed relationship.

alternative hypothesis, or research hypothesis The hypothesis that the researcher wants to support and that predicts a significant difference

exists between the groups being compared.

ANOVA (analysis of variance) An inferential statistical test for comparing the means of three or more groups.

applied research The study of psychological issues that have practical significance and potential solutions.

archival method A descriptive research method that involves describing data that existed before the time of the study.

bar graph A graphical representation of a frequency distribution in which vertical bars are centered above each category along the x-axis and are separated from each other by a space, which indicates that the levels of the variable represent distinct, unrelated categories.

basic research The study of psychological issues in order to seek knowledge for its own sake.

behavioral measures Measures taken by carefully observing and recording behavior.

between-groups sum of squares The sum of the squared deviations of each group's mean from the grand mean, multiplied by the number of participants in each group.

between-groups variance An estimate of the effect of the independent variable and error variance.

between-participants design An experiment in which different participants are assigned to each group.

Bonferroni adjustment Setting a more stringent alpha level for multiple tests to minimize Type I errors.

case study method An in-depth study of one or more individuals.

causality The assumption that a correlation indicates a causal relationship between two variables.

ceiling effect A limitation of the measuring instrument that decreases its ability to differentiate between scores at the top of the scale.

checklist A tally sheet on which the researcher records attributes of the participants and whether particular behaviors were observed.

class interval frequency distribution A table in which the scores are grouped into intervals and listed along with the frequency of scores in each interval.

closed-ended questions Questions for which participants choose from a limited number of alternatives.

cluster sampling A sampling technique in which clusters of participants that represent the population are used.

coefficient of determination (r^2) A measure of the proportion of the variance in one variable that is accounted for by

429

another variable; calculated by squaring the correlation coefficient.

Cohen's d An inferential statistic for measuring effect size.

cohort A group of individuals born at about the same time.

cohort effect A generational effect in a study that occurs when the eras in which individuals are born affect how they respond in the study.

college sophomore problem An external validity problem that results from using mainly college sophomores as participants in research studies.

conceptual replication A study based on another study that uses different methods, a different manipulation, or a different measure.

confound An uncontrolled extraneous variable or flaw in an experiment.

construct validity The degree to which a measuring instrument accurately measures a theoretical construct or trait that it is designed to measure.

content validity The extent to which a measuring instrument covers a representative sample of the domain of behaviors to be measured.

continuous variables Variables that usually fall along a continuum and allow for fractional amounts.

control Manipulating the independent variable in an experiment or any other extraneous variables that could affect the results of a study.

control group The group of participants who do not receive any level of the independent variable and serve as the baseline in a study.

convenience sampling A sampling technique in which participants are obtained wherever they can be found and typically wherever is convenient for the researcher.

correlated-groups design An experimental design in which the participants in the experimental and control groups are related in some way.

correlated-groups t test A parametric inferential test used to compare the means of two related (within- or matched-participants) samples.

correlation coefficient A measure of the degree of relationship between two sets of scores. It can vary between 21.00 and 11.00.

correlational method A method that assesses the degree of relationship between two variables.

counterbalancing A mechanism for controlling order effects either by including all orders of treatment presentation or by randomly determining the order for each participant.

criterion validity The extent to which a measuring instrument accurately predicts behavior or ability in a given area.

cross-sectional design A type of developmental design in which participants of different ages are studied at the same time.

debriefing Providing information about the true purpose of a study as soon after the completion of data collection as possible.

deception Lying to the participants concerning the true nature of a study because knowing the true nature of the study might affect their performance.

degrees of freedom (df) The number of scores in a sample that are free to vary.

demographic questions Questions that ask for basic information such as age, gender, ethnicity, or income.

dependent variable The variable in a study that is measured by the researcher.

description Carefully observing behavior in order to describe it.

descriptive statistics Numerical measures that describe a distribution by providing information on the central tendency of the distribution, the width of the distribution, and the shape of the distribution.

difference scores Scores representing the difference between participants' performance in one condition and their performance in a second condition.

diffusion of treatment A threat to internal validity in which observed changes in the behaviors or responses of participants may be due to information received from other participants in the study.

directionality The inference made with respect to the direction of a causal relationship between two variables.

discrete variables Variables that usually consist of whole number units or categories and are made up of chunks or units that are detached and distinct from one another.

disguised observation Studies in which the participants are unaware that the researcher is observing their behavior.

double-barreled question A question that asks more than one thing.

double-blind experiment An experimental procedure in which neither the experimenter nor the participant knows the condition to which each participant has been assigned; both parties are blind to the manipulation.

ecological validity The extent to which research can be generalized to real-life situations.

effect size The proportion of variance in the dependent variable that is accounted for by the manipulation of the independent variable.

empirically solvable problems Questions that are potentially answerable by means of currently available research techniques.

equal unit size A property of measurement in which a difference of 1 is the same amount throughout the entire scale.

error variance The amount of variability among the scores caused by chance or uncontrolled variables.

eta-squared (η^2) An inferential statistic for measuring effect size with an ANOVA.

exact replication Repeating a study using the same means of manipulating and measuring the variables as in the original study.

expectancy effects The influence of the researcher's expectations on the outcome of the study.

experimental group The group of participants who receive some level of the independent variable.

experimental method A research method that allows a researcher to establish a cause-and-effect relationship through manipulation of a variable and control of the situation.

experimenter effect A threat to internal validity in which the experimenter, consciously or unconsciously, affects the results of the study.

explanation Identifying the causes that determine when and why a behavior occurs.

external validity The extent to which the results of an experiment can be generalized.

face validity The extent to which a measuring instrument appears valid on its surface.

factorial design A design with more than one independent variable.

factorial notation The notation that indicates how many independent variables are used in a study and how many levels are used for each variable.

field studies A method that involves observing everyday activities as they happen in a natural setting.

floor effect A limitation of the measuring instrument that decreases its ability to differentiate between scores at the bottom of the scale.

focus group interview A method that involves interviewing 6 to 10 individuals at the same time.

F-ratio The ratio of between-groups variance to within-groups variance.

frequency distribution A table in which all of the scores are listed along with the frequency with which each occurs.

frequency polygon A line graph of the frequencies of individual scores.

grand mean The mean performance across all participants in a study.

histogram A graphical representation of a frequency distribution in which vertical bars centered above scores on the x-axis touch each other to indicate that the scores on the variable represent related, increasing values.

history effect A threat to internal validity in which an outside event that is not a part of the manipulation of the experiment could be responsible for the results.

hypothesis A prediction regarding the outcome of a study that often involves the relationship between two variables.

hypothesis testing The process of determining whether a hypothesis is supported by the results of a research study.

identity A property of measurement in which objects that are different receive different scores.

independent-groups t test A parametric inferential test for comparing sample means of two independent groups of scores.

independent variable The variable in a study that is manipulated by the researcher.

inferential statistics Procedures for drawing conclusions about a population based on data collected from a sample.

informed consent form A form given to individuals before they participate in a study to inform them of the general nature of the study and to obtain their consent to participate.

Institutional Review Board (IRB) A committee charged with evaluating

research projects in which human participants are used.

instrumentation effect A threat to internal validity in which changes in the dependent variable may be due to changes in the measuring device.

interaction effect The effect of each independent variable across the levels of the other independent variable.

internal validity The extent to which the results of an experiment can be attributed to the manipulation of the independent variable rather than to some confounding variable.

interrater reliability A reliability coefficient that assesses the agreement of observations made by two or more raters or judges.

interval scale A scale in which the units of measurement (intervals) between the numbers on the scale are all equal in size.

interview A method that typically involves asking questions in a face-to-face manner that may be conducted anywhere.

interviewer bias The tendency for the person asking the questions to bias the participants' answers.

knowledge via authority Knowledge gained from those viewed as authority figures.

knowledge via empiricism Knowledge gained through objective observations of organisms and events in the real world.

knowledge via intuition Knowledge gained without being consciously aware of its source.

knowledge via rationalism Knowledge gained through logical reasoning.

knowledge via science Knowledge gained through a combination of empirical methods and logical reasoning.

knowledge via superstition Knowledge based on subjective feelings, belief in chance, or belief in magical events.

knowledge via tenacity Knowledge gained from repeated ideas and stubbornly clung to despite evidence to the contrary.

kurtosis How flat or peaked a normal distribution is.

laboratory observation Observing the behavior of humans or other animals in a contrived and controlled situation, usually the laboratory.

Latin square A counterbalancing technique to control for order effects without using all possible orders.

leading question A question that sways the respondent to answer in a desired manner.

leptokurtic Normal curves that are tall and thin with only a few scores in the middle of the distribution having a high frequency.

Likert rating scale A type of numerical rating scale developed by Rensis Likert in 1932.

loaded question A question that includes nonneutral or emotionally laden terms.

longitudinal design A type of developmental design in which the same participants are studied repeatedly over time as they age.

magnitude (1) A property of measurement in which the ordering of numbers reflects the ordering of the variable. (2) An indication of the strength of the relationship between two variables.

mail survey A written survey that is self-administered.

main effect An effect of a single independent variable.

matched-participants design A type of correlated-groups design in which participants are matched between conditions on variable(s) that the researcher believes is (are) relevant to the study.

maturation effect A threat to internal validity in which participants' naturally occurring changes could be responsible for the observed results.

mean A measure of central tendency; the arithmetic average of a distribution.

mean square An estimate of either total variance, variance between groups, or variance within groups.

measure of central tendency A number that characterizes the "middleness" of an entire distribution.

measure of variation A number that indicates the degree to which scores are either clustered or spread out in a distribution.

median A measure of central tendency; the middle score in a distribution after the scores have been arranged from highest to lowest or lowest to highest.

mesokurtic Normal curves that have peaks of medium height and distributions that are moderate in breadth.

mode A measure of central tendency; the score in a distribution that occurs with the greatest frequency.

mortality (attrition) A threat to internal validity in which differential dropout rates may be observed in the experimental and control groups, leading to inequality between the groups.

multiple-baseline design A single-case or small-n design in which the effect of introducing the independent variable is assessed over multiple participants, behaviors, or situations.

multiple-baseline design across behaviors A single-case design in which measures are taken at baseline and after the introduction of the independent variable at different times across multiple behaviors.

multiple-baseline design across participants A small-n design in which measures are taken at baseline and after the introduction of the independent variable at different times across multiple participants.

multiple-baseline design across situations A single-case design in which measures are taken at baseline and after the introduction of the independent variable at different times across multiple situations.

multiple-group time-series design A design in which a series of measures are taken on two or more groups both before and after a treatment.

narrative records Full narrative descriptions of a participant's behavior.

naturalistic observation Observing the behavior of humans or other animals in their natural habitats.

negative correlation An inverse relationship between two variables in which an increase in one variable is related to a decrease in the other and vice versa.

negatively skewed distribution A distribution in which the peak is to the right of the center point and the tail extends toward the left or in the negative direction.

negative relationship A relationship between two variables in which an increase in one is accompanied by a decrease in the other.

nominal scale A scale in which objects or individuals are assigned to categories that have no numerical properties.

nonequivalent control group posttest-only design A design in which at least two nonequivalent groups are given a treatment and then a posttest measure.

nonequivalent control group pretest/posttest design A design in which at least two nonequivalent groups are given a pretest, then a treatment, and finally a posttest measure.

nonmanipulated independent variable The independent variable in a quasi-experimental design in which participants are not randomly assigned to conditions but rather come to the study as members of each condition.

nonparametric test A statistical test that does not involve the use of any population parameters, μ and σ are not needed, and the underlying distribution does not have to be normal.

nonparticipant observation Studies in which the researcher does not participate in the situation in which the research participants are involved.

nonprobability sampling A sampling technique in which the individual members of the population do not have an equal likelihood of being selected to be a member of the sample.

normal curve A symmetrical bell-shaped frequency polygon representing a normal distribution.

normal distribution A theoretical frequency distribution that has certain special characteristics.

null hypothesis The hypothesis predicting that no difference exists between the groups being compared.

observational method Making observations of human or other animal behavior.

one-tailed hypothesis (directional hypothesis) An alternative hypothesis in which the researcher predicts the direction of the expected difference between the groups.

one-way randomized ANOVA An inferential statistical test for comparing the means of three or more groups using a between-participants design and one independent variable.

open-ended questions Questions for which participants formulate their own responses.

operational definition A definition of a variable in terms of the operations (activities) a researcher uses to measure or manipulate it.

order effects A problem for within-participants designs in which the order of the conditions has an effect on the dependent variable.

ordinal scale A scale in which objects or individuals are categorized and the categories form a rank order along a continuum.

parametric test A statistical test that involves making assumptions about estimates of population characteristics, or parameters.

partial correlation A correlational technique that involves measuring three variables and then statistically removing the effect of the third variable from the correlation of the remaining two.

partially open-ended questions Closed-ended questions with an open-ended "Other" option.

participant observation Studies in which the researcher actively participates in the situation in which the research participants are involved.

participant (subject) variable A characteristic of the participants that cannot be changed.

Pearson product-moment correlation coefficient (Pearson's r) The most commonly used correlation coefficient when both variables are measured on an interval or ratio scale.

percentile rank A score that indicates the percentage of people who scored at or below a given raw score.

personal interview A survey in which the questions are asked face to face.

person-who argument Arguing that a well-established statistical trend is invalid because we know a "person who" went against the trend.

phi coefficient The correlation coefficient used when both measured variables are dichotomous and nominal.

physical measures Measures of bodily activity such as pulse or blood pressure that may be taken with a piece of equipment.

placebo An inert substance that participants believe is a treatment.

placebo group A group or condition in which participants believe they are receiving treatment but are not.

platykurtic Normal curves that are short and relatively more dispersed (broader).

point-biserial correlation coefficient The correlation coefficient used when one of the variables is measured on a dichotomous nominal scale and the other is measured on an interval or ratio scale.

population All the people about whom a study is meant to generalize.

positive correlation A direct relationship between two variables in which an increase in one is related to an increase in the other and a decrease in one is related to a decrease in the other.

positively skewed distribution A distribution in which the peak is to the left of the center point and the tail extends toward the right or in the positive direction.

positive relationship A relationship between two variables in which an increase in one is accompanied by an increase in the other.

post hoc test When used with an ANOVA, a means of comparing all possible pairs of groups to determine which ones differ significantly from each other.

posttest-only control group design An experimental design in which the dependent variable is measured after the manipulation of the independent variable.

prediction Identifying the factors that indicate when an event or events will occur.

pretest/posttest control group design An experimental design in which the dependent variable is measured both before and after manipulation of the independent variable.

principle of falsifiability Stating a scientific theory in such a way that it is possible to refute or disconfirm it.

probability The expected relative frequency of a particular outcome.

probability sampling A sampling technique in which each member of the population has an equal likelihood of being selected to be part of the sample.

pseudoscience A claim that appears to be scientific but that actually violates the criteria of science.

public verification Presenting research to the public so that it can be observed, replicated, criticized, and tested.

qualitative research A type of social research based on field observations that are analyzed without statistics.

qualitative variable A categorical variable for which each value represents a discrete category.

quantitative variable A variable for which the scores represent a change in quantity.

quasi-experimental method Research that compares naturally occurring groups of individuals; the variable of interest cannot be manipulated.

quota sampling A sampling technique that involves ensuring that the sample is like the population on certain characteristics but uses convenience sampling to obtain the participants.

random assignment Assigning participants to conditions in such a way that each has the same probability as all others of being placed in any condition.

random sample A sample achieved through random selection in which each member of the population is equally likely to be chosen.

random selection A method of generating a random sample in which each member of the population is equally likely to be chosen as part of the sample.

range A measure of variation; the difference between the lowest and the highest scores in a distribution.

rating scale A numerical scale on which survey respondents indicate the direction and strength of their response.

ratio scale A scale in which in addition to order and equal units of measurement there is an absolute zero that indicates an absence of the variable being measured.

reactivity A possible reaction by participants in which they act unnaturally because they know they are being observed.

regression analysis A procedure that allows us to predict an individual's score on one variable based on knowing one or more other variables.

regression line The best-fitting straight line drawn through the center of a scatterplot that indicates the relationship between the variables.

regression to the mean A threat to internal validity in which extreme scores upon retesting tend to be less extreme, moving toward the mean.

reliability An indication of the consistency or stability of a measuring instrument.

representative sample A sample that is like the population.

response bias The tendency to consistently give the same answer to almost all of the items on a survey.

restrictive range A variable that is truncated and has limited variability.

reversal design A single-case design in which the independent variable is introduced and removed one or more times.

sample The group of people who participate in a study.

sampling bias A tendency for one group to be overrepresented in a sample.

scatterplot A figure that graphically represents the relationship between two variables.

self-report measures Usually questionnaires or interviews that measure how people report that they act, think, or feel.

sequential design A developmental design that is a combination of the cross-sectional and longitudinal designs.

single-blind experiment An experimental procedure in which either the participants or the experimenter are blind to the manipulation being made.

single-case design A design in which only one participant is used.

single-group posttest-only design A design in which a single group of participants is given a treatment and then tested.

single-group pretest/posttest design A design in which a single group of participants takes a pretest, then receives some treatment, and finally takes a posttest measure.

single-group time-series design A design in which a single group of participants is measured repeatedly before and after a treatment.

skeptic A person who questions the validity, authenticity, or truth of something purporting to be factual.

small-n design A design in which only a few participants are studied.

socially desirable response A response that is given because a respondent believes it is deemed appropriate by society.

Spearman's rank-order correlation coefficient The correlation coefficient used when one or more of the variables are measured on an ordinal (ranking) scale.

split-half reliability A reliability coefficient determined by correlating scores on one half of a measure with scores on the other half of the measure.

standard deviation A measure of variation, the average difference between the scores in the distribution and the mean or central point of the distribution or more precisely the square root of the average squared deviation from the mean.

standard error of the difference between means The standard deviation of the sampling distribution of differences between the means of independent samples in a two-sample experiment.

standard error of the difference scores The standard deviation of the sampling distribution of mean differences between dependent samples in a two-group experiment.

standard normal distribution A normal distribution with a mean of 0 and a standard deviation of 1.

static item A type of item used on a checklist on which attributes that will not change are recorded.

statistical significance An observed difference between two descriptive statistics such as means that is unlikely to have occurred by chance.

stratified random sampling A sampling technique designed to ensure that subgroups or strata are fairly represented.

subject (participant) effect A threat to internal validity in which the participant, consciously or unconsciously, affects the results of the study.

survey method Questioning individuals on a topic or topics and then describing their responses.

systematic empiricism Making observations in a systematic manner in order to test hypotheses and refute or develop a theory.

systematic replication A study that varies from an original study in one systematic way—for example, by using a different number or type of participants, a different setting, or more levels of the independent variable.

telephone survey A survey in which the questions are read to participants over the telephone.

test A measurement instrument used to assess individual differences in various content areas.

testing effect A threat to internal validity in which repeated testing leads to better or worse scores.

test/retest reliability A reliability coefficient determined by assessing the degree of relationship between scores on the same test administered on two different occasions.

theory An organized system of assumptions and principles that attempts to explain certain phenomena and how they are related.

third-variable problem The problem of a correlation between two variables being dependent on another (third) variable.

total sum of squares The sum of the squared deviations of each score from the grand mean.

Tukey's honestly significant difference (HSD) A post hoc test used with ANOVAs for making all pairwise comparisons when conditions have equal n.

two-tailed hypothesis (nondirectional hypothesis) An alternative hypothesis in which the researcher predicts that the groups being compared differ but does not predict the direction of the difference.

Type I error An error in hypothesis testing in which the null hypothesis is rejected when it is true.

Type II error An error in hypothesis testing in which there is a failure to reject the null hypothesis when it is false.

undisguised observation Studies in which the participants are aware that the researcher is observing their behavior.

validity An indication of whether the instrument measures what it claims to measure.

variable An event or behavior that has at least two values.

variance The standard deviation squared.

within-groups sum of squares The sum of the squared deviations of each score from its group mean.

within-groups variance The variance within each condition, an estimate of the population error variance.

within-participants design A type of correlated-groups design in which the same participants are used in each condition.

z-score (standard score) A number that indicates how many standard deviation units a raw score is from the mean of a distribution.

INDEX